readings
on
social
change

prentice-hall international, inc., London

prentice-hall of australia, pty. ltd., Sydney

prentice-hall of canada, ltd., Toronto

prentice-hall of india (private) ltd., New Delhi

prentice-hall of japan, inc., Tokyo

readings
on
social
change

Wilbert E. Moore
Russell Sage Foundation

Robert M. Cook
Yale University

prentice-hall, inc. / englewood cliffs, new jersey

prentice-hall readings in modern sociology series
Alex Inkeles, Editor

© 1967 by
PRENTICE-HALL, INC., Englewood Cliffs, N.J.

Library of Congress Catalog Number: 67–10033

Printed in the United States of America C–76134

Current Printing (Last Digit)

10 9 8 7 6 5 4 3 2

preface

The growing scholarly interest in the analysis of social change is perhaps overdue, as major and minor social transformations are clearly evident in the crude world of experience. In the small book to which the present one is something of a companion (Wilbert E. Moore, *Social Change*, 1963) it was argued that the tardiness of scholars, particularly of sociologists, in attending to change has been partly owing to certain inhibitions intrinsic to their theoretical stances. Be that as it may, not all scholars have shared in the neglect. We have tried to assemble here, from various sources and various scholarly traditions, studies which, taken together, range widely over the social cosmos and over the temporal spectrum of change.

In general organization we have followed the pattern of the book noted above, but we have not viewed our mission as finding material that would "fill in the details" omitted because of the brevity of that book. Rather, we have sought both supplementary and complementary substantive data and approaches.

Though we expect the primary classroom use of this book to be in sociology courses, and though we do not seriously suffer from some variety of sociologists' self-hate, our prejudice has been in the direction of finding mature statements by historians and biologists and others who share our concern for change. We are relying on the professor and on the textual organization of reliable summaries by a single hand to provide most of the theoretical and conceptual coherence to the provocative materials we have here gathered together. Our introductions to the several chapters will provide a kind of rationale for our selections, but that of course is not binding.

Since a reader is an assembly of the work of others, the task of putting one together properly stands not very high on the scale of relative scholarly values. We should not have it otherwise. But that does not absolve us from all responsibility, or from the elementary civility of giving credit where credit is due. We wish to record our deep gratitude to authors and publishers for permission to use the selections presented here. Suitable citations appear with each selection; this more general acknowledgment is recorded freely, and indeed a bit insistently. It is of course the authors' book, not ours.

ROBERT M. COOK

WILBERT E. MOORE

table of contents

**readings
on
social
change**

the normality of change

one

The view of social change as something that happens *to* societies and lesser social systems, to the exclusion of what happens *within* them, is consistent with certain conventions in social analysis, but will not do as an adequate conception of the course of events. In the book to which this volume is a companion, Moore's *Social Change,* the intrinsic sources of change are discussed in terms of inherent flexibilities in social systems and the universal gap between the ideal and the actual in human affairs.

Here we present several other approaches to the normality of change. The first and last selections, by Myrdal and Guessous, respectively, discuss the uses and abuses of stable equilibrium models of social systems, whereby change is exceptional and produces reactions that restore an essentially stationary state. Myrdal underscores the importance of cumulative change rather than restoration of a prior order. Guessous attends to the works of leading contemporary social theorists, and with great critical clarity shows the shortcomings of equilibrium theory. The selection by Myrdal, from a book that has become a classic in other respects, is itself an early and influential critique of equilibrium models.

Between Myrdal's early critique and the contemporary one by Guessous are several selections that do not assume a stable equilibrium, but rather develop notions of intrinsic change. Smelser outlines the sources of collective behavior and deals with sequences rather than cross-sectional factors. His "value-added" concept is similar to Myrdal's concept of cumulation. Smelser's approach, however, is much more determinate: "The sufficient condition for final production . . . is the combination of *every* necessary condition, according to a definite pattern."

Note the similarity of this to Marx:

No social order ever perishes before all the productive forces for which there is room in it have developed; and new, higher relations of production never appear before the material conditions of their existence have matured in the womb of the old society itself. Therefore mankind always sets itself only such tasks as it can solve; since, looking at the matter more closely, it will always be found that the task itself arises only when the material conditions for its solution already exist or are at least in the process of formation.

This notion is somewhat less complex than Myrdal's, which includes interaction effects (feedback), as well as multiple starting points and paths. Cumulation also figures in Marxist views of social change—here summarized in two relatively short statements—but with the distinctive emphasis being given to "materialism" as a prime mover and to dialectical processes or *dis*continuities in the pace of change.

Although Guessous is highly critical of equilibrium analysis, he demonstrates that charges of "static bias" lack sophistication—there are a number of changes that equilibrium analysis can and does handle.

The selections presented here only suggest the extent to which the *functional* model of society is under attack, with non-Marxists now paralleling a long-standing Marxist tradition. Though the attack is nearly devastating, we have as yet no emergent theory that will treat social systems as interconnected sets of social *processes*, including both stability and change—the latter cyclical, evolutionary, and revolutionary.

Incidentally, the coincidence of theoretical attacks on self-equilibrating models of social systems with the conspicuous reality of large-scale and widespread social change (discussed in Chapters Four and Five) invites the suspicion that the scholarly developments may owe as much to the course of events as to the course of analytical progress.

A Methodological Note
on the Principle of Cumulation

GUNNAR MYRDAL

In social science we have been drawing heavily on the notions and theories of the much farther developed natural sciences, particularly physics. The notion of equilibrium, for instance, has been in all our reasoning for centuries. Actually it is present in most research of the present day, even when it is not formally introduced. In most social research we have restricted our utilization of the equilibrium notion to that simple and static variant of it, the *stable equilibrium*. It is this equilibrium notion which is implicit in the sociological constructions of "maladjustment" and "adjustment" and all their

several synonyms or near-synonyms, where equilibrium is thought of as having a virtual reality in determining the direction of change.[1] We propose the utilization of *other equilibrium notions* besides this simplest one. For dynamic analysis of the process of change in social relations, it is highly desirable that we disengage our minds from the stable equilibrium scheme of thinking. The other types of equilibrium notions are often better descriptions of social reality than the stable one.

Gunnar Myrdal, *et al.*, "A Methodological Note on the Principle of Cumulation," *An American Dilemma*, pp. 1065-1070. Copyright 1944 by Harper & Brothers. Reprinted by permission of Harper & Row, Publishers.

[1] These equilibrium concepts have been used also as vehicles for introducing hidden valuations—i.e., bias—into research. . . . Our interest . . . is directed only upon their usefulness as theoretical tools. To explain these other notions it is convenient to think in terms of analogies. The stable equilibrium is like a hanging pendulum, unmoving, and with no tendency to move unless jolted.

If we succeed in placing a pencil upright on its end, it is also in equilibrium, but an unstable one, a "labile status" of balancing forces, as we easily find if we touch it. No "adjustment," "adaptation," or "accommodation" toward the original position will follow the application of a push, but only an accelerated movement *away* from the original state of balance. A third type of equilibrium is present when a pencil is rolling on a plane surface: it may come to rest anywhere. A fourth type is what we might call "created equilibrium," that is, arranging a disordered pile of pencils into a box by intelligent social engineering.

The most important need is to give place in our hypothetical explanatory scheme to a rational recognition of the cumulation of forces. In one branch of social science, economics, these various types of equilibrium notions have lately been used with great advantage. The principle of cumulation has given us, for the first time, something which approaches a real theory of economic dynamics.[2] . . . The following brief notes are intended to give an abstract clarification of the theory [of the "vicious circle"] and a perspective on some of its future potentialities as a method of social research.

In considering the Negro problem in its most abstract aspect, let us construct a much simplified mental model of dynamic social causation. We assume in this model society of our imagination a white majority and a Negro minority. We assume, further, that the interrelation between the two groups is in part determined by a specific degree of "race prejudice" on the side of the whites, directed against the Negroes. We assume the "plane of living" of

the Negroes to be considerably lower than that of the whites. We take, as given, a mutual relationship between our two variables, and we assume this relationship to be of such a type that, on the one hand, the Negroes' plane of living is kept down by discrimination from the side of the whites while, on the other hand, the whites' reason for discrimination is partly dependent upon the Negroes' plane of living. The Negroes' poverty, ignorance, superstition, slum dwellings, health deficiencies, dirty appearance, disorderly conduct, bad odor, and criminality stimulate and feed the antipathy of the whites for them. We assume, for the sake of simplicity, that society, in our abstract model, is in "balance" initially. By this we mean that conditions are static, that our two variables are exactly checking each other: there is—under these static conditions—just enough prejudice on the part of the whites to keep down the Negro plane of living to that level which maintains the specific degree of prejudice, or the other way around.

If now, in this hypothetically balanced state, for some reason or other, the Negro plane of living should be lowered, this will—other things being equal—in its turn increase white prejudice. Such an increase in white prejudice has the effect of pressing down still further the Negro plane of living, which again will increase prejudice, and so on, by way of mutual interaction between the two variables, *ad infinitum*. A cumulative process is thus set in motion which can have final effects quite out of proportion to the magnitude of the original push. The push might even be withdrawn after a time, and still a permanent change will remain or even the process of change will continue without a new balance in sight. If, instead, the initial change had been such a thing as a gift

[2] For a simplified model of cumulative economic causation, see Gunnar Myrdal, *Monetary Equilibrium* (London: William Hodge & Co., Ltd., 1939), 24ff.

a methodological note on the principle of cumulation   3

from a philanthropist to raise the Negro plane of living, a cumulative movement would have started in the other direction, having exactly the same causal mechanism. The vicious circle works both ways.

The Negroes' "plane of living" is, however, a composite entity. Let us, while retaining our major assumptions, approach a more realistic conception by splitting up this quantity into components, assuming that the cumulative principle works also in their causative interrelations. Besides "relative absence of race prejudice on the side of whites," we introduce a number of variables: levels of "Negro employment," "wages," "housing," "nutrition," "clothing," "health," "education," "stability in family relations," "manners," "cleanliness," "orderliness," "trustworthiness," "law observance," "loyalty to society at large," "absence of criminality," and so on. All these variables—according to our hypotheses —cumulate. In other words, we assume that a movement in any of the Negro variables in the direction toward the corresponding white levels will tend to decrease white prejudice. At the same time white prejudice is assumed to be, directly or indirectly, one of the causative factors effective in keeping the levels low for the several Negro variables. It is also our hypothesis that, on the whole, a rise in any single one of the Negro variables will tend to raise all the other Negro variables and thus, indirectly as well as directly, result in a cumulatively enforced effect upon white prejudice. A rise in employment will tend to increase earnings; raise standards of living; and improve health, education, manners, and law observance, and vice versa; a better education is assumed to raise the chances of a higher salaried job, and vice versa; and so all the way through our whole system of variables. Each of the secondary changes has its effect on white prejudice.

If, in actual social life, the dynamics of the causal relations between the various factors in the Negro problem should correspond to our hypotheses, then—assuming again, for the sake of simplicity, an initially static state of balanced forces—*any change in any one of these factors, independent of the way in which it is brought about, will, by the aggregate weight of the cumulative effects running back and forth between them all, start the whole system moving* in one direction or the other as the case may be, with a speed depending upon the original push and the functions of causal interrelation within the system.

Our point is not simply that many forces are "working in the same direction." Originally we assumed that there was a balance between these forces, and that the system was static, until we introduced one push coming in at one point or the other. When the system starts rolling, it is true that *the changes in the forces*—though not all the forces themselves—work in one direction; but this is because the variables are assumed to be interlocked in such a causal mechanism that a change of any one causes the others to change *in the same direction*, with a secondary effect upon the first variable, and so on.

We may further notice that the "balance" assumed as initial status was not a stable equilibrium at all—of the type which is tacitly assumed in the notions of "maladjustment," "adjustment," "accommodation," "social lag" —and, further, that in our scheme of hypotheses there is not necessarily assumed to exist any new "balance," or "equilibrium," or "harmony," toward which the factors of the system "adjust" or "accommodate." In the utilization of this theoretical model on problems of actual social reality, the initial state of labile balance, which we assumed for simplicity in our demonstration, will of course never be found. What we shall have to study are *processes of systems actually rolling* in the one direction or the other, systems which are constantly subjected to all sorts of pushes from outside through all the variables, and which are moving because of the cumulative effect of all these pushes and the interaction between the variables.

The individual factors into which we split the Negroes' plane of living can of course be split again, and it is the purpose of scientific analysis to do so. The causal relations between the subfactors, and between them and all other factors, will be assumed to be ruled by the same cumulative principle. White race prejudice, here assumed as the "cause" of discrimination, is not a solid and static factor. To begin with, it depends upon discrimination itself. If, for some reason—for example, the demand of the employer during a war emergency, or the ruling of a trade union—white workers actually come to work with Negroes as fellow workers, it has been experienced that prejudice will often adjust to the changed amount of discrimination. White prejudice itself can be split into a great number of beliefs and valuations; to a degree, both of these two types of factors are dependent upon each other, . . . and, consequently, are under the rule of the cumulative principle.

Throughout this treatise on the Negro problem the model of dynamic causation—and the implied skepticism toward the idea of stable equilibrium—is kept steadily in the back of our mind. A main viewpoint in our study of every single factor in the Negro problem is thus its interrelation with all other factors and their cumulative effect upon the status of the Negro.

The principle of cumulation allows us to see that there is sense in the general notion of the "status of the Negro." We should, indeed, have liked to present in our study a general *index*, year by year or at least decade by decade, as a quantitative expression of the movement of the entire system we are studying: the status of the Negro in America. Such an index would have about the same significance as the general indices of production or prices or any other complex systems of interdependent variables. The index is an average. It should, for the same principal reasons, have to be broken down for regions, classes, and items, and this breaking down would have the same scientific function in an analysis. It would give quantitative precision to the concept of the general status of the Negro—a concept which, because of the cumulative principle, we cannot escape. And it always clarifies our reasoning to be compelled to calculate a quantitative value for a notion we use. Materials for such an index of (relative and absolute) Negro status are, to a great extent, available, and the general theory of the index offers a methodological basis for its construction. But the work of constructing and analyzing a general index of Negro status in America amounts to a major investigation in itself, and we must leave the matter as a proposal for further research.

Our chief task is to analyze the causal interrelation within the system itself as it works under the influence of outside pushes and the momentum of ongoing processes within. The system is much more complicated than appears from our abstract representation. To begin with, all factors must be broken down by region, social class, age, sex, and so on. As what we are studying is a race relation, the number of combinations increases by multiples for each classification applied. White prejudice, for instance, varies not only with the status of the white man, but also with the Negro's social class and the field of Negro behavior in relation to which race prejudice is active. There are also Negro prejudices in the system.

Each factor has its peculiarities and irregularities. White prejudice, for instance, changes not only as a reaction to actual changes in Negro plane of living, but also to expectations of such changes. The latter reaction may be totally different from the former: a higher plane of living among Negroes, when it is actually achieved, may be expected to effect a *decrease* of white prejudice, but the *expectation* of it for the future might *increase* prejudice, particularly in the South (even if its long-run effects—when it actually comes—will be, as we have assumed, a decrease of prejudice). It is possible, finally, that certain social classes of whites—say poor whites in the South— even in the fairly long-range perspective will react with increased prejudice against the Negro's approaching the white man's status.

The system thus becomes complicated, but the fundamental principle of cumulative causation remains. The scientific ideal is not only to define and analyze the factors, but to give for each one of them a measure of their actual quantitative strength in influencing the other factors, as well as a measure of their ability to be influenced themselves by outside forces. The time element becomes of paramount importance in these formulas. As we have exemplified for the factor of white prejudice, the effects might have different signs in the short and in the long run. Even when this is not the case, the effects will be spread differently along the time axis. A rise of employment, for instance, will almost immediately raise some standards of living, but

change[s] in levels of education or health are slow to be achieved, and their effects back on the other factors are in turn delayed, which slows up the whole process of cumulation. The system regularly develops under a great multitude of different outside pushes, primarily directed against almost every single factor. The actual pushes go in both directions, thus often *turning the system around on its axis as it is rolling.* Ideally, the scientific solution of the Negro problem should thus be given in the form of an interconnected series of quantitative equations, describing the movement of the actual system under various influences. That this complete, quantitative, and truly scientific solution is far beyond the horizon does not need to be pointed out. But in principle it is possible to execute, and it remains as the scientific ideal steering our endeavors.

This conception of a great number of interdependent factors, mutually cumulative in their effects, disposes of the idea that there is *one* predominant factor, a "basic factor." This idea— mainly in the form of a vague conception of economic determinism—has been widely accepted in the writings on the Negro problem during the last decade. As we see the methodological problem, this one-factor hypothesis is not only theoretically unclear but is contradicted by easily ascertainable facts and factual relations. As a scientific approach it is narrow.[3]

---

[3] The usual economic one-factor theory is available in two extreme versions, depending upon the type of political teleology involved: (1) a radical Marxist version, where the expectation is an economic revolution which will change everything and even eradicate race prejudice; (2) a liberalistic version which does not expect an economic revolution and which —as the assumption is that no significant change can be brought about except by tackling the "basic factor," the economic system— is pessimistic about any type of induced

The theoretical system of dynamic social causation we have selected corresponds more closely to the practical man's common sense ideas about things than it does to the apprehension of reality met in many scientific writings on the Negro problem. The social scientist tends to rely too much on static notions and *a priori* to give too dominant a role to a "basic factor." The professional philanthropist, the Negro educator, the Negro trade unionist, the leaders of Negro defense organizations like the NAACP, the Urban League, or the Interracial Commission, and, indeed, the average well-meaning citizen of both colors, pragmatically applies this same hypothesis.[4] To use once more our parallel from modern economic theory: when the economists during the last two decades abandoned the classical static equilibrium approach and went ahead to construct a dynamic theory of causal interrelations on a process of change, what they actually did was to apply the pragmatic notions of bankers, businessmen, and labor leaders and try to systematize them. This revolutionized economic theory and had great importance for the scientific planning of economic policy. A rational strategy in the Negro problem also assumes a theory of dynamic causation.

change. There are all sorts of intermediary positions and also compromises toward recognizing that factors other than the economic one have some influence. But the one-factor theory always implies a fatalistic tendency and prevents a rational conception of interdependence and cumulative dynamic causation. . . .

[4] The best formulation of our hypothesis available in the literature is, thus, to be found in a book by a practical man writing without scientific pretensions but out of lifelong experiences: "There is a vicious circle in caste. At the outset, the despised group is usually inferior in certain of the accepted standards of the controlling class. Being inferior, members of the degraded caste are denied the privileges and opportunities of their fellows and so are pushed still further down and then are regarded with that much less respect, and therefore are more rigorously denied advantages, and so around and around the vicious circle. Even when the movement starts to reverse itself—as it most certainly has in the case of the Negro—there is a desperately long unwinding as a slight increase in good will gives a little greater chance and this leads to a little higher accomplishment and that to increased respect and so slowly upward toward equality of opportunity, of regard, and of status." [Edwin R. Embree, *Brown America* (New York: The Viking Press, Inc., 1931), p. 200.] To this it should only be added that even if the unwinding process is working with time lags so is the opposite movement. In spite of the time lags, the theory of the vicious circle is a cause rather for optimism than for pessimism. The cumulative principle works both ways.

The Determinants of Collective Behavior

NEIL J. SMELSER

The Organization of Determinants

. . . What determines whether an episode of collective behavior *of any*

Neil J. Smelser, *Theory of Collective Behavior*, pp. 12-20. © 1963 by Neil J. Smelser. Reprinted with permission of The Free Press of Glencoe, Inc., and Routledge & Kegan Paul, Ltd.

sort will occur? What determines whether one type *rather than another* will occur? Many of the existing answers to these questions are unsatisfactory scientifically. As Strauss has observed, many students of panic have failed to distinguish any specific and determinate set of conditions for the occurrence of panic above and beyond a simple list of possibly operative factors:

The conditions of panic can be roughly classified into three categories: physiological, psychological, and sociological. Physiological factors are fatigue, undernourishment, lack of sleep, toxic conditions of the body, and the like. Psychological factors are surprise, uncertainty, anxiety, feeling of isolation, consciousness of powerlessness before the inevitable expectancy of danger. Sociological factors include lack of group solidarity, crowd conditions, lack of regimental leadership in the group. An effective statement of the mechanics of panic causation cannot be made by merely listing the factors entering into that causation when these factors are as diverse in character as they seem to be. A student seeking a genuinely effective statement of panic causation would attempt to find what is essential to these diverse conditions and tie these essential conditions into a dynamic statement of the development and outbreak of the panic occurrence.[1]

These determinants must be organized. Each must be assigned to its appropriate contributory role in the genesis of panic. A mere list will not suffice.

Even more, we must organize the determinants precisely enough so that panic is the *only* possible outcome; we must rule out related outbursts. To quote Strauss again:

. . . The conditions of panic which have been noted, because they are not genuine causative conditions, are conditions for more than panic. That is to say, the conditions for panic which are listed in the literature are not conditions for panic specifically; they are also conditions for other kinds of closely related phenomena. . . . The thin line between the occurrence of panic and the occurrence of . . . other types of nonrational behavior is attested to by the rapid shifts from one of these forms to another in battle—from collective exaltation to panic, from panic to collective fascination, and the like.

In a genuine sense, then, the causes for panic are not specific causes. They are also conditions for other types of collective behavior.[2]

We need, then, a *unique* combination of determinants which yields a *unique* outcome, panic. We must systematize the determinants, and note the changes in the combinations of determinants which produce different outcomes.

Similar problems of explanation arise in connection with social movements. In examining the anthropological literature on messianic movements, Barber concludes that there exists a "positive correlation of the messianic movement and deprivation [of various types]."[3] The first difficulty in attempting to assess this correlation—assuming that it exists—is that "deprivation" is a vague term. A statement of the kinds of deprivation is necessary. In addition, there are many types of messianic movements; some are associated with a positive sense of regeneration of society, others with passive resignation. Finally, as Barber notes, messianism is not the only response to deprivation; among "several alternative responses" he mentions "armed rebellion and physical violence" and "depopulation." Thus, in spite of Barber's correlation, there remain several kinds and levels of deprivation and several responses besides messianism. This is what we mean when we say that there exists a residue of indeterminacy in the connections between determinants and outcomes in the field of collective be-

[1] A. Strauss, "The Literature on Panic," *Journal of Abnormal and Social Psychology,* **39** (1944), 324.

[2] *Ibid.,* 324-325.

[3] B. Barber, "Acculturation and Messianic Movements," *American Sociological Review,* **6** (1941), 663-669.

havior. To reduce this residue is one of the major tasks of this study.

The Logic of Value-Added

The scheme we shall use to organize the determinants of collective behavior resembles the conception of "value-added" in the field of economics.[4] An example of the use of this term is the conversion of iron ore into finished automobiles by a number of stages of processing. Relevant stages would be mining, smelting, tempering, shaping, and combining the steel with other parts, painting, delivering to retailer, and selling. Each stage "adds its value" to the final cost of the finished product. The key element in this example is that the earlier stages must combine *according to a certain pattern* before the next stage can contribute its particular value to the finished product. It is impossible to paint iron ore and hope that the painting will thereby contribute to the desired final product, an automobile. Painting, in order to be effective as a "determinant" in shaping the product, has to "wait" for the completion of the earlier processes. Every stage in the value-added process, therefore, is a necessary condition for the appropriate and effective addition of value in the next stage. The sufficient condition for final production, moreover, is the combination of *every* necessary condition, according to a definite pattern.

As the value-added process moves forward, it narrows progressively the range of possibilities of what the final product might become. Iron ore, for instance, is a very general resource, and can be converted into thousands of different kinds of products. After it is smelted and tempered into a certain quality of steel, the range of possible products into which it might enter is narrowed considerably. After it is pressed into automotive parts, it can be used for very few products other than automobiles. If we were to view the finished automobile as the "outcome" to be explained and the stages of value-added as "determinants," we would say that as each new stage adds its value, the "explanation" of the outcome becomes increasingly determinate or specific. As the value-added process develops, it allows for progressively fewer outcomes other than the one we wish to explain.

This logic of value-added can be applied to episodes of collective behavior, such as the panic or the reform movement. Many determinants, or necessary conditions, must be present for any kind of collective episode to occur. These determinants must combine, however, in a definite pattern. Furthermore, as they combine, the determination of the type of episode in question becomes increasingly specific, and alternative behaviors are ruled out as possibilities.[5]

---

[4] For an elementary account of the nature of value-added, cf. P. A. Samuelson, *Economics: An Introductory Analysis*, 4th ed. (New York: McGraw-Hill Book Company, 1958), pp. 187-188.

[5] This methodological position has been developed by Meyer and Conrad with reference to explanation in economic history. "If [the economic historian's] intention is indeed to know about and explain specific historical events, then it is our contention that he must follow the rules of scientific explanation. To explain an event one must be able to estimate a range of admissible possibilities, given a set of initial conditions and a causal or statistical law. . . . Like other economists and other scientists, it must be [the economic historian's] aim to narrow the range of possibilities, to explain why the particular realized development did in fact occur." J. R. Meyer and A. H. Conrad, "Economic Theory, Statistical Inference, and Economic History," *Journal of Economic History*, 17 (1957), 532. For a mathematical formalization of such logic, cf. M. E. Turner and C. D. Stevens, "The Regression Analysis of Causal Paths," *Bio-*

The following are the important determinants of collective behavior:

1. Structural Conduciveness

We read that financial booms and panics, fashion cycles and crazes do not plague simple, traditional societies; we also read that America as a civilization is prone to such seizures, and that, within America, places like Los Angeles and Detroit are especially productive of bizarre movements. Are such statements true, and if so, why? Do certain structural characteristics, more than others, permit or encourage episodes of collective behavior? To illustrate this condition of structural conduciveness with respect to the occurrence of financial panic, let us assume that property is closely tied to kinship and can be transferred only to first-born sons at the time of the death of the father. Panic under such conditions is ruled out, simply because the holders of property do not have sufficient maneuverability to dispose of their assets upon short notice. Under conditions of economic pressure, certain responses are possible—for instance, a movement to change the customs of property transfer —but not panic. The structure of the social situation does not permit it. At

the other extreme lies the money market, in which assets can be exchanged freely and rapidly.

Conduciveness is, at most, permissive of a given type of collective behavior. A money market, for instance, even though its structure is conducive to panic, may function for long periods without producing a crisis. Within the scope of a conducive structure, many possible kinds of behavior other than panic remain. We must narrow the range of possibilities. In order to do so, we add several more determinants. In this way we make more probable the occurrence of that event (e.g., panic) which is merely possible within the scope of conduciveness.

2. Structural Strain

Financial panics develop when loss or annihilation threatens the holders of assets. Real or anticipated economic deprivation, in fact, occupies an important place in the initiation of hostile outbursts, reform movements, revolutionary movements, and new sects as well. Extreme religious movements seem to cluster among deprived groups such as colonial populations, the disinherited members of a society, and recent migrants. Race riots follow population invasions and new kinds of cultural contacts. . . .

In explaining any case of collective behavior (a panic, for instance), we must consider the structural strain (the threat of economic deprivation, for instance) as falling *within the scope established by the condition of conduciveness*. Otherwise this strain cannot be a determinant of panic, however important it may be as a determinant of some other kind of behavior. It is the *combination* of conduciveness and strain, not the separate existence of either, that radically reduces the range of possibilities of behavior other than panic.

metrics, **15** (1959), 236-258. Our approach also seems consistent with two general remarks made recently by Morris Ginsberg on the problem of social change. The search for social causation (or explanation), he maintains, involves a search for "an assemblage of factors which, in interaction with each other, undergo a change of character and are continued into the effect." Such processes of social causation, moreover, often have a "cumulative and frequently circular character." "Social Change," *British Journal of Sociology*, **9** (1958), 220-223; see also R. M. MacIver, *Social Causation* (Boston: Ginn & Co., 1942), pp. 251-265. Thus it may be possible to treat many types of social change other than collective behavior by this value-added conception. Cf. N. J. Smelser, *Social Change in the Industrial Revolution* (Chicago: University of Chicago Press, 1959), pp. 60-62.

3. Growth and Spread of a Generalized Belief

Before collective action can be taken to reconstitute the situation brought on by structural strain, this situation must be made meaningful to the potential actors. This meaning is supplied in a generalized belief, which identifies the source of strain, attributes certain characteristics to this source, and specifies certain responses to the strain as possible or appropriate. . . . The growth and spread of such beliefs are one of the necessary conditions for the occurrence of an episode of collective behavior.

Many generalized beliefs, however, enjoy a long existence without ever becoming determinants of a collective outburst. Throughout history, for instance, men have harbored superstitions about creatures from other planets, their powers, and their potential danger. Only on very specific occasions, however, do such beliefs rise to significance as determinants of panicky flights. These occasions arise when the generalized beliefs combine with the other necessary conditions of panic.

4. Precipitating Factors

Conduciveness, strain, and a generalized belief—even when combined—do not by themselves produce an episode of collective behavior in a specific time and place. In the case of panic, for instance, these general determinants establish a predisposition to flight, but it is usually a specific event which sets the flight in motion. Under conditions of racial tension, it is nearly always a dramatic event which precipitates the outburst of violence—a clash between two persons of different race, a Negro family moving into a white neighborhood, or a Negro being promoted to a traditionally white job. These events may confirm or justify the fears or hatreds in a generalized belief; they may initiate or exaggerate a condition of strain; or they may redefine sharply the conditions of conduciveness. In any case, these precipitating factors give the generalized beliefs concrete, immediate substance. In this way they provide a concrete setting toward which collective action can be directed.

Again, a precipitating factor by itself is not necessarily a determinant of anything in particular. It must occur in the context of the other determinants. A fist fight, for instance, will not touch off a race riot unless it occurs in the midst of—or is interpreted in the light of—a general situation established by conduciveness, strain, and a generalized belief.

5. Mobilization of Participants for Action

Once the determinants just reviewed have been established, the only necessary condition that remains is to bring the affected group into action. This point marks the onset of panic, the outbreak of hostility, or the beginning of agitation for reform or revolution. In this process of mobilization the behavior of leaders is extremely important.

6. The Operation of Social Control

In certain respects this final determinant arches over all the others. Stated in the simplest way, the study of social control is the study of those counter-determinants which prevent, interrupt, deflect, or inhibit the accumulation of the determinants just reviewed. For purposes of analysis it is convenient to divide social controls into two broad types: (a) Those social controls which minimize conduciveness and strain. In a broad sense these controls *prevent* the occurrence of an episode of collective behavior, because they attack very nonspecific determinants. (b) Those social controls which are mobilized only *after* a collective episode has begun to materialize. These determine how fast, how far, and in what directions the episode will develop. To assess the effectiveness of the second kind of controls, we shall ask how the appropriate agencies of control—the police, the courts, the press, the religious authorities, the community leaders, etc.—behave in the face of a potential or actual outburst of collective behavior. Do they adopt a rigid, uncompromising attitude? Do they vacillate? Do they themselves take sides in the disturbance? . . .

By studying the different combinations of these six determinants, we hope to provide the best possible answer to the explanatory questions posed at the beginning of this section: What determines whether an episode of collective behavior *of any sort* will occur? What determines whether one type *rather than another* will occur? By utilizing these analytically distinct determinants, moreover, we shall be better equipped to untangle those complex empirical situations (e.g., wars, depressions) in which many different types of collective behavior unfold simultaneously.[6]

[6] For an account of the parade of outbursts during the early part of World War I in England, cf. W. Trotter, *Instincts of the Herd in Peace and War* (London: Macmillan & Co., Ltd., 1922), pp. 140-141. For other characterizations of the clustering of collective behavior, cf. L. Whiteman and S. L. Lewis, *Glory Roads: The Psychological State of California* (New York: Thomas Y. Crowell Company, 1936), pp. 4-5; K. G. J. C. Knowles, " 'Strike-Proneness' and its Determinants," *American Journal of Sociology*, **60** (1954-55), 213; J. W. Thompson, "The Aftermath of the Black Death and the Aftermath of the Great War," *American Journal of Sociology*, **32** (1920-21), 565. At the level of social movements, "it is rare for a mass movement to be wholly of one character. Usually it displays some facets of other types of movement, and sometimes it is two or three movements in one." E. Hoffer, *The*

Value-Added and Natural History

According to the logic of the value-added approach, any event or situation, in order to become a determinant of a collective episode, must operate within the limits established by other determinants. At first glance this approach is very similar to the widespread "natural history" approach to collective behavior. In its simplest form, this approach involves the claim that there exist certain empirical uniformities of sequence in the unfolding of an episode of collective behavior. A classic model of the stages of a social movement is the sequence developed by Dawson and Gettys—the sequence beginning with a "preliminary stage of social unrest," passing through a "popular stage of collective excitement" and a "stage of formal organization," and finally reaching a kind of terminal point of "institutionalization." The entire sequence introduces some new institutional form—a sect, a law, a new kind of family structure, or a political reform.[7] A comparable model for revolutions is Crane Brinton's suggestive sequence involving first economic and political weakness of the old regime in the midst of general prosperity; disaffection of specific groups, especially the intellectuals; transfer of power, rule of the moderates; accession of the extremists and the reign of terror and virtue; and finally, a period of relaxation of some of the revolution's excesses, institutionalization of some elements of its program, and a return to many of society's old ways.[8] Many

True Believer (New York: New American Library, 1958), p. 26.

[7] C. A. Dawson and W. E. Gettys, *An Introduction to Sociology* (New York: The Ronald Press Co., 1929), pp. 787-803.

[8] *The Anatomy of Revolution* (New York: Vintage Books, Inc., 1957). See also P. A. Sorokin, *The Sociology of Revolution* (Philadelphia: J. B. Lippincott Co., 1925); L. P.

investigators, following the pioneer work of Prince, have used the logic of natural sequence to account for the events during and after disasters.[9] Dahlke has suggested a typical sequence of events leading to a race riot.[10] Recently Meyersohn and Katz have attempted to outline the natural history of the adoption of fads.[11] In most of these accounts it is not stated whether the temporally prior stages are necessary conditions for the later stages.

To appreciate the difference between the value-added and the natural history approaches, let us return to the analogy of the production of an automobile. In one respect the stages of value-added can be described as a natural history. The ore is smelted before the steel is shaped; the steel is shaped before the paint is applied, and so on. It is possible, however, that the paint itself has been *manufactured* prior to the shaping of the steel. This circumstance complicates the simple account of a natural history. Now we must consider the paint to have been in existence—dormant, as it were, as a determinant—*before* the preceding de-

terminant. The paint can be activated as a determinant, however, only after the steel has been shaped and readied for painting. In the value-added process, then, we must distinguish between the *occurrence* or *existence* of an event or situation, and the activation of this event or situation as a determinant. The value-added logic implies a temporal sequence of activation of determinants, but any or all of these determinants may have existed for an indefinite period before activation.

The same logic governs the explanation of an episode of collective behavior. A simple natural history approach to panic would involve an account of one event or situation (for example, the closing off of exits) followed by a second (the growth of fear), followed by a third (a shout or loud noise), followed by yet another (someone starting to run), and so on. Under the value-added approach, these events or situations would become activated as determinants in a certain temporal order, but any of them might have been in existence already. The fear of entrapment, for instance, is a near-universal fear which has endured through the ages. It is activated as a determinant of panic, however, only after conditions of conduciveness and strain (danger) have been established. Even precipitating factors need not occur at a specific moment in time. A loud explosion may have occurred some time in the past without causing any particular alarm. Once certain determinants of panic have accumulated, however, this explosion may be remembered and reinterpreted (i.e., activated as a determinant) in the light of the new situation. The logic of value-added, in short, does posit a definite sequence for the activation of determinants but does not posit a definite sequence for the empirical establishment of events and situations.

Edwards, *The Natural History of Revolution* (Chicago: University of Chicago Press, 1927); R. D. Hopper, "The Revolutionary Process: A Frame of Reference for the Study of Revolutionary Movements," *Social Forces,* **28** (1950), 270-279.

[9] S. H. Prince, *Catastrophe and Social Change* (New York: Columbia University Press, 1920); for more recent use of the concept, cf. W. H. Form and S. Nosow, with G. P. Stone and C. M. Westie *Community in Disaster* (New York: Harper & Row, Publishers, 1958), and L. J. Carr, "Disaster and the Sequence-Pattern Concept of Social Change," *American Journal of Sociology,* **38** (1932-33), 209-210.

[10] H. O. Dahlke, "Race and Minority Riots—A Study in the Typology of Violence," *Social Forces,* **30** (1951-52), 419-425.

[11] R. Meyersohn and E. Katz, "Notes on a Natural History of Fads," *American Journal of Sociology,* **62** (1956-57), 594-601.

Finally, certain *single* empirical events or situations may be significant as *several* determinants of collective behavior. A severe financial crisis, for instance, may create widespread economic deprivation (structural strain) and at the same time may touch off one or more outbursts (precipitating factor). A long-standing religious cleavage, such as that between Protestants and Catholics, may be frustrating for each group (structural strain); the same cleavage may harbor hostile sentiments within each group toward the other (generalized beliefs). Under the appropriate conditions these latent determinants may be activated to contribute to a collective outburst. We must always distinguish clearly, therefore, between the empirical occurrence or existence of an event or situation, and its significance as one or more determinants in the value-added process.

Marxism

KARL MARX

. . . The general result at which I arrived and which, once won, served as a guiding thread for my studies, can be briefly formulated as follows: In the social production of their life, men enter into definite relations that are indispensable and independent of their will, relations of production which correspond to a definite stage of development of their material productive forces. The sum total of these relations of production constitutes the economic structure of society, the real foundation, on which rises a legal and political superstructure and to which correspond definite forms of social consciousness. The mode of production of material life conditions the social, political, and intellectual life process in general. It is not the consciousness of men that determines their being, but, on the contrary, their social being that determines their consciousness. At a certain stage of their development, the

Karl Marx, "Preface to a Contribution to the Critique of Political Economy," in *Karl Marx and Frederick Engels: Selected Works* (Moscow: Foreign Languages Publishing House, 1962), **I**, 362–364. Reprinted by permission of the publisher.

material productive forces of society come in conflict with the existing relations of production, or—what is but a legal expression for the same thing—with the property relations within which they have been at work hitherto. From forms of development of the productive forces these relations turn into their fetters. Then begins an epoch of social revolution. With the change of the economic foundation the entire immense superstructure is more or less rapidly transformed. In considering such transformations a distinction should always be made between the material transformation of the economic conditions of production, which can be determined with the precision of natural science, and the legal, political, religious, aesthetic, or philosophic —in short, ideological forms in which men become conscious of this conflict and fight it out. Just as our opinion of an individual is not based on what he thinks of himself, so can we not judge of such a period of transformation by its own consciousness; on the contrary, this consciousness must be explained rather from the contradictions of material life, from the existing conflict between the social productive forces and the relations of production. No social order ever perishes before all the productive forces for which there is room in it have developed; and new, higher relations of production never appear before the material conditions of their existence have matured in the womb of the old society itself. Therefore mankind always sets itself only such tasks as it can solve; since, looking at the matter more closely, it will always be found that the task itself arises only when the material conditions for its solution already exist or are at least in the process of formation. In broad outlines Asiatic, ancient, feudal, and modern bourgeois modes of production can be designated as progressive epochs in the economic formation of society. The bourgeois relations of production are the last antagonistic form of the social process of production—antagonistic not in the sense of individual antagonism, but of one arising from the social conditions of life of the individuals; at the same time the productive forces developing in the womb of bourgeois society create the material conditions for the solution of that antagonism. This social formation brings, therefore, the prehistory of human society to a close.

The Essence of Historical Materialism

A Revolutionary Upheaval in Man's View of Society

From ancient times men have sought for answers to the questions: Are social systems a matter of accident or are they the result of some invisible yet powerful causes? Is it possible to change these systems, to achieve well-being and freedom for all and not only for the minority? If so, how? And who will lead humanity to the achievement of these much-desired aims? And finally, which way is humanity going—toward a golden age of progress or toward stagnation and decline?

Thinkers of all times and all nations have tried to answer these questions. But for many centuries their theories and conceptions were invariably overthrown not only by the criticism of other scholars, but also by the criticism of time, by the whole development of

Fundamentals of Marxism-Leninism (Moscow: Foreign Languages Publishing House, 1963), pp. 116-125. Reprinted by permission of the publisher.

history. In the field of social studies the path to knowledge has proved particularly long and arduous.

The point is that the life of society is a great deal more complex than the development of nature. Within the limits of our direct observation the phenomena of nature recur comparatively uniformly, regularly, and this makes it easier to understand their essence. But to trace a similar regularity, a similar recurrence in the life of society is far more difficult. This naturally makes it harder to understand and hinders us in detecting any definite law in its development.

There is another distinction of no less importance. In nature, we have to deal with the operation of impersonal, elemental forces. In the history of society, we are dealing with the actions of people, who are endowed with consciousness and willpower and are always pursuing some kind of aim. At first glance it would appear that in this field the main task is to elucidate the motives that make people act, to find out what aims a certain person has set himself, and this will tell us why he acted in one way and not another. This kind of psychological explanation of the life of society, which was predominant in pre-Marxist sociology and prevails to this day in bourgeois theories of society, is superficial and insufficient.

Of course everyone is guided in his actions by certain motives and pursues certain aims. But first, the question arises why a particular man should have those particular motives and aims, and not others. And secondly, even a superficial acquaintance with history shows that the aims and interests of different people, and, consequently, their actions, have always come into conflict, and that the ultimate result of this conflict—a historical event—is often very different from what any of its individual participants intended.

Thus many of those who took part in the French Revolution of 1789-94 thought that they were establishing the reign of reason and eternal justice, creating a society based on natural equality and the inalienable rights of man. Very soon, however, it transpired that they were in practice merely clearing the way for the class domination of the bourgeoisie. In place of the old inequality—between feudals and serfs —there came a new inequality—between the bourgeoisie and the workers.

This contradiction between the conscious activity of each separate individual, on the one hand, and the spontaneity of social development as a whole, on the other, was detected long before Marx. But the philosophers were unable to give a correct explanation of it. In their examination of the actual course of history they got no further than conjectures about the aims and motives of certain historical

figures and thus turned the historical process into a mass of chance occurrences. Those of them who attempted to regard history as a process governed by necessity very soon lapsed into fatalism and began to regard it as a result of the action of some external force (God, the "absolute idea," "the universal mind," and so forth) that was supposed to determine men's actions.

The idealist view of history fostered by the very complexity of social development has been vigorously encouraged by the exploiting classes, who have an interest in concealing the true causes of economic and social inequality, the causes responsible for the wealth and power of some and the poverty and lack of rights of others. Thanks to the efforts of these classes, idealist views of society influence people to this day and are widespread in the capitalist countries.

A fundamental revolutionary upheaval in the very approach to the study of social problems was needed in order to explain what it is that conditions people's ideas, opinions, and conscious actions. This upheaval became possible only after the establishment of capitalism had laid bare the material economic roots of the class struggle, after the working class had stepped into the historical arena as the first class in history which . . . not only does not fear a consistently scientific explanation of society, but has a direct interest in such an explanation.

Only in these historical circumstances did the way lie open for the scientific achievement of Marx and Engels, who extended dialectical materialism to the study of society and its history and evolved a scientific theory of the general laws of social development. This theory is *historical materialism, the materialist conception of history*.

The revolution wrought by Marx and

Engels in social science lies primarily in the fact that they proved that there are no mysterious supernatural forces at work in society, and showed that men are themselves the makers of their history. This struck a crushing blow at all mystical views of society and paved the way for understanding history as a natural process not requiring any interference from without.

On the other hand, Marxism proved that people make their history not arbitrarily but on the basis of the objective material conditions they have inherited from past generations. This struck a mortal blow at voluntarism and subjectivism and paved the way for understanding history as a process governed by natural laws. In appraising the significance of the Marxist theory for the science of society, Lenin wrote that this materialist theory "for the first time made a *scientific* sociology possible . . . that only the reduction of social relations to production relations and of the latter to the level of the productive forces, provided a firm basis for the conception that the development of formations of society is a process of natural history."[1]

Marx formulated the initial proposition of historical materialism as follows: "It is not men's consciousness that determines their being, but, on the contrary, their social being that determines their consciousness." In other words, in society, as in nature, being, material life, is primary, is the determining factor in relation to spiritual life, to consciousness.

According to Marxism, social consciousness is the sum total of the political and legal theories, the religious, philosophical, and moral views of a given society; in addition, social consciousness includes the social sciences,

[1] V. I. Lenin, *Collected Works*, I (Moscow: Foreign Languages Publishing House, n.d.), 140-141.

art, and social psychology (social feelings, moods, customs, and so on). Social being, on the other hand, is the material life of society in all its complexity and with all its contradictions.

What exactly is meant by the material life of society, which, as historical materialism has established, determines the whole face of society, its structure, its views, and its institutions?

The Mode of Production as the Material Basis of the Life of Society

The primary component of the material life of society is the labor activity which people devote to the production of the necessities and comforts of their life—food, clothes, housing, etc. This activity is an eternal natural necessity, an essential condition on which the very existence of society depends. As Engels says, mankind must first of all eat, drink, have shelter and clothing, before it can pursue politics, science, art, religion, etc.

The geographical environment, on the one hand, and population, on the other, form the natural material prerequisites for the process of production. However, although these natural material conditions exercise a considerable influence on the course of social development, either accelerating or delaying it, they do not form the basis of the historical process. Different social systems can exist in one and the same natural environment, and density of population has an unequal effect in various historical circumstances.

Unlike animals, which passively adapt themselves to the external environment, man exercises an active influence on his environment and obtains the material values needful to his life by means of labor, which presupposes the use and making of special instruments. Society cannot arbitrarily choose these instruments. Every fresh generation that enters life inherits the instruments of production that have been created by the efforts of previous generations and carries on production with the help of these instruments, only gradually improving and changing them.

Moreover, the development of these instruments follows a definite sequence. Humanity could not, for example, pass straight from the stone axe to the atomic power station. Each new improvement and invention can be made only on the basis of those that have preceded it, and must rest upon gradually accumulated production experience, the labor skills and knowledge of the people of the given country, or of another, more advanced country.

But the instruments of labor do not function of themselves. The principal part in the process of production is played by human beings, the working people, who are able to create and use these instruments because they possess definite skills and working experience.

The means of production created by society, and above all the instruments of labor by which material wealth is created, and the people carrying out the process of production on the basis of a certain degree of production experience, constitute the *productive forces* of society.

The material life of society is not, however, confined to its productive forces.

Production is carried on not by an isolated individual like Robinson Crusoe on his uninhabited island. It always has a *social* character. In the process of producing material wealth, people, whether they like it or not, find themselves in some way or other linked with one another, and the labor of each producer becomes a part of the social labor.

Even in the early stages of history, people had to unite in order to survive, and with the help of the most primitive instruments to obtain the means of subsistence in combat with wild beasts, the elements, and so on. With the development of the social division of labor this dependence of some people on others increased. Thus with the appearance of craftsmanship the peasants began to depend on the craftsmen, while the craftsmen depended on each other and on the peasants, and so on. The producers thus find themselves linked together in manifold relationships.

These relationships are not confined to the ties between producers engaged in various branches of production. At a certain stage of development of the productive forces . . . the ownership of all or, at any rate, the basic means of production is separated from the direct producers and becomes concentrated in the hands of a few members of society. From then on the producers and the instruments of labor cannot unite and the process of production cannot begin unless the owners of the means of production and the producers enter into certain relations. The relations that are established between people in the course of production become the relationships between *classes*—large groups of people, some of whom own the means of production and appropriate for themselves the results of the labor of others who are deprived of the means of production either completely or partially and are compelled to work for the former. In capitalist society, for example, the capitalist class does not work, but by owning factories, mills, and railways, it can appropriate the fruits of the workers' labor. And the workers, whether they like it or not, can earn a living only by selling their labor-power to the capitalist, since they are deprived of the means of production.

The relationships that people enter into in the course of producing material values were called by Marx and Engels *production relations.* They are also called economic relations.

The production relations are formed independently of human consciousness, and in this sense have a material character. The character of production relations is determined by the level of development and the character of the productive forces. The economic relations peculiar to, let us say, slave-owning would be impossible in primitive society. In the first place, the instruments of labor were then so simple to produce (the club, the stone axe) that almost anyone could make them, so that exclusive, private ownership of these instruments was impossible. And secondly, men could not exploit each other because at the level of productivity which then existed they produced only just enough to live on and it was physically impossible to support parasitic classes.

From this example alone it is evident that the relations which people enter into in the process of production, and also the productive forces, exist not isolated from one another but in a definite unity. This unity of the productive forces and production relations is expressed by historical materialism in the concept of the *mode of production.*

How Production Develops

From the most ancient times to our day social production displays incontestible progress, the constant replacement of one mode of production by another, higher one.

How does this development take place? What moves it forward?

The facts show that the sources of the development of production are to be sought not outside but within that development itself. This was emphasized by Marx, who defined history as the "self-developing social state"[2] of mankind.

In the process of labor, people act upon external nature and change it. But while influencing nature they at the same time change themselves. They accumulate experience of production, labor skills, and knowledge of the world around them. All this makes it possible to improve the instruments of labor and the ways of using them, to invent new instruments, and to introduce various improvements in the process of production. And each improvement or invention of this kind brings in its train fresh improvements, which sometimes effect a real revolution in the techniques and productivity of labor.

As has been shown already, however, production inevitably presupposes certain relations not only between man and nature, but also between the people who take part in production. These relations in their turn exert an influence on the development of the productive forces. They determine the stimuli of the activity of those who are directly engaged in production and of the classes that have command of the instruments of labor. On the nature of the production relations depend the economic laws of every mode of production, the living and working conditions of the workers, and other factors influencing the development of the productive forces.

Interaction of Productive Forces and Production Relations

The unity of the productive forces and production relations that is expressed in the mode of production in no way excludes the possibility of contradictions between them.

The causes that bring about these

---

[2] Karl Marx and Friedrich Engels, *Selected Works,* **I** (Moscow: Foreign Languages Publishing House, 1958), 351.

contradictions lie in the fact that the two elements of the mode of production—production relations and productive forces—develop in different ways. Generally speaking, the techniques, production skills, and working experience that people possess—whether it is a matter of history as a whole or of one mode of production taken separately—improve and increase more or less constantly. They are the most mobile, changing element of production.

As for the production relations, although during the existence of a given mode of production they undergo certain changes, their essential nature remains unchanged. Thus, for example, the state-monopoly capitalism of the present day . . . is distinctly different from the capitalism of the nineteenth century. However, the basis of capitalist production relations—private ownership of the instruments and means of production—remains the same and, consequently, the basic laws of capitalism still hold good. Radical changes of production relationships are bound to have the character of a leap, a break in gradualness, which entails the *liquidation* of the old production relations and their replacement by new ones, i.e., the appearance of a new mode of production.

Hence it is clear why any harmony between the production relations and the character of the productive forces in the history of each mode of production can be only transient, temporary, until the socialist epoch is reached. Usually such harmony exists only in the initial stage of development of a mode of production, the stage that is marked by the establishment of new production relations corresponding to the given level of development of the productive forces. After this, however, the development of technology and the accumulation of labor skills, experience, and knowledge do not come to a

stop, but are as a rule accelerated, thus graphically demonstrating the positive effect of production relations on the development of the productive forces. When production relations correspond to these forces, their development proceeds comparatively smoothly and without hindrance.

But the development of the production relations themselves cannot follow constantly that of the productive forces. In class society these relations, having once arisen, become consolidated legally and politically in forms of ownership, in laws, in class politics, in the state and other institutions.

With the growth of the productive forces the discrepancy that inevitably arises between them and the production relations eventually develops into a conflict, since the obsolete production relations hinder the further development of the productive forces.

Thus the relations of feudal society based on the feudal lord's ownership of land and the personal dependence of the peasants on the feudal lords did at one time correspond to the productive forces which society had at its disposal, and therefore aided their development. But in the age when industry (manufacture, followed later by machine industry) began to forge ahead at enormous speed, the situation changed. Serfdom became a brake on the growth of industry, which needed workmen who would, on the one hand, be personally free and, on the other, not possess any means of production, and whom hunger would drive to the mills and factories to work under the yoke of the capitalist. A striking example of the discrepancy between production relations and productive forces is shown by modern capitalism, under the conditions of which the vastly increased socialization of production is constricted within the narrow framework of private capitalist ownership.

This discrepancy finds expression in destructive crises, wars, the slowing up of economic development, and so on.

The conflict between production relations and productive forces leads to a sharpening of the contradictions in various spheres of the life of society, and above all between classes, some of which are interested in the old production relations, while others are interested in the new production relations that are maturing.

Sooner or later this conflict is resolved by the revolutionary abolition of the old production relations and their replacement by new ones corresponding to the character of the productive forces that have grown up, and to the requirements of their further development. A new mode of production arises. There begins—at a higher level—a new cycle of development, which passes through the same stages and, in the case of societies composed of antagonistic classes, again culminates in the destruction of the old and the birth of a new mode of production.

Basis and Superstructure

The state of the productive forces determines, as we have seen, the character of men's production relations, i.e., the economic structure of society. This economic structure in its turn constitutes the *basis*, the foundation, on which there arise many kinds of social relations, ideas, and institutions. The ideas of society (political, legal, philosophical, religious, etc.), the institutions and organizations (state, Church, political parties, etc.) which arise on a given basis, constitute the *superstructure* of society. The theory of basis and superstructure explains how in the final analysis the mode of production determines all aspects of social life and reveals the link between the socioeco-

nomic relations and all the other relations of a given society.

Every society known to history has its specific basis and corresponding superstructure.

The social division of society, its class composition, depends on the dominant form of ownership, and this class composition in its turn determines the character of the society's political institutions and legal standards. A monarchy is inconceivable under socialism, and universal suffrage would be impossible in a slave-owning society. Feudal production relations presuppose . . . not only the material but also—in one form or another—the personal dependence of the peasant on the land owner (serfdom). In feudal law this is expressed in the form of legal inequality between peasants and feudals.

The transition to capitalist production relations brought changes also in legal relations. The substitution of the "discipline of hunger" for direct coercion and personal dependence found its juridical expression in the fact that the law formally declared the equality of worker and capitalist. But since bourgeois law is based on the system of private property the equality it proclaims, in reality, merely strengthens the dominant position of the property-owning classes. Consequently political and legal relations are derived from economic relations and are determined by them.

The same must be said for philosophical, religious, moral, artistic, and other social ideas and conceptions. We know, for example, that in primitive society the prisoners who were captured during wars between various tribes were killed and sometimes even eaten. Later on it became customary to turn them into slaves. Why did such a "softening" of social morals take place? Because the growth of labor productivity had made possible the appropriation of the labor of others, the exploitation of man by man. And it was on this economic basis that the new customs and new views characteristic of the epoch of slavery were born.

The changes in the production relations that occur under socialism bring about a radical change in the views, morals, and standards of conduct of the members of society. Under capitalism, speculation is considered just as much a profession as, say, the profession of doctor or barrister, a profession which at best may be controlled by regulations (operating in favor of the large-scale speculators against the smaller ones), but always remains legal, just as the institutions (the stock exchange, for example) which serve this form of activity are legal. It could not be otherwise in a society based on the exploitation of the labor of others, where money is the highest value, the measure of all virtue. Under socialism, however, such activities are not only morally condemned by society, they are also punishable by law.

From the fact that the basis determines the superstructure it follows that every change of basis, i.e., of production relations, entails a change of superstructure, radical changes in the sphere of the state, law, political relations, morals, and ideology. The superstructure in its turn exercises an influence on production relations and can either delay or accelerate their replacement. It is quite clear, for example, that the political institutions of the modern bourgeoisie (the state, above all), its law and ideology, are playing an important part in the preservation of capitalist ownership and delaying its long overdue replacement by socialist (public) ownership.

In the superstructure of any class society the ideas and institutions of the ruling class are dominant. But in addition to these the superstructure also includes the ideas and organizations of the oppressed classes, which help these classes to fight for their interests.

Thus the fact of the division of bourgeois society into workers and capitalists is sooner or later reflected in the consciousness of both classes. The result of this is that alongside the class ideology and organizations of the bourgeoisie—its state, political parties, press, etc.—there also appear and develop in society the ideology and organizations of the working class. The workers sooner or later become conscious of themselves as a special class, they become aware of their common interests and of the incompatibility of these interests with those of the capitalists. Awareness of class interests results in the workers beginning to unite for a joint struggle against the capitalists. The advanced section of the working class unites in a political party; trade unions and other mass organizations of the working people are created. The relations binding the proletarians in a class organization—political party, trade unions—are relations that must pass through people's consciousness before becoming established, for the workers join a party consciously, out of ideological considerations and of their own free will. Class solidarity develops among the workers and they acquire a morality of their own that is opposed to the ruling bourgeois morality.

Thus on the real basis of class relations there arises a whole pyramid of different world outlooks, social attitudes, political and other organizations and institutions, everything that goes to make up the concept of the superstructure.

In no society is the combination of its various aspects—the productive forces, economy, politics, ideology, etc. —a matter of accident.

The character of the productive forces and the level of their development predetermine the relations into which people enter in the process of production, and these relations form the basis on which a distinct political and ideological superstructure arises. Every society therefore constitutes an integral organism, a so-called *socioeconomic formation*, i.e., a definite historical type of society with its own characteristic mode of production, basis, and superstructure.

The concept of the socioeconomic formation is of enormous significance for the whole science of society. It makes it possible to understand why, in spite of an immense variety of concrete details and peculiarities, all peoples travel what is basically the same path. The history of every people is ultimately conditioned by the development of the productive forces, which obeys the same internal laws. The development of society proceeds through the consecutive replacement, according to definite laws, of one socioeconomic formation by another. Moreover, a nation living in the conditions of a more advanced formation shows other nations their future just as the latter show that nation its past.

The doctrine of socioeconomic formations tears the mystical veils from the history of humanity and makes it comprehensible and knowable. "The chaos and arbitrariness that had previously reigned in the views on history and politics gave way to a strikingly integral and harmonious scientific theory, which shows how, in consequence of the growth of productive forces, out of one system of social life another and higher system develops . . ." (*V. I. Lenin*).[3]

[3] V. I. Lenin, *The Three Sources and Three Components of Marxism* (Moscow: Foreign Languages Publishing House, 1959), p. 9.

A General Critique of Equilibrium Theory

MOHAMMED GUESSOUS

Introduction

Kingsley Davis once wrote: "It is only in terms of equilibrium that most sociological concepts make sense. Either tacitly or explicitly anyone who thinks about society tends to use the notion. The functional-structural approach to sociological analysis is basically an equilibrium theory."[1] The pervasive use of equilibrium models is,

Adapted from Mohammed Guessous, *Foundations for a General Theory of Social Change* (Princeton: Center of International Studies, Princeton University, forthcoming).

[1] Kingsley Davis, *Human Society* (New York: The Macmillan Company, 1949), p. 634.

indeed, true not only of sociology, but of economics, political science, anthropology, and psychology as well.

In the most general terms, a system is said to be in equilibrium when its component parts are so compatible with each other that, barring an outside disturbance, none of them will change its position or relation to the others in any significant way. An equilibrium system is said to be stable when a slight change in external conditions creates internal variations whose own effect is equal and opposite to the initial disturbance, thereby moving the system back to its former position of rest (e.g., a ball in a funnel). It is said to be unstable when the initial disturbance creates a movement that feeds on its own relationships, thereby displacing the system further and further from its former position of rest (e.g., a ball on the small end of a funnel). Equilibrium is said to be neutral when the initial disturbance is not countered but does not produce a self-perpetuating movement either: the system simply moves to a new position and stays there (e.g., a ball in a box of sand). These standard definitions show that whoever identifies equilibrium with stability is actually substituting a particular instance for the whole class of equilibrium systems.

A theory of social equilibrium is a theory that seeks to uncover the general conditions for the maintenance of a society in stable equilibrium, and to specify the mechanisms by which that stability is preserved or re-established after the occurrence of outside disturbances. The statements that are produced by such a theory must be viewed, not as descriptions of what actually happens in most (or all) societies, but as speculative outlines of what society *would be* like *if it were* to function as an equilibrium system. The ultimate purpose—and justification—of such an exercise is to lay the basic foundations for a general theory of social systems. Although "functionalism" can be conceived in terms so broad as to make it almost synonymous with any sociological analysis,[2] it is nevertheless true to

say that most social scientists have tended to equate "functional theory" with equilibrium theory as defined above, and to understand the "functional" explanation of a pattern of behavior as being a demonstration of the manner in which it contributes to the maintenance of social stability.[3] The writings of Talcott Parsons and his associates constitute a particularly clearcut example of an attempt to develop a theory of social equilibrium along functionalist lines. For the sake of clarity as well as brevity, our critique of equilibrium theory will therefore draw most heavily upon Parsons' work.

Change Within Equilibrium Systems

The central problem of this essay may be formulated as follows: Change constitutes one of the most pervasive, persistent, and essential characteristics of social life everywhere. No theory is really a general theory of social systems unless it is able to provide explanations for the repeated occurrence of various kinds of changes in those systems; or else, it must show that these changes are only passing phenomena—unusual and temporary deviations from the postulated course of events—and/or that they are produced by fluctuations in nonsocial factors. How does equilibrium theory—particularly as exemplified in Parsons' work—fare when subjected to such a test?

A serious examination of this question reveals that the widespread complaints about a "static bias" in Parsons' work (or, more generally, in function-

[2] See, for example, Marion J. Levy, *The Structure of Society* (Princeton: Princeton University Press, 1952), Chap. 2; Robert K. Merton, *Social Theory and Social Structure* (New York: The Free Press of Glencoe, Inc., 1957), Chap. 1; Kingsley Davis, "The Myth of Functional Analysis as a Special Method in Sociology and Anthropology," *American Sociological Review*, 24 (December, 1959), 757-772; Francesca Cancian, "Functional Analysis of Change," *American Sociological Review*, 25 (December, 1960), 818-827.

[3] See George C. Homans, *The Human Group* (New York: Harcourt, Brace & World, Inc., 1950), pp. 307-308; Talcott Parsons, *The Social System* (New York: The Free Press of Glencoe, Inc., 1951), pp. 383-384; Carl G. Hempel, "The Logic of Functional Analysis," in L. Gross, ed., *Symposium on Sociological Theory* (New York: Harper & Row, Publishers, 1959), esp. pp. 293-297.

alist writings) are either trivial, or meaningless, or false unless they are carefully qualified and specified. Parsons' examination of the conditions for social stability *does* permit the formulation of many propositions about patterns of change in social life; and this is as it should be, because an investigation of the general bases for social stability necessarily requires a survey of the forces that threaten as well as those that preserve the stability of the social system. More specifically, it can be shown that an equilibrium theory like that of Parsons is logically capable of providing reasonable explanations for at least three types of determinate changes in the flow of social life—namely, (1) changes that are *necessary* for the maintenance of social stability; (2) other changes that are *compatible with* the maintenance of social stability; (3) and finally, limited, temporary, and reversible *fluctuations* around the equilibrium position of the social system. A full demonstration and evaluation of these assertions would be impossible within the confines of this short essay.[4] All we can do here is to provide some very brief, and inevitably ambiguous, sketches of the kinds of arguments that could be used for such a demonstration.

1. First, one might argue that the maintenance of social stability must be viewed, not as a smooth, continuous, and nearly automatic process, but rather as a dynamic, never-ending struggle, as a shaky balance which often threatens to collapse and escapes it only *in extremes*. This line of analysis leads to the contention that a society will not remain stable over a long time unless it is able and willing to undergo two kinds of changes in its compo-

nents: (a) periodic sequences of structural differentiation, involving the emergence of new, specialized subsystems of norms, resources, and activities able to cope with particular problem areas within the social system; and (b) the institutionalization of periodic "phase-movements," whereby the focus of collective concern would alternatively shift from one set of norms, demands, and functional problems to another set which is no less important but which could not be handled simultaneously.

2. One might further argue that most social systems are bound to progressively change in the direction of an ever-more rational implementation of their institutionalized goals and values (e.g., replacement of existing means to valued ends by newer and progressively more efficient ones; continuous search for alternative structures that could carry out given functional requirements in an ever-more efficient manner, etc.). These patterns of change—which may be labelled as cumulative growth (or social development)—can be subsumed under a slightly modified version of equilibrium theory, i.e., by assuming society to be in dynamic, rather than static, equilibrium. Within the latter framework, cumulative growth is tolerable so long as it proceeds in a relatively gradual, orderly, and predictable way, thus allowing the social system to absorb it without disruption of its basic values and structures. The social system assumed to be in stable equilibrium would be defined here, not by a specific set of concrete structures and processes, but by a whole range of permissible variations, by a system of immanent potentialities.

3. One might, finally, contend that the normal flow of social life is most likely to deviate from the ideal conditions for stable equilibrium in certain

---

[4] Evidence for these assertions is extensively reviewed in Chap. 2 [of the book from which this selection was adapted].

predictable ways (i.e., through failures in the socialization process, indeterminacies in normative expectations, inconsistencies among institutionalized norms and values, and tensions between human needs and the demands for social conformity); that the deviations from equilibrium produced by these internal disturbances will usually be small, confined to particular problem areas, and soon reversed through the reactivation of social control mechanisms; and that the long-run over-all effect of such fluctuations upon the core structures and values of the social system will usually be trivial.

A General Critique of Equilibrium Theory

The real trouble with an equilibrium theory like that of Parsons is that *its underlying premises allow it to give a reasonably adequate account of only some of the changes that are known to occur regularly in social life, but not of others, and that its failure in the latter respect probably prevents it from providing an adequate framework for a general theory of social systems.*

There is, indeed, one whole class of changes which an equilibrium theory like that of Parsons does not account for—namely, *changes that involve a transformation of the fundamental structure of society,* and which are usually described under such labels as "structural change," "social revolution," "change of the system," etc. We refer here to pervasive, discontinuous, and cumulative changes which, having affected many actors in many contexts of their lives, bring about a radical reorganization of the over-all system of values, norms, and resources, and so displace the equilibrium point of society that *"the new one cannot be reached from the old one by infinitesimal steps.* Add successively as many

mail coaches as you please, you will never get a railway thereby."[5] This matter of structural change can be illustrated through the use of an example from mathematics. Assume an equation of the form $Y = a + bX$. This equation involves two groups of relations: first, the value of Y at any moment will depend upon the value of X; the latter, called a variable, is expected to take different values in the course of time. The second element of this equation is a and b, called constants or parameters because they are not expected to vary in any short period: they symbolize what we have called the fundamental structure of society. Now, the system described by this equation can undergo two types of changes: on the one hand, successive changes in X will yield different values of Y, but these varying values stem from the *same fixed framework:* the equation remains the same; the fundamental relations remain constant throughout these variations in X and Y. What we have called structural change would be represented here by a change in the constants or parameters (or again, by a change in the form of the equation, e.g., from a linear to a binomial function).[6] After a social

[5] Joseph A. Schumpeter, *The Theory of Economic Development* (Cambridge: Harvard University Press, 1951), p. 64n.

[6] For further comments on this notion of structural change, see Parsons, *op. cit.,* p. 481; Talcott Parsons and Neil Smelser, *Economy and Society* (New York: The Free Press of Glencoe, Inc., 1957), pp. 247-248; A. R. Radcliffe-Brown, *A Natural Science of Society* (New York: The Free Press of Glencoe, Inc., 1957), p. 87; Lewis A. Coser, "Social Conflict and the Theory of Social Change," *British Journal of Sociology,* **8** (September, 1957), 197-207, esp. 201-202; Fritz Machlup, "Structure and Structural Change: Weaselwords and Jargon," *Zeitschrift für Nationalekonomie,* **18** (August, 1958), 280-298; Raymond Firth, *Social Change in Tikopia* (London: George Allen & Unwin, 1959), pp. 340-342; E. K. Francis,

system has undergone the latter kind of change, the *same* stimulus may have implications markedly *different* from what they were before that change occurred (e.g., an item which was eufunctional for the system may cease to be so, and vice versa). Parsons' theory, as well as any other variant of equilibrium theory, is logically prevented from showing how this kind of structural change could arise from the normal operation of society. They may concede the probable emergence of internal disturbances, but must insist that the latter alone can never alter the determinate fundamental relations that characterize the social structure. They may allow for some gradual and orderly development of the immanent potentialities of a social system, but must stop short of showing how the normal flow of social life could lead to a transformation of the system of potentialities itself. In short, their commitment to a model of stable equilibrium logically requires them to argue that, if left to itself, a society would essentially live in its own eternal present.

Within the framework of an equilibrium theory like that of Parsons, there logically remains one point of view from which the problem of structural change can be analyzed—by relating it to the *influence of powerful exogenous forces*. The latter refer to variations in the physical environment; to changes in the genetic constitution of human organisms and/or in the distribution of genetic components within a given population; to autonomous cultural innovations adopted under the influence of charismatic leaders; and especially to changes induced by other social sys-

tems through cross-cultural contact and diffusion.[7] The disruptive influence of these exogenous forces may be subsumed under a slightly modified version of the equilibrium model, i.e., *by assuming society to be "stable in the small" only.* That is to say, one may argue that the stability attributed to the social system does not necessarily imply that the latter will be able to resist and overcome every possible kind of outside interference. Rather, the system's ability to maintain some constancy of internal relations will usually hold for only a limited and well-defined range of variations in the external situation. Thus as soon as environmental disturbances go beyond the "margin of safety" characteristic of that system, they will inevitably overcome its internal control mechanisms, and irremediably displace it further and further from its initial position of rest.

This view of structural change as due to the influence of powerful exogenous forces was represented, in the early stages of development of the sociological discipline, by a great many mechanistic theories that sought to explain social behavior by the influence of demographic, climatic, geological, and biological factors.[8] A similar "external-

---

[7] See Talcott Parsons, "An Outline of the Social System," in Talcott Parsons, *et al.*, *Theories of Society* (New York: The Free Press of Glencoe, Inc., 1961), I, 71, 78-79.

[8] For reviews and further discussion, see, for example, Pitirim A. Sorokin, *Contemporary Sociological Theories* (New York: Harper & Row, Publishers, 1928); Newell LeRoy Sims, *The Problem of Social Change* (New York: Thomas Y. Crowell Company, 1939), Part II; W. F. Cottrell, *Energy and Society* (New York: McGraw-Hill Book Company, 1955); Sol Tax, ed., *Evolution after Darwin*, 3 vols. (Chicago: University of Chicago Press, 1960); M. F. Ashley Montagu, ed., *Culture and the Evolution of Man* (New York: Oxford University Press, 1962); Theodosius Dobzhansky, *Mankind Evolving* (New Haven: Yale University Press, 1962).

"Prolegomena to a Theory of Social Change," *Kylos*, 14 (1961), 213-233; J. A. Ponsioen, *The Analysis of Social Change Reconsidered* (The Hague: Mouton & Co., 1962), pp. 17-18.

istic" explanation of structural change pervades the overwhelming majority of contemporary discussions of this subject. Most of these discussions view social systems as devoid of any capacity for bringing about a fundamental transformation of their own structures; they argue that structural transformation comes primarily from the fact that those same systems are continuously pushed and pulled by unruly and unpredictable external forces; and they differ from earlier mechanistic theories only in that they have shifted from emphasis upon biological and inorganic factors to an overwhelming preoccupation with another exogenous source of structural change—what they interchangeably call "diffusion," "culture-contact," "acculturation," "Westernization," "imperialism," "the international Communist conspiracy," the action of "subversive elements" and "outside agitators," etc.[9] For example,

Foster states: "Notwithstanding the importance of local innovation and discovery, as we have indicated, the major force in culture change is borrowing; members of the group appropriate forms of behavior they first encounter in alien societies. . . . Contact between societies is the single greatest determinate of culture change."[10] And Murdock seems to echo the same argument when he maintains that "it is doubtful whether there is a single culture known to history or anthropology that has not owed at least 90 per cent of its constituent elements to cultural borrowing."[11] This very widespread view of the primary sources of structural change involves a number of fundamental difficulties which we shall now quickly review.

To interpret structural change in this manner is an abdication of analytical responsibility, because *the behavior of exogenous forces is assumed to be indeterminate from the point of view of the theory of social systems.* (This does not preclude the possibility of a determinate analysis of these forces when a different system is taken as the reference point.) A knowledge of the laws of operation of a social system in stable equilibrium provides no basis for predicting the occurrence, intensity, and timing of external disturbances. This ultimately implies the

---

[9] For a sample of the immense literature on this subject, see Alexander Goldenweiser, *et al.*, *Culture: The Diffusion Controversy* (New York: W. W. Norton & Company, Inc., 1927); Melville J. Herskovits, *Acculturation* (Locust Valley, N.Y.: J. J. Augustin, Inc., Publisher, 1938); Pitirim A. Sorokin, *Social and Cultural Dynamics*, IV (New York: American Book Company, 1941), Chap. 13; Bronislaw Malinowski, *The Dynamics of Culture Change* (New Haven: Yale University Press, 1945); Edward H. Spicer, ed., *Human Problems in Technological Change* (New York: Russell Sage Foundation, 1952); H. Ian Hogbin, *Social Change* (London: C. A. Watts & Co., Ltd., 1958); Daniel Lerner, *The Passing of Traditional Society* (New York: The Free Press of Glencoe, Inc., 1958); Leonard W. Doob, *Becoming More Civilized* (New Haven: Yale University Press, 1960); Egbert de Vries, *Man in Rapid Social Change* (New York: Doubleday & Company, Inc., 1961); Warren G. Bennis, *et al.*, *The Planning of Change* (New York: Holt, Rinehart & Winston, Inc., 1961); George M. Foster, *Traditional Cultures and the Impact of Technological Change* (New York: Harper & Row, Publishers, 1962); Everett M. Rogers, *Diffusion of Innovations* (New York: The

Free Press of Glencoe, Inc., 1962); Bert F. Hoselitz and Wilbert E. Moore, eds., *Industrialization and Society* (The Hague: Mouton & Co., 1963); Ward H. Goodenough, *Cooperation in Change* (New York: Russell Sage Foundation, 1963); Cyril E. Black and Thomas P. Thornton, eds., *Communism and Revolution* (Princeton: Princeton University Press, 1964); Peter Worsley, *The Third World* (London: George Weidenfeld and Nicolson, Ltd., Publishers, 1964).

[10] George M. Foster, *op. cit.*, p. 25.

[11] George P. Murdock, "How Culture Changes," in H. L. Shapiro, ed., *Man, Culture and Society* (New York: Oxford University Press, 1956), p. 254.

doctrine that anything can happen in human history; that the course of historical changes like the Renaissance, the French Revolution, the transition from feudalism to capitalism, or the present transformation of traditional societies, depends upon mere chance, the free decisions of men, or the dictates of a divine "Prime Mover;" that sequences of structural change are only unusual and abnormal phenomena; that they are mere exceptions to the smooth course of events postulated by the equilibrium model—exceptions which are brought about by single, individual, nonrepetitive events that may be amenable to historical analysis but not to theoretical generalization. The tenability of this doctrine is clearly contradicted by most historical data available to us. For example, Sorokin's wide-ranging researches in Western social history from 600 B.C. to 1933 revealed that the societies in his sample tended to experience a serious internal disturbance *every four to seven years on the average,* and that the magnitude of these disturbances had fluctuated from century to century much less than is usually believed. His concluding comments on these findings are worth quoting at length:

The fact that these phenomena occur so frequently confirms our conclusions that they are inseparable from the very existence and functioning of social bodies. If this be so, then it is evident that the usual method of accounting for these phenomena as the fault of a government, an aristocracy, or a mob, or of revolutionaries, or any other group, as due to this or that set of special conditions and factors—in brief, the habit of regarding disturbances as something quite abnormal and in need of being explained by special extraordinary factors and the faults and misdeeds of various agencies or individuals—is superficial and unscientific. Disturbances seem to be no less "normal" than periods of order, only less frequent,

and seem no more to need a special explanation than order does. Their "causes" are as deep in social life itself as the "causes" of internal peace. A set of special conditions, like a poor government, a selfish aristocracy, stupid mobmindedness, poverty, and war, may play a secondary role in reinforcing or weakening, accelerating or retarding, disturbances, but these are only secondary factors. Even without them, disturbances, like storms, would frequently occur.[12]

In short, if we were to take Parsons' view of structural change seriously, we would have to give up any hope of ever achieving some reasonably adequate understanding of the myriads of structural transformations that have been experienced by human societies through the ages, and we would be especially handicapped in our efforts to understand our modern era, whose most distinct characteristic is a revolutionization of practically every aspect of man's experience in nearly every single society on the face of this earth. Neither has Parsons himself made any secret of this fundamental shortcoming. He argued in 1951 that *"a general theory of the processes of change of social systems is not possible in the present state of knowledge.* The reason is very simply that such a theory would imply complete knowledge of the laws of process of the system, and this knowledge we do not possess. The theory of change in the structure of social systems must, therefore, be a theory of particular subprocesses of change *within* such systems, not of the over-all processes of change *of* the systems as systems." He later added: "When such a theory [of structural change] is available the millennium for social science will have arrived. This

12 Pitirim A. Sorokin, *Social and Cultural Dynamics* (New York: American Book Company, 1937), **III**, 504; Sorokin's evidence is presented in *ibid.,* Chaps. 12-14.

will not come in our time and most probably never."[13]

These difficulties are amply documented in available discussions of social change by Parsons and his associates. For example, in discussing how a process of structural differentiation begins, Parsons simply writes: "We may start with the *postulation* of a deficit of input at the goal attainment boundary of the social system which is *postulated* as undergoing a process of differentiation. . . ."[14] Again, his analysis of the genesis of motivation to deviance begins with the statement: "Let us *assume* that, *from whatever source*, a disturbance is introduced into the system, of such a character that what alter does leads to a frustration, in some important respects, of ego's expectation system vis-à-vis alter."[15] Indeed, Parsons' so-called "paradigm of deviant behavior," as well as other well-known discussions of the same subject by Merton and Dubin,[16] turn out to be no more than *descriptive typologies* of what kinds of normative deviations *could* occur in a society. Dubin was very explicit on this point. He wrote: "This is *not* a theory of *how* deviant behavior occurs, nor *why* it occurs. It is simply a descriptive typology of the range of mutually exclusive types of nonconforming behavior."[17] In his more empirically oriented writings, Parsons does discuss the problem of structural change, and he often does so with a great deal of insight and acumen.[18] But what is most striking about these essays is the manner in which they make use of many ideas and hypotheses that are hardly compatible with Parsons' own theoretical scheme. "Indeed," as Gouldner pointed out, "the extent to which Parsons' efforts at theoretical and empirical analysis of change suddenly lead him to enlist a body of Marxist concepts and assumptions is nothing less but bewildering. . . . It almost seems as if two sets of books were being kept, one for the analysis of equilibrium and another for the investigation of change."[19] At other times, the problem of structural change is deftly "swept under the rug" by simply denying that any such change has happened in the phenomenon under study. Thus Parsons and White recently maintained that the paramount value system of American society has *not* undergone any fundamental change in the last century.[20]

[13] Talcott Parsons, *The Social System, op. cit.*, pp. 486 and 534, respectively.
[14] Talcott Parsons, "Some Considerations on the Theory of Social Change," *Rural Sociology*, **26** (September, 1961), 229, italics added.
[15] *The Social System, op. cit.*, p. 252, italics added.
[16] See *ibid.*, Chap. 7; R. K. Merton, *op. cit.*, Chaps. 4-5; R. K. Merton, "Social Conformity, Deviation and Opportunity Structures," *American Sociological Review*, **24** (April, 1959), 177-189; Robert Dubin, "Deviant Behavior and Social Structure," *ibid.*, **24** (April, 1959), 147-164; Marshall B. Clinard, ed., *Anomie and Deviant Behavior* (New York: The Free Press of Glencoe, Inc., 1964).
[17] Robert Dubin, *op. cit.*, 163.

[18] See, for example, Talcott Parsons, *Essays in Sociological Theory*, rev. ed. (New York: The Free Press of Glencoe, Inc., 1954), and *Structure and Process in Modern Societies* (New York: The Free Press of Glencoe, Inc., 1960).
[19] Alvin W. Gouldner, "Some Observations on Systematic Theory, 1945-55," in Hans L. Zetterberg, ed., *Sociology in the United States of America* (Paris: UNESCO, 1956), p. 41.
[20] Talcott Parsons and Winston White, "The Link Between Character and Society," in S. M. Lipset and L. Lowenthal, eds., *Character and Social Structure* (New York: The Free Press of Glencoe, Inc., 1961), esp. pp. 100, 103. Contrast this assertion with the other essays in *ibid.*, to which may be added: Elting E. Morison, ed., *The American Style* (New York: Harper & Row, Publishers, 1958); Richard T. La Piere, *The Freudian Ethic* (New York: Duell, Sloan & Pearce, Inc., 1959); and Herbert Marcuse, *One-Dimensional Man* (Boston: Beacon Press, 1964); Parsons has even maintained that the basic value system of Christianity has *not* undergone any fundamental change *from the time*

Many proponents of equilibrium theory tend to accept the fairness of the above indictment, but they add that the latter theory "is by no means devoid of relevance to the analysis of such processes of [structural] change, processes which pose precisely the most difficult empirical problems we have in our field. We definitely have *something* to say about these problems."[21] That "something" invariably revolves around the method of comparative statics, which was generally defined by Samuelson as "the investigation of changes in a system from one position of equilibrium to another without regard to the transitional process involved in the adjustment."[22] That is to say, although we may not be able to predict the occurrence, intensity, or timing of processes of structural change, our knowledge of the relations among variables in a state of equilibrium will still allow us to formulate a theory of the social system's *responses* to *given* disturbances. Assuming certain disturbances as given, the method of comparative statics proceeds then to a formal exploration of the ways in which these disturbances affect the behavior of the equilibrium system and of its various components. This method is very widely used in the sociological literature. But it unfortunately involves a number of quasi-insuperable difficulties which we will now quickly review.

In the first place, the method of comparative statics allows for only one pattern of systemic reaction to a disturbance—that of movement to a new position of rest. It thus neglects the important case in which the initial disturbance calls forth supporting changes, thereby moving the system further and further from its former position of rest without any prospect of stabilization in sight. Secondly, that method pays no attention to the temporal sequence of transition from one equilibrium position to another: it only describes what the system will be like once it has reached a new position of rest. The neglect of these two important questions reveals a number of untenable premises that underlie this whole procedure and that are rarely brought into the open:

(*a*) This may imply the assumption that disruptive disturbances occur only on rare occasions, and that each of them has ample time to work itself out before a new disturbance takes place. Upon this view, social change is interpreted as an intermittent process between extended periods of stationariness; it is viewed as a revolution or mutation which occurs in one stroke and, through a sudden and cataclysmic upheaval, quickly and decisively affects all the parts of a social system. Curiously enough, many Marxian theorists seem to subscribe to this same viewpoint when they insist that there can be no "real" social change without a revolution, and that the transition from one social form to another always occurs rapidly and abruptly by way of a leap.[23] This over-all view of social life is blatantly contradicted by numerous facts of daily observation as well as by a mass of historical evidence. Most structural transformations never occur in one stroke; they usually take a long

---

of *Christ to the present.* See his "Christianity and Modern Industrial Society" in Edward A. Tiryakian, ed., *Sociological Theory, Values, and Sociocultural Change* (New York: The Free Press of Glencoe, Inc., 1963), pp. 33-70.

[21] Talcott Parsons, *The Social System, op. cit.,* p. 534.

[22] Paul A. Samuelson, *Foundations of Economic Analysis* (Cambridge: Harvard University Press, 1947), p. 8; see *ibid.,* Chap. 2.

[23] See Gustav A. Wetter, *Dialectical Materialism* (New York: Frederick A. Praeger, Inc., 1958), esp. pp. 325-329, and the comments in Ralf Dahrendorf, *Class and Class Conflict in Industrial Society* (Stanford: Stanford University Press, 1959), pp. 130-133, 210.

time to come about, and their cumulative effects become clearly noticeable only over a long stretch of history.[24] Pigou, an advocate of the theory of equilibrium in economics, has further pointed out that in the real world "the new stationary state, to which a given shift in the governing conditions points, is never attained in fact; for some new disturbance always intervenes. Thus its history is not made up of periods of stationariness . . . and periods of transition. Transition rules always; stationariness never; the long run never comes." And Pigou heroically added in conclusion to his whole book on *The Economics of Stationary States*: "It follows that the analysis worked out in this book cannot by itself make any large direct contribution to the study of real life. It provides a taking-off place, but little more; a first stage only, which needs extensive supplement. The building is much more than the foundation. But, nonetheless, to take pains over the foundation is not to waste time."[25]

(*b*) An analysis of structural change by means of the method of comparative statics usually says nothing about the temporal sequence of the transition from one equilibrium state to another; nor does it investigate differentials in

the speed with which the component parts of the system react to a given disturbance. Failure to analyze this question implicitly commits proponents of that method to a number of alternative assumptions. One such assumption would be that the variables of the system will instantaneously adjust themselves to any change in conditions. Instantaneity means here that "no matter how small the duration of t [time] is taken to be, the time necessary for a new adjustment to occur is so much smaller that it can be neglected."[26] It would logically follow from this assumption that the social system will never deviate from its equilibrium state for even a single moment! Alternatively, one might understand the silence maintained around this question to imply the assumption that all the component parts of the social system will adjust to a given disturbance in an equal time span and/or with equal reaction speeds. This assumption is highly unrealistic; commitment to it would prevent us from analyzing some of the most crucial processes by which change in the structure of society occurs (e.g., it does not allow for slow, delayed, or staggering adjustment, for differences in the speeds at which the relevant adjustment processes operate in different parts of the social system, etc.). One final possible interpretation of this question would be to argue that the analysis of change within the framework of an equilibrium theory will, strictly speaking, apply only in the long run. That is to say, the theo-

[24] For some supporting evidence, see Pitirim A. Sorokin, *Society, Culture and Personality* (New York: Harper & Row, Publishers, 1947), Parts VI-VII; Oscar Halecki, *The Limits and Divisions of European History* (New York: Sheed & Ward, 1950); George Boas, "Historical Periods," *Journal of Aesthetics and Art Criticism*, 11 (March, 1953), 248-254; Dietrich Gerhard, "Periodization in European History," *American Historical Review*, 61 (July, 1956), 900-913; Alexander Gerschenkron, "On the Concept of Continuity in History," *Proceedings of the American Philosophical Society*, 106 (April, 1962), 195-209.

[25] Arthur C. Pigou, *The Economics of Stationary States* (London: Macmillan & Co., Ltd., 1935), p. 264.

[26] Robert E. Kuenne, *The Theory of General Economic Equilibrium* (Princeton: Princeton University Press, 1963), pp. 461-462; see also Melvin W. Reder, *Studies in the Theory of Welfare Economics* (New York: Columbia University Press, 1947), esp. pp. 108-109; and John C. Harsanyi, "Explanation and Comparative Dynamics in Social Science," *Behavioral Science*, 5 (April, 1960), 136-145.

rist deliberately places himself within the long run; he allows for enough time to evolve during which the system will have made full adjustments to a given disturbance. This is the least objectionable of the assumptions heretofore reviewed. It underlies most theories of stages in the development of some social process; and it looms behind most of our earlier comments about structural differentiation, phase movements, cumulative growth, and fluctuations around the equilibrium position of the social system.

(c) Finally, by failing to analyze the path of transition from one equilibrium state to another, proponents of the method of comparative statics implicitly assume that the probability for a system to reach a new position of rest does not depend upon its following any particular route or sequence of reactions to a given disturbance, and that the same position of rest may be reached in a variety of ways. This was, indeed, the view taken by Bertalanffy in his discussion of the "principle of equifinality." In his own words:

A profound difference between most inanimate and living systems can be expressed by the concept of *equifinality*. In most physical systems, the final state is determined by the initial conditions. Take, for instance, the motion in a planetary system where the positions at time t are determined by those of a time to, or a chemical equilibrium where the final concentrations depend on the initial ones. If there is a change in either the initial conditions or the process, the final state is changed. Vital phenomena [including social systems, M.G.] show a different behavior. Here, to a wide extent, the final state may be reached from different initial conditions and in different ways. Such behavior we call equifinal. . . . In an open reaction system, irrespective of the concentrations in the beginning or at any other time, the steady-state values will always be the same, being determined only by the constants of reactions and of the inflow and outflow.[27]

The applicability of this principle of equifinality to social systems cannot be viewed as self-evident; it must constitute a question for empirical investigation, not a dogma to be taken for granted by theoretical *fiat*; and it must meet objections like those formulated by David Easton when he wrote:

What is often neglected in connection with the equifinal steady state is that this is a peculiarity only of one kind of system and is not necessarily true of all systems, such as the social. Indeed, economists have long been able to demonstrate that path taken toward equilibrium may in fact influence the final position of rest; at times it may even forever prevent the attainment of equilibrium. Perhaps it is true that all organic systems are equifinal, but we already have evidence from economic theory that this is not necessarily the case under all circumstances for social systems.[28]

Conclusion

Parsons and Shils once claimed that their theoretical scheme is "concerned equally with the conditions of stability and the conditions of change. It is equally concerned with slow cumulative change and with sudden or fluctuating change. . . ."[29] Our brief discussion has shown that, when understood as referring to the actual or potential development of a sufficient

[27] Ludwig von Bertalanffy, "The Theory of Open Systems in Physics and Biology," *Science*, 111 (January 13, 1950), 25.

[28] David Easton, "Limits of the Equilibrium Model in Social Research," *Behavioral Science*, 1 (April, 1956), 99-100.

[29] Talcott Parsons and E. A. Shils, "Values, Motives, and Systems of Action," in Parsons and Shils, eds., *Toward a General Theory of Action* (New York: Harper & Row, Publishers, 1962), p. 230.

body of substantive propositions about well-known patterns of social change, the above claim is and will remain untenable as long as it is tied to the conception of society as an equilibrium-maintaining system. More particularly, we have seen that an equilibrium theory like that of Parsons can neither explain the occurrence of radical changes in society nor account for the phenomena which accompany them; it says next to nothing about what happens when a social system is in disequilibrium, and only tells us what that system will be like if and when it has reached a new position of rest.

The real trouble with equilibrium theories is not simply that they distort reality. Every exercise in theory building—to use Lord Morley's aphorism about politics—is bound to be "one long second-best, where the choice often lies between two blunders." Oversimplification is inevitable, but some oversimplifications may be less enlightening and less fruitful than others. The basic objection to equilibrium theory is, rather, that it systematically emasculates and ignores some of the most essential characteristics of social life. It is tied to the image of a society whose historical development holds no surprises. Nothing new and unique, no important transformations ever happen in the normal world of equilibrium theory. Society stands still even as it revolves; it will change only to the extent and with the effect of preserving its fundamental structure unchanged; the rhythm of its future will be the beat of its present—unless it is shattered by the sudden eruption of explosive and unpredictable external forces. . . .

When its failures with respect to the problem of structural change are added to some of its other shortcomings which we cannot review here,[30] it will

then become clear that equilibrium theory provides neither an adequate basis for, nor even a stepping stone toward, the development of a general theory of social systems. The latter task cannot be undertaken until we have performed a radical reconstruction of the whole body of modern social theory—including changes in our initial and subsidiary assumptions, in the leading questions to be asked of social reality, in the factors to be singled out for special emphasis, and

---

[30] For some useful critiques of various other aspects of equilibrium theory, see Pitirim A. Sorokin, "Le Concept d'équilibre est-il nécessaire aux Sciences Sociales?," *Revue internationale de sociologie*, 44 (September-October, 1936), 495-529, and *Social and Cultural Dynamics, op. cit.*, Vol. IV, esp. pp. 587-600, 677-693; Robert Goetz-Girey, "Statique et dynamique économiques dans la science allemande contemporaine," *Revue d'économie politique*, 50 (July-August, 1936), 1308-1330; Simon Kuznets, *Economic Change* (New York: W. W. Norton & Company, Inc., 1953), esp. Chap. 1; Jules Henry, "Homeostasis, Society and Evolution: A Critique," *The Scientific Monthly*, 81 (December, 1955), 30-309; Hans H. Tock and Albert H. Kastorf, "Homeostasis in Psychology: A Review and Critique," *Psychiatry*, 18 (February, 1955), 81-91; D. Easton, *op. cit.*; R. C. Davis, "The Domain of Homeostasis," *Psychological Review*, 65 (January, 1958), 8-13; Evon Z. Vogt, "On the Concepts of Structure and Process in Cultural Anthropology," *American Anthropologist*, 62 (February, 1960), 18-33; J. C. Harsanyi, *op. cit.*; Wilbert E. Moore, *Social Change* (Englewood Cliffs, N.J.: Prentice-Hall, Inc., 1963); Pierre L. van den Berghe "Dialectic and Functionalism: Toward a Theoretical Synthesis," *American Sociological Review*, 28 (October, 1963), 695-705; Henri Lefelvre, "Réflexions sur le structuralisme et l'histoire," *Cahiers internationaux de sociologie*, 35 (July-December, 1963), 3-24; Raymond Firth, *Essays on Social Organization and Values* (London: The Athlone Press, 1964), Chap. 1; Renate Mayntz, "On the Use of the Equilibrium Concept in Social System Analysis," *Transactions of the Fifth World Congress of Sociology*, Vol. IV (International Sociological Association, 1964), pp. 133-153; [the book from which this selection was adapted], esp. Chaps. 2-5.

in our current interpretations of well-known facts and situations. This is just another way of saying that we may not yet have even begun to ask the most crucial questions about social behavior, let alone to answer them; that today's social theorist is still presented with a job and a half, and that he still has a long way to go before the proverbial labors are able to produce insights into social life which are both significant and enlightening.

the qualities of change

two

Alterations in the way men behave and the way their organized life more or less assembles itself can be distinguished in a variety of ways. Most of these distinctions lend themselves readily to common-sense designations: large-scale and small-scale, long-term and short-term. Others require a somewhat deeper penetration into issues—for example, whether change goes in a consistent direction, at a consistent pace, and always moves forward or simply turns on itself, with boring repetition.

Thinking about change makes no sense at all—is indeed impossible—without some conception of the passage of time. And time is a subject that has fascinated (and eluded) philosophical thinkers for a long time. One of the most sensible, if occasionally difficult, statements that has come to our attention is that of a physicist, Richard Schlegel, who turns our statement about the relation of time and change the other way around. Change, he perceptively argues, is essential to the conception of time. Indeed, in his view, our conception rests upon two "kinds of physical change, cyclic and noncyclic, in the natural world that we know." He rejects the notion of "absolute time," or any *real* time outside of these physical processes.

The directionality of change is addressed from different perspectives by an historian of science, Price, and by a sociologist, Sorokin. Price has demonstrated again that many social processes can be fitted with exponential and logistic curves, a further confirmation of the significance of cumulation, noted in the preceding chapter. On the other hand, in his analysis of "saturated science," Price gives us one way in which Sorokin's "principle of limits" operates.

Lest we regard all of man's valued concerns as being on the ascendant, at an accelerating speed, Sorokin reminds us of ambiguities and uncertainties, of reversals in the course of events. His notion that change is an unfolding of the "inherent potentialities" of a system, and that each supersystem possesses the "germs of its own decline," appears to be right out of Marx. On the other hand, the intersection of cyclical and linear changes, which combine to form "varyingly recurrent processes," parallels Schlegel's analysis of physical change.

We have, then, a view of cumulative change, whether continuous or discontinuous, and a view of change that is far less regular. A tolerance for complexity is the first essential component of the scientific mind. The notion that some doctrines may be true and others false may first occur to one, and properly. The notion that seemingly contradictory doctrines are simultaneously true, because they relate to different orders of the world of experience, must also be seriously entertained. We suggest that this is the situation with respect to Price's and Sorokin's differing views of the directionality of change.

Time and Physical Process

Time and Physical Change

Time is associated in an essential way with the changing characteristics of the natural world. If a region or village has seemed not to change we say that for it "time has stood still." This very usage reflects the idea that the changing of the world is a concomitant of the passage of time.

We might ask: Does the world change because time moves on, or does time move on because there is change? The answer must be that time arises from changes that occur. To answer otherwise would be to assume that there is a time entity that is prior to the events of the natural world. We are here assuming contrariwise, that time is an aspect of the natural world, coexistent with that world but not prior to it. Evidence against the existence of time that is prior to events will be given later. . . .

It is not difficult to perceive that the existence of time is related to the existence of change, and yet, it may seem that change is not the essential element of time. A quality of persistence or extension—of "everything not happening at once"—seems to be the most fundamental and essential characteristic of time. That is, if the natural world changes it presents a succession of different states or conditions. The capa-

Richard Schlegel, *Time and the Physical World* (East Lansing: Michigan State University Press, 1961), pp. 1-16. Reprinted by permission of the publisher.

bility of presenting such a succession requires that nature possess a property of taking on or displaying more than one state. This property might be called "capability of showing change," and we could then say that we find time in the world because the world possesses the "capability of showing change."

It should be made clear, however, that the possibility of presenting a succession of different states would not ensure the existence of physical time. We can think of a universe in which there is no change whatsoever, although there is a possibility of change being introduced; such a universe would be one which possesses the "capability of showing change" but in actuality presents only a single state. In this universe there would be no time. An intuitive feeling that a changeless universe would in fact still have a time progression associated with it is an expression of our mental habits. The world we live in indubitably does present a succession of different states, and we are therefore accustomed to considering time and change to be necessary attributes of existence. But a universe which in all of its parts showed no change whatsoever would not have a time measure associated with it, for there would be nothing about the universe that could distinguish one state as being at a different time than any other state.

We will say, then, that change in the

time and physical process   **37**

natural world is essential for the existence of time. We realize that "capability of showing change" is a more fundamental natural property than the actual showing of change, but since such a capability is not alone sufficient for the existence of time, we will stipulate natural change as the first element in the constituting of time.

Some hypothetical examples of the physical situations which we have suggested may be helpful. A universe which presents states which are successively different is well known to all of us; for on levels of observation from the ultramicroscopic to the astronomical the natural world about us is one of changing properties. A large mass of homogeneous matter, idealized as being in mechanical and thermal equilibrium and with no interaction of any kind with the surrounding universe, would be a domain in which there is no change of any kind. Hence *within* that domain we could even say that there is no time, although the domain be surrounded by a changing world in which there is proper time measure. The introduction of, say, a heat source into the domain would give rise to a succession of different states as the material continually grew warmer; this succession would constitute an element of change, and therefore a time element, in the domain. The entire universe, similarly conceived as homogeneous matter in an equilibrium state, would be a universe possessing the "capability of change" but with no time property.

To illustrate the meaning of a universe without the property of presenting successive and different states we might think of a world which has only a momentary existence, in terms of the time sense of our actual universe, or of a universe which is such that changes cannot occur in it. A physical world which existed, for instance, only as do the photons in a flash of light which is quickly absorbed would be a world with little possibility for existing in different states. Or, a universe in which the constituent entities—the atoms say—could not possibly move relatively to each other and could not take up or lose energy of any kind would also be a world which did not possess capability for change, and hence would be a world in which time did not exist. Such a world, of quiet atoms in constant energy states, is of course far different from the actual world about us.

Clocks and Cyclical Processes

Physical change of any kind whatsoever may be considered as giving rise to a time that is not yet differentiated, or not yet measured in defined units. For the setting up of a measure of time passage we use physical change of a special kind; we define time units in terms of processes of change which are *cyclical* in a uniform manner. A cyclical process of a physical system (by system we merely mean a chosen group of material entities) is a process in which the system repeatedly goes from some initial state 0, through intermediate states 1, 2, 3, ... n, and then again to the original state 0. A selected cyclic process may be taken as a basis of time measure; the time unit is defined as the duration of one (or any other chosen number) of the cycles of the process, and the time extent of a noncyclic process of interest may be determined by finding how many cycles of the cyclic process occur between the initial and final states of the noncyclic process. The cyclic process that is so used as a time measure is the essential process of a *clock*.

The first cyclical process to serve man as a time measure was almost surely the rotation of the earth on its axis. The alternation of day and night presents a natural time measure for the noncyclical changes of nature, and historically the day must have been the first time unit. The seasonal changes associated with the orbital revolutions of the earth, and the phase changes in the moon resulting from its revolution, have of course provided two other obvious natural cycles that have long served as units of time measure.

In our society today we use a variety of cyclical processes as bases for clocks. The pendulum clock uses a simple cycle of back-and-forth mechanical motion. The rate of an electric clock rests on the cyclical electrical potential variations in the supplied electric power, those variations themselves being a reflection of the revolutions of the moving elements in the powerhouse alternators. Some clocks of high accuracy utilize the semielastic oscillations of a crystalline material as the basic cyclic process, and the most accurate clock at present available—the cesium[1] clock—depends for its rate regulation on the precessional motion of nucleus and outer electron in the cesium atom.

Whatever natural cycle is used for a clock, it must satisfy the primary condition of being a uniform cyclic process; that is, any one cycle must be the same as any other. If we have an established cyclical process which we have set up as a satisfactory standard time unit, we can say of any other cyclic process that it is uniform if each of its cycles occurs in the same interval of time. The cyclic processes which are used in good clocks obviously must have this property of uniformity. A

[1] L. Essen and J. V. L. Parry, *Nature*, **176** (1955), 280; *Philosophical Transactions of the Royal Society of London*, **250** (1957), 45-69. See also Harold Lyons, "Atomic Clocks," *Scientific American* (February, 1957).

cyclical process like the revolving of a wheel on an axle, such that the wheel first spins at a high angular velocity but then because of frictional effects gradually rotates more slowly, would obviously not be a uniform cyclic process.

The establishing of a standard time unit based on a uniform cyclical process raises the question: How may we know when the chosen process is uniform? If there is no time standard prior to the standard process which defines the time unit, may not that standard process actually vary from cycle to cycle? The answer to this question is twofold. In the first place, any process chosen to be the standard one for defining the time unit will be examined for any possibility of known physical influences which might cause one cycle of the process to be different from another. Thus the axial rotation of the earth is known to be not an exactly uniform cyclic process because, for one reason, the ocean tides constitute a kind of earth to moon-and-sun frictional effect that over a long period of time affects the earth's axial rotation. Likewise, it has been found that the earth's orbital rotation about the sun is subject to slight perturbing influences. A clock based on an atomic cyclical process, on the other hand, is presumably based on a process which can be maintained virtually free of perturbing interference. On physical grounds a crystal or atomic clock, therefore, is in principle to be preferred as an ultimate time standard over an astronomical cyclic process; the atomic process is a simple or "pure" natural process, whereas a process like the earth's rotation is compounded of one major cyclic process with several minor processes that become not quite trivial when a very high degree of uniformity from cycle to cycle is desired. In practice, however, we are by no means ready to give up astronomical cycles as standards for time measurement.

But the consideration of directly physical criteria is associated with a second way of determining whether or not a given cyclic process is uniformly cyclical. Since there are cyclic processes in nature, we can test the uniformity of any one process by observing the consistency of its cyclic frequency with the frequency of other presumably uniform cycles. Thus we find that the axial and orbital rotation frequencies of the earth, the frequency of revolution of the moon, the frequency of a constant amplitude pendulum swing, and many atomic and electromagnetic wave frequencies all bear to a certain degree of accuracy a constant ratio to each other. At any investigation that we make we find, say, that a given pendulum swings through 86,400 cycles while the earth revolves once on its axis. Or a kind of yellow light is consistently found to result from 4.4×10^{19} electromagnetic wave oscillations during a suitably determined revolution of the earth on its axis.

These various cyclic phenomena seem manifestly to be uniform in their cycles because the duration of a cycle of any one of the phenomena is some constant fraction or multiple of the duration of a cycle of any other of the phenomena. Having established a group of cyclic phenomena—that is, that group of processes whose cycles are in constant frequency or time ratio to each other—we can determine whether or not any newly considered phenomenon is a cyclic process by observing whether or not its cyclic frequency is of constant ratio to any of the processes of the group. Thus the simple timing with a clock of a rotating wheel establishes whether or not the wheel's rotation is a uniform cyclic process; the process of the clock which is being used has presumably already been established as a member of the group of natural uniform cyclical processes.

What we are saying here is that by a consistency criterion we distinguish those processes which are uniformly cyclical from natural processes generally. The physical criteria for uniformity may then be applied to members of the cyclical group, so as to determine which are most free from disturbing physical influences and will therefore present in their behavior virtually only a single and uniform cyclical natural process. In practical work, the consistency condition is determined not so much by direct observation as through the mediation of a physical theory; the cyclical motions that are accurately described by theory are members of a consistently uniform set of motions (assuming of course that the theory is consistent). This point has been well discussed in connection with man's actual timekeeping by G. M. Clemence, who states:[2] An invariable measure of time is ". . . a measure that leads to no contradiction between observations of celestial bodies and the rigorous theories of their motion; yet more precisely, it is the measure of time defined by the accepted laws of motion."

Clemence points out that the irregular fluctuations in the earth's rate of rotation have been established by comparison with other planetary or satellite motions.

Among the motions in the solar system that can be observed accurately enough to be used as clocks are the rotation of the earth, the earth's revolution around the sun, the revolution of the moon around the earth, that of Mercury and Venus around the sun, and the four large moons of Jupiter around that planet. Of these

[2] "Time and Its Measurement," *American Scientist*, **40** (1952), 260.

nine clocks it is found that eight agree with one another, and the outstanding disagreement is the rotation of the earth.[3]

The decision that it is the earth's axial rotation which is irregular rests on the small likelihood that every one of the other eight motions would be irregular by the same amount of time (the amount of the earth's irregularity). One can of course then look for physical reasons for the earth's irregularity, and in finding such one further strengthens the choice of the other motions as the properly uniform ones. But in any case—and this is the relevant point—the uniform cycles are chosen as defining a time unit because with that unit the entire theory of celestial motions becomes consistent with observation (or, if one likes, the set of theoretically expected uniform cycles are then found consistently to be so).

We can argue that our choice of time unit is arbitrary, and we have merely *defined* which cycles constitute the set of uniform cycles. In a nonpractical sense this is true: any cycle, even one that is highly irregular by our present time standards, could in principle be chosen as setting our time standard. Various other cycles would then be found to vary in odd ways; each day, for example, might differ widely from its predecessor in length. But for the actual description and theory of celestial motions, time units have been used which give us a large group of cyclical motions that are uniform from one cycle of a motion to the next, as compared with other similarly uniform motions and in accordance with physical theory. The uniformity that is found rests in part, then, on theory, which may be considered as a kind of extended definition, but also in part on the nature of our physical world.

[3] *Ibid.*

Conceivably, the motions of all physical bodies might be so chaotic that no theory could be found, and no associated time unit, which would enable us to find cyclical processes that possess any kind of uniformity. In fact, as has been noted, it is otherwise: with a theory of motion that is correctly descriptive, at least as far as it goes, we do find astronomical and atomic cycles which are among themselves consistently uniform from one cycle to the next.

It may be objected that the consistency criterion for cyclic uniformity is invalid, in that *all* of the cycles of the group of uniform cycles might be varying in tempo. Thus it has been proposed that time might everywhere "dilate" or "contract," and yet we would be unaware of the change because of the uniformity of the effects [;] if all processes began going only half as fast as formerly, our mental processes as well as all physical processes would be equally affected and the world would seem quite as before. Such a hypothetical *universal* variation in time rate is actually of uncertain meaning, for a proposed time change which is in principle not observable would be without significance except in a context of physical theory. We shall, however, consider this possibility in two specific ways, and shall find that in neither case is our criterion for uniformity invalidated.

First, we might think that every time-keeping process is speeded up, so that, for example, a given revolution of the moon about the earth which previously required T seconds now takes only $T/2$ seconds. All other processes would be similarly quickened. This speeding up may be regarded, however, as nothing more than a redefinition of time units. Since our time unit has only the warrant that it gives us consistency or uniformity among cycles as prescribed by theory, there is no physical import to the question of what is *the* length of a time unit; for there is no process over and beyond the natural systems of our world in terms of which that length may be defined. We might redefine our time unit, choosing the "dubsec" in place of the second, with one "dubsec" equal to two seconds. Time values, expressed in the new unit, would numerically equal one-half of time values in terms of seconds, but there would be no disturbance of the consistency relations that had been found, in terms of the chosen time standards, among natural cycles.

Second, we might in a speculative way consider that some timekeeper exists outside the domain of the natural universe, and that by the measure of his time processes the tempo of all of the physical processes of nature is changed. We now find that such a universal variation in our chosen group of uniform cyclic processes would require drastic revisions in natural law. As an example, let us assume that all physical processes are to be doubled in tempo, so as to occur in "half of their previous time." A swinging pendulum, then, for which the frequency is $(\frac{1}{2}\pi)$ $\sqrt{g/l}$, where g is the gravity acceleration of a mass and l is the length of the pendulum, would begin to swing at twice its previous rate provided that the gravitational constant g were quadrupled in value. But also the velocity which a body reaches in time t in falling from rest under the influence of gravity is gt; that is, the velocity is proportional to g and not to $\sqrt{g}$. Therefore, the fourfold increase in g which caused the frequency of the pendulum swing to be doubled would cause the velocity acquired by a falling body to be quadrupled, in a given time t is measured by the "outside" timekeeper. Within our natural domain, to be sure,

a change in the value of g would not bring temporal inconsistencies, but for the hypothetical outside observer the change would, we see, have varying influences on the time rates of different processes.

Countless other illustrations may be devised to show that we could not get a universal change in all physical processes and maintain our present form of physical law. We could not do this because different processes do not in general depend on the same mathematical power of the various physical constants. Hence the change in constants which would be required to give changes in tempo would of necessity give different changes to different processes. A somewhat more involved example of dependence of time rate on physical constant than the pendulum-falling body illustration is provided by the effects of the value for the heat energy released by the oxidation of carbon. This heat energy is perhaps a factor in the time rate of human physiological performance, and it is certainly a major factor in determining the rate at which an automobile moves. But the increase in oxidation energy value which would double the speed of a car motor (and which would have to vary from car to car!) would certainly not have a doubling effect on the speed of physiological processes. We may indeed conclude that the notion of a physical but undetectable universal change in time rate of all natural processes has the characteristics of an absurdity.

Natural Law and Cyclic Processes

The uniform cyclic processes of nature provide us, then, with a clear and definite time measure. Noncyclic processes of change may be given a time length, by reference to the cyclic processes in terms of which a time unit is defined.

Time's apparent quality of being all-pervading and of possessing an essential evenness of flow rests essentially on the existence of uniform cyclic processes everywhere in nature. Were there not such cycles presented to us, the passage of time would be associated with noncyclic change, and time would certainly have a haphazard, irregular quality—resulting from things happening now rapidly, now slowly, and differently at one place than another.

The fact that there are cyclic processes which give rise to our time concept must be considered to be one of the major generalizations that we can make about the natural world. The fact that the various uniform cyclic processes do bear a constant frequency ratio to each other is a further general property of nature of the widest significance. This fact is related to what is sometimes expressed as the "uniformity of nature" or the "order of natural law." What we do find is that two given cyclic processes, say the orbital revolution of the earth and the oscillating motion of a prescribed pendulum, have within a certain narrow range the same frequency ratio at any investigation that is made of the ratio. A similar constancy of ratio is found for other cyclic processes, in atomic as well as terrestrial and astronomical domains. The constancy is so universally found for a given ratio of cyclic frequencies that we confidently assume the constancy to exist everywhere in the universe. Further, we confidently and usually justifiably assume that noncyclic processes have a similar uniformity, such that similar natural processes will always occur in the same time interval, as measured by standard cyclic processes.

We see, then, that our experience of time as regular, as having equivalent units, rests on the uniformity of repeated process that does exist in nature; or we can say that our concept of time would not be as it is were it not for the order of nature. The orderliness of nature may be said in turn to rest on the fact that natural processes occur in accordance with descriptive natural laws which mankind has been able to discern. These laws take various forms, and the set of natural laws is certainly not unique; there are later-nature sets of laws by which the phenomena of a given domain may be described and predicted with a high degree of accuracy. Yet for any given domain of experience, there is usually a preferred set of descriptive natural laws, and these laws—as accurate descriptions of nature —describe the cyclic and noncyclic phenomena that are observed to occur.

We have discussed in the previous section the possibility of a universal, consistent change in the frequencies of all cycles, and we saw that the possibility of such a change is physically unreasonable. A different possibility, however, is that one or some of the cyclic processes of nature might undergo change in frequency, as a result of slow changes in the laws of nature or in the fundamental physical constants. Such changes would of course have discernible effects, in that there would be resulting changes in the frequency ratios of various processes. It is a matter of speculation whether or not such changes occur; certainly the customary assumption of physicists in their work is that the laws of nature are not changing.

There are, however, cosmological theories in contemporary physics which do require that as the universe evolves, in the manner presented by the theory, there will be relative changes in the values of the physical constants.[4] For

[4] See H. Bondi, *Cosmology* (New York:

example, the late E. A. Milne devised a cosmology which required in effect two time scales, one for electromagnetic processes and one for mechanical processes, to state briefly the distinction between the two scales. At various stages in the development of the universe the ratio between the scales would differ, with the result that, in effect, the frequency ratio of a given kind of light waves and a prescribed mechanical oscillator would vary. In quite a different manner Professor P. A. M. Dirac has presented a theory which relates the gravitational constant to other basic constants of the universe, in such a way that with the presumed expansion of the universe the gravitational constant would be decreasing in magnitude. A pendulum clock, as timed by an atomic-oscillations clock, would therefore have run faster a billion years ago than today; or a solar system of the same masses and kinetic energies as our present system would have different orbital sizes and frequencies a billion years ago than it has today.

A further development of the Dirac suggestions has been carried out by Pascual Jordan. He assumes a total constant energy for the universe, with a balance between the (negative) gravitational potential energy of a body and its positive mass energy; new matter may then enter the universe, without violation of conservation of energy. In Jordan's theory, the universe is steadily growing in total mass and in size, and, as in the Dirac theory, gravitational attraction between particles is

Cambridge University Press, 1952). Also, E. Teller, "On the Change of Physical Constants," *Physical Review*, **73** (1948), 801; R. H. Dicke, "Principle of Equivalence and the Weak Interactions," *Review of Modern Physics*, **29** (1957), 355, and "Gravitation—An Enigma," American Scientist, **47** (1959), 25.

growing smaller relative to electrical attraction.

Absolute Time

The possibility of changes in physical laws or constants—although important for the problem of the age of the universe—need not detain us longer at this point. From any practical considerations of timekeeping, even of the highest accuracy, the possibility of changes in frequency ratio is unimportant, since no discernible changes are expected in any theory except over periods of millions of years. The theoretical possibility does emphasize, however, the manner in which we do base our time concepts on the cyclic processes which exist in nature. We can speak of the frequency of some one cyclic process changing with respect to the frequency of another process, but we cannot speak in any absolute sense of a cycle's changing in frequency, because we have no absolute measure of time.

Until a few decades ago the view was common among physicists that there existed in nature a "stream of time" which moved evenly forward and provided a common coordinate to which all events could be referred with respect to their time relationships. This view seems to have had some acceptance in Greek times (as indicated by the *Timaeus* of Plato) and it was made a part of physical theory in the seventeenth century by the chief author of physics, Isaac Newton. Newton spoke of time as a stream that "of itself and from its own nature flows equably without regard to anything external."[5] Time so conceived is our *absolute time* which would exist in a world without change or matter. There is an implica-

[5] Isaac Newton, *Principia*, Scholium to the Definitions.

tion in the notion of absolute time that there exists in some manner a great master clock, over and below the natural events of the world, and that this clock keeps a time that is everywhere flowing, independently of the events of the world.

. . . The theory of relativity specifically invalidates the absolute time concept; for that theory predicts differences in rate of physical process, for a given physical system, under varying conditions of motion, and the existence of these differences has been confirmed experimentally. But even without referring to the theory of relativity we find reasons for rejecting the absolute time concept. We find cyclical processes in nature, but we find them to be of varying frequencies, and any one process may be varied in value, in practice, or in theory, by variation of the physical parameters that characterize the system which undergoes the process. We do not, then, find any "master cyclic process" which serves as a master clock that is reflecting an all-pervading absolute time flow.

We might say that since there are uniform frequency ratios among the various cyclical processes—neglecting relativity theory effects—we may assume an absolute time which is regulating these processes. We, however, gain nothing by way of scientific explanation in making such an assumption, since there is no observable physical process, corresponding to that assumed absolute time flow, which is additional to the observed processes. On the other hand, in taking the point of view that time is an aspect of physical process, we can understand time as a part of the total unity—the natural world—which we are trying to understand. Further, certain hypothetical extreme conditions of nature—as a state of no change whatsoever—then carry with them changes in our time concept,

as will be discussed in the final section. . . . On an assumption of absolute time—which is in fact not justified in any event by observation—all possible conditions and processes of nature must be fitted into a concept of time which cannot be altered, whatever the ultimate state of change or not-change in the universe may be found to be. To forbid any modification of a concept by further experience is altogether counter to proper scientific procedure.

Time Measurement and Noncyclic Processes

We have emphasized the role of cyclic processes in providing both clocks and a standard unit for time measurement. The question may well be asked: Could we not equally well use a noncyclical natural process for a time measure? We can think of a clock's being made, for instance, from the natural decay of a radioactive isotope.[6] Such a process is uniform, in that a constant fraction of a given sample will always decay in a given unit of time. Or, somewhat more crudely, we might think of a process like the weathering of a rock as providing a time measure. A fairly constant stream of water, for example, might in each year wash away the same depth of rock over which the water is flowing.

In the examples cited, however, we think of a noncyclic process as serving as a clock, on the basis of a calibration which utilizes a time standard derived from cyclical processes. The question which we wish to answer is whether or not noncyclic processes alone could serve as primary standards and clocks in our time measurement. If this were

---

[6] J. A. Carroll has discussed in detail how a clock could be made of two radioactive materials with different decay constants: *Nature*, **184** (1959), 260.

to be done we would expect to be able to find in nature a number of processes which are noncyclic but yet are undergoing change in some uniform manner; these processes would serve as clocks and time standards, as do in fact the various natural cyclical processes. And just as noncyclic processes are satisfactorily described by time units and natural laws which are the same as those for cyclic processes, we would expect that if noncyclic processes were the primary ones for time measurement the cyclic processes could be accurately described in terms of time units based on the noncyclic processes.

Experience indicates, however, that uniform noncyclic processes of change are not abundant in our natural world. Even approximately uniform noncyclic processes, like the weathering of rocks, are not obvious, and noncyclic processes, which depend on a few simple physical parameters and are therefore highly uniform, are rare in nature. The decay of radioactive materials is one such process, and the apparent recessional motion of galaxies, with a velocity directly proportional to their distance from the earth, is a second. Both of these processes are fairly subtle ones to discern, and it is safe to say that if man had had to depend on them as bases for clocks he would have been a long time indeed in conceiving of time as being in any way uniform and capable of quantitative division. However, the theoretical possibility of basing our time measure on one of the few uniform, natural noncyclic processes cannot be denied. It is true that there are contrived noncyclic processes which serve as clocks—the hourglass and water clock are examples—but they were invented by men who had gained their time concept from the natural cyclic processes.

With respect to the concept of time, a striking feature of our universe is that it does present cyclic processes in abundance; and hence the universe does readily suggest a time concept which implies persistence of entities through uniform, successive time intervals. Noncyclic processes are ones in which a system is continuously being carried into states which are different from all previous states of the system. If all the processes of nature were of this kind—like the radioactive decay and galactic recession processes—the world would always be changing, and it would be perhaps difficult even to identify any persisting aspect of nature. The fact, however, that many processes are cyclic reassures us that absence of change is characteristic of at least parts of our universe, for in a cyclic process each state of a system is a return to a previous state. Those same cyclic processes then which give us a time measure are also essential for our changing universe's possessing elements of permanence and stability.

The Origins of Time

We have seen that there are two essential physical requirements for our time concept: processes of change which give rise to successive differences in states of the world, and cyclic phenomena, among those processes, which give a basis for time measurement. If there were change only, without the cyclic phenomena, we would not have a time concept similar to the one we do have, for we would have no sense of time as being composed of uniform and equivalent units. We have also the theoretical, rather unlikely, possibility of a time measurement being based primarily on uniform, noncyclic processes; with that possibility there are still two requirements for our time concept, but a group of uniform noncyclic processes is substituted among the various processes of change for the group of uniform cyclic processes.

It is perhaps an aid in understanding the nature of our time concept to consider hypothetical extreme conditions in our world, with respect to the two requirements. If change alone, without the presence of a group of clearly uniform processes, will not give us our time concept, we may next ask: What would be the effect of there being uniform processes of change only? Our actual world contains uniform cyclic processes among the various processes of change. If the world contained only cyclical changes, would we still have our time concept? The answer must be "No." For unless the various cyclic processes interacted or continuously changed their phase relations so as effectively to produce noncyclic change, a world which was dominated by cyclic processes would continuously return to previous states and there would be no sense of a progressively increasing sequence. For illustration we might think of our terrestrial world as being such that there were no indications of geological evolution, so that the only observed changes in landscape were the seasonal ones, identically repeated each year. Further, we think of there being no biological evolution and no significant social change, so that each generation of animals and men remains as in preceding generations. There would then be a sense of time, and of going in the extreme case where each generation lived exactly as any other in a world that was the same for each generation, there would be no time that progressively increased from generation to generation.

In considering a purely cyclic universe, we must be on guard, as also in the instance of a universe of no change whatsoever, against the notions of time which have become intuitive with us. We tend to think that time always is going on, no matter what is happening in the universe. In fact, however, if the world went through equivalent cycles repetitively, there would be nothing to give rise to a concept of one cycle's being earlier or later than another, and there would be no criterion for distinguishing any one cycle from another. The changes within a cycle would give a sense of temporal succession, within the cycle, but beyond one cycle a purely cyclic process itself may be considered to be an atemporal process.

Any physical process that is purely cyclical may be treated as being an atemporal process as long as it is considered only in its own domain, without reference to the larger, temporal universe surrounding it. The successive oscillations of a photon as it moves through a vacuum, for example, are identical, and there is no change that gives a time coordinate. The motion of an electron about a nucleus, or the cycles of two isolated astronomical bodies rotating about each other, have a similar atemporal quality. On interaction with other systems these purely cyclic processes may become noncyclic and thereby gain a temporal character.

The cyclic process, then, can become a temporal process only by reference to noncyclic processes. We may refer to the latter as *progressively* changing processes, in contrast to the cyclic processes in which we do not have progressive change except within any one cycle. We have seen that the progressively changing process does not give us our time concept because change in general does not provide a basis for time standardization and measurement. But likewise, uniform cycles of change will not by themselves give us our time concept, because without progressive change there is no distinction of any one cycle from another. Time has its origin *in the existence of both kinds of physical change, cyclic and noncyclic, in the natural world that we know.*

Conceivably, the world might be such that it contained progressive change, with a sufficient number of uniform noncyclic processes that time measurement could be based on these uniform processes rather than on cyclic processes. Our time concept, however, is so clearly based on uniform cyclic processes, in a universe that presents an abundance of such processes, that we shall neglect the hypothetical possibility of standardizing uniform noncyclic processes and henceforth confine discussion to the cyclic processes in regard to the providing of time standards and clocks.

Our natural world does seem to be one which is obviously undergoing progressive change. The evolution of species, the geologic changes in the earth, the evidences of development in the stars: these are all processes of noncyclic, progressive change. Even the life of any one human being is emphatically this way, with its differing states of growth, maturity, and deterioration. And yet throughout the natural fabric of progressive change there are woven countless cyclic processes, constant in their frequency ratios, in terms of which man can measure the stages of progressive change. We could state the matter with alternate emphasis, and point out that we find cyclic processes everywhere in nature, but also, along with these phenomena there are progressively changing processes which give us that sense of the world's moving from state to state—or from time to time—by which we are able to discern two successive cycles as occurring at different times.

* * * * *

Progressive change is perhaps the dominant element in our experience,

of the two that give rise to our time concept. And yet to a small child, for example, whose life is evenly passing from day to day, there is almost a complete absence of a sense of time's "moving on." Rather, the world is made of units each very much like the other, and later experience must teach the awareness of progression and change that comes with adulthood. Even in one's adult life, and in a society that changes as much from one generation to the next as Western societies have done in recent decades, contemplation of the repetition of generations brings some sense of time's not moving on, of the atemporal quality of cyclic process. For one's parents and grandparents, and so on back, in many essential ways lived much as we do, facing the same situations of life that are the lot of us today.

Contrariwise, we well know that our grandparents' generation is earlier in time than ours of today, because of the progressive changes that have occurred in the intervening years. Likewise, we confidently assign a later date to each successive revolution of the earth about the sun; each of the cycles of that process, in our scientific experience, is indeed closely equivalent to any other, but progressive changes from cycle to cycle on the earth, as well as in the universe at large, prevent the earth's revolving from being a purely atemporal process. And so it is throughout our experience: the natural world presents both progressively changing and cyclic processes, and we have a time concept which implies both a going-on change of the world and a presence of equivalent time units for the measuring of any process of change.

It has sometimes been argued that the origin of time rests on the existence of a causal relationship among all physical events. This point of view has been stressed by Hans Reichenbach, in his book *The Direction of Time,* in which he states that ". . . time order is reducible to causal order."[7] In one sense a physicist can scarcely disagree with such a statement, because we would not accept a time order among events if the order violated physical causality relations. But on the other hand, it clearly is not necessary (and I do not believe Reichenbach wished to imply this) for us to know what the causal connections are between events if a time concept is to be established by those events: primitive man achieved a notion of time, without any very exact knowledge of causal relations between events.

. . . We have discussed the foundations in physical phenomena of our time concept. These are the bases, we believe, on which the concept does in fact rest, and it is because of these characteristics of the physical world that we have our time concept. Further, it seems evident that this concept is prior to any detailed knowledge of physics.

[7] Hans Reichenbach, *The Direction of Time* (Berkeley: University of California Press, 1956), p. 25.

Diseases of Science

DEREK J. DE SOLLA PRICE

The use of a mathematical and logical method is so deeply embedded within the structure of science that one cannot doubt its power to bring order into the world of observation. Perhaps the best classical statement of this is given by Plato in his *Laws,* where he remarks that "arithmetic stirs up him who is by nature sleepy and dull, and makes him quick to learn, retentive, and shrewd, and aided by art divine he makes progress quite beyond his natural powers."

This is amply demonstrated by the rich return whenever the scientific methods of measurement and mathematical treatment have been used, be they within the sciences as in biology, or in human affairs as in economics and other segments of what was once called political arithmetic. It does not of course follow that quantification followed by mathematical treatment is in itself a desirable and useful thing. The pitfalls are many; for example, it is almost certainly an arbitrary if entertaining procedure to grade the various geniuses that the world has seen and give them so many marks out of a hundred for each of the qualities they have demonstrated or failed to demonstrate.

Now the history of science differs remarkably from all other branches of history, being singled out by virtue of its much more orderly array of material and also by the objective criteria which exist for the facts of science but not necessarily for the facts of other history. Thus we can be reasonably sure what sort of things must have been observed by Boyle or Galileo or Harvey, in a way that we can never be sure of the details of Shakespeare's life and work. Also, we can speak certainly about the interrelations of physics, chemistry, and biology, but not so positively about the interdependence of

Derek J. de Solla Price, *Science Since Babylon* (New Haven: Yale University Press, 1961), pp. 92-124. Reprinted by permission of the publisher.

the histories of Britain, France, and America.

Above all, there is in the field of science a cumulative accretion of contributions that resembles a pile of bricks. Each researcher adds his bricks to the pile in an orderly sequence that is, in theory at least, to remain in perpetuity as an intellectual edifice built by skill and artifice, resting on primitive foundations, and stretching to the upper limits of the growing research front of knowledge.

Now, seemingly, by means of the art divine of arithmetic, an array so orderly is capable of some sort of exact analysis which might progress beyond the natural powers afforded us by the usual historical discussions. It is perhaps especially perverse of the historian of science to remain purely an historian and fail to bring the powers of science to bear upon the problems of its own structure. There should be much scope for a scientific attack on science's own internal problems, yet, curiously enough, any such attack is regarded with much skepticism, and the men of science prefer, for the most part, to talk as unskilled laymen about the general organizational problems with which science is currently beset.

Fortunately, it happens that the most revealing issues in the history of the last few centuries of science have much in common with the basic problems currently afflicting the structure and organization of science. Both considerations concern what one might well call the "size of science"—the magnitude of the effort in terms of numbers of men working, papers written, discoveries made, financial outlay involved. For the history of science, the treatment of such magnitudes by a process of refined head counting and suitable mathematical manipulation may provide one much-needed way of viewing the forest of modern science

without the distraction of the individual trees of various separate technicalities. Provided only that we take the precaution to link the results at every possible stage with such information as we have already gleaned from purely historical considerations of the evidence, it might do much to amplify that evidence. It is in a very similar way that economic history can augment social history and provide a new and more nearly complete understanding of processes that previously were only partly intelligible on qualitative lines.

Before entering this region, I must post a caveat with respect to the claim that such an analysis might have direct bearing on our understanding of present problems and future states of science. Whatever our reasons for accepting the study of history as a legitimate and valuable activity of scholars and teachers, one of the claims not customarily made is that of direct utility. We do not advise that a good grounding in history can make one an efficient politician. We do not maintain that the historian is the possessor of any magic crystal ball through which he can look into the future. If I suggest that the history of science is perhaps more useful than most other histories, it is only because of the peculiar regularity and verifiability of its subject matter. Since such oddities exist, however, it is useful to stretch the method to the full and examine critically any benefits which might thereby accrue.

For a preliminary exercise in the internal political arithmetic of science, let us first examine the history of the vital process that made science assume a strongly cumulative character. The origin of this was in the seventeenth-century invention of the scientific journal and the device of the learned paper—one of the most distinct and fundamental innovations of the Scientific Revolution. The earliest surviving journal is the *Philosophical Transactions of the Royal Society of London*, first published in 1665.[1] It was followed rapidly by some three or four similar journals published by other national academies in Europe. Thereafter, as the need increased, so did the number of journals, reaching a total of about one hundred by the beginning of the nineteenth century, one thousand by the middle, and some ten thousand by 1900. According to the *World List of Scientific Periodicals*, a tome larger than any family Bible, we are now well on the way to the next milestone of a hundred thousand such journals.

Now this provides a set of heads that are reasonably easy to count. For the earlier period there exist several lists giving the dates of foundation of the most important scientific serial publications; for more recent years we have the *World List* and similar estimates. Of course there is some essential difficulty in counting *Physical Review* as a single unit of the same weight as any *Annual Broadsheet of the Society of*

Leather Tanners of Bucharest, but for a first order of magnitude, there seems no overriding difficulty in selecting which heads to number.

If we make such a count extending in time range from 1665 to the present day, it is immediately obvious that the enormous increase in the population of scientific periodicals has proceeded from unity to the order of a hundred thousand with an extraordinary regularity seldom seen in any manmade or natural statistic. It is apparent, to a high order of accuracy, that the number has increased by a factor of ten during every half-century, starting from a state in 1750 when there were about ten scientific journals in the world. From 1665 to 1750, the birth span of the first ten journals, the regularity is not quite so good, but this indeed is exactly what one might expect for a population that was then not large enough to treat statistically. No sort of head counting can settle down to mathematical regularity until the first dozen or so cases have been recorded.

The detail at the beginning of the curve of growth is rather revealing in terms of its historical implications. Starting in 1665, the curve proceeds for a couple of decades as if there had been healthy growth. By that time, the growth acts as if it had started from a first journal at a date nearer to 1700 than 1665. Thus the curve indicates that, in some sense, the scientific journal was born a little too soon. The first publications were demonstrably precursors rather than true originators of the process. This is particularly interesting when one considers the difficult periods which the Royal Society and the other academies experienced once the initial flush of enthusiasm had passed. They went through grave crises and had to suffer rebirth early in the eighteenth century.

---

[1] The most readable recent account of the genesis of the Royal Society and its *Philosophical Transactions* is Dorothy Stimson, *Scientists and Amateurs* (New York: Henry Schuman, Inc., 1949). For the other national societies, the standard secondary source is Martha Ornstein, *The Role of Scientific Societies in the Seventeenth Century*, 3rd ed. (Chicago: University of Chicago Press, 1938). The only good general history of the later history of the scientific periodical is a short article by Douglas McKie in "Natural Philosophy Through the Eighteenth Century and Allied Topics," commemoration number to mark the 150th anniversary of the *Philosophical Magazine* (July, 1948), 122-131. See also John L. Thornton and R. I. J. Tully, *Scientific Books, Libraries and Collectors* (London: Chaucer House, 1954), esp. Chap. 8, "The Growth of Scientific Periodical Literature," which cites several further references.

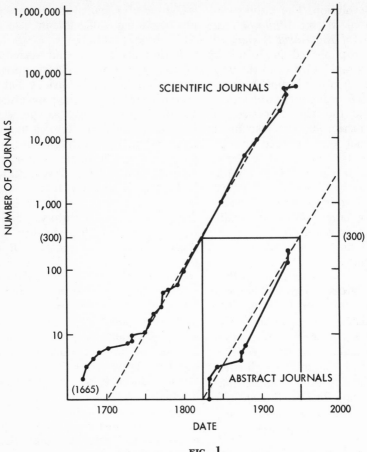

FIG. 1.

In the course of this proliferation of the scientific journals, it became evident by about 1830 that the process had reached a point of absurdity: no scientist could read all the journals or keep sufficiently conversant with all published work that might be relevant to his interest. This had, in fact, been an attendant worry from the very beginning of the operation, and the first duty of the earliest journals was to review all published books and all papers which had appeared in the organs of the other national academies. But by about 1830 there was clearly trouble in the learned world and, with an assemblage of some three hundred journals being published, some radically new effort was needed. Yet again there was an invention as deliberate and as controversial as the journal itself: the new device of the abstract journal appeared on the scene.

Now a single abstract journal could never suffice, and in accordance with the convenient compartmentalization of science current by this time, further abstract journals were created to fill the needs of the various specialist groups. Because it presented a solution to the crisis, the abstract journal removed the pressure, and the number of plain journals was enabled to grow un-hampered. This growth has continued to the present day. On account of this proliferation, however, the number of abstract journals has also increased, following precisely the same law, multi-plying by a factor of ten in every half-century. Thus by about 1950 we reached the point at which the size of the population of abstract journals had attained the critical magnitude of about three hundred. This is of course the reason why during the last decade scientists have been concerned about the need for abstracts of abstracts, call-ing this an "information problem" which seems to require some process of electronic sorting of abstracts as a means of coping with the rising flood of literature.

It is interesting to reflect that, on the basis of this historical evidence, one can show that any new process would bear the same relation to abstracts as the abstracts have to original papers. This relation involves a compression by a factor of about three hundred—the number of journals that seem to have necessitated the coming into being of each abstract journal.

Now it seems that the advantage at present providable by electronic sort-ing may be of a considerably smaller order of magnitude—perhaps a factor of the order to ten. If this is so, it fol-lows that the new method must be no more than a palliative and not the radical solution that the situation de-mands. It can only delay the fateful crisis by a few paltry decades.

The seriousness of the crisis is evi-dent from the change in form and function of physics papers in recent years. Collaborative work now exceeds the single-author paper, and the device of prepublications duplicated sheets circulated to the new Invisible Col-leges has begun to trespass upon the traditional functions of the printed paper in a published journal.[2] If we do not find some way of abstracting the abstracts, it may well happen that the printed research paper will be doomed, though it will be difficult to rid ourselves of the obsession that it seems vital to science.

The most remarkable conclusion ob-tained from the data just considered is that the number of journals has grown exponentially rather than line-arly. Instead of there being just so many new periodicals per year, the number has doubled every so many years. The constant involved is actually about fifteen years for a doubling, cor-responding to a power of ten in fifty years and a factor of one thousand in a century and a half. In the three hun-dred years which separate us from the mid-seventeenth century, this rep-resents a factor of one million.

---

[2] The new Invisible Colleges, rapidly grow-ing up in all the most hard-pressed sections of the scholarly research front, might well be the subject of an interesting sociological study. Starting originally as a reaction to the communication difficulty brought about by the flood of literature, and flourishing mightily under the teamwork conditions induced by World War II, their whole *raison d'être* was to substitute personal contact for formal communication among those who were really getting on with the job, making serious ad-vances in their fields. In many of these fields, it is now hardly worthwhile embarking upon serious work unless you happen to be with-in the group accepted and invited to the annual and informal conferences, commuting between the two Cambridges, and vacationing in one of the residential conference and work centers that are part of the international chain. The processes of access to an egress from the groups have become difficult to un-derstand, and the apportioning of credit for the work to any one member or his subteam has already made it more mean-ingless than before to award such honors as the Nobel Prize. Are these "power groups" dangerously exclusive? Probably not, but in many ways they may turn out to be not wholly pleasant necessities of the scientific life in its new state of saturation.

One can be reasonably surprised that any accurate law holds over such a large factor of increase. Indeed, it is within the common experience that the law of exponential growth is too spectacular to be obeyed for very long. Large factors usually introduce some more-than-quantitative change that alters the process. Thus if only the Indians had been wise enough to bank at compound interest the small sum for which they sold the island of Manhattan, it would now, at all reasonable rates of interest, have grown to be of the same order of magnitude as the present real estate value of that area.

Now not only is it therefore quite exceptional that anything could have grown so regularly from unit size to the order of hundreds of thousands, but it is altogether remarkable that this particular curve should be a normal, compound interest, exponential law of growth rather than any of the other alternatives that exist, some of them more simple, some more complex. The exponential law is the mathematical consequence of having a quantity that increases so that the bigger it is the faster it grows. The number of journals has behaved just like a colony of rabbits breeding among themselves and reproducing every so often. Why should it be that journals appear to breed more journals at a rate proportional to their population at any one time instead of at any particular constant rate?

It must follow that there is something about scientific discoveries or the papers by which they are published that makes them act in this way. It seems as if each advance generates a series of new advances at a reasonably constant birth rate, so that the number of births is strictly proportional to the size of the population of discoveries at any given time. Looking at the statistics in this light, one might say that

the number of journals has been growing so that every year about one journal in twenty, about 5 per cent of the population, had a journal-child—a quotient of fecundity that is surely low enough to be reasonable but which must inevitably multiply the population by ten in each succeeding half-century.

The law of exponential increase found for the number of scientific journals is also obeyed for the actual numbers of scientific papers in those journals. In fact, it seems an even more secure basis to count the heads of whichever papers are listed by one of the great abstract journals or bibliographies than to take a librarian's list of the journals themselves. A list of papers is likely to be a little more comprehensive and more selective than any list of journals which may from time to time publish scientific papers immersed in nonscientific material.[3] As a good speci-

---

[3] In addition to the examples here cited, there are several known to me in standard bibliographies of the sciences and commentaries thereon. For X-ray crystallography there is the graph reproduced by William H. George in *The Scientist in Action* (London: Williams & Norgate, Ltd., 1938), p. 232, Fig. 27 [taken from the bibliography by Wyckoff, *The Structure of Crystals*, 2nd ed. (New York: Chemical Catalogue Company, Inc., 1931), pp. 397-475]. For experimental psychology see Robert S. Woodworth, *Experimental Psychology* (New York: Holt, Rinehart & Winston, Inc., 1938), p. iii. For astronomy there is the monumental work of Houzeau and Lancaster, *Bibliographie générale de l'astronomie* (Brussels: 1882), II, 71. This last is especially remarkable for the fact that it shows the full time scale, beginning with a slow exponential growth (about forty years for a doubling) and then changing to the modern normal rate (about fifteen years to double) just at the time of the first astronomical periodical publications in the early nineteenth century. For chemical papers see the analysis by Laurence E. Strong and O. Theodor Benfey, "Is Chemical Information Growing Exponentially?" in *Journal of Chemical Education*, 37 (1960), 29.

men of the result of such a statistical investigation of numbers of scientific papers, there is next presented a curve showing the numbers of papers recorded by *Physics Abstracts* since it came into being in 1900. In the earliest decade, this journal's main function was to record electrical engineering papers, and not before World War I did it find it useful to list the physics section separately; we therefore ignore the mixed data before 1918.

It is, however, quite remarkable that from 1918 to the present day the total number of physics papers recorded in the abstracts—clearly a rather complete and significant selection—has followed an exponential growth curve to an order of accuracy which does not fluctuate by more than about 1 per cent of the total. There are now about 180,000 physics papers recorded in these volumes, and the number has steadily doubled at a rate even faster than once every fifteen years. In this curve, one particular side effect is worth noting. The data show that during World War II, in the period 1938-48, the production of physics papers was reduced to reach a minimum of very nearly one-third of what it normally would have been. In the whole decade including the war, some 60,000 instead of 120,000 papers came out.

Two diametrically opposed conjectures have been made with respect to the effect of the war upon science. The one school would argue that the enormous stimulation of giant projects like that of the atomic bomb helped science in a way that no peacetime activities could have afforded. The other school says that the mobilization of men and money for purpose of war effort rather than for scientific advance was a diversion, an actual retardation instead of an acceleration of science. The graph shows immediately that neither of these things happened—or, rather, if they did, they balanced each other so effectively that no resultant effect is to be found. Once science had recovered from the war, the curve settled down to exactly the same slope and rate of progress that it had before. It had neither a greater nor a less initial slope; it is exactly as if the war loss had not occurred. The present curve runs accurately parallel to its projected pre-war course.

Returning to the main investigation, we can note that once again the accuracy of exponential growth is most surprising, especially because of the large factor involved, and also because its regularity is so much greater than one normally finds in the world of statistics. I might add that exactly the same sort of result occurs if one takes the head count for scientific books or for abstracts of chemical, biological, or mathematical papers.[4] It may also be

Since my first publication on this subject [in *Archives internationales d'histoire des sciences*, **14** (1951), 85-93] extended and republished in a more popular form in *Discovery* (June, 1956), 240-243, there have come to my notice about thirty such analyses, all with similar results. It seems beyond reasonable doubt that the literature in any normal, growing field of science increases exponentially, with a doubling in an interval ranging from about ten to about fifteen years.

[4] The figures for book publication and the size of libraries are the subjects of many investigations, several of them instigated by worried librarians charged with the management of their monster. Perhaps the best selection of data is in F. Rider, *The Scholar and the Future of the Research Library* (New York: Hadham Press, 1944). Roughly speaking, both the world population of book titles and the sizes of all the great libraries double in about twenty years (estimates usually range from seventeen to twenty-three years). If we allow that in some five hundred years of book production there must have been some twenty-five doubling periods, this will give about $2^{25}=30,000,000$ books alive today, a figure conforming well with normal estimates. In the *Third Annual Report of*

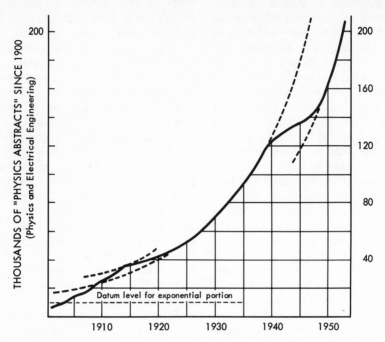

FIG. 2. Total number of *Physics Abstracts* published since January 1, 1900. The full curve gives the total, and the broken curve represents the exponential approximation. Parallel curves are drawn to enable the effect of the wars to be illustrated.

found in the bibliographies which exist for particular specialties within any of these domains. One may, in fact, with a suitably documented topic, perform such a mathematical analysis and thereby demonstrate very clearly the successive phases: first, precursors; then, a steady state of exponential growth; next, a decline to linear growth, when no new manpower is entering the field; and finally, the collapse of the field, when only a few occasional papers are produced, or an alternative revival, should it suddenly take on a new lease

of life, through a redefinition of its content and mode of operation.

So far we only have the very crudest measure of the size of science; there has been no discussion of the relation between the number of papers and the number and quality of the scientists working and the research they produce. It is relatively easy to establish a relationship between scientists and their papers. For example, one can readily take an index volume for several years of publication in a particular journal or over a whole field and count the number of men who published but one paper, those with two, three, and so on. This has been done many times, and for my present purpose, it will suffice to cite Lotka's Law of Productivity,[5] which states that the number

the Council on Library Resources (period ending June 30, 1959), where such data are presented, I find a wistful comment that deserves repetition: "The world's population is laid to rest each generation; the world's books have a way of lingering on." Such is the stuff of cumulative growth, the distinction of scholarship in general, but of science in particular.

[5] Lotka's Law was first published in "The Frequency Distribution of Scientific Pro-

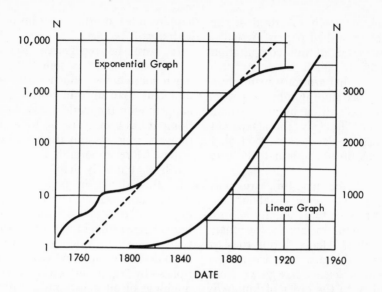

FIG. 3. Total number of papers published in the field of mathematical theory of determinants and matrices, plotted exponentially (left) and linearly (right). There are three stages in the growth, the first an irregular period of precursors and a slightly premature beginning, from 1740 to about 1800. The next stage is one of pure exponential growth from 1800 to about 1880 and the last is a period of linear growth extending from 1880 to the present. In the exponential portion there is a doubling every twelve years. In the linear portion the growth maintains its value at 1880, i.e., about thirty-five papers per year, or roughly one dozen full-time workers in the field.

of authors publishing just N papers is proportional to $1/N^2$. Thus if you have a certain chance of producing one paper during your lifetime, you have one-quarter that chance of producing two, one-ninth for three, one-hundredth for ten, and so on.

Again, this is a reasonably expected

ductivity," *Journal of the Washington Academy of Sciences*, 16 (1926), 317. It is commented upon as an example of an almost universal distribution law in George K. Zipf, *Human Behavior and the Principle of Least Effort* (Reading, Mass.: Addison-Wesley Pub. Co., Inc., 1949), pp. 514-516 (some of the theory and examples are not entirely trustworthy). An independent and more mathematical formulation in terms of skew distribution functions and their theory may be found in Herbert A. Simon, *Models of Man, Social and Rational* (New York: John Wiley & Sons, Inc., 1957), pp. 160-161, where further source materials are cited.

mathematical law, but it is surprising to see that it seems to be followed to much greater accuracy than one might predict. Once more, it is surprising to find that this seems to be a universal law. Thus it is obeyed equally well by data taken from the first few volumes of the seventeenth-century *Philosophical Transactions* and by those from a recent volume of *Chemical Abstracts*. The distribution of productivity among scientists has not changed much over the whole three hundred years for which papers have been produced.

As a result of the constancy of this law, it is possible to say that over the years there have been about three papers for every author. If we care to define a scientist as a man who writes at least one scientific paper in his lifetime, then the number of scientists is always approximately one-third of the number of published papers. Actually, the mathematics of this computation is not quite trivial; it is necessary to make a somewhat arbitrary assumption about the maximum number of papers that could be written by any man in one lifetime.[6] Happily, the agreement with statistical data is so good that assumptions do not appear to be very critical.

Having established this, we may transfer all our remarks about the growth of scientific literature into equivalent remarks about the man-power involved. Hence during the last three hundred years, the size of the labor force of science has grown from the first few to the order of hundreds of thousands. Now this is something so familiar, it seems, from discussion of the explosion of the world population, and from the well-known troubles of libraries, which seem to be doubling in size every few decades, that it may look as if we are merely making new soup with old bones.

To state it a little more dramatically, however, we may remark that at any time there coexist in the scientific population scientists produced over, let us say, the last forty years. Thus at any one time, about three doubling periods' worth of scientists are alive. Hence some 80 to 90 per cent of all scientists that have ever been are alive now. We might miss Newton and Aristotle, but happily most of the contributors are with us still!

It must be recognized that the growth of science is something very much more active, much vaster in its problems, than any other sort of growth happening in the world today. For one thing, it has been going on for a longer time and more steadily than most other things. More important, it is growing much more rapidly than anything else. All other things in population, economics, nonscientific culture, are growing so as to double in roughly every human generation of, say, thirty to fifty years. Science in America is growing so as to double in only ten years—it multiplies by eight in each successive doubling of all nonscientific things in our civilization. If you care to regard it this way, the density of science in our culture is quadrupling during each generation.

Alternatively, one can say that science has been growing so rapidly that all else, by comparison, has been almost stationary. The exponential growth has been effective largely in increasing the involvement of our culture with science, rather than in contributing to any general increase in the size of both culture and science. The past three centuries have brought science from a one-in-a-million activity to a point at which the expenditure of several per cent of all our national productivity and available manpower is entailed by the general fields of science and its closely associated applications.

An excellent example of such concentration is the electrical engineering industry, the technology of which is more implicitly scientific than any other. Published manpower figures show the usual exponential increase, acting as if it started with a single man ca. 1750 (the time of Franklin's experiments on lightning) and doubling until there were two hundred thousand

---

[6] So far as I know, the record for meaningful scientific publications in huge quantities is held by William Thompson, Lord Kelvin. From about 1840 to 1870 he produced about 8.5 papers per year, thereafter until his retirement some 15.0 per year (for a period of about thirty years), then about 5.0 per year until his death in 1907; in all a total of about 660 papers in one lifetime, a working average of one fine paper per month, year in and year out. Almost every one of these would be viewed by any reasonable critic as a major scientific contribution.

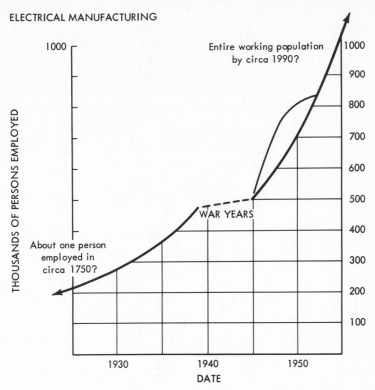

THOUSANDS OF PERSONS EMPLOYED

Entire working population by circa 1990?

About one person employed in circa 1750?

WAR YEARS

DATE

1930   1940   1950

FIG. 4. Adapted from figures published by *The Manchester Guardian* for March 20, 1956: "The Electrical Industry Today," by Dr. Willis Jackson, F.R.S.

people employed in 1925 and an even million by 1955. At this rate, the whole working population should be employed in this one field as early as 1990.

Returning for a moment to the history of the process rather than its statistics, it seems reasonable to identify by name this growth of science and its associated technologies from the small beginning to its present status as the largest block of national employment. It is the process we call the Industrial Revolution, if one thinks in terms of technology, or the Enlightenment, if one stresses the cognitive element. The movement started in Europe in the mid-seventeenth century and reached large proportions measurable by thousands, rather than units, in the late eighteenth and early nineteenth centuries. Thus our various graphs of

cumulative growth may be regarded as charting quantitatively the course of this Industrial Revolution and Enlightenment and providing a key to the various dates and phenomena associated with their progress.

It is instructive in this study to compare the growth charts of Europe with those for the United States. All the available statistics show that the United States has undergone the same sort of accurately exponential proliferation as Europe. The difference is, however, that once the United States started, it made its progress by doubling in scientific size every ten years rather than every fifteen. This was remarked upon already in 1904, in a brilliant essay in *The Education of Henry Adams* (Chap. 34). The explanation of the rate difference is difficult, but the fact seems quite clear. Once the United States had, so to speak, decided to get down to a serious attempt at scientific education, research, and utilization, it was able to carry through this process at a rate of interest considerably higher than that in Europe.

A great part of the explanation is probably due not to any special and peculiar properties of the American way of life as compared with the European but merely to the fact that this country was expanding into a scientific vacuum. Furthermore, it was doing it with the help of that high state of science already reached and held as a common stock of knowledge of mankind at the date when the United States started its process. Europe had to start from the beginning, and by the eighteenth or nineteenth century it had a considerable accretion of tradition and established institutions of science and technology.

Whatever the reason, the United States continued to expand at this rate faster than Europe, and eventually it acquired an intensity of science in society that became greater than that of Europe. One can consider the scientific advancement of Russia in exactly the same way. In Tsarist Russia science was not altogether inconsiderable—it partook of the general level of Europe —but after 1918 a determined effort was made to expand science. Again the statistics show that the advance had been very accurately exponential, and that the doubling time is of the order of some seven years rather than the ten of the United States and the fifteen of Europe. Again, one can attribute this in large part not to any particular excellence of the Russians or to a degree of crash programing but rather to the fact that if they wanted to do the job at all, there was only one way of doing it, and this involved being able to start from a world state of scientific knowledge that was considerably higher for them than for the start of the United States.

Lastly, we take the case of China. Here we have an even more recent start and, consistent with the theory, we see that the statistics in that country indicate a doubling every five years. As an indication of this, it has already just become necessary and advisable to prepare running English translations of the chief Chinese scientific journals, as we have now been doing for the Russian literature over some few years. Again, rather than attribute any particular high quality to the Chinese, I would suggest that they are simply expanding into a large scientific vacuum, starting at a higher level than any of the earlier protagonists.

The whole thing is like a gigantic handicap race in which the country that starts last must necessarily have the highest initial speed, and it seems fairly conclusive that this speed can readily be maintained—it certainly has been by America—so that the state of science must eventually reach the concentration that we see in the most highly developed countries. It is reasonable to suppose from the very universality of science and from its supranational qualities that it is much more likely for the world to reach a state of uniform development and exploitation in this direction than in many another. The handicap race of Industrial Revolutions has indeed been so well designed that it seems likely that all runners will come abreast, reaching a size of science proportional to their total populations, at much the same time, a time not too many decades distant into the future.

Because of the obvious importance of the scientific race between the United States and Russia, and that which may well occur between these countries and China, this study of the

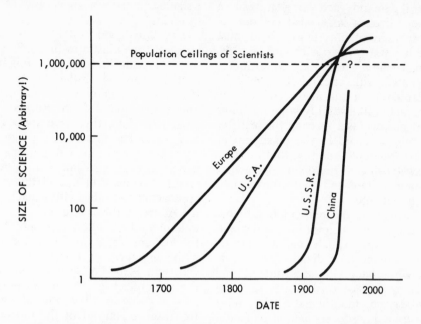

FIG. 5. Schematic graph of the rise of science in various world regions. The measures, the shapes of the initial portions of the curves, and the way in which the curves turn over to their respective ceilings toward the top are all merely qualitative.

natural history of Industrial Revolutions clearly needs more attention. The modern scientific development of Japan would provide an excellent case history. The very slow beginnings in modern India might throw light on what it is that constitutes a true onset of this sort of exponential Industrial Revolution.

Having now discussed the historical origins and statistical progress of the device of the scientific paper and the profession of the scientist, we must next consider the decline and fall of these things. It is indeed apparent that the process to which we have become accustomed during the past few centuries is not a permanent feature of our world. A process of growth so much more vigorous than any population explosion or economic inflation cannot continue indefinitely but must lead to an intrinsically larger catastrophe than either of these patently apparent dangers.

To go beyond the bounds of absurdity, another couple of centuries of "normal" growth of science would give us dozens of scientists per man, woman, child, and dog of the world population. Long before that state was reached we should meet the ultimate educational crisis when nothing might be done to increase the numbers of available trained professionals in science and technology. Again, to take a reasonably safe exaggeration, if every school and college in the United States were turned to the exclusive production of physicists, ignoring all else in science and in the humanities, there would still necessarily be a manpower shortage in physics before the passage of another century.

The normal expansion of science that we have grown up with is such that it demands each year a larger place in our lives, a larger share of our resources. Eventually that demand must reach a state where it cannot be satisfied, a state where the civilization is saturated with science. This may be regarded as an ultimate end of the completed Industrial Revolution. Thus that process takes us from the first few halting paces up to the maximum of effort. The only question that must be answered lies in the definition of that saturated state and the estimation of its arrival date.

Fortunately, the mathematical theory is again most helpful if we demand only an approximate picture and require no maze of detail. Exponential growths that become saturated and thereby slowed down to a steady level are very common in nature. We meet them in almost every field of biological growth or epidemiology. The rabbit population in Australia or the colony of fruit flies in a bottle all grow rapidly until some natural upper limit is reached. In nearly all known cases, the approach to the ceiling is rather strikingly symmetrical with the growth from the datum line.[7] The curve of growth is a sigmoid or logistic curve,

S-shaped, and even above and below its middle.

The only good historical example known to me illustrates the decline of the European Middle Ages, followed by the beginning of the Renaissance. If one makes a graph of the number of universities founded in Europe, arranged by date, the curve splits into two parts. The first part is a sigmoid curve starting at A.D. 950, growing exponentially at first but falling away rapidly by about 1450, and thereafter approaching a ceiling with equal rapidity. Added to this is a second exponential curve, doubling more rapidly than the first and acting as if it had started with a first member, a new style of university in 1450. The lesson is obvious: the old order began to die on its feet and, in doing so, allowed a quite new, Renaissance concept of the university to arise.

It is a property of the symmetrical sigmoid curve that its transition from small values to saturated ones is accomplished during the central portion (halfway between floor and ceiling) in a period of time corresponding to only the middle five or six doubling periods (more exactly, 5.8), independent of the exact size of the ceiling involved. Thus the time at which the logistic curve has fallen only a few per cent below the expected, normal exponential curve represents the onset of the process. Three doubling periods later, the deficiency is 50 per cent, the sigmoid curve reaching only half the expected height. Thereafter, the sigmoid curve becomes almost flat, while the exponential curve continues its wild increase. One must therefore say that only some three doubling periods intervene between the onset of saturation and absolute decrepitude.

For science in the United States, the accurate growth figures show that only about thirty years must elapse between

[7] A collection of such sigmoid graphs showing autocatalytic growth is to be found in Alfred J. Lotka, *Elements of Mathematical Biology* (New York: Dover Publications, Inc., 1956), Chap. 7, Figs. 4-8. In the same work, p. 369, Fig. 71 is another sigmoid graph, this one indicative of technological rather than scientific growth, that of the total mileage of American railroads. The osculating tangent (straight line through the midpoint of the S-curve) acts as if it is started *ca.* 1860 and attained saturation (at some 300,000 miles) *ca.* 1920. This, then, is the *effective* span of this aspect of the Industrial Revolution in America. At least this method has the advantage over many historical discussions in suggesting some decent and objective criterion for what constitutes an effective beginning and an effective end to the process. The same criterion distinguishes capricious precursors from true originators.

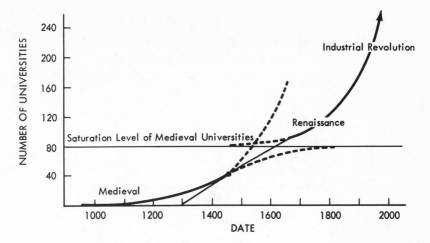

FIG. 6. Number of universities founded in Europe. From the foundation at Cairo in 950 up to ca. 1460 there is pure exponential growth, doubling in about one hundred years. Thereafter saturation sets in, so that the mid-region of the sigmoid extends from 1300 to ca. 1610. Between 1460 and 1610 is a period of transition to the new form of universities, a growth that also proceeds exponentially as if it has started from unity ca. 1450 and doubling every sixty-six years. There is probably an even greater transition to yet faster growth starting at the end of the Industrial Revolution.

the period when some few per cent of difficulty is felt and the time when that trouble has become so acute that it cannot possibly be satisfied.[8] It seems quite apparent from the way in which we have talked, from time to time in recent years, about manpower difficulties in science that we are currently in a period in which the onset of a man-

---

[8] To be more exact, the standard equation for a sigmoid curve is $y = (1 + e^{-x})^{-1}$, where $x = k \ (t - t_0)$. Its osculating tangent intersects the abscissa at $x = -2$, and the line $y = 1$ at $x = 2$. In the former place, at $x = -2$, $y = 0.12$, whereas the plain exponential function $Y = e^z$ has the value $Y = 0.135$. y is therefore some 12.0 per cent of Y below the value of Y; at $x = o$ we have $y = 0.5$ but $Y = 1.0$, a falling of some 50 per cent below expectation. Each unit of x corresponds to 1.45 doubling periods, or a factor of $e = 2.718$. The four units of the middle portion of the curve therefore correspond to 5.8 doubling periods, and the interval between a shortage of 12.0 per cent and that of 50 per cent is only 2.9 doubling periods.

power shortage is beginning to be felt. We are already, roughly speaking, about halfway up [to] the manpower ceiling.

The historical evidence leads one to believe that this is no incidental headache that can be cured separately by giving science an aspirin. It is just one symptom of a particularly deep-rooted disease of science. Perhaps it is more a natural process than a disease, though clearly we participants in the process are ill-at-ease as a result. It is essential to the nature of the case that science go through a period of vigorous growth and that there has now come a sort of postadolescent hiatus, and the growth is done and science has its adult stature. We must not expect such growth to continue, and we must not waste time and energy in seeking too many palliatives for an incurable process. In particular, it cannot be worthwhile sacrificing all else that humanity holds dear in order to allow science to grow

diseases of science   63

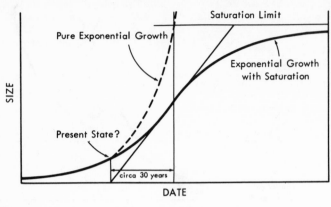

SIZE

Pure Exponential Growth

Saturation Limit

Exponential Growth
with Saturation

Present State?

circa 30 years

DATE

FIG. 7.

unchecked for only one or two more doubling periods. It would seem much more useful to employ our efforts in anticipating the requirements of the new situation in which science has become, in some way, a saturated activity of mankind, taking as high a proportion of our expenditure in brains and money as it can attain. We have not reached that stage quite yet, but it is only a very short time before we will—less than a human generation. In the meantime, we must certainly do what we can to provide the aspirin of more and better scientists, but we must also face the larger issue ahead.

What makes it particularly exciting is that the bending of the curve toward a ceiling is happening just at that time when the handicap race of the various Industrial Revolutions has been run out and ended in a close finish. In previous decades the runners have been far apart; now they are bunched together and their speeds no longer have much effect. To think out the consequences of this, we must now examine the feeling of living in a state of saturated science.

Some of the effects are already apparent and may be amenable to historical analysis and even statistical treatment. If the cumulative expansion of science rapidly outpaces all efforts we can make to feed it with manpower, it means that more and more things will arise naturally in the life of science and require attention that cannot be given. There will be too many discoveries chasing too few workers. At the highest level we must come to a situation at which there are too many breakthroughs per square head. In all previous times, for each breakthrough, such as that of X-rays in 1895, there were many large groups of physicists who could attack the new problem and start to work on it. Already in our own times we have a decrease of this. In any particular area of breakthrough there are initially fewer capable specialists, and many of these are faced with the prospect of having too many interesting tidbits on their own plate to feel the need to go elsewhere, however exciting that might seem.

It may be remarked that this specialization may also be measured, and if you do it in any reasonable way, it appears to lead to the result that it, too, is doubling in every decade or so. As the amount of knowledge increases, each man must occupy a smaller and smaller segment of the research front. This, again, is not a process that can continue indefinitely; eventually a point of no return is reached at which the various disadvantages of acute specialization became too marked. Cross-fertilization of fields decreases and so thereby does the utility of the science. The more rapidly moving research front tends to leave behind such specialists, in increasing numbers, to while out their years of decline in occluded pockets.

Thus far nothing has been said about the quality of research as opposed to its quantity. This is of course much more difficult to determine and would repay much more serious investigation than it has ever had. Various measures are possible. One may study the growth of only important discoveries, inventions, and scientific laws, rather than all such things, important and trivial; any count of this sort immediately shows that the growth, though still exponential, possesses a doubling time that is much longer than that of the gross growth of science. The actual stature of science, in terms of its achievements, appears to double within about one generation (some thirty years) rather than in the ten years that doubles numbers of papers and numbers of scientists.[9]

[9] It is difficult to be precise about this law; so far, I feel, one may have only reasonable certainty that the stature of science, however one defines it, grows some two or three times more slowly than any measure of gross size. One need not argue about the exact size of the constant involved. What is particularly impressive is that the cost of science, in terms of expenditure in money and national income, grows much *faster* than the gross size. Indeed, Strong and Benfey suggest [*Journal of Chemical Education*, 37 (1960), 29] that United States research and development costs double every six years, whereas the persons listed in *American Men of Science* double only in twelve years. Thus it would seem that the cost goes up as the square of the number of men working, and the number of men increases as the square or cube of their effectiveness in increasing the stature of science. We have therefore a fourth- or

In its stature, science grows much more nearly in keeping with all else in our society: size of population, economic wealth, activity in the arts. In size, however, it must undergo something like three doublings for each of these other generations. Perhaps it is not entirely wrong to see this as a consequence of the cumulative structure of science. If it grows like a pile of stones or bricks, then the pile keeps the same pyramidal shape. Its height measures the stature of science and its attainment; in this it grows at the same general rate as our culture at large. However, to make the pyramid twice as high, its volume must be multiplied by eight, the cube of two. It must undergo three doublings for every doubling of the height. The number of bricks of scientific knowledge increases as the cube of the reach of that knowledge.[10]

Even if this is only a most approximate law, based on rather tenuous hypotheses and measurements, it nevertheless constitutes a powerful law of diminishing returns in the world of sci-

sixth-power law of rapidly diminishing returns. To proceed with rocketry at ten times the present effectiveness would cost, say, ten thousand or perhaps a million times as much money! To return to the measurement of the stature of science, it may be noted that on the basis of such subjective lists of "important" discoveries as those of L. Darmstaedter and of P. Sorokin, the evidence seems to agree that there was quite normal exponential growth, doubling in about 120 years for all the period up to about 1660, and then again normal growth doubling every thirty years from that time to the present day.

[10] This "fortuitous" agreement with a popular and picturesque model leads one to wonder whether some of the other highly descriptive phrases which scientists habitually apply to their tactics can have more than casual usefulness. Is, for example, the geographic simile (fields of work, borderline investigations, difficult territory) a suitable description of the topology of the connectivity of learning?

ence. This finding may be easily strengthened by an analysis of the distribution in quality of scientific men. It has been proposed, on the basis of statistical investigations of the number of times that various papers were used by other people, that an inverse square law of goodness holds here as it did for productivity. For every single paper of the first order of importance there are four of secondary quality, nine of the third class, and so on. Much of the same result is obtained if one regards the spread in the scientific population as similar to that as the upper tail of a normal distribution curve of some sort of intelligence quotient.

However you do it, it seems inevitable that to increase the general number of scientists you must cut off a larger section of the tail, rather than increase the thickness of the same section of tail. Probably it follows that to double the population of workers in the few highest categories, there must be added some eight times their number of lesser individuals. At a certain point it becomes rather futile to worry about improving the standard of the low-grade men, since it is unlikely that one can tamper very much with a distribution curve that seems much the same now as it was in the seventeenth century, much the same in America as in Europe or as in Russia. Minor differences in quality of training there might be, but to work on the research front of modern science demands a high minimum of excellence.

Thus science in an age of saturation must begin to look rather different from its accustomed state. I believe it is without question that the occurrence of such a change must produce effects at least as disturbing to our way of life as an economic depression. For one thing, any slackening of the research pace of pure science must be reflected quite rapidly in our advancing tech-

nology, and thereby in our economic state.[11] It is difficult to say just what form this effect might take. Clearly there is no direct, one-to-one relationship of pure science to technology. Even if there were declared a sudden moratorium on pure scientific research, or (what is more plausible) an embargo on growth that allowed all such work to continue but without the habitual 6 per cent yearly increase in manpower, there would still be enough of a corpus of knowledge to provide for technological applications for several generations to come. As Robert Oppenheimer has expressed it: "We need new knowledge like we need a hole in the head."

There is, however, a snag in the argument as expressed above, for in the past the expansion of science and of technology have proceeded hand in hand, and it has been only the sorry task of the historian to point out examples where the one or the other has taken the leading role—an evaluation in most cases that has been revised back and forth several times each decade. I suspect, because of this intimate relationship, that although technology might be left with a great bulk of pure science waiting to be applied, any decrease in the acceleration of science will prove an unaccustomed barrier to industry, and that the flow of new ideas into industry will in some indeterminate way suffer and drop spectac-

[11] For such an analysis of the role of research in economic growth, see Raymond H. Ewell, in Chemical and Engineering News, 33 (July 18, 1955), 2980-2985. Ewell makes a good case for the growth rate of individual industries and the gross national product both being directly proportional to the growth rate of expenditure on research and development. In detail, some 10 per cent increase in the cost of science is needed to produce the national economic growth rate of 3 per cent; that is, the scientific budget seems to increase as the cube of the general economic index.

ularly. We are now geared to an improvement of technology at a rate of some 6 to 7 per cent per annum, and a decline in this must affect all our lives. Then again, if manpower is chronically to be in short supply in the world of science, it will follow that *what* we do is much more important than *how much* we do it.

It follows also that the good scientist will be increasingly in demand and in power, since it must become ever more apparent that it is he who holds the pursestrings of civilization in the era we have entered. Indeed, if it were not for the well-established reluctance of scientists to enter the political arena, one might boldly predict that the philosophers are about to become kings—or presidents at least.

In a saturated state of science there will be evident need to decide, either by decree or by default, which jobs shall be done and which shall be left open—remembering always that an ever-increasing number of possible breakthroughs must be left unexploited. It is most doubtful whether this can be best done by considering merely the utility to society of the job in itself. In the history of science, it is notorious that practical application has often grown out of purely scientific advance; seldom has pure research arisen from a practical application by any direct means. I would be cautious here, for there are too many violent views in such areas, and the truth is certainly no unmixed extreme. But even so, it would be foolhardy to direct all medical research to work on cancer, or all physicists to work on missiles and atomic power.

If such fields are rich and important at the moment, it is evident that they have not always been so, that they will probably appear in a different light a few decades hence. In this future state, we might perchance depend on fields that are currently being starved through diversion of the funds elsewhere. If at any time in the future we wish to change, even if the demand is great, we might have already committed our resources in such a way that they cannot be converted to the new projects. Not only is science changing more and more rapidly; it is entering a completely new state.

In this new state, our civilization will rise or fall according to the tactics and strategy of our application of our scientific efforts. It is anarchical to decide such issues by merely letting ourselves be ruled by the loudest voices. It may or may not be worthwhile to support missile research to the hilt, but no man can make such a decision without considering the possibility that this work will ruin the chances of half a dozen other fields for an entire generation. In a condition in which so much of our scientific research is supported by military contract and federal projects, it seems no man's business to consider the possible damage which could come in our new saturated state.

If the supply of research cannot simply be allowed to follow the ephemeral demand, it seems also that we can no longer take the word of the scientists on the job. Their evaluation of the importance of their own research must also be unreliable, for they must support their own needs; even in the most ideal situation they can look only at neighboring parts of the research front, for it is not their own business to see the whole picture. Quite apart from the fact that we have no national scientific policy, it is difficult to see any ground on which such a policy might be based. It is difficult to take advice from either the promoters of special jobs or from the scientists themselves, for their interests might well be opposed, might well be irrelevant, to the needs of the nation as a whole.

The trouble seems to be that it is no man's business to understand the general patterns and reactions of science as the economist understands the business world. Given some knowledge of economics, a national business policy can be formulated, decrees can be promulgated, recessions have some chance of being controlled, the electorate can be educated. I do not know, indeed, whether one might in fact understand the crises of modern science so well as to have the power to do anything about them. I must, however, suggest that the petty illnesses of science—its superabundance of literature, its manpower shortages, its increasing specialization, its tendency to deteriorate in quality—all these things are but symptoms of a general disease. That disease is partly understood by the historian, and might be understood better if it were any man's professional province to do so. Even if we could not control the crisis that is almost upon us, there would at least be some satisfaction in understanding what was hitting us.

Reasons for Sociocultural Change and Variably Recurrent Processes

PITIRIM A. SOROKIN

Principle of the Immanent Change of Systems and Supersystems

Having analyzed sociocultural changes—their forms, directions, and rhythms—we must now inquire into their causes. Why are sociocultural phenomena not static? Why do not sociocultural changes pursue a uniform linear or cyclical course instead of exhibiting varying rhythms and tempos? As Aristotle rightly observed: "We cannot feel that we understand a thing until we can give an account of its causes and its *modus operandi*."[1]

Most of these questions are satisfactorily explained by two general principles or uniformities: by the principle of immanent change of sociocultural systems, assisted by the principle of facilitating external factors, and by the

Pitirim A. Sorokin, *Society, Culture and Personality*, pp. 696-706. Copyright 1947 by Harper & Brothers. Reprinted by permission of Harper & Row, Publishers.

[1] Aristotle, *The Physics*, 194b.

principle of limit in its three fundamental forms.

1. Any system, especially a sociocultural system, being a "going concern," incessantly functioning, inevitably changes as long as it continues to exist and function, even if it is placed in a wholly static environment.[2] Change is an inherent property of all functioning systems. The most efficient automobile engine is bound to change if it is left running, even under the best conditions. Likewise any biological organism or system inevitably changes as long as it lives, even if the external conditions are static. As the experiments of S. Metalnikov and others show, the simplest organisms, such as the amoeba

[2] For a development of this and subsequent statements cf. my *Social and Cultural Dynamics* (New York: American Book Company, 1940), Vol. IV, Chaps. 12-13; also for a history of theories of immanent change and examples of contemporary explanations of business fluctuations and political and other transformations.

or paramecium caudalum, having re-acted to a given stimulus A, react to the same stimulus a second time in a different way, although the stimulus and the other conditions of the environment may remain unchanged; their third reaction is different from the second, and so on.[3]

To reiterate, the cause of the changes in a social system is inherent in the system itself. Whether the system is scientific or religious, aesthetic or philosophical, whether it is represented by a family, a business firm, an occupational union, or a state, it bears within itself the seeds of incessant change, which mark every action and reaction even in a fixed environment.

2. An additional reason for the change of a sociocultural system is its milieu, which is made up mainly of a multitude of other changing systems and forces. The total constellation of interacting systems necessarily intensifies the process of change inherent within each member system. Thus the change implicit in a family or a scientific or philosophical system is stimulated through the interaction with other families or the state and with other scientific or philosophical systems.

3. The immanent change of a sociocultural system or supersystem means, furthermore, the generation of a series of consequences affecting and largely determining its subsequent career. The effects of a given change are not evanescent. In most cases they are lasting and engender a cumulative series of consequences, even if the environment remains static. Thus the marriage of a member of a family or the division of the family property produces a train of consequences that induce further changes in the family. The consequences of a war do not cease with the armistice and peace, but usually continue to operate long after the end of the war.

4. Hence changing immanently and generating a cumulative series of consequences of each change, a system incessantly transforms both itself and its milieu.

5. Through this incessant generation of consequences attending each of its changes a system perceptibly determines the character and course of its own future career. The whole series of changes it undergoes throughout its existence is to a large extent *an unfolding of its inherent potentialities*. From an acorn can spring only an oak. From the seed of any organism can emerge only the respective organism. In spite of the vicissitudes of their subsequent life history, the main line of the changes which such organisms undergo is merely the result of the inherent properties of the seed. The same is true of sociocultural systems. For instance, implicit in the family system are the main lines of its subsequent development; the course of the change of a family is different from that of a political party or state, regardless of its environment. Likewise the course of the changes experienced by a musical system is different from that of a scientific or ethical system. As we shall see, the forms of change of "univariant" sociocultural systems are different from those of "bivariant" or "multivariant" systems; the forms, rhythms, periodicities, and directions of their quantitative and qualitative changes differ in each system according to its nature. In this sense any sociocultural system largely molds its own destiny.

6. This fundamental characteristic of systems or supersystems does not preclude the influence of external—geographic, biological, and sociocul-

[3] Cf. S. Metalnikov, *La Lutte contre la mort* (Paris, 1937), p. 74 and Chaps. 1-7; also K. Goldstein, *The Organism* (New York: American Book Company, 1939), *passim*.

tural—factors. However, their role consists largely (*a*) in the acceleration or retardation of the immanent change of a system; (*b*) in facilitating or hindering the realization of its potentialities; (*c*) in the suppression, distortion, or overdevelopment of some of its characteristics; (*d*) in a modification of its secondary traits, or in its mutilation or destruction. External factors cannot transform a given system into something fundamentally different from its essential nature, cannot make it unfold properties which it does not possess, cannot radically alter its immanent course. They can crush the system, or they can use its components—its members and some of its vehicles and meanings—for the creation of another system. This means, however, not the radical transformation of a given system into another quite different one, but rather the substitution of another in its place. No external conditions can force a corn seed to grow into a rosebush, or transform a scientific system into a symphony or a work of sculpture, a novel into a law code, or a family into a political party or a state. External factors can promote or hinder the full development of an oak or a scientific theory; they can accelerate or retard their growth; they can merge the family with a political party, thus making a multibonded group out of two unibonded groups, or they can crush systems and groups. That is all.

The outlined functions of external factors concern equally the geographic, the biological, and even the sociocultural factors external to a given system. Geographic factors exert a perceptible influence upon the distribution of population; upon the character of dwellings, roads, means of transportation, clothing, and food and drink. But they do not rigorously determine the forms of population groups, the essential architectural forms of buildings, or the essentials of food and drink and modes of transportation. They influence to some extent wealth, the distribution of industry, and the seasonal fluctuation of business; possibly (though more questionably) vital processes—energy, efficiency and mental creativity, forms of disease, and the like. This influence is neither decisive nor rigorous. Changing sociocultural conditions convert into wealth materials which under other circumstances are not regarded as potential wealth. Mental creativity, health, and sickness depend still less upon geographic conditions. As for religion, science, philosophy, the fine arts, law and ethics, language, politics, and economics, probably only certain subsidiary traits are determined by geographic factors. The essential nature of these systems and their changes depend little upon geographic factors.[4] The various effects of geographic conditions do not exceed the formulated functions of external factors so far as sociocultural systems are concerned. In regard to cultural congeries their effects may be somewhat more decisive.

What has been said of geographic factors applies to biological forces external to a system. The biological factor of heredity is an internal factor of a sociocultural system because human beings, with their hereditary properties, are

[4] For a detailed study of the relationship between various geographic factors and diverse sociocultural phenomena, cf. my *Contemporary Sociological Theories* (New York: Harper & Row, Publishers, 1928), Chaps. 2-3. . . . Among the works published recently G. Dykmans, *Introduction critique à la science économique*, 2 vols. (Brussels: 1945) gives the most complete survey, criticism, and bibliography dealing with the role of geographic factors; Dykmans' conclusions agree in all essential respects with those arrived at in my *Theories*. L. Deschesne's *La Localisation des diverses productions* (Brussels: 1945) furnishes a very detailed study of the effects of geographic conditions upon the localization of industry, together with the most highly generalized rational principles of such localization and of sociocultural ecology.

components of sociocultural systems. The effects of other biological factors, such as density of population, natural selection, and the so-called "struggle for existence," are confined to the outlined effects of external factors.[5]

More decisive is the influence of sociocultural factors external to a given system or supersystem. But even this is confined to the enumerated functions of external forces. Only when a given system actually becomes a part of a larger system or of a supersystem does it begin to change in close accord with all the parts of the larger system or the supersystem.

7. This means that any system (or subsystem or supersystem) possesses a certain measure of self-determination and a certain margin of autonomy from the operation of external forces in its functioning and changes. The degree of self-determination and the margin of autonomy differ for different systems, depending upon their nature, their milieu, and other conditions.

(a) Other conditions being equal, the lowest degree of self-determination and the narrowest margin of autonomy are found among unorganized groups and cultural congeries; they are the prey of external forces.

(b) In systems of the same kind the degree of self-determination and the margin of autonomy tend to increase with a better organization of the groups and with a closer integration of the cultural systems.

(c) In subsystems and systems that are a part of a larger system or a supersystem, the self-determination and the margin of autonomy of each are limited not only by external forces but also by the other subsystems and systems of the more inclusive system. Each part retains a certain degree of autonomy, but this is restricted by the close meaningful and causal interdependence of the parts upon one another and upon the system as a whole. Hence the component parts tend to change in togetherness often synchronously, though at somewhat different rates.

8. So far as the self-determination of any system is equivalent to its freedom, it is free, within the margin of its autonomy, from the deterministic influence of external forces. The systems are somewhat indeterminate also in the sense that the very notion of the potentialities of a system necessarily contains a marginal element of indeterminacy. A potentiality A with traits $a, b, c, d, \ldots n$ implies the possibility of a realization of traits a and c in one case; of a, d, and n in another; of b, c, and d in a third, etc. Thus the potentialities of the system permit a measure of choice in the realization of its secondary traits.

9. Beyond the limits of self-determination and the margin of autonomy the life course of systems is determined by external factors and by other systems with which they are united into a more comprehensive system. Principles 8 and 9 thus afford a definite answer to the question: Are social and cultural systems deterministic or indeterministic? Each system is in part self-deterministic, or free, and in part deterministic, unfree.

This conclusion appears to be much sounder than many others, for instance, those that claim the complete determinism of sociocultural systems or their complete indeterminism and freedom of will; or such theories as that of A. Eddington, who postulates chance or indeterminacy for inorganic phenomena and an "objective law of direction" for organic and superorganic phenomena,[6] or that of Max Planck and others,

[5] For a detailed analysis and criticism of the role of biological factors, together with the relevant literature, cf. my *Theories*, Chaps. 4-7.

[6] Cf. A. Eddington, *The Philosophy of*

who proclaim the rule of "statistical and dynamic determinism" in the inorganic world, with regions of "ego" and "free will" exempt from such determinism.[7] All such theories are both one-sided and in certain respects inconsistent.[8]

10. Since every system changes immanently and since it changes also under the influence of changing external factors and of changes in the supersystem to which it belongs, it can never return to its original state, can never reproduce itself in absolutely identical fashion. *Hence the strictly cyclical conception of the change of systems is untenable. The principle of immanent change emphatically contradicts it.*

The Principle of Limits

The principle of limits is the second general principle or law that accounts for an enormous number of characteristics of sociological change, particularly of rhythms and of variations in recurrent trends, and for the improbability of any permanent linear course of change in sociological systems. The principle of limits exhibits the following three main forms.

1. Limits in Causal-Functional Relationship of Interdependent Variables

According to the first form of the principle of limits the causal-functional relationship between two or more variables A and B has certain definite limits; beyond a given value of A and B it ceases to exist or undergoes a radical change. Within certain limits the more firmly we strike a piano key, the louder the resulting sound. Beyond this point the result will be not a louder sound but merely a broken keyboard.

The physicochemical and biological sciences are well aware of the principle of limits in the causal-functional relationships of their variables. They have formulated a number of general principles relative to the "stability limit" (Knorr and others), "critical temperature," "critical pressure," "critical concentration," and the like, representing points beyond which the causal-functional relationship between the given variables either undergoes a radical change or ceases to exist. For example: "Chemical reactions do not take place completely in one direction, but proceed only to a certain point and there make a halt." Thus the upper limit in the vaporization of water or the equilibrium between liquid and vapor is reached at the critical temperature of 364.3 degrees and the critical pressure of 194.6 atmospheres. At higher temperatures no pressure, however great, can induce the liquid phase. Such limits are typical of a vast number of causal-functional relationships between physicochemical variables.[9]

Sociologists and social scientists are imperfectly aware of this principle. When they formulate valid or invalid causal relationships between business depression and criminality, prosperity and the birth rate, poverty and the

Physical Science (New York: The Macmillan Company, 1939), pp. 61, 89-90, *et passim.*

[7] M. Planck, *Where Is Science Going?* (New York: W. W. Norton & Company, Inc., 1932), pp. 145-169, and A. Lotka, "Evolution and Thermodynamics," *Science and Society*, 8 (1944), 169ff.; J. Frank, *Fate and Freedom* (New York: Simon & Schuster, Inc., 1945).

[8] For the fluctuation of deterministic and indeterministic conceptions in their application to the ideational and sensate supersystems, cf. my *Dynamics*, Vol. II, Chap. 9.

[9] A. Findlay, *The Phase Rule and Its Applications* (London: Longmans, Green & Company, Ltd., 1904), pp. 96, 200, 234, *et passim.* W. Gibbs's phase rule and the theorems of Van Hoff, Le Chatelier, and others present the general principles of such limits.

mortality rate, education and criminality, economic conditions and the forms of the arts, farm income and illiteracy, and so on, they rarely mention any limits within which the causal relationship between their variables holds. They seemingly assume that it has no limits no matter what values we assign to the variables.

On the basis of both logic and observed facts it is reasonably certain that in practically all causally connected sociocultural variables there are limits beyond which the causal-functional relationship ceases or else assumes another character. Poverty below the level of physiological necessity depresses the birth rate and increases the mortality rate; an improvement in material well-being up to and above the level of physiological necessity causes an increase in the birth rate and a decrease in the mortality rate. However, there are limits beyond which a further improvement of material conditions does not lead to a further rise of the birth rate or decline of the mortality rate; it may even produce the opposite results. The same is true of practically all causal relationships between sociocultural variables; they apparently all have their limits. A precise causal formula demands, therefore, the specification of the limits within which it is valid and beyond which it becomes invalid. This principle of limits in causal-functional relationships is one of the reasons why most sociocultural processes have their "optimum" points and fluctuate without any definite trend between certain limits in their direction and course.

2. Limits in Linear Direction of Sociocultural Change

Contrary to the claims of a host of biological and social "linearists," the theory of a permanent linear trend of biological evolution or sociocultural progress is hardly tenable on either logical or empirical grounds. In virtually every sociocultural process there are limits for a linear trend. Within a limited time and a limited segment of the process some linear trend is possible, but it is scarcely possible for an unlimited period or for the entire process.

A linear sociocultural change is a complicated variety of the uniform rectilinear motion observed in mechanics. Newton's law declares that such motion is possible only when there is no interference from external forces, or when the moving body is completely isolated from all environmental factors, or when all the external forces at any moment mutually cancel one another and permit the body to move according to the law of inertia, uniformly and rectilinearly. The motion of material bodies, including the heavenly bodies, is, however, not subject to these conditions. Gravitational forces, for instance, interfere with it and divert it into a circular or elliptical orbit.

Still less do these conditions apply to sociocultural phenomena. They are subject to the constant operation of physical, biological, and sociocultural factors. No systems or congeries exist in a vacuum, isolated from the forces of the environment. Nor do the innumerable forces external to a changing sociocultural phenomenon perpetually annul one another. Moreover, even if this were true, the principle of immanent change would preclude the possibility of limitless linear trends in the change of sociocultural systems and congeries.[10]

These logical reasons are well corroborated by factual evidence. Practically all the permanent linear trends

---

[10] There are many other reasons for this conclusion. For a more precise elaboration of this and subsequent statements, cf. my *Dynamics*, Vol. IV, Chap. 14.

postulated by biological and social scientists have proved spurious when subjected to the acid test of empirical observation.

3. Limited Possibilities of Basic Variations of Systems

Since every empirical sociocultural system is finite, and since there are limits beyond which any further change renders it unrecognizable and unidentifiable, therefore it is capable of only a limited number of basic variations or types of change. Having exhausted these types, the system either disintegrates or repeats these types in a new setting, with different secondary characteristics. Hence on the one hand the recurrence, or rhythm, of sociocultural processes, and on the other the variations in their course.

Natural scientists are thoroughly familiar with the principle in question, and, in contrast to social scientists, they incessantly apply it. Every physicist knows that water has only three basic types, or phases, of variation—vapor, liquid, and solid—which are repeated endlessly. Chemical systems with more than one component exhibit a greater number of phases and greater degrees of "freedom" in their changes; but, according to W. Gibbs's formula: $P + F = C + 2$, or $F = C + 2 - P$ (where P denotes the number of phases, F the degree of freedom, and C the number of components of the system); virtually all chemical systems are limited in their transformations and therefore repeat their phases in time and space.[11]

Similarly, the number of basic physical forms of energy, such as heat, sound, electricity, and magnetism, is strictly limited; therefore they endlessly recur in the physical world. The same is true of biological systems; whether it is the number of species, or the number of dominant characteristics or variations of a given species, or the number of fundamental biological processes (adaptation, natural selection, the struggle for existence, reproduction, and so on), they are all limited in their fundamental types, and therefore recur in time and space.

No less true is this of sociocultural systems. Whatever classification of the basic types of *economic organization* is adopted, these rarely exceed six or eight in number, as in the classification given by K. Bücher, G. Schmoller, E. Meyer, and W. Sombart, who list hunting, the collecting of natural products, pastoral life, agriculture, and industry. If a given economic system runs through all these types and continues to exist, it must necessarily repeat them, with variations. Similarly, the cardinal types of the *family* and *marriage* do not exceed ten in number. The same is true of the chief types of *political regimes* and the *forms of government*; the five forms given by Plato and the six of Aristotle and Polybius embrace all the principal variations. No different is the situation with respect to the basic forms of *religion, language and writing, ethics and law, philosophy,* or the *fine arts.* The same is true of *technological systems* (as illustrated by the paleolithic, the neolithic, the copper, the bronze, the iron, and the machine age), and of systems of mechanical energy.

[11] Cf. A. Findlay, *op. cit.*, pp. 16ff. H. Poincaré rightly stresses the importance of the limited number of chemical elements, whose recurrence makes possible the science of chemistry. If, instead of 92 chemical elements, there were 92 billions, "each time we picked up a new pebble, there would be a strong probability of its being composed of an unknown substance. In such a world there would be no science." Even life itself would hardly be possible under such conditions. For a further comment on this statement, cf. P. L. du Noüy, *Biological Time* (London: Methuen & Company, Ltd., 1936), p. 34.

Even if we take *the main patterns of minor social and cultural* phenomena, such as styles of dress and coiffure,[12] of arrow points, of sword handles, and of drums, or systems of matrilineal and patrilineal descent and forms of kinship, we find that they too are limited and therefore repeat themselves in secondary variations at various periods in various societies.

Summarizing, the basic forms of almost all sociocultural phenomena are limited in their number; hence they inevitably recur in time, in rhythmic fashion, and in the course of their changes do not follow a strictly linear trend.[13]

Immanent Change and Limits and Rhythms of Sociocultural Processes

From the principle of the immanent change of systems, re-enforced by the ever-changing constellation of external factors, there follows the impossibility of an absolutely cyclical direction of change.

The principle of immanent change, re-enforced by that of limits (in its three forms), precludes a limitless linear direction of change in sociocultural systems. Theoretically such a limitless trend is possible in the case of an "in-

variant" social system, that is, one which possesses only a single basic type, variant, or phase, which cannot change into any other form, variant, or phase.[14] Even an "invariant" sociocultural system can pursue a linear trend only in a vacuum or in a milieu where all the external forces cancel one another out. Such a theoretical case is hardly ever realized in the sociocultural universe. First, we are not sure that there are any invariant sociocultural systems; second, the necessary milieu, with a mutual annulment of all the external forces for an indefinite period, does not exist; third, it is certain that no sociocultural system operates in a vacuum, completely isolated from all external forces. Hence such unlimited linear directions are hardly possible in the actual change of a sociocultural system. What may resemble a limitless linear trend is likely to be merely a limited trend of considerable duration exhibiting many deviations from strict linearity even within this segment, and becoming explicitly nonlinear when a longer period is considered. Even such possibly linear processes as the increase of the population of the earth, the multiplication of inventions and discoveries, and the intensification of social differentiation and division of labor are, in fact, linear in only a limited sense; viewed even in their known span of existence, they reveal many deviations from linearity, and if considered from the standpoint of their entire life history, they would probably be found to pursue a parabolic course or to fluctuate without any definite trend.[15] Ninety-nine per cent

---

[12] G. Glotz remarks that the modern Parisian coiffure and dress are strikingly similar to those of the Minoan culture. [*La Civilisation égéenne* (Paris: 1923), pp. 88ff.] W. Deonna gives a large number of such recurrences in dress, coiffure, manners, etc. (*L'Archéologie*, 3 vols., *passim*.)

[13] For a development of this proposition, cf. my *Dynamics*, Vol. IV, pp. 701ff.; A. Goldelweiser, "The Principle of Limited Possibilities," *Journal of American Folklore*, **26** (1913), 259-290; R. Thurnwald, "The Spell of Limited Possibilities," *American Sociological Review*, **2** (1937), 195-203; and R. Lowie, "On the Principle of Convergence in Ethnology," *Journal of American Folklore*, **25** (1912), 37ff. For other literature, cf. my *Dynamics*, Vol. IV, pp. 704ff.

[14] The term "invariant" is borrowed from Gibbs's phase rule. It designates chemical systems that do not possess any degree of freedom, whereas chemical systems that possess two or more degrees of freedom are designated, respectively, as "univariant," "bivariant," and "multivariant." (Cf. A. Findlay, *op. cit.*, pp. 17ff.)

[15] Cf. my *Dynamics*, Vol. IV, pp. 715-726.

of all other linear "laws of evolution and progress" are definitely untenable, figments of the imagination of theorists rather than accurate formulae of the actual direction of sociocultural processes.

This generalization applies also to the laws of the "universal stages" through which mankind as a whole or a given society or cultural system is supposed to pass. Apart from the sequence of phases of repeated rhythms, no such law of stages has been established. When empirically tested, most of such laws, including Comte's law of three stages, Spencer's law of evolution, and hundreds of similar laws of historical development, prove untenable.[16]

---

[16] Recently L. A. White attempted to defend such linear laws of evolution and of the universal linear sequence of its stages. He is right so far as he asserts that many evolutionists do not claim that every culture or society passes through these stages in their universal sequence. He fails, however, to demonstrate what exactly are these evolutionary stages and who and what passes through them, and where. "The evolutionists described the development of writing as follows: first there was picture writing; out of it grew a form of rebus writing; and out of this emerged the alphabet. What they have done is to describe a cultural process; they have said that these stages follow one another in this order. They have said nothing about any tribe or nation, or about the order in which it might acquire one or another of these forms of writing." (L. White, "Diffusion vs. Evolution," *American Anthropologist*, 47 [1945], 343ff. Cf. also his "History Evolutionism and Functionalism," *Southwestern Journal of Anthropology*, 1 [1945], 221-246.) This order of emergence of the forms of writing is the best case cited by White in support of his claim. Taking his statement at its face value, we are entitled to conclude that even this sequence of the forms of writing is not a universal law of evolution; for many tribes and nations have not passed through this sequence. Those which have done so represent neither mankind as a whole nor even the majority of social groups. Therefore they give only a partial, limited sequence of no more general significance than the following sequences: picture writing, alphabetic form, rebus writing,

The *number of phases* in the rhythm of a given sociocultural process roughly corresponds to the number of basic types or variations of a given system. If the system is "univariant" and has two basic types, then its rhythm will exhibit two phases, such as the sequences increase and decrease, materialism and idealism, peace and war, depression and prosperity, or the diurnal-nocturnal rhythm of activity and rest. If the system is multivariant and has, say, six main types or variants, such as the Aristotelian forms of government (monarchy, tyranny, aristocracy, oligarchy, democracy, mob rule), then its changes will present a six-phase rhythm, and so on. If one knows how many fundamental variants a given system possesses, one can predict what kind of rhythm, with how many phases, it will display in the course of its existence. This statement must, however, be ac-

---

alphabetic form; alphabetic form only; picture writing only; rebus writing only. We have no reason to elevate one of the sequences—say, picture, rebus, and alphabetic writing—into a universal law of evolution, leaving the other sequences in the inferior position of a mere deviation from the alleged universal law. Furthermore, even the allegation that there first appeared picture writing, then rebus writing, and finally alphabetic writing is a mere guess. Third, even if they did emerge in that order, such an emergence, happening only once in the course of history, in no way establishes a law of evolution. Again, the fact that the classical Greek style of architecture was followed in turn by the Romanesque, Gothic, baroque, rococo, and other styles does not establish a law of architectural evolution. To elevate such a local, particularized sequence into a law of evolution of architecture means to deprive the term "law of evolution" of its central meaning. The overwhelming majority of social and cultural forms exhibit no universal stages of evolution. White is correct in distinguishing repeated sociocultural processes from unique historical events and from nonrhythmic, ever-varying processes; but his valiant effort to champion the linear laws of evolution, with their universal stages, is futile.

cepted with certain reservations. Sociocultural systems are much less rigid than chemical systems, and the sequence of their phases is more variable. For instance, between clear-cut phases of economic prosperity and depression there may be intermediate "bridges" that cannot be properly designated as either definite prosperity or definite impoverishment. In bivariant system with three basic variants, these are repeated again and again, but not necessarily in the same order; between these phases there may be subsidiary phases.

The *less numerous the principal variants* of a given sociocultural system, the *simpler, more pronounced, and more readily observable are its rhythms.* If it has only two main variants and consequently a two-phase rhythm, this rhythm repeats itself more frequently and is hence more easily observed and apprehended than one with 500 phases in a system with 500 basic variants.

In systems with a *large number of main variants the rhythm is so complex, consisting of so many phases, that we can hardly grasp its nature or observe its recurrence.* The change of such systems, even if they have a fairly definite rhythm, appears nonrhythmical and nonrecurrent. It suggests an ever-new process, without any repetitions or recurrences, incessantly varying and unpredictable.

The two preceding propositions explain why many sociocultural processes appear unique at any moment of their existence. They account also for the actual novelty of most sociocultural processes considered not only in their main aspects, but in all their secondary and detailed characteristics. Since the number and variety of these secondary characteristics are enormous, and since the conditions of the milieu are also highly varied, the number of combinations of these secondary traits and of the milieu is practically unlimited. In

respect to the secondary traits of a system and of its milieu we cannot expect any repeated uniformity, any recurrent rhythms. It is only in its main types or variants that the history of a system repeats itself in the form of recurrent rhythms, and even these can be properly apprehended only if the basic variants and the phases of the rhythm are not too numerous. Thus the total change of most systems reconciles the two extremes; it is in part a repetition of the old, and in part ever new. The new factors preclude a recurrence of identical cycles.

Understood in the above sense, the dominant form of the direction of sociocultural processes is neither permanently cyclical nor permanently linear, but varyingly recurrent, with incessant modifications of the old themes.

The task of the historical, ideographic, or individualizing sciences consists in the description of the new, unique features of a given system, whereas the task of sociology and of the nomographic, or generalizing, sciences consists in the observation and abstraction of repeated uniformities in the process of change, of established rhythms, however approximate and subject to variation these uniformities may be.

Backward Glance, in Light of Immanent Change and Limits

These principles sum up what we have met in the study of the fluctuations of virtually all the preceding social, cultural, and personal processes. We have observed that social organization, differentiation, and stratification grow immanently until they reach their optimum point in a given group; when the optimum point is exceeded, groups generate forces that inhibit further differentiation and stratification. On the other hand, when immobility persists too long, social systems generate forces working for differentiation. If systems do not succeed in regaining their optimum equilibrium, they tend to disintegrate. The same immanent reaction of systems and the same fluctuation between the optimum limits have been observed in the alternations of freedom and restraint, of expansion and contraction of governmental regimentation, of increase and decrease of mobility, etc. Too much sensate freedom, laissez faire, or mobility generates forces within a system that tend to limit these factors and to reverse the trend. Conversely, too much restraint, governmental regimentation, or immobility elicits the opposite reaction in favor of more freedom, less governmental control, and greater mobility.

We have seen also how and why compulsory or even contractual relationships contain within themselves the seeds of their own destruction and of their transformation into a different kind of social relationships. The same has been demonstrated with respect to the leading cultural systems and supersystems. Each of the principal supersystems possesses the germs of its own decline. With the development, and especially the overdevelopment, of a sensate, ideational, or even idealistic supersystem these germs develop, become more virulent, and eventually undermine the supersystem and pave the way for the emergence and growth of a different system. Even if the external milieu were completely static, each supersystem would immanently follow this course, just as a human organism inevitably pursues its predetermined course from childhood to old age.

The principles of *immanent causes* and of *limits* must be and are applied to explanation of all such sociological phenomena as changes of political or economic systems, business cycles, changes in styles of art or in patterns of cultural growth in various preliterate groups, the rise and decline of historic civilizations, or the maintenance of social equilibrium. Thus the overwhelming majority of theories of the business cycle find its cause in the immanent forces of the capitalist system of economy that inherently generates waves of prosperity and depression (the theories of M. Tugan-Baranovsky, A. Spiethoff, G. H. Hill, J. Schumpeter, M. Bouniatian, A. Aftalion, A. H. Hansen, E. Wagemann, and others).[17]

Geographic, biological, and other forces external to an economic system play merely the role of accelerating (facilitating) or retarding (hindering) factors, or, in extreme cases, that of catastrophic agents. Even in a static milieu, fluctuations of the capitalistic economic system would inevitably occur. Regardless of the milieu, the capitalist system bears within itself the seeds of its own destruction. Hegel and Marx are correct in predicting its immanent, or "dialectical," self-destruction.

Similarly, any political regime, religious creed, or style of art is immanently bound to change and eventually to bring about its own decline. Plato and Aristotle demonstrated this principle in their analysis of how and why each political regime—whether it be an aristocracy or timocracy, oligarchy or monarchy, democracy or tyranny—generates the forces of its own destruction.[18] When anthropologists declare that the nature of the initial culture of a given preliterate group "defines the situation" and becomes the decisive determining factor in the subsequent development of such a culture, they are merely enunciating the principle of im-

17 Cf. my *Dynamics*, Vol. IV, pp. 660ff., and Theories, pp. 120ff.
18 Cf. Plato, *The Republic*, Books VII and VIII; also Aristotle, *Politics*, Book V, *passim*.

manent self-determination and development of cultures.[19]

When Toynbee, Spengler, Danilevsky, *et al.* seek to explain why civilizations decline and disintegrate, they unanimously affirm that they perish "not through murder but through suicide" immanently generated by each civilization in the process of its growth. When social scientists speak of social, economic, or political "equilibria," they all apply the principle of immanent self-adjustment of social, economic, or political systems. The very statement that any social system, when disturbed, tends to re-establish its initial position, or to restore its equilibrium, is a clear-cut formulation of the principle of immanent change and self-adjustment.[20]

Decline of Systems and Exhaustion of Their Creative Forces

Viewed ontologically, the decline of most cultural systems and supersystems is due largely to the growing inadequacy of their intrinsic values—their deviation from genuine reality—or to the exhaustion of their creative functions. Millions of uncreative systems arise, flourish for a time, and quickly disappear. The longevity of most cultural systems and supersystems is due to the fact that they embody genuine reality and values; in other words, that they are creative.

---

[19] Cf. W. I. Thomas, *Primitive Behavior* (New York: McGraw-Hill Book Company, 1937) Chap. 2; R. Lowie, "Some Problems in Ethnology," *American Anthropologist*, 14 (1912), 68-71; C. Wissler, "Ceremonial Bundles of the Blackfoot Indians," *Anthropological Papers of the American Museum of Natural History*, 7 (1912), 100-106; and F. Znaniecki's "closed system" in *The Method of Sociology* (New York: Holt, Rinehart & Winston, Inc., 1934), pp. 11ff.

[20] For an analysis of equilibrium theories, cf. my *Dynamics*, Vol. IV, pp. 677-693.

Being, however finite, limited in the quantity and quality of the true reality-value which they embody, they unfold in the course of their existence merely the potentialities of their finite system of values. Having fulfilled this mission, they eventually become devitalized, a liability rather than an asset. When they have reached this point, their decline is inevitable. Through sheer inertia they may perpetuate their existence for a brief period, an existence (to use Toynbee's phrase) which is rather "death in life" than actual life. Ultimately they are banished from the stage of history and relegated to a "museum" status.

A pertinent illustration of this generalization is afforded by our supersystems. In spite of the richness of their values, even they are finite, each incorporating only one aspect of ultimate truth, reality, or value. The ideational supersystem unfolds the supersensory and superlogical aspect of the infinite manifold; the sensate supersystem, its sensate aspect; the idealistic supersystem, its rudimentary idealistic aspect. Having fulfilled its mission, each supersystem becomes increasingly sterile and progressively hinders the emergence of a new and vital supersystem representing an aspect of reality largely neglected during the domination of its predecessor. Such a situation presents, as it were, an ultimatum to the society and culture in question; they are forced either to replace the exhausted supersystem with a creative one or else to become stagnant and fossilized. Some cultures succeed in making the necessary substitution and survive. Others perish or else become fossilized, being converted into mere raw material, so to speak, for more creative cultures.

When the sensate supersystem of the Creto-Mycenaean culture was exhausted, it was replaced by the creative ideational supersystem of the Greeks.

When this declined, it was superseded by the idealistic supersystem of the fifth century B.C. Being highly unstable and fragile, this, in turn, gave way to the sensate supersystem of the period from the third century B.C. to the fourth A.D. By the fourth century A.D. this supersystem had become depleted, and it was replaced by the ideational Christian supersystem of the Middle Ages. By the thirteenth century the latter had fulfilled its mission and was succeeded by the idealistic and then by the sensate supersystem of the last five centuries. Each supersystem, during its ascendance and at its climax, has been marked by creative genius. Each has contributed immeasurably to humanity's store of truth, beauty, and goodness.

The rhythmic succession of the supersystems is hence not a monotonous, cyclical recurrence, but an ever-creative process constituting a progressive realization of the infinite manifold in the empirical world of humanity.

The contemporary sensate system, in its virile stages, contributed markedly to the values of science and technology, the fine arts, and, in lesser degree, philosophy and ethics. But it is clearly approaching the end of its career; indeed, it is rapidly crumbling under our very eyes. In its present decadent phase, characterized by increasing wars and revolutions, by the perversion of science in the interest of ever more lethal weapons of destruction, by progressive sensualism and the like, it has begun to menace the further existence of humanity. If civilization is not to perish, our moribund sensate supersystem must be replaced by a new ideational or idealistic supersystem. Sooner or later such a supersystem will emerge, destined to continue the creative role of the superorganic on this planet.

small-scale change

three

Change is very much part of the quality of human life, when that life is examined in detail. We mark off the flow of time into conventional units, such as years, seasons, months, weeks, days, hours, and so on. Related conventions assign different activities to different time units, although unexpected events may also occur. Many changes are so regular in their recurrence that they are a major component of predictable order, and scarcely to be regarded as change in the sense of altered roles, rules, or conditions of action. This is one type of small-scale change to which we have not given attention in our selections.

Another conception of small-scale change, and that is the one offered here, refers to changes within groups and organizations rather than societies, cultures, or civilizations.

The complaint was registered in the book *Social Change* that much of the research categorized as "group dynamics" had little relevance either to the structure of groups or to the dynamic properties of group structure. The selection from Mills is clearly innocent of these charges. Using the metaphor of the life cycle (which in its original meaning is another example of small-scale, repetitive change in our first sense), Mills is concerned not only with changes in the perceptions and personalities of participants, but also in the creation and extinction of the group as a collectivity.

Endless (and often meaningless) repetition is one of the commonly assumed characteristics of bureaucracies, that is, large administrative organizations. Yet despite their resistance to change, from whatever source, bureaucracies too are marked by detectable, and predictable, dynamic patterns. The selection by Moore presents some of those patterns in the setting of the business corporation.

Toward a Conception of the Life Cycle of Groups

THEODORE M. MILLS

One of the more deeply perplexing and taxing experiences for the person

Theodore M. Mills, *Group Transformation* (Englewood Cliffs, N. J.: Prentice-Hall, Inc., 1964), pp. 65-80. Reprinted by permission of the author and the publisher.

entering a learning group . . . is the speed at which events, in kaleidoscopic confusion, appear. Often it is expressed in images of "jungle noises," "being at sea," "horses off in all directions," "being shot at from all quarters," "a mess, a mess, a mess," and so on. "We have never, don't now, and will never know what is going on, and if someone says he can untangle it, that just makes it worse." One might imagine similar images going through the mind of a totally naïve person at his first baseball game. Events appear strangely confused, disordered, and unpredictable. Only after one conceives *the game* do these events take their meaningful and enjoyable place in an ordered pattern. Only then do certain events become significant, central, and exciting—though perhaps still unpredictable.

The experienced group leader, or the well-trained observer, has at least an implicit conception of what goes on in men's minds and something of what transpires in groups. By deciphering the multifaceted meaning of comments, he discerns more order and patterns than can the initiate. In fact, a number of teachers, therapists, observers, and social scientists have sensed the existence of certain structures and of ordered change in these structures. Currently, there is a variety of formulations which attempt to make clear the phases, developmental sequences, cycles, or the like through which groups tend to go. The authors of these schemes perhaps share the assumption that a "game"—albeit ingenious and complicated—is being played and that random-like events will become more ordered, more meaningful, more significant once the "game" is conceived, formulated, and understood.

Quite appropriately, these preliminary conceptions of systems in change vary according to the type of group and its goal and according to the professional role or theoretical interest of their authors. For example, for short-term, intellectual, problem-solving groups, Bales conceives of phases in terms of the intellectual processes of orientation, evaluation, and decision,

these being paralleled by an increase in socioemotional issues.[1] For groups training normal adults in human relations, Thelen and Dickerman formulate four phases: (1) members' attempt to establish their customary place in the power hierarchy; (2) leader's rejection of this hierarchy and of authoritarian goals, resulting in frustration and conflict; (3) cohesion and complacency; harmony at all costs; (4) combination of group-centeredness and serious efforts at "work."[2] Phases in his therapy groups are formulated by Mann as (1) hostility serving to bind members through mutuality of feelings, (2) anxiety about closeness, (3) personal mutual analysis, and (4) personal mutual synthesis.[3] Bennis has revised the two-phase (six subphase) conception of group development of Bennis and Shepard into three phases: (1) oral-inclusion, (2) anal-responsibility, and (3) phallic-intimacy.[4] Aiming at a more abstract level, Parsons, Bales, and Shils suggest an ever-ascending spiral created by four-stage cycles, the stages being addressed to the problems of (1) adaptation, (2) goal reduction, (3) integration, and (4) emotional expression and maintenance of patterns;[5]

[1] Robert F. Bales and F. L. Strodtbeck, "Phases in Group Problem Solving," *Journal of Abnormal and Social Psychology*, **46** (1951), 485-495.

[2] H. Thelen and W. Dickerman, "The Growth of a Group," *Educational Leadership*, **6** (1949), 300-316. In these references on group development, I am indebted to the work of Warren G. Bennis in a working paper on group development (1957a) and in some problems and research gaps in group development (1957b), Group Research Project, Massachusetts Mental Health Center.

[3] James Mann, "Group Therapy with Adults," *American Journal of Orthopsychiatry*, **23** (1953), 332-337.

[4] Bennis, 1957a.

[5] Talcott Parsons, Robert F. Bales, Edward A. Shils, *Working Papers in the Theory of Action* (New York: The Free Press of Glencoe, Inc., 1953), pp. 163-269.

more recently Parsons has presented a more refined conception of the cycle.[6]

Perhaps these examples are enough to suggest the enormous utility of a clearly conceived, comprehensive model of the major sequences in group structure and process. Enough is known from observation and experience to say that groups are inherently complex systems with a vast number of variables changing simultaneously. Valuable as knowledge of the correlation between two or three of them might be, there remains the question of the place of one correlation within a set of many; and insightful though the comprehensive clinical analysis of the motivation of one event, or of the motivational system of one member, might be, there remains the question of its ramifications in an interdependent system. Though current models may be open to justifiable criticism because of bias and gaps, as they are improved they can help the practitioner place a single event or variable within a multivariate context and relate the here and now both to the past and to the future, much as the fan does with his fairly complex model of the game of baseball.

The discussion of the life cycle of learning groups presented [below] was prompted, first, by the desire to understand more clearly how readings in content analysis are associated with major changes in the group and, second, by the need, in my opinion, to emphasize certain processes which have been observed in learning groups but which have not found their way into current conceptions of phases,

cycles, and developmental sequences. The first of these is the process of forming indigenous norms, that is, of giving up preconceived normative notions, of creating normlessness, of experimenting with and selecting new ones, and of refashioning them through experience. One part of this process of course is the creation and modification of the full set of role relations within the group. In most current formulations, these processes, which are difficult to tie down empirically, are excluded. Problem-solving sequences, such as those of Bales, for example, deal with frequencies of types of behavior in an extranormative sense. Unincorporated within the hypothesis are questions of what members believe the behavior should be and whether or not it coincides with contractual relations within the group. Moreover, although sequences in therapy groups may trace the rise and fall of anxiety, rarely is there consideration of the anxiety-reducing function of entering into a contract with one's "rival" or with one's "master." Changes in norms and changes in motivational states are intimately related. For these reasons, the discussion of the life cycle emphasizes normative processes.

The second emphasis is upon *partial* consummation. Until much more is understood about human behavior, and insofar as members of learning groups realize what is *not* known by them or by anyone else, there is an incompleteness to their experience. They may have started on an enterprise, but by no means do many groups feel that they have gained total wisdom. In terms of initial and even subsequent expectations, members ordinarily feel that they have fallen short of the group goal. Consummation in learning groups is partial and fragmentary, as it may be in therapy groups. In spite of this limitation, however, current formula-

[6] Talcott Parsons, "Pattern Variables Revisited," *American Sociological Review*, **25** (August, 1960), 467-483. See also Talcott Parsons, "The Point of View of the Author," in *The Social Theories of Talcott Parsons*, ed. Max Black (Englewood Cliffs, N.J.: Prentice-Hall, Inc., 1961), pp. 311-363.

tions, without an important exception, portray in the way persons and the group change an eventual climb to an ideal peak. The picture is of members who express themselves freely and discern accurately while they listen, comprehend, and achieve consensual validation—this while the group becomes integrated. Some characteristic final phases illustrate the point: *The Working Group* (Bach),[7] *Combination of Group-Centeredness and Serious Efforts at "Work"* (Thelen and Dickerman),[8] *Focus of Responsibility Becomes Fixed in Group* (Gordon),[9] *Personal Mutual Synthesis* (Mann),[10] *Productive Collaboration* (Semrad and Arsenian),[11] *Integrative* (Coffey and Leary).[12]

Whether the formulations refer to groups far more successful than those observed by the author, or whether the formulation expresses what should happen rather than what in fact does happen, remains to be learned from further rigorous empirical examination. Until such time, the discussion of the life cycle notes some of the effects partial consummation has had upon the learning groups observed by the author.

The third emphasis is upon the fact that most learning groups terminate. Anticipating this death and handling its reality is an important issue to those

[7] George R. Bach, *Intensive Group Psychotherapy* (New York: The Ronald Press Company, 1954), pp. 268-293.

[8] Thelen and Dickerman, *op. cit.*

[9] Thomas Gordon, *Group-Centered Leadership* (Boston: Houghton Mifflin Company, 1955), Chap. 10.

[10] Mann, *op. cit.*

[11] Elvin V. Semrad and John Arsenian, "The Use of Group Processes in Teaching Group Dynamics," in *The Planning of Change*, ed. Warren G. Bennis, Kenneth D. Benne, and Robert Chin (New York: Holt, Rinehart & Winston, Inc., 1961), pp. 737-743.

[12] H. S. Coffey, *et al.*, "Community Service and Social Research," *Journal of Social Issues*, 6 (1950), 25-37.

who commit themselves to the group. Though separation anxiety and the process of termination are familiar to many therapists and trainers, they have not gained an important place in the formulations of group development, phase sequences, and so forth. Why this is so is probably not a simple matter. It may be associated with the desire to think only about positive aspects at the end of the group's life; it may result from the pervasive and culturally patterned denial of death in our society; or it may be rooted in an underlying sociological assumption that while persons die, institutions and societies live on. In any case, no formulation, to my knowledge, adequately accommodates group mortality. Some, in fact, would seem to require fundamental modification to make room for processes of dissolution, liquidation, and separation.

Emphasis upon norms, imperfect consummation, and dissolution should not be interpreted as an exclusion of other issues and processes which have already been summarized in developmental sequences. The following discussion, in fact, assumes, is indebted to, and builds upon the perceptive and stimulating conceptions of Bennis and Shepard, Semrad and Arsenian, Parsons, Bales, and Shils, and seeks by its special emphasis to add its contribution to a comprehensive formulation. At the same time, the emphases are based upon the belief that the realities of group process are such that a comprehensive model must be in terms of a life cycle—group formation and group dissolution—rather than simply a progressive development toward some implicitly desired state.

Issues and Activities in the Life Cycle of Learning Groups

There are five principal periods: (1) the encounter, (2) testing boundaries and modeling roles, (3) negotiating an indigenous normative system, (4) production, and (5) separation. For each period, the central issues, the predominant activity, and the group properties which emerge as a consequence are briefly suggested. The discussion does not attempt to include all areas, issues, or mechanisms—for example, certain sources of personal anxiety and their defenses, the progress of role differentiation and the probable structures, the more complex patterns of symbolic manipulation, and the process of member and group clarification. Instead, it presents a likely course in terms of selected variables. Moreover, it does not attempt to follow through the fate of groups which vary from this particular course or to specify the fate of those which become arrested at particular points along the way.

The Encounter

Issues. The first issue is whether or not a group will actually materialize. Will a sufficient number of persons return and continue to attend? Second, and if they do, to what degree will the arrangements and procedures that are worked out be conducive to accomplishing the announced aim.

For a prospective member, the first issue is: Do I want to belong to the group in view of what the experience might demand and what it might give? Second, am I capable of being a member? Am I, for example, able to see what I don't want to see, to do what I prefer not to do, to be appraised by those I don't want to judge me? Looking far ahead, will what I can give be valued by others?

Activities. Among characteristic responses to these issues are the following:

NAÏVE ACTIVISM. Based upon preconceptions of group discussion, of human behavior, of one's role in similar contexts, and supported by the hope that

these conceptions handle most contingencies, members rush into the task.

DISILLUSIONMENT. Due to the almost universal inadequacy of the preconceptions, to a growing awareness that to embrace a task is not the same as performing it, and to an uncertainty arising from the value differences among members, disillusionment occurs.

RETRENCHMENT. As a consequence of disillusionment, members withdraw from the more complicated areas of the task and suppress their more personal thoughts.

Emergent properties. If the enterprise continues, the following new components or states are likely to exist.

Within the group, there is a state of anomie. Preconceived notions about what should be felt, said, and done and about the roles of member and instructor are found inadequate and inappropriate and hence must be given up. Since there is no indication from any authoritative source concerning what notions might or should take their place, anomie exists.

Persons arrange a new contract with themselves, as it were. They enter an arrangement whereby they agree to give more to the group than they receive immediately, and they leave themselves more than usually vulnerable, intellectually and emotionally.

In short, the group emerges from the encounter with certain members making long-term investments and committing themselves to a state of anomie.

Testing Boundaries and Modeling Roles

Issues. A central issue of a group in such a state is to determine the scope of anomie. Of the previous ideas about what the group should be and about what should be done, how many are to be given up, how many modified, how many retained? How extensive is the uncertainty? how deep the involvement? how threatening the process? A second issue is the character of the arrangement that might replace anomie. What constitutes a learning group? What is involved in creating a productive and satisfying arrangement?

For a group member, the central issue is: Can I try new stances, new roles, when chance of success is low and risk of failure is high? Can I go ahead without authoritative approval and disapproval as a guide? To what extent dare I risk being called a fool? *Activities.* With a distant goal, but with no normative guides from any source, one likely set of responses is (1) to retest pragmatically the limits of preconceived ideas, and (2) to model new behavioral roles so that their scope, their effectiveness, and their appropriateness may be experienced and judged by members. Boundary testing and role modeling are likely to be oriented to the following issues:

COMMITMENT. The importance of the group to oneself may be tested by being absent; the importance of one's own performance, by giving one's very best ideas or by remaining silent; the worth of the performance of others, by overt challenge or by silent critique. The strength of others' commitment is tested and gauged.

AUTHORITY. The apparent discrepancy between the expected and the announced role of the instructor is tested by attempts to manipulate him into the more conventional active, directive, appraising, and nurturant role, or by taking his role, or by organizing a substitute authority structure. Tests are made of the members' fantasy of him as omnipotent and omniscient and of them, in relationship to him, as ignorant and impotent. Unbelieving, they test, above all, the instructor's assertion that he will not legislate for them and give to them a new system. In the course of these attempts, the roles modeled include the rebellious, the recalcitrant, the doctor's helper, the usurper, the silent supporter, and the independent student.

INTIMACY. Tests are made for an equitable, comfortable distance between members, often by approaching too close and pulling too far away. Similar tests are made of (1) the limits of self-revelation and of what one can tolerate seeing in others, (2) the range of tolerance of similarities and of differences among members, (3) the lasting power of one's initial likes and dislikes and of one's admiration and devaluation of others, and (4) the solidarity of subgroups which might offer security. Modeled roles may include the cold and the detached, the intimate and the anaclitic, the open and the personal, the fellow student and the colleague. Testing and modeling are oriented to the definition of acceptable boundaries of particularistic, diffuse, and affective interpersonal relations.

WORK. What more exactly is involved in "understanding human behavior"? The process of seeking knowledge is tested by trying to let the facts speak for themselves, by simply accepting or rejecting a case instead of understanding it, by trying to explain a case from the application of a single theory or set of concepts, and by attempting to exhaust the material from an analysis of only the conscious level. Testing all the way, the group members move facing backward into work. Tests seek those circumstances which give absolute certainty to one's interpretation. Tests explore how infinite the regression is when one attempts to understand another's attempt to understand someone's attempt to report events. Modeled roles are those of jurist, academician, romanticist, scientist, poet, philosopher, and artist. Since the issue of exploring what the group might or wants to become is critical, discussion of external matters, such as cases or events of community and nation, become screen discussions within which the exploration of the group's future continues. Issues of commitment and authority are explored and tested in this substitute context. For this reason, there is ambiguity concerning what a speaker is referring to, and there is no distinction between the feelings about external objects and about internal ones.

In summary, processes during this second phase are devoted to testing boundaries and modeling possibilities in respect to *personal commitment, authority, intimacy,* and *work.* Exploration permeates the boundary between the group and the external situation so that these distinctions are not clear.

Emergent properties. The following new components, or states, are likely to exist as residues of experimentation.

Since testing boundaries, modeling roles, and formulating conclusions from these activities *are* part of the process of learning about human behavior, there exists—though perhaps still unformulated—a notion of what it takes to be productive and a feeling of satisfaction in having begun to learn. Therefore, there vaguely exists a sense of goal direction, a sense that is based pragmatically upon the group's experience.

Consequently, there also exist grounds not only for selecting those issues which are relevant to the goal but for evaluating the possible alternative ways of handling issues. There exist, in other words, both motivation and a rudimentary set of values to guide the formation of a new normative system.

Negotiating an Indigenous Normative System

Issues. Having dropped certain preconceptions, displayed a range of possibili-

ties, experienced progress in learning, intellectually and emotionally, and gained a sense of goal direction, the group's central issue is to legislate an enabling set of norms. How are values and preferences to be formulated into ideas concerning what should and should not be done, and concerning what sorts of interpersonal relations should prevail?

For a group member, the central issues are: Can I perform the student role in this group and still be the kind of person I am and want to be? Is the role which is preferred both creative and compatible with my needs and capacities?

Activities. With a rudimentary but pragmatically based sense of the legitimate and the preferred, the group is likely to negotiate a new set of norms and to select agents who sanction and control on behalf of these norms. Whereas earlier roles of experimenter and explorer were modeled, now roles of sanctioner and controller are modeled. Negotiations focus upon the following familiar issues:

COMMITMENT. Attempts are made to establish the criteria for group membership. The right of members to consume time to make a personal point, the right of silent members to receive without giving, the right of absent members to return without paying a price, these rights are all challenged. The uncommitted portions of the group and of persons are sought out, and loyalty tests are administered. Members testify to their own loyalty.

AUTHORITY. The group revolts overtly against the instructor, thereby transforming the fantasy of instructor-omnipotence and member-impotence into a new set of ideas concerning what members can and should do independently of the instructor. Membership entails guilt over revolt and responsibility for making decisions. Both students and instructor now have a right and an obligation to make decisions instrumental to the group goal, and the instructor is obligated to protect those who seek to engineer such decisions. The taboo against expressing negative reactions against the instructor is attenuated.

INTIMACY. The experience of learning something by collaborating results in the inhibition of intimacy is its aim; that is, being close for its own sake is differentiated from being close enough to produce something of value. The latter becomes the basis of the new normative relationship. Differences among members, as persons and in their roles, tend to become tolerable and admitted (providing there is some indication that each contributes toward effective goal reduction). Persons who remain alien in this respect become crucial issues; they either come around or are ostracized. These negotiations eventuate, first, in roles which approximate collaborating ones and, second, in an attenuation of the taboo against expressing positive feelings.

WORK. Having discovered that some behavior of some members is insightful, instructive, and productive, the group attempts to follow their lead. It practices creating fantasy material and interpreting it as a means of discovering more about what is going on in the group. In another direction, it examines carefully the basic facts in cases and expresses a desire to hear tape recordings of its own procedures. On the one hand, all data (ideally) become relevant; on the other, the canons of observation, interpretation, and formulation are (ideally) retained.

Emergent properties. From the viewpoint of the group as a whole, the following new components are important.

A nucleus of persons is committed to a rudimentary normative system. These norms are based both upon pragmatic tests of what the group can do and what it needs to do to accomplish its goal.

A set of conditions are formulated which members must fulfill before they take group time and before their roles are allowed to become differentiated.

A new role relationship arises between member and instructor which replaces the previous image of impotence confronting omnipotence. Members are obligated to inquire and to decide; the instructor is obliged both to protect the innovator and to back up those who exercise control in behalf of the new norms.

A new role relationship among members distinguishes the instrumental from the personal. Though obliged to work together, members are not obliged to like one another, nor are they prevented from doing so. Though obliged to reveal those feelings which are essential to an understanding of the cases and the groups' processes, members remain free to express or not to express those personal likes and dislikes peripheral to the group's task.

A new conception of the group's task arises. Figure and ground begin to separate. Replacing the image of a formless, boundless mass of data, projections, interpretations, and fantasies is a notion of the relevance of facts, the value of interpretations, and the fruitfulness of formulations. Usefulness replaces certainty as a criterion.

A concept arises of the group as a unique entity distinct from the constituent personalities and from all other groups. It could now be named. The boundary between group and nongroup is confirmed, as evidenced, for example, by the impossibility of admitting a stranger and by the unavoidable pain at the loss of a member.

In short, in this phase the group seeks to define and to legislate what it should be. As it evaluates, selects, and decides, it inadvertently becomes something special—it becomes a unique system with its own values, norms, internal arrangements, and outlook on the external world.

Production

Issues. Having become a group of a special kind, its new issue is what it can produce. Can its observations and interpretations stand up to tests against reality? Can its formulations be communicated, understood, remembered, and transmitted to others? Can it create something of lasting value?

For a member, the issues are: Can I communicate ideas which are both relevant and in such a form that they can be tested against reality? Can I hear, evaluate, and test someone else's ideas?

Activities. Though by no means for the first time, but with new determination, members apply what they know about the processes of observation, emotional expression, interpretation, formulation, and testing.

OBSERVATION. To what extent are observations complete and accurate? What cues and signals does one tend to miss?

EMOTIONAL EXPRESSIONS. To what extent are the feelings experienced by members, by authors, or by persons in the cases conveyed for what they are? What is repressed? What is distorted? What is projected?

INTERPRETATION. On how many levels and in terms of what facets might one interpret an event? What is a statement saying about the case? about the speaker? about the group?

FORMULATION. By what gift or skill are ideas which come from the concrete and the particular transformed into ones which are helpful in clarifying or explaining disparate data? How does one translate what is learned into ideas that can be conveyed and tested for both their relevance and their lasting value?

TESTING. By reference to basic data—whether it be tapes of their own sessions, facts as reported in cases, or of some other sort—observations, interpretations, and formulations are impersonally tested for completion, accuracy, and usefulness.

INTERNAL CHECKS. Since tests show the effect of various defenses upon the working processes, the group tends to establish internal checks against denial, distortion, intellectualization, and projection. Statements are screened as they are produced, and members are ranked according to their contact with reality.

DIAGNOSIS. Members attempt to assess what is in the here and now that either disrupts or facilitates the working process and, consequently, they seek to understand more fully how group process affects the learning process.

Emergent properties. Ordinarily, the production test causes a revision of certain components:

The nature of the task is redefined. It is more difficult than it seemed.

The aspiration level of the group is lowered. The revised goal is to understand something about limited aspects of human and group processes.

Norms governing what should or should not be expressed are relaxed. ("Deviant" behavior might be productive after all.)

Central cultural themes are formed around those interpretations and formulations which have been found insightful, helpful, and apparently of lasting value. Since these themes have, in a sense, saved the group, members gather them and husband them. They symbolize what the group wishes itself to be.

The group as a whole becomes an object of negative feelings. Members are disillusioned with its resources and its potential.

At the same time, the intellectual boundaries between fact and fantasy, between group process and content of statements, between the internal group and the external objects, and between a gratifying statement and one based on reality are clearer. The distinctions have been clarified by the testing that has gone on.

In short, during this phase the group puts itself to the test of producing something of general and lasting value. Rallying around a set of central insights, salvaged from the test, it emerges disillusioned and less ambitious, but intellectually keener.

Separation

Most training and learning groups run by a fixed schedule. The first and last meeting date is known. Consequently, quite irrespective of how the group has done and what it aspires to do, the fact of separation forces a complex set of demands and issues, some of which are briefly noted below.

Issues. Two central issues exist for the group as a whole. First, can it create something of value that will not die; and, second, how are the boundaries between the group and other objects to be dissolved in time for the last meeting?

For a member, the first issue is: How can I recollect within the allotted time my attachments to others and to the group? Second, am I able to carry away the group's valuables, as well as its finished and unfinished business?

Activities. WORK. Effort, sometimes compulsive, is spent generating new interpretations and formulations which might hold the key or the secret. The history of the group is reviewed and successful episodes are codified. Paralleling this effort is an attempt to understand what the group is (more than what it can do) by understanding the way it dies.

INTIMACY. Members withdraw first by expressing their deepest feelings, positive or negative, about one another, then by expressing positive feelings. The boundary between group members and others is dissolved by bringing friends in as visitors and by recounting fully to outside friends what is going on in the group.

AUTHORITY. The attempt to dissolve the boundary between the instructor as authority and other authorities takes the form of asking him to state once and for all that his role is artificial, not real, that the course from the beginning has been an experiment, and that if he were truly himself he would not do what he has done.

COMMITMENT. Members review their roles and what they have given and received from one another. They seek a confirmation that their choice to join the enterprise was a wise one. Positive feelings about the experience are aroused and members thank one another for contributions.

Yearning for a benediction from some source, the group dies.

Emergent properties. What is left:

A group that is dead and cannot be revived. Individual fantasies of a future reunion.

Within persons, a tendency, on occasion, to model their emotional and intellectual processes of experiencing, observing, interpreting, formulating, and so forth after the pattern of processes which occurred in the group. Individual members tend, on occasion, to operate as the group as a system operated.

A tendency in some members to create groups in which they can reenact the instructor's role.

A tendency in some members to induce their friends to re-enact their own role by joining the course.

Angry feelings toward the instructor for beginning something he should know could not be finished. Anger toward themselves for committing themselves to such an enterprise. Some sense of accomplishment.

Evolution, Revolution, Reaction

WILBERT E. MOORE

Wherein the forces that produce change within corporations are identified, including periodic and only partially successful attempts to suppress sin.

If change is a law of life, its lawful characteristics, the orderly qualities of social transformation, are only slightly understood. Most "models" of corporate behavior or of other administrative organizations, are "static." That is, they deal with enduring features of corporate life, with relationships that, persisting through time, are nearly timeless. Tomorrow follows today as today followed yesterday with comforting or dismaying regularity. Yet corporations are no more exempt than individuals or families or nations from past history and present perils, from accumulation and erosion, from slow evolution and rapid mutation.

Change is a producer of tensions and uncertainty but also a reliever of them. Persistence, though possibly dull, has the great advantage of permitting predictability of human conduct, an assurance that the same people and the same groups will behave in much the same way from day to day and year to year. Without considerable persistence, social organization becomes impossible and human life intolerable. Orderly change also permits predictability, the

Wilbert E. Moore, *The Conduct of the Corporation* (New York: Random House, Inc., 1962), pp. 191-201. Reprinted by permission of the publisher.

forecasting that tomorrow will be different in about the direction and degree that today differed from yesterday. Even orderly change, however, is tension producing if for no other reason than because of the continuous adjustment it requires. In addition, in any complex organization it is impossible to find or even to imagine a change that does not affect some interest adversely. Even an across-the-board increase in wages and salaries will affect the relative or absolute differences in income to the disadvantage of those at the top or those at the bottom.

The example of income increases illustrates how change may alleviate tensions, however. The equity of a given income distribution is much less likely to be questioned if all are experiencing a favorable change than if only some people get a raise or no one does. Adversity, and especially adversity as compared with the past or with "reasonable" expectations for the present, is more likely to produce discontent than is the relative degree of prosperity. "Equal sacrifices" are harder to implement and accept than possibly unequal benefits.

Complete certainty is almost as intolerable as complete uncertainty. The quest for a change of pace by people caught in routinized jobs, the introduction of elements of risk or uncertainty in situations providing only a boring regularity, offer testimony to the need for change as a way of alleviating strain as well as a source of further tension. Points of tension or strain, possibly the result of past changes, provide hospitable environments for further change. Order and regularity, though necessary, do not reign unchallenged either in fact or in principle.

The Paths of Progress

Some organizational changes are essentially evolutionary in nature. That is, they represent the gradual transformation of the organization in response to its own characteristics and its adjustment to relatively stable environments. Some persistent problems of organization, for example, though never finally "solved," provide the basis for the continuous quest for further approximations to perfection. The troubled question of the relations between individuals and organizations and the manifold ways in which competition and conflict plague a nominally cooperative system provide challenges that will normally lead to changes in both doctrine and practices.

On a visit to the River Rouge plant of the Ford Motor Company several years ago I casually observed the entrance to a suite of offices designated "Employee Relations." That was normal enough. But a hundred yards farther along in the seemingly endless building a somewhat more imposing group of offices was identified as "Management Relations." From the old days of "scientific management" concerned only with improving the productivity of manual workers, we have now progressed to a concern with the nature of organization itself, including the manager's relations with it.

Organizations also tend to accumulate a body of customary law. Since the formal law is never complete and exact, preventing any latitude or uncertainty, decisions become doctrines and practices become precedents. Lore is added to law and eventually takes on the aura of law and perhaps even its reality, if a challenge is made and defeated by citing the long-established practice as the basis for affirming its binding quality. The rules may be silent on the right of appeal for an employee who is dismissed and has no union spokesman. If, however, a higher officer and an "unbroken" line of predecessors have insistently announced an "open door policy" with regard to subordinates, the practice of appeal may well become a genuine right.

Some corporate changes, though evolutionary in the sense of gradual change consistent with past trends, may have a high component of purpose, that is, of deliberate alteration. Corporate missions or objectives are often rather vague (for example, good corporate citizenship) or open-ended (for example, profit maximization). The sharpening of objectives and their translation into specific goals for specific future periods become a steady source of fairly orderly "progress." This process is enchanced by more or less constant emphasis on implementing the doctrines of efficiency and rationality. The injunction to "find a better way" may apply to almost any phase of operations, from the muscular movements of the production worker to the cerebrations of the expert on organization.

We have, then, the paradox that organizational evolution may occur by the accumulation of precedents, which are essentially "conservative" in nature, and by the improvement of techniques, which are essentially "liberal" in character. The paradox often becomes an overt contradiction, as when the innovation challenges practice based on precedent and either interrupts one evolutionary trend by establishing another or fails through rejection by conservative opinion. The appeal to experience is always a strong enemy of the appeal to reason, for experience often wears the cloak of rationality to cover the irrational sentiment that attaches to tradition.

The paths of progress are not entirely smooth and may appear so only much later and in retrospect, when the difficulties that seemed to loom so large can be regarded as temporary, the outcome inevitable, and the struggles or delays downgraded or quietly forgotten. The great advantage of the historian is that he knows the outcome of the events that he seeks to interpret, but to the participant without the gift of superior foresight the outcome may be very much in doubt.

All continuing complex organizations tend to add to their original mission, to accumulate functions. Some of these additional functions may be thought of as instrumental, as aiding the principal purpose, but in ways not precisely demonstrated. Others may simply be viewed as good in their own right and, resources permitting, worthy of pursuit. Thus corporate aid to higher education may evolve from specific scholarships for students in technical fields represented by the company, through aid for continuing research in the colleges and universities to encourage the progress of useful knowledge, to general support for all branches of knowledge without precise expectations of company benefits. Personnel policies may evolve from those designed to increase the employee's productivity to those designed to encourage his general growth as a social being.

When the future causes the past, as it does in a sense when change is deliberately planned and implemented, conventional notions of causation are upset. When conservative restraint—the expression of alarm by asking "whither are we drifting?"—appeals to the future to inhibit the present, conventional causation is reversed by a "feedback" from what has not yet happened to that which is now proposed.

One of the main pressures for organizational change is the deliberate cultivation of growth. This is commonly justified by an aphorism that is accepted as unqualified wisdom, another law of life. This admonition is "grow or die." Biological organisms are mortal and have in any event highly variable characteristics of growth (and decline), so the notion is not even a very good analogy. Corporations may survive by growth or despite it. They may survive by maintaining a stable size and, not rarely, by judicious contraction. Growth, as with human obesity, may very well shorten the corporation's life expectancy rather than build up its increasing strength for dealing with the hazards of the environment. Many a company has been tempted into expansion out of all reason by forecasting an endless growth of the market at an accelerating rate or by venturing into totally unfamiliar markets where the opportunities for profits appeared greater than in the intensive cultivation of what the company was already prepared to do.

The objective falsity or exaggeration of a human belief does not as such destroy its significance. Men act in accordance with their beliefs whether those be true, false, or incapable of objective judgment (such as the belief in life after death). Acting in accordance with their beliefs, corporation executives generally equate progress with growth and then attempt to fulfill their aspirations by expanding their enterprises. The company that does so, and the company officers that do so, may be accorded recognition for their success by other true believers. This is clearly one of the strongest forces for continuous change in the contemporary corporation. It affects participants at nearly every level and in nearly every functional position. Each year should be better than the last, and the phrase "bigger and better" tends to be redundant, because bigger equals better. The objective basis of this belief is, to repeat, extremely shaky and relatively dependent on a multitude of variable conditions in the corporation's external environment and internal structure.

The distortion of nostalgia, which leads to the notion that progress consists of going backward, of recapturing the simpler past, may be equaled by distortion of dreams of future greatness. Size may prevent excellence rather than achieve it. There are other ways to grow—for example, in wisdom and virtue—besides just getting bigger.

Fashions and Fads

It appears to me that a great deal of organizational change in large corporations is imitative in character. That is, some one persuades Company A that it is important to have a special department to deal with the theory of organization and management itself. Company B, seeing this development, reasons that Company A must have made a thorough study and reached a decision only after mature consideration. Under this assumption there is no need for Company B to make its own study or linger long over the decision. It adds its own staff. Company C finds this reasoning even more persuasive, since two companies have added the new department. By the time Company E gets into line, there will be enough technical people in similar positions to form an association, hold meetings, and read learned papers to one another. Meanwhile the organizational specialists in Company A or B will have studied enough and heard so much from their compatriots in other companies that they will want to spread the good word more widely in their own companies. After all, what is the use of having experts on management if they have no effect on those who are doing the managing? The next move then is a kind of staff and command school or an advanced management program, not for the young recruits from the campuses but for the men who need "retreading" to broaden their vision and skills. Soon no self-respecting company of substantial size can be without an advanced management training program.

The initial impulse to many organizational changes is less important than the quick way in which an innovation becomes a fashion. Some are more properly called fads, that is, they last a very short while and are replaced by something newer and even more stylish. A number of years ago training programs in "sound economic principles" were all the rage, although the principles were straight out of nineteenth-century textbooks and had almost no bearing on the conduct of the corporation. Currently, decision-making games are in vogue, but I expect the novelty to wear off and the tired businessman can go back to playing Monopoly with his children instead of playing business strategies with his colleagues.

It is rather hard to find true business fads, as a matter of fact, because most organizational innovations have hardy survival qualities. Employee counseling, for example, which was an outgrowth of the cynical views of manipulation of workers' sentiments that the Western Electric researchers concluded was at the base of informal organization, still has its sponsors and staff in the Bell System, despite the subsequent progress in comprehending the motivations of workers and managers alike. Even when they pass from the center of the stage, the faddish schemes do not leave the theater. The ephemeral character of fashion and fad is thus applicable only to a part of the organizational changes in the corporate world. "Old agencies never die," and few in fact fade away. Their claims to provide cure-alls are likely to be downgraded, but some seeming virtue remains, and so do their supporters. There is enough uncertainty as to just what *is* worthwhile not to take undue chances.

Drift and Reconstruction

The organization being prior to the man, the position more enduring than its incumbent, a succession of officeholders has little theoretical consequence for the ongoing system. Each comes, plays his part, moves on to other roles, and is followed by another bit player to take his turn. Yet individuals do differ, despite valiant efforts to cast them into molds, and the molds do permit a little freedom to the man who is being shaped. A man never really leaves a position to his successor precisely as he received it from his predecessor. He will have added a little or subtracted a little from his duties, he will have changed directions at least slightly, and he may have actually set records difficult for anyone else to match, let alone improve upon.

Some consequences of turnover are fairly cyclical in character. "A new broom sweeps clean," goes the adage, and often the new appointee is expected to make a number of changes during a short time just after his appointment. This is his opportunity to make his weight felt, to establish expectations for himself and others. Reorganization is likely to be easier then, not only because it is expected, but also because the reorganizer will not yet

have had time to become personally involved with the people who will suffer from the change. The dull hand of sympathy often restrains the man who "knows all the circumstances," but the stranger can protect himself from sentiment by ignorance.

There is one particular cycle of growth and reorganization that operates in executive offices. The corporate executive is the residuary legatee of unsolved problems. Thus when new agencies are established or new functions added, they may not be neatly assignable to a part of the organization as it already exists. The alternative, and it is a frequent one, is to attach the new unit to the executive office. Thus for any given executive, his number of direct subordinates and the range of their functions is likely to increase during his tenure in office.

The time of succession in the chief executive office often becomes a time for tidying up the organization and reducing the direct responsibilities of the executive. Occasionally I have seen this reorganization substantially accomplished by the outgoing officer anticipating his retirement. He wants, he says, to leave a neat organizational structure for his successor. He doubts, he means, that the man who follows him is half the man that he is and had better be relieved of some of the responsibilities that the retiring man has capably carried. There is every reason to expect the new man to go through the same cycle, for he will acquire responsibilities by default if not by intent.

The new executive commonly attempts to refurbish the "old line" contacts with major divisions and other interests of central importance to the executive function. His time, interest, and accessibility almost inevitably decline as he discovers that new problems preoccupy him. The aura of good feeling gradually evaporates as some new palace crowd stands between the king and his traditional subjects. Even old-timers, forgetful of past cycles and disappointments, may be repeatedly trapped into believing that "this time it will be different." In detail it certainly will be, but in general it is likely to be the same old story with a slightly new cast of characters.

The Cycle of Sin and Penance

Corporations, like individuals, are unlikely to maintain a steady state of virtue. In some respects their conduct reminds one of the small-town sinner who gets "saved" annually at a rousing revival meeting but backslides and needs a new treatment the next year.

The commonest corporate example of backsliding and salvation is in the abuse of "indulgence." A ten-minute coffee break gradually extends to three-quarters of an hour, at which juncture someone in authority decides things have got out of hand. A new and firm edict is issued that, let us say, a fifteen-minute break is the maximum tolerable limit, with the threat that the privilege will be withdrawn altogether if further abused. Generally, this is an idle threat, as the next repetition of the cycle will demonstrate.

Psychologists sometimes use the term "perseveration" to refer to actions carried to ridiculous extremes. The one-martini, hour-and-a-half lunch may be extended to the three-martini, three-hour lunch before a man's colleagues or boss exercise, respectively, informal or formal control. Competitive systems occasionally become perseverative to the point where the defeat of the enemy takes precedence over the object of the game.

Because the removal of privileges is always more resented than failing to accord them in the first place, it might appear that preventive action should be taken when a clearly sinful drift begins. The problem is where to draw the line. The manager scarcely wants to appear stuffy and ridiculous, and he probably keeps hoping for corrective self-discipline. This is not a wholly impossible dream, for self-discipline or "group controls" may occur. Often, however, no one quite knows where virtue ends and sin begins until, by any standard, the line has been passed some distance back. The progress toward general slackness may be very gradual, with each day's behavior looking very much like that of the day before (but not the month or year before). Where does one draw the line between the box of cigars to the purchasing agent and the air-conditioned Cadillac? At what point do arriving late and leaving early constitute perfunctory performance? What is the precise difference between the easy good fellowship at an office Christmas party and a drunken orgy? Commonly an extreme instance of misconduct is required to trigger a conservative retreat, a new set of rules, or even prohibition of the privilege altogether.

Extreme misconduct, particularly if it is accompanied by adverse publicity —attempts to "hush it up" having failed—are likely to lead to righteous moralizing on the part of officials and the conspicuous imposition of penance.

A few years ago a sales division of a large electrical company was caught supplying call girls to customers at conventions. The divisional manager and several subordinates were disciplined, and top company officials declared themselves forthrightly against sin. More recently the president of one of the "big three" automobile companies was fired for awarding supply contracts to companies in which he had a substantial interest. In this case other company officials were opposed to "conflict of interest."

Virtually every company has its nurtured memories of "Black Thursdays," when heads rolled, houses were cleaned, and moral austerity imposed. Such memories of course rarely lose content as the story is retold, but they may lose a firm coincidence with fact.

The heads that roll may not be those of the "real" culprits but of those "responsible." This is one of the costs of power. For the external public, the punitive actions must be made to appear "appropriate." For the members of the corporation, somewhat less cynical standards are needed, as punishment should be reasonably just to have its effect in maintaining the morals of other potential sinners. Thus public and private justice may not coincide, but a conspicuous dismissal and inconspicuous re-employment may satisfy the demands of both.

Conservative revolutions may be about as temporary as the moral fervor of the backsliding convert. Yet at least in the corporate case there is likely to be a residue of restraint. As long as personal capacities for mischief and various organizational pathologies persist, conspicuous instances of misconduct may occur again, but commonly not the same ones or of the same degree that caused the last bloodletting. The corporation's capacity to change includes the capacity to create or harbor new ways of misbehaving, leading to new reactions, and so on and on down the vistas of the future. The thought is not entirely comforting, but not entirely dismaying either.

changes in societies

four

"As we begin the discussion of social change in . . . *societies,* we encounter a domain prominently occupied by historians" (Moore, *Social Change,* p. 69). Though the historians' occupancy of this domain is not preemptive, as the cited discussion goes on to point out, it is perhaps fitting to lead off our selections on societal changes by a notable example of comparative history: Palmer's treatment of an era of "democratic revolutions." Although Palmer deals with a period of large-scale and rapid change, which would prompt many scholars to use the term *revolution,* his precise focus is on changes in the basis of political authority or legality, which is an exact use of the term.

If the rapid alteration in the situation of the American Negro is not exactly revolutionary, there are nonetheless prominent elements of changes in power as well as changes in other social dimensions. Rose traces the consequences for the Negro of secular changes in American society, and then goes on to note systematically the gains and impediments in various programs of deliberate change. Rose was one of Myrdal's principal collaborators on *An American Dilemma,* and the changes described in his paper in many ways fit the model proposed by Myrdal in his "Note on the Principle of Cumulation," reproduced in Chapter One. Students of change and persons concerned with public policy may both now question whether the course of change affecting the American Negro may "dampen off," and thus also fit a logistic curve and the "principle of limits."

Population trends are among the secular changes in American society, particularly when viewed in the aggregate. Fertility trends and migratory movements of course represent summary measures of individually motivated acts, which in turn may be traced back to various structural pressures and constraints. Hauser's discussion of the "population explosion" is less concerned with causes than with consequences, the latter ranging from patterns of consumption to urban congestion. Yet he does attend to the interaction and feedback effects among demographic, economic and cultural variables. His discussion of the Negro population explosion is of particular import for questions about future patterns of segregation and discrimination in the United States. For example, we seem to be moving toward all-Negro inner cities, which could offset the legal changes that discourage segregation.

In the final selection of the chapter we become, once more, revolutionary. The Committee on the Triple Revolution explores the intersection of changes in the technology of production, and, if you will, of destruction, with changes in human rights. (Hauser's analysis is an important complement to this discussion, which largely neglects the consequences of population growth for the changes it describes.)

Thus we again pick up the theme of alterations in the distribution of power, and particularly the critical position of the American Negro in that transformation. Can the Human Rights Revolution be seen as a continuation and extension of the Age of the Democratic Revolution? Is it possible that the cumulative, interactive effects of the trends described in the Triple Revolution will result in a transformation of societies as basic as that of the Industrial Revolution (described in the following chapter)?

The Age of the Democratic Revolution

R. R. PALMER

A young Philadelphian of good family, Thomas Shippen, in the course of a visit to Europe, where he cultivated the acquaintance of "titled men and ladies of birth," bore a letter of introduction to Thomas Jefferson, the American Minister to France, who presented him at the court of Versailles. They arrived, one day in February, 1788, "at ½ past 10 and were not done bowing until near 2." Young Shippen chatted with the Papal Nuncio and the Russian Ambassador, who "was very polite," and on meeting a woman and her two daughters who were all countesses he was introduced with all his "titles," which he thought most people believed to be hereditary. He was then paired with a German princeling for presentation to the king, who mumbled a few words while hitching on his sword. It all made the young man very conscious of his American nationality. He was "revolted" at the king's arrogance, but even more "mortified at the suppleness

R. R. Palmer, *The Age of the Democratic Revolution* (Princeton: Princeton University Press, 1959, 1964), pp. 3-13, 20-23, 572-575. Reprinted by permission of the publisher.

and base complaisance of his attendants." Such oriental splendor he thought worth seeing—once. It set him to thinking, for, as he wrote to his father, he detected ennui and uneasiness on the faces at court, and was more convinced than ever that "a *certain degree of equality* is essential to human bliss."

The underlining was Shippen's own. He added that America was peculiarly fortunate, since it provided the degree of equality that made for happiness, "without destroying the necessary subordination." No doubt his taste for equality had its limits. Descended on his mother's side from the Lees of Virginia, and on his father's from one of the founders of Pennsylvania, Thomas Shippen belonged socially to the groups that had provided many officers of government in America, and it was in fact on this ground, according to the etiquette at Versailles, that he was thought, as a mere republican, to have sufficient rank for presentation at court. On the other hand, Shippen's own father, a prominent doctor, had been a revolutionary of sorts, having acted as chief medical officer in the Continental army. More generally, the point is that even Americans of aristocratic standing or pretensions looked on the Europe of 1788 with a certain disapproval.

This little scene at Versailles, revealed in the new edition of the *Papers of Thomas Jefferson*,[1] may serve to introduce some of the themes of the following pages, bringing together, as it does, Europe and America, monarchy and republicanism, aristocracy and an emerging democracy, and reflecting certain predilections or biases which the author at the outset confesses to sharing, without, he hastens to add, writing from any such point of view in the social scale as that of the Shippens of Philadelphia.

Let us pass from the concrete image to the broadest of historical generalizations. The present work attempts to deal with Western civilization as a whole, at a critical moment in its history, or with what has sometimes recently been called the Atlantic civilization, a term probably closer to reality in the eighteenth century than in the twentieth.[2] It is argued that this whole civilization was swept in the last four decades of the eighteenth century by a single revolutionary movement, which manifested itself in different ways and with varying success in different countries, yet in all of them showed similar objectives and principles. It is held that this forty-year movement was essentially "democratic," and that these years are in fact the Age of the Demo-

[1] Julian P. Boyd, ed., *The Papers of Thomas Jefferson* (Princeton: Princeton University Press, 1950-   ), XII, 502-504.

[2] See the paper prepared by Professor J. Godechot and myself for the international historical meeting at Rome in 1955: "Le Problème de l'Atlantique du xviiie au xxe siècle," in *Relazioni del X Congresso Internazionale di Scienze Storiche*, 5 (1955), 175-239.

cratic Revolution. "Democratic" is here to be understood in a general but clear enough sense. It was not primarily the sense of a later day in which universality of the suffrage became a chief criterion of democracy, nor yet that other and uncertain sense, also of a later day, in which both Soviet and Western-type states could call themselves democratic. In one way, it signified a new feeling for a kind of equality, or at least a discomfort with older forms of social stratification and formal rank, such as Thomas Shippen felt at Versailles, and which indeed had come to affect a good many of the habitués of Versailles also. Politically, the eighteenth-century movement was against the possession of government, or any public power, by any established, privileged, closed, or self-recruiting groups of men. It denied that any person could exercise coercive authority simply by his own right, or by right of his status, or by right of "history," either in the old-fashioned sense of custom and inheritance, or in any newer, dialectical sense, unknown to the eighteenth century, in which "history" might be supposed to give some special élite or revolutionary vanguard a right to rule. The "democratic revolution" emphasized the delegation of authority and the removability of officials, precisely because . . . neither delegation nor removability were much recognized in actual institutions.

It is a corollary of these ideas that the American and the French revolutions, the two chief actual revolutions of the period, with all due allowance for the great differences between them, nevertheless shared a good deal in common, and that what they shared was shared also at the same time by various people and movements in other countries, notably in England, Ireland, Holland, Belgium, Switzerland, and Italy, but also in Germany, Hungary, and

Poland, and by scattered individuals in places like Spain and Russia.

The Revolution of Western Civilization

To obtain the right perspective on the whole era it is necessary to begin by looking at its climax at the end. This came with the wars of the French revolution from 1792 to 1800 or 1801. . . . The whole period can best be understood by remembering the unprecedented struggle in which it ended. This struggle had in it something universal; as Burke said, there had been nothing like it since the Protestant Reformation had thrown all Europe into a commotion that overran all political boundaries.[3]

Burke himself, when he died in 1797, was so afraid of invasion and revolution in England that he gave orders for his remains to be secretly buried, lest triumphant democrats dig them up for desecration. Revolution broke out in Ireland in 1798. Dutch historians speak of revolution in the Netherlands in 1795, when the Batavian Republic was founded, and of a more radical movement of 1798. The Swiss feel that they were revolutionized in the Helvetic Republic of 1798. Italian writers speak of revolution at Milan in 1796, at Rome in 1797, at Naples in 1798. The Cisalpine, Roman, and Parthenopean republics were the outcome. In the German Rhineland there were some who demanded annexation to France, or, that failing, the establishment of a revolutionary "Cisrhenane," or Rhine-

land Republic. Elsewhere in Germany the disturbance was largely ideological. The philosopher Fichte, an ardent revolutionary thinker, found it "evident" in 1799 that "only the French Republic can be considered by the just man as his true country." The city of Berlin was notably pro-French. In Poland, revolution reached a climax in 1794 with Kosciusko. In Hungary in the same year seventy-five members of a republican conspiracy were arrested. In Greece, in 1797, delegates from Athens, Crete, Macedonia, and other parts of the Greek world met at a secret conclave in Morea; they planned an uprising of all Greeks against the Ottoman Empire, if only the French would send weapons, ammunition, and a few units of the French army. A Russian found that the "charm of revolution" had penetrated "deep into Siberia."

And at the other extremity of Western civilization, in the thinly settled American West, long after the Terror in France is supposed to have brought Americans to their senses, there was still so much lingering pro-French feeling, so much democratic and republican sentiment, so much inclination to break away from the allegedly aristocratic East, that the outgoing president, George Washington, in his Farewell Address, earnestly begged his Western countrymen to put their trust in the United States. In 1798 the popular hero, George Rogers Clark, holding a commission as brigadier general in the army of the French Republic, attempted a secret recruiting of Kentuckians to invade and "revolutionize" Louisiana, which was then Spanish, and meant the whole territory west of the Mississippi. Blocked by an unsympathetic United States government, he fled to St. Louis, where, on the uttermost fringes of the civilized world, there was a society of French *sansculottes* to receive him.

[3] The present section draws heavily on my two articles, "Reflections on the French Revolution," in *Political Science Quarterly*, 67 (1952), 64-80, and "The World Revolution of the West, 1763-1801," *ibid.*, 69 (1954), 1-14. See also, for bibliography, my "Recent Interpretations of the Influence of the French Revolution," in *Journal of World History*, 2 (1954), 173-195.

At Quebec in 1797 a man was hanged, drawn, and quartered as a dangerous revolutionary. At Quito, in what is now Ecuador, the first librarian of the public library was tortured and imprisoned for political agitation. A republican conspiracy was discovered at Bahia, in Brazil, in 1798. A Negro at Buenos Aires testified that Frenchmen in the city were plotting to liberate slaves in an uprising against the Spanish crown. In the High Andes, at the old silver town of Potosí, far from foreign influences on the coasts, the governor was horrified to discover men who toasted liberty and drank to France. The British government, in 1794, a year before occupying Cape Town, feared that there were too many "democrats," eager to welcome the French, among the Dutch at the Cape of Good Hope.[4]

---

[4] For the incident about Burke in the preceding paragraphs see T. W. Copeland, *Our Eminent Friend Edmund Burke: Six Essays* (New Haven: Yale University Press, 1949), p. 90; for the quotation from Fichte, J. Droz, *L'Allemagne et la révolution française* (Paris: 1949), p. 279; for other countries mentioned, P. F. Sugar, "The Influence of the Enlightenment and the French Revolution in Eighteenth-Century Hungary," *Journal of Central European Affairs,* **17** (1958), 348-352; A. Dascalakis, *Rhigas Velestinlis: La Révolution française et les préludes de l'indépendance héllénique* (Paris: 1937), p. 15; M. M. Shtrange, *Russkoye Obshchestvo i Frantsuzkaya Revolyutsiya* (Moscow: 1956), p. 61; A. P. Whitaker, *The Mississippi Question 1795-1803* (New York: Appleton-Century-Crofts, 1934), p. 155; W. Kingsford, *History of Canada,* 10 vols. (London: 1887-1898), VII, 440-451; E. Clavéry, *Trois Précurseurs de l'indépendance des démocraties sud-américaines: Miranda, Nariño, Espejo* (Paris: 1932); A. Ruy, *A primeira revoluçao social brasiliera, 1798* (Rio de Janeiro: 1942); R. Caillet-Bois, *Ensayo sobre el Rio de la Plata y la Revolucion francesa* (Buenos Aires: 1929), pp. 76-77, 106-107; and for the Cape of Good Hope, Great Britain, Historical Manuscripts Commission, *The Manuscripts of J. B. Fortescue Preserved at Dropmore* (London: 1892-1927), II, 645.

All of these agitations, upheavals, intrigues, and conspiracies were part of one great movement. It was not simply a question of the "spread" or "impact" or "influence" of the French revolution. Not all revolutionary agitation since 1918 has been produced by the Kremlin, and not all such agitation in the 1790's was due to the machinations of revolutionary Paris. It is true, and not without contemporary significance, that persons of revolutionary persuasion were able to install revolutionary regimes only where they could receive help from the French republican army. But revolutionary aims and sympathies existed throughout Europe and America. They arose everywhere out of local, genuine, and specific causes; or, contrariwise, they reflected conditions that were universal throughout the Western world. They were not imported from one country to another. They were not imitated from the French, or at least not imitated blindly. There was one big revolutionary agitation, not simply a French revolution due to purely French causes, and foolishly favored by irresponsible people in other countries.

This universal agitation was clear enough to contemporaries, but has not been well presented by the historians. The old classic, Sorel's *L'Europe et la révolution française,* of which the first volume appeared in 1885, is in the older tradition of diplomatic history and international relations. It can by its very title convey a false impression, if it suggests a struggle between the French revolution and "Europe," since the struggle was primarily between a revolutionary French government and the conservative governments and governing classes of Europe, with many Frenchmen opposed to the revolution, and many other Europeans and Americans in favor of it. At a more specialized level, there has been much research and writing in many countries. There are, for example, excellent studies of the Jacobin clubs in France, of the democratic-republican societies in the United States, and of the radical societies in Great Britain, and we know that there were similar political clubs, at the same time, in Amsterdam, Mainz, Milan, and elsewhere. But only very recently has Professor Godechot undertaken to study such clubs as a whole, comparing their membership, their methods, and their stated aims. In all countries it has been the national history that has mainly occupied attention. The literature on the French revolution is enormous, but most of it is focused on France. Italians have published abundantly on their *triennio*, the three revolutionary years in Italy from 1796 to 1799. Swiss, Belgians, Dutch, Irish, and many others have provided a wealth of materials on their respective histories at the time. The years from 1763 to 1800 have always been a staple of American historiography. But the work has been carried on in national isolation, compartmentalized by barriers of language or the particular histories of governments and states. All acknowledge a wider reality, but few know much about it. . . .

Recently, probably because we live in a period of world revolution ourselves, there has been more tendency to see an analogous phenomenon at the close of the eighteenth century. Alfred Cobban and David Thomson in England have spoken of a kind of Democratic International at that time, and Louis Gottschalk of Chicago has stressed the idea of a world revolution of which the American and French revolutions were a part. Only certain French scholars in the last decade, Lefebvre, Fugier, Godechot, have undertaken to develop the idea in de-

tail.[5] Godechot's recently published two volumes are a remarkable work, built upon extensive and difficult researches, and analyzing the revolutionary social classes, organizations, clubs, methods, propaganda devices, ideas, objectives, and achievements with great care. They are largely confined, however, to the parts of Europe actually occupied by French armies during the revolutionary wars, and are limited in time to the decade from 1789 to 1799; and they seem to represent a compromise, in the author's mind, between the idea of expansion of a primarily French revolution and the idea of a more widespread upheaval in which the French revolution was the greatest single eruption. Planned as they are, they give proportionately little attention to the English-speaking world and to Germany and Eastern Europe; and the American revolution, its effects in Europe, and the political problems and disturbances of various European countries before the war of 1792 appear only allusively as a background.

It may be said, and it is of course true, that even if there is a world revolution in the twentieth century, its existence is of not the slightest relevancy, one way or the other, as evidence of any comparable movement at the close of the eighteenth. There is in America, and always has been, a strong body of opinion holding that the American and French revolutions were phenomena of altogether different kinds. There have always been British and European observers who have

[5] G. Lefebvre, *La Révolution française* (Paris: 1951) in the series *Peuples et civilisations*, Vol. XIII; A. Fugier, *La Révolution française et l'Empire napoléonien* (Paris: 1954) in the series edited by P. Renouvin, *Histoire des relations internationales*, Vol. IV; and especially J. Godechot, *La Grande Nation: L'Expansion révolutionnaire de la France dans le monde de 1789 à 1799* (Paris: 1956), 2 vols.

maintained that the agitation for parliamentary reform in England or Ireland, or the political overturns of the Dutch, Swiss, or Italians, were not truly revolutionary in any meaningful or modern sense. It is admittedly [our] purpose . . . to persuade to a contrary opinion. It is not necessary, however, to reject such ideas as simply mistaken, or to insist upon similarities where none exist. All that is necessary, or even desirable, is to set up a larger framework, or conceptual structure, in which phenomena that are admittedly different, and even different in very significant ways, may yet be seen as related products of a common impulse, or different ways of achieving, under different circumstances and against different degrees of opposition, certain recognizably common goals.

Revolution, it must be admitted, has become a distasteful word in many quarters. Americans may feel a troubled sympathy for anticolonialist movements in Asia or Africa, and a more unanimous enthusiasm for such abortive revolutions as those attempted in Hungary or Poland in 1956; but the successful and threatening revolution of our own time, "the revolution" par excellence, is the one represented by Communist parties, Soviet republics, and, at least allegedly, the social doctrines of Karl Marx. To this revolution most readers . . . , as well as the author, feel a certain lack of cordiality. Some would dismiss all revolutions as dangerous and delusive, or even make of conservatism a kind of basic philosophy. In this case it becomes necessary —for Americans—to argue that the American revolution was not really a revolution, but a conservative movement. . . . My own belief is that opposition to one revolution is no reason for rejecting all revolutions, that the value of conservatism depends on the value of what is to be conserved, that

revolution must be appraised according to the ethical content and feasibility of its aims, and in terms of probable alternatives and real choices at the moment; and that the true matter for moral judgment, or for political decision, is not between the old and the new, or the conservative and the revolutionary, but the actual welfare of human beings as estimated by a reasonable calculation of possibilities in particular situations.

The parallels between the Russian and the French revolutions, or between the twentieth-century and the eighteenth-century upheavals, are plainly apparent and cannot be honestly denied. In both there is the same story of collapse of the old system, seizure of power by new and unauthorized groups, extermination of the old institutions; confiscation, emigration, terror; attack upon the Church; consolidation of the new regime in a powerful country, with the setting up of dependent states in adjacent regions; agitation threatening all established governments, frontiers, interests, classes, and views of life; cleavage of opinion, and formation of loyalties and aversions, that overrun all political borders and divide all states within. We do not like this today, and we are embarrassed to find it happening in the name of liberty and equality in the decade of the 1790's. We are further embarrassed by taunts from the Left, of Marxists who say that the proletarian today is only trying to do what the bourgeois once did; or that the bourgeois today, for obvious reasons, is trying to deny his own revolutionary background and suppress even the memory of it, lest it set a bad example.

It is the weakest of all replies to hold that revolution under any conditions is a sad mistake. Perhaps we should not be too squeamish; perhaps we should admit that we "bourgeois" entered upon a revolutionary era some two centuries ago. We should admit that it resembles the revolutionary era of the twentieth century. We should then add that the resemblances are largely formal, more of pattern than of substance, and involving abstractions. All wars are alike in being wars, and there is even such a thing as military science; but not all wars, or all combatants, are alike in their effects upon mankind. All revolutions resemble one another as revolutions, and there is probably even a science or technique of revolution as such; but it does not follow that all revolutions have the same effects. It is permitted to believe that a better society, more humane, more open, more flexible, more susceptible to improvement, more favorable to physical welfare and to the pursuit of higher concerns, issued from the democratic revolution of the eighteenth century than from the Communist revolution of the twentieth. It is not necessary to idealize either. It is enough to say that revolution is like war, occurring when all compromise breaks down, and representing a violent clash between two or more groups over the structure of the whole society to which each belongs. We may indeed write the history of a war, or a revolution, in which we constantly deprecate the resort to violence, regret the loss of individual liberties, comment on the bad feeling between the participants, and note how all other pursuits become subordinated to one single, overwhelming end. We would not thereby much elucidate the war, or the revolution; we would only be saying that we preferred peace, or that in a better world neither war nor revolution would ever be necessary.

The exact relationship of the Russian to the French revolution has in recent decades been the subject of much careful examination. Two tend-

encies may be perceived: the one to associate, the other to dissociate, the two revolutions. By an "associationist" view I would not mean such an attempt as Crane Brinton's in his *Anatomy of Revolution,* in which the author looks for a pattern of revolutionary process as such, by comparative study of the English, American, French, Russian, and other revolutions. I would mean rather a view in which the French revolution is seen as a kind of origin, partial cause, or distant prefiguration of the Russian revolution, which insists upon Jacobinism as the Communism of the eighteenth century, or sees a kind of continuing linear process in which the Russian revolution is in some way a consequence of the French, or presents a more highly developed stage of the same process. This was of course the view of Marx, Lenin, and Trotsky, as it is of modern Soviet scholars; it is also the view of many warmly anti-Soviet and anti-Communist writers, notably of Professor Talmon of the Hebrew University at Jerusalem, who traces the "origins of totalitarian democracy," or Soviet Communism, back to Robespierre and Rousseau.[6] There are nowadays many others for whom Robespierre and Rousseau figure more as ancestors of totalitarianism than of democracy.

It is true that Marx and his followers were close students of the French revolution, and learned a good deal from it; this is, if anything, a good reason for the rest of us to make an independent study of the subject. It is also true that the Communist movement would never have taken form as it did except for the prior occurrence of the French revolution—as of much else in the preceding history of Russia and of Europe. It is even true that the

[6] J. L. Talmon, *The Rise of Totalitarian Democracy* (Boston: Beacon Press, Inc., 1952).

Jacobins were in some ways something like the Communists; but, not to dwell on the difference in their actual principles, the fact that the Jacobin clubs were the products of the French revolution rather than the producers of it, never had any international organization, lasted only five years, and were closed down by revolutionaries themselves, should give pause to those wishing to pursue this parallel beyond a certain point.

"Dissociation" of the French and Russian revolutions, at a serious level, rests upon observations of the following kind: First, the subsequent cult of the revolution was a different thing from the French revolution itself. This was emphasized, for example, by the late Professor Griewank of Jena. Strongly inclined to Western democratic and humane values, Griewank believed that the French of the revolution thought in relatively practical terms of rational politics and the needs of war, and that the ballooning up of the revolution into a vast, fearsome, perpetual, gigantic, and all-consuming force was the work in part of counter-revolutionaries who wished to discredit the real aims of the French revolution, in part of romantic philosophers, and in part of rebellious spirits in those countries, like Germany, where real revolution had had the least effect.[7] It is apparently a fact that the modern or Communist revolutions have been, so far, least successful precisely in those countries where the eighteenth-century or democratic revolution produced the most significant changes. Related to this is the thought of the American scholar T. H. von Laue, who has suggested a significant difference of kind between the Russian, Asian, and twentieth-century revolutions on the one

hand, and the French, Western, and eighteenth-century revolutions on the other. Where the latter, he holds, arose as indigenous developments of their own culture, reflecting the growth of values, knowledge, and aspirations having deep native roots, the twentieth-century revolutions, whether in Russia or China or formerly colonial areas, are alike in having been precipitated by contacts with an outside or foreign civilization, and by the stresses, maladjustments, feelings of backwardness, and other ambivalences ensuing thereupon.[8] The French of 1789 might feel that in respect to government or personal rights they were less favored than the British or the Americans. Like all peoples, they had been exposed to influences from outside. But the French revolution grew directly out of earlier French history. The French were untroubled by any feeling of backwardness; they did not have to strain to keep up in a march of progress. The same is generally true of the Western world at the time. The eighteenth century saw the revolution of the Western world; the twentieth century, the revolution of the non-Western.

* * * * *

In Western civilization, in the middle of the eighteenth century, there was no novelty in discussions of liberty, or human equality, or law, or limited government, or constitutional rights, or the sovereignty of the people. Greek and medieval philosophy, Roman law, Christian theology, and baronial rebellions had all made contributions to one such idea or another. A marked democratic movement had expressed itself in the English revolution during the

[7] K. Griewank, *Der neuzeitliche Revolutionsbegriff: Entstehung and Entwicklung* (Weimar: 1955).

[8] T. H. von Laue, "Die Revolution von aussen als erste Phase der russischen Revolution," in *Jahrbücher für die Geschichte Osteuropas*, 4 (1956), 138-158. Mr. von Laue is an American scholar writing in German.

1640's, and the history of many European towns was full of clashes between populace and patricians. Such popular movements, however, had been local, sporadic, and unsuccessful; and of general ideas, such as ultimate human equality, or government with the consent of the governed, it is well known that the more general such ideas are the more variegated and contradictory may be the actual practices with which men learn to live. Actual practice, about 1750, was such that certain old ideas, or old words and phrases, took on a new application and a wider and more urgent meaning.

If we say that a revolutionary era began about 1760, it is not because any persons or any organizations intended or worked in advance for a revolution. The modern conception of a revolutionary movement is the result, not the cause, of the revolutionary era that we are discussing. "Revolution" was a familiar word, but it usually meant no more than the revolving fortunes of governments, without great impersonal causes or any long-run direction; one might speak of Chancellor Maupeou's "revolution" in France in 1770, or the King of Sweden's "revolution" of 1772. The situation that began to develop about 1760 was revolutionary in a deeper way.

By a revolutionary situation is here meant one in which confidence in the justice or reasonableness of existing authority is undermined; where old loyalties fade, obligations are felt as impositions, law seems arbitrary, and respect for superiors is felt as a form of humiliation; where existing sources of prestige seem undeserved, hitherto accepted forms of wealth and income seem ill-gained, and government is sensed as distant, apart from the governed and not really "representing" them. In such a situation the sense of community is lost, and the bond between social classes turns to jealousy and frustration. People of a kind formerly integrated begin to feel as outsiders, or those who have never been integrated begin to feel left out. As a group of Sheffield workingmen demanded in 1794: "What is the constitution to us if we are nothing to it?"[9]

No community can flourish if such negative attitudes are widespread or long-lasting. The crisis is a crisis of community itself, political, economic, sociological, personal, psychological, and moral at the same time. Actual revolution need not follow, but it is in such situations that actual revolution does arise. Something must happen, if continuing deterioration is to be avoided; some new kind or basis of community must be formed.

. . . It has often been said, on the authority of no less a person than Alexis de Tocqueville, that the French revolution was over before it began, that it was the work of men's minds before they made it the work of their hands. This idea can be misleading, for with it one may miss the whole reality of struggle. The revolution was not merely the attempt to realize in practice ideas which had already conquered in the realm of thought. No ideas had "conquered"; there was no "climate of opinion" of any specific social or political content. The revolution was a conflict between incompatible conceptions of what the community ought to be, and it carried out with violence a conflict that had already come into being. There is no reason to suppose (if we put aside historical metaphysics) that one side in this conflict was moribund, the other abounding with vigor; one, old and doomed in any case to extinction, the

---

[9] An address to the British nation, printed with *Proceedings of a Public Meeting at Sheffield . . . 7 April 1794* (Sheffield: 1794), p. 41.

other, new and already riding upon the wave of the future. It is sufficiently enlightening to see it simply as a conflict, in which either antagonist would prevail at the expense of the other. It is hoped that readers . . . , whichever way their own sympathies may lie, may at least agree, upon finishing it, on the reality of the conflict.

In the absence of better words, and not wishing to invent more colorless sociological terms, we think of the parties to this essential conflict, so far as they may be reduced simply to two sides, as the proponents of "aristocratic" and "democratic" forms of the community, emotionally overcharged or semantically ambiguous though these words may be. It is held that both democratic and aristocratic forces were gaining strength after about 1760, that revolution came because both were rising, and that they took the form of revolution and counterrevolution at the close of the century, and of democratically and conservatively oriented philosophies thereafter. It follows that conservatism and counterrevolution were no mere "reactions" against revolution, but eighteenth-century forces against which revolution was itself a reaction. This idea is not the invention of the present author: recent works on the American revolution emphasize the growing conservatism in British Parliamentary circles before 1775; Professor Valjavec insists that conservatism in Germany antedated the agitation of the 1790's; French historians stress the "aristocratic resurgence" preceding the eruption of 1789.[10]

---

[10] Cf. C. R. Ritcheson, *British Politics and the American Revolution* (Norman: University of Oklahoma Press, 1954); F. Valjavec, *Die Entstehung der politischen Strömungen in Deutschland, 1770-1815* (Munich: 1951); and the writings of Mathiez, Lefebvre, J. Egret, and others on the French Revolution.

. . . [There were] certain "constituted bodies," in Europe and America, most of them predominantly aristocratic in 1760, and including parliaments, councils, assemblies, and magistracies of various kinds. A continuing and universal theme of the period is the attempts of these constituted bodies to defend their corporate liberties and their independence, against either superior authorities on the one hand or popular pressures on the other. Resisting superior authorities, these bodies could be liberal and even revolutionary. The democratic revolutionary movement, however, came into play when persons systematically excluded from these bodies, and not content merely with the independence of these bodies as already constituted, attempted to open up their membership, change the basis of authority and representation, reconstitute the constituted bodies, or obtain a wholly new constitution of the state itself. . . .

* * * * *

In the twentieth century, . . . it is not as easy to generalize about the grand sweep of human events as it once was. It is not easy to summarize what happened in the world of Western civilization in the forty years from 1760 to 1800, or to be certain of the meaning of these years for the subsequent history of mankind. . . . In history, for large ideas, there is no such thing as proof; no view, however much demonstrated, can pretend to be conclusive or final. It is hoped, however, that the reader can now see these events of the eighteenth century as a single movement, revolutionary in character, for which the word "democratic" is appropriate and enlightening; a movement which, however different in different countries, was everywhere aimed against closed élites, self-selecting power groups, hereditary castes, and forms of special advantage or discrimination that no longer served any useful purpose. These were summed up in such terms as feudalism, aristocracy, and privilege, against which the idea of common citizenship in a more centralized state, or of common membership in a free political nation, was offered as a more satisfactory basis for the human community.

What had happened by 1800, even in countries where it was temporarily suppressed, was the assertion of "equality" as a prime social desideratum. It was an equality that meant a wider diffusion of liberty. That the assurance of some liberties meant the curtailment of others was well understood, so that, more on the continent of Europe than elsewhere, the democratic movement brought a consolidation of public authority, or of the state. It was not an equality that could long accept the surrender of liberty; the solution provided by Bonaparte could not prove to be durable. Nor was it an equality that repudiated the power of government; the world of Thomas Jefferson would also pass.

In forty years, from 1760 to 1800, "equality" took on a wealth of meanings, to which few new ones have been added since that time. It could mean an equality between colonials and residents of a mother country, as in America; between nobles and commoners, as in France; patricians and burghers, as at Geneva; ruling townsmen and subject country people, as at Zurich and elsewhere; between Catholic and Protestant, Anglican and dissenter, Christian and Jew, religionist and unbeliever, or between Greek and Turk in Rhigas Velestinlis' memorable phrase. It might refer to the equal right of guildsmen and outsiders to enter upon a particular kind of trade or manufacture. For some few it included greater equality between men and women. Equality for ex-slaves and between races was not overlooked. For popular democrats, like the Paris *sans-culottes*, it meant the hope for a more adequate livelihood, more schooling and education, the right to stroll on the boulevards with the upper classes, and for more recognition and more respect; and it passed on to the extreme claim for an exact equality of material circumstances, which was rarely in fact made during the revolutionary era, but was feared as an ultimate consequence of it by conservatives, and expressed in Babeuf's blunt formula, "stomachs are equal."

Monarchy, religion, the Church, the law, and the economic system—along with the British Parliament, the Dutch Union of Utrecht, the old folk democracies of the upland Swiss, the gentry republic in Poland, and the patrician communes of Italy—were brought into question so far as they upheld inequalities that were thought to be unjust. "Everywhere inequality is a cause of revolution," said Aristotle long ago, and his observation may remain as the last word on the subject. The problem of the historian in deciding upon the causes of revolution, as of rulers in preventing or guiding it, is to identify the sore spots, the political, economic, sociological, or psychological matters which arouse, in a significant number of relatively normal human beings, the embittered sense of inequality which is the sense of injustice.

. . . For Tocqueville the course of all history revealed a continuing movement toward a greater "equality of conditions." In the introduction to his *Democracy in America*, thinking of both France and the United States, and indeed of all Europe since the Middle Ages, he explained his view of world history, in which he was less oracular than Hegel, and less dogmatic than Marx.

"The gradual trend toward equality of conditions," he said, "is a fact of Providence, of which it bears the principal characteristics: it is universal, it is enduring, it constantly eludes human powers of control; all events and all men contribute to its development.

"Would it be wise to think that a social movement of such remote origin can be suspended by the efforts of one generation? Can it be supposed that democracy, after destroying feudalism and overwhelming kings, will yield before the powers of money and business —*devant les bourgeois et les riches?*

"What then does the future hold? No one can say."[11]

Here was no prediction of revolution to come, no conservative theory, as with Friedrich Gentz, that one revolution must lead endlessly to another, to show what a great evil the French revolution had been; no neo-revolutionary message, as with Karl Marx, to show that since one revolution that he called "bourgeois" had occurred, another that he called "proletarian" must surely follow. It was only a prediction that the future would see an increasing equality of conditions, brought about in ways that could not be foreseen, and were not prescribed. It was a prediction that even inequalities of wealth and income, like others, would be reduced either by revolution or otherwise. Such has in fact proved to be the case.

For Tocqueville it was a troubled

anticipation, in which difficulties and losses were to be expected as well as gains. In substance, however, it was the anticipation that had inspired the last days of Condorcet, who had rejoiced to see, in 1794, at the end of the "Progress of the Human Mind," the vision of a future world in which all invidious differences between human beings would be erased.

All revolutions since 1800, in Europe, Latin America, Asia, and Africa, have learned from the eighteenth-century revolution of Western civilization. They have been inspired by its successes, echoed its ideals, used its methods. It does not follow that one revolution need lead to another, or that revolution as such need be glorified as a social process. No revolution need be thought of as inevitable. In the eighteenth century there might have been no revolution, if only the old upper and ruling classes had made more sagacious concessions, if, indeed, the contrary tendencies toward a positive assertion of aristocratic values had not been so strong. What seems to be inevitable, in both human affairs and in social science, must be put in contingent form—if x, then y. If a sense of inequality or injustice persists too long untreated, it will produce social disorganization. In a general breakdown, if a constructive doctrine and program are at hand, such as were furnished in the eighteenth century by the European Enlightenment, if the capacities of leaders and followers are adequate to the purpose, and if they are strong enough to prevail over their adversaries, then a revolution may not only occur and survive, but open the way toward a better society. The conditions are hard to meet, but the stakes are high, for the alternative may be worse.

---

[11] *Démocratie en Amérique,* in *Oeuvres* (Paris: 1951), I, Part I, 4. The standard English translation (Henry Reeve and Phillips Bradley, eds. [New York: Alfred A. Knopf, Inc., 1945], I, 6), by calling *les bourgeois* "tradesmen," betrays its mid-Victorian origin and misses the full relevancy for modern times. . . .

The American Negro Problem in the Context of Social Change

ARNOLD M. ROSE

The "Negro protest" must be seen in the context of the Negro problem in the United States and of the forces of social change operating throughout the society. The protest movement is directed against a situation in American society, and it finds its strengths and its obstacles in that situation, which itself is in a condition of rapid flux. To describe this context systematically would require a lengthy book. In this article I propose merely to paint the situation, and the major changes occurring within it, in crude, broad strokes, so that the subsequent descriptions of various aspects of the Negro protest will have a backdrop.

Major Causes of Change

An analysis of the dynamic forces operating in the present situation inevitably involves the selection of what is most significant in the complexity of current affairs. I give greatest emphasis to forces involving social power, both economic and political, sometimes wielded deliberately but more often impersonally in the form of great trends affecting the whole society. I give smaller stress to changes in public ideologies and least weight to factors usually singled out as "psychological" —although it seems to me that a better

Arnold M. Rose, "The American Negro Problem in the Context of Social Change," *The Annals of the American Academy of Political and Social Science,* 357 (January, 1965), 1-17. Reprinted by permission of the author and *The Annals.*

sociopsychological analysis than is dominant today in academic circles would not separate the individual psychological factors from those involving social power and ideologies.

The major forces causing the rapid change in race relations since 1940 seem to have been continuing industrialization and technological advance, the high level of mobility among the American people, economic prosperity, the organization and political education of minority groups, an increased American awareness of world opinion, consistent support for civil rights on the part of the Supreme Court and a lesser support from the other branches of the federal government and the Northern state governments, and the propaganda and educational efforts for more equal implementation of civil rights. Some of these forces are likely to continue to exert the same pressure as in the recent past; others are likely to change in their influence, and new forces are likely to have increasing influence.

Industrialization and Technological Progress

Industrialization has created changes in race relations in several ways. First, it has eliminated cotton agriculture as the dominant source of Southern wealth. Racism grew up as an American ideology partly in response to the need to maintain a reliable and permanent work force in the difficult job of growing cotton. While American Negro slavery was older than extensive cotton agriculture, it took on major economic and political significance in connection with the rise of "King Cotton" after 1793, and the patterns of discrimination and prejudice that have persisted to the present day took their form originally in the cotton-growing areas. Cotton agriculture remained a dominant element in the economy of the Southern states until the 1930's, but then it lost its pre-eminence because of the diversification of agriculture and the rise of manufacturing. The continuation of racism after the displacement of cotton as "king" is an example of the sociological principle that ideologies continue after the conditions that gave rise to them cease to exist. Nevertheless, the decline of cotton agriculture permitted other forces to weaken racism.

Industrialization prompted a sizable move of people from rural areas into the cities, where they found factory jobs and entered service occupations. Urbanization has always been associated with the weakening of traditional social structures. The caste system governing the relations between whites and Negroes in the South had its birth in the rural areas and imposed its structure upon a relatively static rural society. When Negroes moved into the cities—and even in the South the majority of them now live in cities—the elaborate requirements of the caste system could hardly be maintained. Relationships in the city are too casual and too functional to require the constant manifestations of subordination on the part of Negroes that characterized the rural caste system. Segregation became more physical than symbolic, and behind the walls of segregated isolation, Negroes were better able to build resistance to subordination.

Industrialization also brought about emigration from the South. While the great migration of Negroes was to the Northern cities until about 1940, it became increasingly a westward migration after that. The migration was of course partly due to the lag in Southern industrialization, but even with that now being overcome, the especially strong discrimination against Negroes in the South has motivated their continued migration out of the region. The majority of Negroes, however, no longer live in the Deep and Upper South—the old Border states have realigned themselves largely with Northern states—and the outward migration must necessarily slow down. The main significance of the northward and westward migration for the Negroes was that it separated them from the full-blown caste system of the South, even though they met other forms of discrimination and prejudice in the other regions of the country. In the North—which, for this purpose, includes the West also—they vote freely and have the almost full protection of the laws and the law enforcement machinery. They, as well as the whites, get a better education in the North, and this has been a major factor in improving their status. Thus Negroes have been much better able to improve their condition in the North, and they have used their improved condition—especially their vote—to help Negroes still living in the South.

Technological progress has been an important—though not the sole—factor which has contributed to the high level of prosperity since 1940. The prosperity and the almost full employment associated with it during the period 1940-1954 have been especially beneficial to Negroes. Measurements vary, but it has been estimated that the rise of average real income among Negroes since 1940 has been two to three times that among whites, though practically all of that improvement occurred before the economic recession of 1955.

As the average income of Negroes is still significantly below that of the whites, the rapid improvement of their economic condition must be seen against the backdrop of great economic discrimination and poverty in the pre-1940 period. The prospects for further automation and the industrial use of nuclear energy will involve still higher productivity and a higher standard of living for employed workers in the future—and Negroes are no longer excluded from the general economic improvement, especially in the North. The rise in average family income among Negroes since 1935 has meant not only a fuller participation in the material benefits of the modern economy, but also a greater opportunity to obtain more education and other cultural benefits. It should also be remembered that continuing general prosperity among whites has tended to reduce one major source of frustration among whites, which sometimes contributes to scapegoating and race baiting.

Technological change—especially in the form of automation—is having another effect—partly negative—on the position of Negroes in the United States. As a relatively unskilled element in the work population, the Negro is often the most rapidly displaced worker when changing technology requires an upgrading of skills. This process is aggravated by the fact that many Negroes are relative newcomers to the ranks of Northern industrial workers, and therefore have the lowest seniority and least protection from unionization. Hence Negroes are the hardest hit by technological unemployment. Technological change and low seniority have, for all practical purposes, replaced discrimination as the main force in excluding Negroes from factory jobs in the North and West. Thus Negroes constitute a dispropor-

tionately large number of the "permanently unemployed," and their rate of becoming unemployed was about double that of white workers during the several recessions that have occurred since 1955. In July, 1963, 11.2 per cent of the Negroes in the labor force were unemployed, compared to 5.1 per cent among whites. Occupational training for Negroes is crucial. If minority workers get new job training, they will cease to be subject to special handicaps and will substantially close the gap between them and the already skilled workers of the majority group, who now also need retraining.

Protest and Pressure Associations

The development of an educated élite and of a lively sense of group identification among Negroes has significantly impelled American race relations into a more equalitarian direction since the turn of the century. A wide range of protest and pressure associations have exerted their influence, sometimes with and sometimes without collaboration of liberal whites. Although this movement was quite highly developed by 1940, it has taken on some significant additional elements since then. The nonviolent resistance technique—as a means of achieving desegregation borrowed from Gandhi, who was himself influenced by Thoreau—was apparently first used in the United States in 1942, by the then newly organized Congress on Racial Equality (CORE) in Chicago. Applied first in selected Northern cities, it was gradually tried in the Border states and did not begin work in the South until about 1954. The technique caught nationwide attention in 1955 with the spontaneous and independent development of the Montgomery, Alabama, bus strike, led by the Reverend Martin Luther King. After the successful conclusion of this effort, King organized the Southern Christian Leadership Conference (SCLC), which worked for desegregation in other Southern cities. In 1960, the CORE technique of "sit-ins," used for years on an interracial basis, was adopted spontaneously by groups of Southern Negro college students and employed all over the South with considerable success. These students formed the Student Nonviolent Co-ordinating Committee (SNCC), and a sympathetic group of Northern students—both white and Negro—formed the Students for Integration (SFI) and the Northern Student Movement (NSM) to provide moral and physical aid to the Southern SNCC and to CORE. The NSM also conducts an educational program for culturally deprived Negro children in certain Northern cities.

The significance of all these organizations was not simply that the Gandhian technique of nonviolent resistance was successfully added to the repertory of those seeking equal rights for Negroes, but also that large sections of the Negro masses were now directly participating in the efforts for the improvement of their status. The new organizations, rivals to some extent among themselves, placed themselves in partial opposition to the older NAACP and Urban League because their more traditional techniques of legal action in the courts and negotiation with whites in positions of power did not lend themselves to direct, local participation. The competition was healthy, however, for while the Negro youth and some lower income persons joined the newer organizations, the growing Negro adult middle class was stimulated to give increasing support to the older organizations. In the summer of 1963, all these organizations—supported by significant segments of organized religion and labor—joined forces to promote a dramatic "March on Washington."

Violence as a technique for changing the pattern of race relations was also developed in the post-World War II period. Some of this was a purely spontaneous response to white violence and did not take an organized form, as in the case of the Jacksonville, Florida, Negroes in March, 1964, who rioted and destroyed white property when a Negro woman was killed by a white man. But of greater significance was the acceptance of a philosophy of violence by a small number of fairly well-educated Negroes, such as the group led by James Lawson of the United African Nationalist Movement, and by small numbers of poorly educated Negroes in the Muslim Brotherhood, the African Nationalist Pioneer Movement, and other nationalist organizations.

While cold conflict with white America had been found among the Negro lower class ever since the Garvey movement of the 1920's, it was never so well organized as in the Black Muslim movement ("Temple of Islam") of the 1950's and 1960's. This disciplined organization, probably reaching a membership of 100,000 by 1960, had as its stated goal a segregated territory within the United States, and it espoused—vaguely, in order not to violate the law—future violence to attain this goal. In 1964, one of its leaders, Malcolm X of New York, broke off from the parent movement headed by Prophet Elijah Muhammed to head a movement promising more immediate violence.

These were the new organized power currents that developed among Negroes in the post-World War II era. While not all of them sought integration, all of them did seek equality. They suggested a heightened group identification and impatience among

Negroes,[1] and since they occurred at a time when desegregation was becoming a reality, they suggested that Negroes themselves—while hastening the demise of discrimination—might delay integration in its final stages. That is, group identification may become so strong that Negroes, like American Jews, may not want full integration.

Effects of World War II

As the Negro population was becoming more politically alert to the possibilities of changing race relations, the white population was becoming more aware of the need to change its traditional ways of associating with and thinking about Negroes. Perhaps the most important force here was the Second World War itself. It transformed the United States from an isolated and isolationist nation into a leading power with responsibilities in every part of the world. The American people had to see themselves as other people saw them, and they found the world's major criticism to be America's handling of its racial violence. Newspapers in every country reported on American discrimination and racial violence. A significant number of Americans became aware of this criticism, and it had a profound effect on their consciences. World reaction gained even greater significance as the colored nations of Asia and Africa, formerly under colonial rule, gained their independence. As the United States government partly realigned its foreign policy toward these new nations, it was obliged to encourage a more equalitar-

---

[1] The crescendo of Negro opposition to discrimination during the 1950's and 1960's, which reached the proportions of what was called a "Negro Revolt" by the summer of 1963, surprised many white Americans. Increased group identification, resulting in protest on the part of Negroes, was predicted in my book, *The Negro's Morale* (Minneapolis: University of Minnesota Press, 1949).

ian treatment of nonwhite minorities at home. The formation of newly independent African nations after 1957 increased race pride among American Negroes and strengthened their drive toward equality.

The Second World War and its aftermath brought unprecedented numbers of Americans in touch with other peoples. The Armed Services transported millions of Americans to Europe and Asia, and the tourist trade sent millions more to all parts of the world. Asiatics and Africans, especially students, began to visit the United States in significant numbers. A colored man on the downtown streets of New York City and Washington, D.C., was almost as likely to be a foreign as a native one, and even Southerners could no longer be sure whether the Negroes they saw in their cities were Americans or Africans. Perhaps more far-reaching was the change in the nation's mass media. Before 1940, newspapers, movies, and radio either ignored the Negro or stereotyped him unfavorably; after 1950, these media paid the Negro —foreign and native—a great deal of objective or favorable attention. Some social science research and certain novels made the Negro almost popular in some mainly intellectual white circles. With the rising living standards of the American Negro and his efforts to integrate himself into American life, white Americans generally were also much more likely to have direct contact with middle-class Negroes.

Federal Government Assistance

The more educated white Americans and those in closest contact with foreign opinion were most involved in the effort to eliminate discrimination and prejudice. This included the chief federal government officials. The United States Supreme Court led the way, perhaps because it was closer to the Constitution, which had been a thoroughly equalitarian document since 1868, and perhaps because it weighted foreign opinion along with domestic white opinion. The Supreme Court had generally sought to guarantee Negroes some legal protection, but it had equivocated until 1944 about the right to vote and about the equal use of public facilities. That year, a unanimous Court—in the case of *Smith vs. Allwright*—declared unequivocally that the "white primary" was illegal, and that other such subterfuges to prevent Negroes from voting in the South were unconstitutional. Since then, the Court has consistently decided, with undivided opinions, that no branch of any government in the United States could practice any discrimination whatsoever on grounds of race or religion.

Perhaps the most important of these decisions was the one handed down on May 17, 1954, which held that it was unconstitutional for the public schools to segregate the races. This decision withdrew the last legal support from the Southern states' effort to segregate public facilities, such as parks, playgrounds, libraries, and bathing beaches, as well as schools. The "separate but equal" doctrine was dead. The decision also applied to privately owned transportation facilities directly engaged in interstate commerce, including rail and bus terminal waiting rooms and restaurants. Only a small proportion of the local governments affected took immediate steps to desegregate, but through various pressures, the elaborate caste system of the South began to be dismantled. After 1954, the federal courts adjudicated many cases that were brought in order to implement the historic decision wiping out "separate but equal" facilities, but it could go no further in principle, for it was now operating in complete accord with

the Constitutional provisions for full equality.

The Executive branch of the federal government began to fulfill its responsibilities for enforcing equality during the 1930's. The Roosevelt Administration (1933-1945) practiced equality in the administration of some of its programs and for the first time hired Negroes in other than custodial or honorary capacities. The main innovation of the Roosevelt era, however, was forced on the President by the combined pressure of all the Negro organizations during the war, namely, the establishment of a Fair Employment Practices Commission (FEPC), which had the task of preventing discrimination in employment by industries holding contracts with the federal government. The Truman Administration (1945-1953) went further in eliminating discrimination in federal employment and in the operation of federal programs, although it lost the FEPC in 1946 through Congressional action. Its main achievements along these lines were the virtual abolition of discrimination and segregation in the armed services and the support and publicity given to the President's Civil Rights Commission. The Eisenhower Administration (1953-1961) continued the existing nondiscriminatory policies and gave administrative support to the courts' rulings on school desegregation —even to the point of calling out federal troops to enforce school desegregation in Little Rock, Arkansas, in 1957. The Kennedy Administration (1961-1963) pumped life into the government committee to enforce nondiscrimination in employment by industries with government contracts— thereby reviving in effect the FEPC for major manufacturing companies— and extended administrative support to the courts' rulings on nondiscrimination by the states and by agencies of interstate transportation. Most important was the 1961 ruling by the Interstate Commerce Commission that rail and bus terminals might not segregate passengers. Further Executive action was taken in late 1962: President Kennedy signed a long-delayed executive order to restrict government guarantees on loans to builders who insisted on excluding Negroes, and the Attorney General began a policy of calling on the National Guard and federal troops to assist in enforcing court orders for school desegregation. In June, 1963, the President responded to the crescendo of Negro protests against discrimination—stimulated by growing unemployment and by the observance of the centennial anniversary of the Emancipation Proclamation—by setting before Congress a comprehensive program of proposed legislation guaranteeing voting rights and desegregation of public schools and prohibiting private enterprises involved in interstate commerce to refuse to do business with Negroes. While the last-mentioned feature had been in the statutes of twenty-eight Northern states since shortly after the Supreme Court (1883) had declared unconstitutional the Civil Rights Act of 1875, Congress regarded it as a drastic innovation and showed a strong inclination to cut down a portion of the President's proposal. After the death of President Kennedy in November, 1963, President Johnson gave even more effective support to the civil rights bill then before Congress, and the bill became law on July 2, 1964.

The Legislative branch has the greatest power but the least achievement, largely because of the presence within it of Southern congressmen. These are a minority but hold the balance of power between the conservatives and liberals—a position they exploit in order to prevent enactment of civil

rights legislation—and they have a disproportionate share of congressional leadership positions because of their seniority. Until 1964, the Congress's main contribution to the equalization of the races was a negative one: it has not sought to reverse the actions of the Judicial and Executive branches—except for killing the FEPC in 1946. In 1957, Congress passed its first statute since the 1870's to enforce civil rights; it was a weak law, which gave federal authorities some power to restrain local polling officials from preventing voting by Negroes. In 1960 it passed a second statute which slightly strengthened this law. It is doubtful that these statutes helped the position of Negroes enough to offset the damage inflicted on other liberal legislation, such as the bill to provide federal aid for education, by the political bargaining that was required. Negroes would be among those helped by the enactment of many bills which Southern congressmen block by deals with the conservatives: scarcely a bill comes before Congress these days—except occasionally in the fields of defense and foreign policy—which does not have a "race angle." Pending legislation that enhances the civil rights of Negroes has usually been killed by the Southern congressional bloc, who extend support to non-Southern conservatives in their opposition to other socially progressive measures, in exchange for help in preventing the passage of civil rights bills. Until the mass civil rights' demonstration of mid-1963, there did not seem to be much hope for significant legislation from Congress.

Some of what Negro leaders want from the federal government can be provided by the Executive branch, and the votes of Negroes are more effective in the presidential elections than in the congressional races. It is doubtful, however, that civil rights groups will diminish their efforts to get federal legislation. The main effort in 1960-1961 was to modify certain procedural rules in the Congress so that substantive civil rights legislation would be easier to pass. By 1963, however, the pressure from an awakening Negro populace—aided by many whites—forced Negro leaders to seek more substantive legislation to outlaw discrimination in voting, education, employment, and business relations.

The Civil Rights Act of 1964, which passed both houses of Congress with overwhelming majorities, despite a Southern filibuster in the Senate and the opposition of the leading contender for the Republican nomination for President, was the most comprehensive legislation to be enacted since post-Civil War days. Its success was due to the active support of President Lyndon Johnson, to demonstrations by civil rights and religious organizations, and to recognition by the congressional leadership of both parties of the facts of social change and of the moral and international issues involved. The main provisions of the eleven titles of the Act were: Title 1 prohibits voting registrars from applying different standards to white and Negro voting applicants and permits the Attorney General to sue in federal courts to enforce this. Title 2 prohibits refusal of service on account of race in hotels, restaurants, gasoline stations, and places of amusement if their operations affect interstate commerce, and it permits the Attorney General to sue in federal courts to enforce this. Title 3 requires that Negroes have equal access to, and treatment in, publicly owned or operated facilities and permits the offended citizen or the Attorney General to sue to enforce this. Title 6 provides that no person shall be subjected to racial discrimination in any program receiving federal aid. Title 7 bars discrimination by employers or unions with twenty-five or more employees or members and places enforcement powers in the hands of both a new commission and the Attorney General. Title 9 permits the federal courts and the Attorney General to intervene in any state suit in which racial discrimination may be involved. If these provisions of the law are enforced, they will wipe out the remnants of the American caste system insofar as law can do so.

State Government Assistance

The Northern state governments and some local governments have been effective sources of change in American race relations. After the federal FEPC was killed by Congress in 1946, New York led the states in passing legislation setting up FEPC's with their jurisdictions. By the late 1950's, many Northern and Western states and cities with a sizable Negro population had such legislation, designed to prevent discrimination in employment: the count in 1963 was twenty states and forty cities with some kind of FEPC law—covering 60 per cent of the total population and about 50 per cent of the minorities. A more difficult problem for the North was discrimination in housing, but in 1958 New York again led the way by making it illegal to discriminate against a person on grounds of race, religion, or nationality in the sale or rental of most categories of housing. By 1963, seventeen states and cities had passed legislation of this sort. It is as yet too early to ascertain the effectiveness of these statutes in eliminating housing discrimination and segregation.

Forces Maintaining Segregation

Such have been the main forces promoting the equalization of Negroes in

American society since 1940. The main forces maintaining the subordination and segregation of Negroes have been those of tradition and the status quo. In 1954, however, a new factor entered which has undoubtedly prevented change from being more rapid than it might otherwise have been. This was the organization of Southern white opposition, mainly in the White Citizens' Councils. There had been no significant organization aiming to hold the Negro in a subordinate position since the decline of the Ku Klux Klan in the late 1920's. Minor and local organizations had made sporadic efforts, but the leading reactionary movements of the period between 1930 and 1954 avoided attacking the position of Negroes. The reaction to the rapid changes of the post-1940 period did not gain organized expression until 1954. Racists did not organize their resistance to changes in the caste system effectively until the very keystone of that system was endangered by the Supreme Court decision to desegregate the public schools. But the economic, political, and legal aspects of the caste system had already changed materially, and the pattern of social segregation had long been threatened before the proponents of the caste system organized themselves to protect it. For twenty-five years, the old racist ideology had found only occasional—and little-heeded—spokesmen, and it was only after 1954 that it was again vigorously reasserted—and this at a time when the original source for this thinking had disappeared, together with most of its material benefits. The ideology of racism was now no longer the response to a conflict between economic and political forces on the one hand and the idealism of the American creed and Constitution on the other, but merely an expression of a traditional psychology.

The South

The Southern resistance movement drew strength from all social classes, but there were also defectors from all classes. Many of the leaders of the White Citizens' Councils were upper class, and they used their economic power to hurt Negroes who sought a greater measure of civic equality. But some of the economic leaders of the South took the position that resistance to the Supreme Court decision disturbed the social peace and was bad for business. They concluded that the South should stop "fighting the War Between the States" and should become forward-looking and efficient. Political and other organizational leaders were similarly divided; while few whites admitted being pro-Negro or in favor of equality, many influential people of the South felt that the Negro could no longer be simply subordinated. It is difficult to know how the less articulate whites of the South divided, but they did divide. While many participated in violent actions to prevent desegregation, a majority of the voters of Little Rock, Arkansas, for example, voted for a school board that had announced its intention to desegregate the public schools in accord with the federal court order. There was similar evidence in other parts of the South that significant numbers of whites were quietly resigned to desegregation. The articulate and organized group, however, was the one that favored the maintenance of the caste system, and it used boycotts, influence on the Southern legislatures, violence, and other means to resist the changes. In general, this group is larger and more effective in the Deep South than in the Upper South; it is of little consequence in the Border states. With some exceptions, the only ones to benefit from the caste system today are those, mainly in the lower classes, who get psychological satisfaction out of a sense of racial superiority. There is also a small, and decreasing, number who benefit economically from the caste system by keeping the Negroes handicapped in job competition.

Some of the leaders of the resistance to change are those who believe that leaders should follow the wishes of the led. But there are also other types of leaders; a few have sought to make money by exploiting the fears of the white South. Another minor type seems to have a psychological need to lead violent movements. Still another rare type hoped to build a full-scale fascist movement out of the Southern resistance to desegregation, and they have had some success in attracting support from extreme right-wing radicals all over the country. But all of them together have not succeeded in stemming the changes in the system of discrimination and segregation. On occasion, a spontaneous leader will lead a day or two of violence, but most of the continuing leaders of the Southern resistance are persons with some traditional and legitimate authority. Imbued with a strong racist ideology, and a strong personal desire to keep the Negro subordinate, they also have a vested interest in keeping things on an even keel, and generally tend to hold their followers back from unplanned violence. Violence directed against Negroes might easily spread to white-owned property and other institutions, and so the traditional leaders try to keep racial agitation in check.

The North

In the North, there is little organized resistance to change in race relations, though there are small property owners' associations that oppose the movement of Negroes into certain neighborhoods and oppose the passage of "fair housing" or "open occupancy" legisla-tion. There are a great number of unorganized white Northerners who resist personal association with Negroes, particularly as neighbors and as social club members. Few Northern whites try to keep Negroes out of coemployment or out of the large, impersonal, voluntary associations, churches, or trade unions, but they still resist intimate association. For a few years following the development of the Southern resistance, there was an unorganized but articulate movement among some Northern leaders to put brakes on the trend toward equalization, particularly as it affected the South. Taking up the Southern theme of "leaving the South alone to work out its own problems," they argued that "both kinds of extremists are dangerous." But the majority of Northern leaders seem to have been persuaded that the South has always moved more rapidly toward better race relations when prodded by the North. The Northern proponents of "moderation" were most articulate in the period 1955-1958, but they probably will be heard again if widespread violence occurs in the South. In 1964, right-wing extremist whites in California and Washington organized to curtail the Fair Housing statutes; they may be the forerunners of larger movements of resistance in the North.

The race relations crisis presents a continuing dilemma for those segments of Northern opinion that have strong ties with the South. This is true not merely for those who have family and personal connections with Southerners, but for Northern businessmen and trade union leaders with Southern branches. The national labor movement, for example, has not moved as forthrightly on integration within its own ranks as might have been expected because of pressures from Southern— and some Northern—locals and because of its hopes of organizing more white Southern workers. In 1959, Negro labor leaders formed the Negro American Labor Council to pressure the AFL-CIO into a position of complete integration. For a period, the leadership of the national labor movement refused to recognize the Negro group except in the critical terms of "dual unionism." By the end of 1961, however, the president of the AFL-CIO, George Meany, verbally capitulated and created organizational machinery to eliminate discrimination and segregation in the member unions. Organized labor remains, however, a divided force on the race issue, not only because of its Southern elements but also because the craft unions in the North refuse to modify their work rules to allow "new elements" into their crafts.

Summary of Progress to 1964

In the dynamic situation created by all these forces, any description of the position of Negroes written at any one moment is bound to be dated before it can be printed. The picture at the beginning of 1964 is here painted in broad strokes, necessarily superficial and incomplete. In 1940 Negroes were excluded from most occupations outside of agriculture and service; by 1960 some Negroes were to be found in nearly every occupation. Between 1940 and 1960 the proportion of white males in the labor force who had white-collar jobs rose from 30.3 to 41.2 per cent, while among nonwhite males the corresponding rise was from 5.0 to 16.0 per cent. At the same time the rise in skilled and semiskilled blue-collar jobs was from 34.3 to 38.6 per cent among white males and from 16.6 to 32.7 per cent among nonwhite males. Considerable employment discrimination remained in the South and even in the Border states, but it was greatly diminished in the Northern and Western states. This did not mean that Negroes were approaching occupational equality, for there was the heritage of inadequate training, low-skill orientations, poor general education, and low seniority. The training lag was the most serious, because union and company seniority rules often made it impossible for Negroes to obtain training for better jobs.

Discrimination in economic benefits provided by the government—poor-relief, unemployment compensation, old-age assistance, public housing, and others—had been all but wiped out, except where there was local control in some Southern communities. A notable exception arose in Louisiana in 1960 where the "Aid to Dependent Children" program was curtailed for mothers who had illegitimate children while receiving ADC aid for their older children. This was applied almost exclusively to Negroes.

Politics

Negroes were voting without restriction in most areas of the Upper South and in some cities of the Deep South. Between 1956 and 1960, while the increase in the total population voting was 8 per cent, the estimated increase in the number of Negroes voting was 16 per cent. The only state that almost systematically excluded Negroes from the polls—as they had been throughout the South in 1940—was Mississippi. Here, and in many rural areas of the other Deep Southern states, they were illegally prevented from voting by the whim of local polling officials and by threats of violence. The poll tax still existed in five states as a requirement for voting, although by the beginning of 1964 a Constitutional amendment was passed to make it illegal for federal elections. Several Southern states had literacy and "understanding" tests for all voting, but they were given to Negroes with discriminatory severity. Negroes occasionally ran for the minor local offices. In Atlanta a Negro was elected to the Georgia state legislature with the aid of white voters. The main changes in Southern politics resulting from Negro voting were the election of liberal Democrats in several states and the breaking of the barriers which hitherto had prevented conservatives from voting Republican.

Hence the two-party system began to develop in the South—especially in Texas and Florida. In the 1948 and 1960 presidential elections, Negro votes in several Southern as well as Northern states provided the margin of victory for the Democratic candidates. In 1963 there were five Negro congressmen and many local public officials, mainly in Northern cities, and Negroes were thoroughly integrated into the local political parties of the Northern states. In Massachusetts in 1962, a Negro was elected to a major state office—attorney general—for the first time since Reconstruction days. Many Negroes were in significant appointive posts, including federal judgeships. The great majority of Negroes were voting Democratic, although there was some evidence of their flexibility in switching party affiliation when a local Republican candidate seemed more pro-Negro than his Democratic counterpart.

In 1964, 90 per cent of the Negroes voted Democratic, and their votes carried a number of "liberal" legislators into office.

Law Enforcement

In 1940, law enforcement in the South was virtually nonexistent when Negroes were the victims—whether whites or other Negroes were the criminals—and brutally severe when whites were the victims and Negroes the law violators. By the 1950's there were many cases, even in the Deep South, of white persons who committed crimes against Negroes being prosecuted and punished, although this was by no means general. Negro criminals whose victims were other Negroes were much more likely to be dealt with properly by law enforcement officials. Practically all Southern cities employed Negro policemen after 1945 to maintain law and order in their Negro communities, and Southern judges were no longer likely to release Negro criminals on the word of a white man. There was still considerable "overenforcement" of the law when Negroes were apprehended for crimes against whites, but civil suits between a white and a Negro were handled much more equitably. Despite the mass violence which attended many instances of desegregation, extralegal violence of the everyday, person-to-person basis which was characteristic of the pre-1940 period was now greatly reduced. Lynching was a rare event after 1950, and even murders of Negro prisoners by white policemen and jailers became infrequent.

Thus even while tension between the races in the South mounted, and the mass violence attending some desegregation got great publicity, total violence declined. This seemed to be due to the fact that potential white perpetrators of violence were aware that they were in some danger of retribution from the law or from retaliating Negroes. In the North, police brutality remained sporadic and individual—it had never been a matter of policy—and there was no evidence of discrimination by judges. While the Second World War years saw some major race riots in the North and West, the formation of interracial citizens' committees in many Northern cities practically eliminated them from 1944 on. The major exception was Chicago and some of its suburbs, where there were numerous small riots all through the 1940's and 1950's when Negroes moved into new residential neighborhoods or attempted to swim at the "white" public bathing beaches.

Social Relations

These changes in the economic, political, and legal spheres were occurring regularly and generally with little public attention or controversy. Changes in the area of social relations, however, were coming about in some areas but not in others, and at times received a great deal of notice. The movement of rural Negroes into the Northern and Southern cities was associated with housing segregation, and housing segregation brought the inevitable segregation of neighborhood facilities, overcrowding, high rents, rundown buildings, slums, and expansion into new neighborhoods attended by conflict with whites. This became the most serious aspect of the race problem, certainly in the North. The chief legal buttress for housing segregation had been the "restrictive covenant," a clause written into a deed for property preventing its resale to members of specified groups, mainly Negroes. In 1948, the United States Supreme Court decided that the racial restrictive covenant was unenforceable in the courts, thus wiping out the legal support for housing segregation and allowing it to rest on voluntary action.

The decision eased the situation for Negroes somewhat, and it was followed by various organized efforts to develop integrated housing in the North. Publicly subsidized housing was no longer segregated, and some privately sponsored integrated housing projects were developed. But the great masses of urban Negroes remained segregated, and there was some evidence that housing segregation was increasing in the South. Negroes themselves fought the

housing restrictions generally only when there was insufficient space to live; only a few of them sought to break the pattern of segregation itself. By the end of the 1950's some Northern states passed statutes making it illegal to refuse to rent or sell housing to Negroes, and generally in the North the space pressures on Negroes eased considerably.

Late in 1962 the President issued an executive order which restricts the lending of money with government guarantees if the housing affected is not available for lease or purchase by minority groups. Political considerations limited the coverage of this order to only about a third of the 90 per cent of all housing units covered by such loans. A full withholding of government credit and guarantees would remove the strongest barrier to housing integration. Whether Negroes would move in large numbers to take advantage of it is more questionable. At this time, residential segregation is one of the most serious and least soluble aspects of the race problem, particularly in the Northern states.

Segregation of other public and privately owned but essentially public facilities remained the effect of housing segregation in the North. This has become known as "de facto" segregation, and there were several local efforts to mix children in the public schools despite the fact that their residences were largely segregated. Forced segregation of schools, playgrounds, restaurants, hotels, and other public and commercial establishments became exceptional in the North as the climate of opinion changed and the old "public accommodations" statutes of the Northern states once again became operative. Some cities began movements to upgrade Negro education—to compensate for cultural deprivation in the family and community—preparatory to initiating programs to end de facto school segregation. In the South, desegregation of these kinds of facilities began as a result of the court decisions and the organized movements already examined.

By 1961, school systems were formally desegregated in all the border states; in many scattered areas of the Upper South and in a few cities of the Deep South there was token desegregation. Violence had attended school desegregation in Dover, Delaware; Clinton and Nashville, Tennessee; Little Rock, Arkansas; and New Orleans, Louisiana. But it was accomplished peacefully and more thoroughly in the larger school systems of Washington, D.C.; St. Louis, Missouri; Dallas and Houston, Texas; and Atlanta, Georgia. By 1961 only Mississippi, Alabama, and South Carolina had none of their schools desegregated, and by 1963 even these had token desegregation in a few schools. There was only spotty and token desegregation in all of the Deep Southern states and some of the Upper South states, but over one-third of all Negro children living in school districts segregated by statute before 1955 were in desegregated schools by 1963.

Desegregation of the other public and the privately owned commercial establishments took roughly the same pattern, though with a few years of delay. In the two years of 1960 and 1961, the sit-in movement opened some restaurants to Negroes in about two hundred cities of the South, and there was continuing desegregation after that. But the majority of restaurants in many of these cities remained segregated, and Negro patronage of the nonsegregated restaurants was rare. Some hotels in the larger Southern cities, such as Houston and Atlanta, quietly desegregated. An issue arose over the exclusion of dark-skinned representatives of foreign nations from the highway restaurants of Maryland, a Border state, and the federal government intervened with partial success. Hotels, theatres, and recreational facilities were opened to Negroes on approximately the same basis as restaurants: in every state but Mississippi and Alabama there were at least some desegregated, but the majority in the Deep South and even some areas of the Upper South remained segregated, and Negro patronage of the desegregated facilities was rare. Interstate transportation was effectively desegregated, and—after the Montgomery, Alabama, bus boycott of 1957—so was the local transportation within many Southern cities.

One of the major gains in the North was the desegregation of most of the major voluntary associations. The major professional associations were desegregated in the South also. Except for weak, formal associations—such as the PTA's—most other Southern voluntary associations remained segregated. Social clubs and informal groups remained segregated throughout the country, with a few exceptions in the North. College fraternities and sororities remained mainly segregated in fact, although a campaign in the North to remove formal barriers was largely successful. Almost the same could be said of the churches, although in mixed neighborhoods, churches sometimes served members of both races.

Interracial marriages were probably on the increase in the North, although they were still not frequent. In the South, interracial marriage continued to be illegal: this was the one type of law discriminating among the races still on the statute books of the Southern states; not even the Negro organizations have sought to challenge it, and hence the courts had no occasion to declare it unconstitutional. The probability is that the courts would declare it unconstitutional, for they had nullified a California statute barring marriage between whites and Orientals. But apparently the Negro leadership thought it unwise to challenge this last formal barrier of the caste system, at least until other forms of desegregation should be accomplished in greater degree. At the present writing (Winter, 1964), there are two cases in the state courts challenging the constitutionality of the laws forbidding interracial marriage.

The formerly elaborate "etiquette of race relations" was crumbling in the South, and it became common to hear Negroes addressed by whites by their formal titles of "Mr.," "Mrs.," and "Miss." The self-demeaning manner of Negroes in the presence of whites disappeared except in the rural areas. With the improvement in occupational opportunities, Negroes were much less likely to be domestic servants. The barriers to serious conversations between the races broke down in the North, but remained in the South. The results of these changes were that Northern whites could perceive Negroes as human beings for the first time, while relations between the races in the South grew cold as they became increasingly restricted to matters of common economic interest. The white Southerners were no longer sure they understood "their" Negroes, and Negroes could no longer be relied on to maintain their "place" in the presence of whites. A Gallup poll taken in July, 1963, showed that 83 per cent of white Southerners expected that there would soon be complete integration of the races in public accommodations, although six years earlier this proportion was only 45 per cent. What is more, 49 per cent expected this integration to be achieved within the coming five years, and only 9 per cent expected it would take longer than twenty years. The same poll showed that 56 per cent of the total population believed that Ne-

groes were treated the "same as whites" in their community, with Negroes in every region outside the South sharing this majority view.

A National Opinion Research Center poll, conducted in December, 1963, showed that 30 per cent of white Southerners accepted *school* integration, as compared to only 2 per cent in 1942 and 14 per cent in 1956. Among white Northerners, the proportions accepting the principle of *school* integration was 75 per cent in 1963, 61 per cent in 1956, and 40 per cent in 1942. Acceptance of *residential* integration among Southern whites rose from 12 per cent in 1942 to 51 per cent in 1963; among Northern whites, it rose from 42 per cent to 70 per cent. Estimates of Negroes' intelligence—as measured by answers to the question, "Can Negroes learn things just as well as whites if they are given the same education and training?"—likewise rose, thus indicating the decline in racism. Among Southern whites, the proportion agreeing rose from 21 per cent in 1942 to 60 per cent in 1963; among Northern whites, the rise was from 50 per cent to 80 per cent.

Future Development

There could be no doubt that the races were moving rapidly toward equality and desegregation by 1964. In retrospect, the change of the preceding twenty years appeared as one of the most rapid in the history of human relations. Much of the old segregation and discrimination remained in the Deep South, and housing segregation with its concomitants was still found throughout the country, but the all-encompassing caste system had been broken everywhere. Prejudice as an attitude was still common, but racism as a comprehensive ideology was maintained by only a few. The change had been so rapid, and caste and racism so debilitated, that this author ventures to predict—if the present trends continue—the end of all legal segregation and discrimination within a decade, and the decline of informal segregation and discrimination to a mere shadow in two decades. The attitude of prejudice might remain indefinitely, but it will be on the minor order of Catholic-Protestant prejudice within three decades. These changes would not mean that there would be equality between the races within this time, for the heritage of past discriminations would still operate to give Negroes lower "life chances." But the dynamic social forces creating inequality will, if the present trends continue, be practically eliminated in three decades. As far as separation of the races without overt discrimination is concerned, this will come for a while to be more associated with Negro group identification than with white exclusionism. It would only be appropriate to guess that most sociologists would find these predictions "optimistic," but then, most sociologists found the predictions contained in *An American Dilemma* of twenty years ago optimistic, and most of these predictions have since come true.

The student of society, who must have historical perspective and be aware of continuities and rigidities in the social structure, may consider the development in American race relations from 1942 to 1964 among the most rapid and dramatic of social changes to have ever been achieved without violent revolution. To the participants themselves the changes did not appear to be so rapid. People generally live from day to day, and from

month to month, without historical perspective, and hence tend not to perceive changes that occur over a period of years. The "social present" usually means much more to people than does social change. Young people who have come to awareness of the world around them during the latter part of the period under consideration see only the conditions of the last few years; for them the conditions of the pre-1940 period are "ancient history," and hence the changes of twenty years are not part of their image of the modern world.

These things are true for all social change. But of particular significance for our analysis is the fact that Negroes *still* experience discrimination, insult, segregation, and the threat of violence, and in a sense have become more sensitive and less "adjusted" to these things. To them the current problems and current conflicts have much more significance than those of ten or twenty years ago. Schooled as they are by the American creed, their standard of comparison for the present situation is not what existed in 1940, but what the Constitution and "the principles of democracy" say should be. Further, most American Negroes are aware of great changes going on in Africa, and in fact are inclined to exaggerate the "improvements" there resulting from the demise of old-fashioned colonialism. From their perspective, the changes occurring in the United States are much too slow; they want "freedom *now*," as the slogan goes. White Americans, who have in mind the United States Constitution and their country's role in a world whose population is two-thirds colored, might agree with them.

The United States Population Explosion:
Consequences and Implications

PHILIP M. HAUSER

I

Increased and widespread attention to the world population explosion and its implications has tended to obscure the fact that the United States is also experiencing a population explosion that is producing severe national problems. Blinded by the short-run gains of national resurgence in population growth, we fail to see its short-range deleterious effects, and ignore its insidious consequences for the longer run.

As a result of the postwar, cold war boom in marriages and babies and continued progress in death control, the United States is now approximating the growth rate it had at the end of the nineteenth century. In the period between 1950 and 1980, the most important impact of our national resurgence in population growth undoubtedly lies in the thrust it has given and will continue to give to the maintenance of a high level of economic activity and economic growth. In the short run, our increased rate of population growth spells expanded market, greater labor input, and larger gross national product.

In 1957, for example, the population of the United States included a labor force averaging 65,000,000 workers. They worked a thirty-hour week, produced a product worth $3.29 per man hour, and generated a gross national product of $434,000,000,000. By 1975,

drawing on projections by the Mc-Graw-Hill Department of Economics,[1] we could have a labor force, reflecting population increase, averaging about 88,000,000 workers. They are likely, with present trends, to be working a thirty-five-and-one-half-hour week, to be producing a product worth $5.14 per man hour (in 1957 dollars), and to be generating a gross national product of $835,000,000,000 (also in 1957 dollars).

In the course of a single human generation, we could double our gross national product. This would be adding to the national product of the United States in one generation an amount greater than the national product of any nation on the face of the earth other than the United States itself. This could follow not only from our rapid population growth but also from continued increase in productivity. The projections, as a matter of fact, indicate a gain by 1975 of some 40 per cent in personal income after taxes (in 1957 dollars).

The businessman is, in general, heartened by considerations such as these, for a fast-growing population accompanied by increased productivity, and therefore income, means rapidly expanding markets. This prospect opens up new fields of investment opportunity for expanded plant and facilities. But this analysis, even while probably reflecting the proper perspec-

Philip M. Hauser, *Population Perspectives* (New Brunswick, N.J.: Rutgers University Press, 1960), pp. 66-91. Reprinted by permission of the publisher.

[1] McGraw-Hill Department of Economics, *The American Economy* (New York: McGraw-Hill Book Company, 1958).

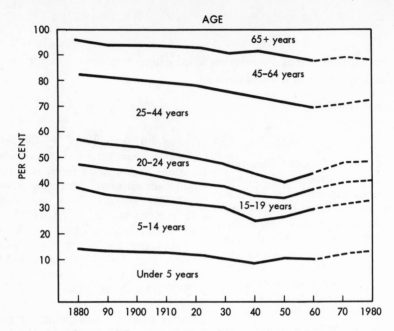

AGE

FIG. 1. Population of the United States by age, 1880 to 1960, and projected to 1980. *Source:* U.S. Bureau of the Census.

tive for the short run, ignores other factors operating to produce longer-range adverse effects, some of which are evident even in the short run.[2]

For example, greatly increased population means, all other things being equal, greatly reduced, nonrenewable natural resources per head, and operation of the law of diminishing returns as an offset to economics of scale. It also means higher densities of population with accompanying gains in potential of interaction, range, and intensity of contacts, increased frictions, and greater tension and frustration in daily living. Growing population den-

[2] For general discussion of population as a factor in the level of United States economy, see conflicting views of J. J. Spengler, "Population Threatens Prosperity," *Harvard Business Review,* **34** (January-February, 1956), 85-94, and Joseph S. Davis, "The Population Upsurge and the American Economy, 1945-80," *Journal of Political Economy,* **61** (October, 1953), 369-388.

sity . . . has been accompanied irresistibly by greater governmental intervention into the economic and social spheres—expanded government functions on the national, state, and local levels. These accompaniments of rapid population increase are operative even in the short run, as are the deleterious consequences resulting from changes in population composition discussed below.

II

Changes in age structure of the magnitude indicated over successive decades (Fig. 1) will necessarily have a profound effect upon many sectors of the American social, economic, and political scene. The differential rates of growth of the various population age groupings will mean differential rates of market expansion to the business community. To business and industry the relatively large increases in the late teen-age population during the sixties mean greatly expanded markets for such things as high school textbooks and other educational equipment, sport clothes, food and drink in teen-age eating places, dance records, jazz bands, and various forms of commercial recreation.

The great boom in young adults, twenty to twenty-four years of age, means a great rise in the number of marriages, and therefore in the demand for the goods and services required in the early years of family formation. Young couples tend to form the basic core of the market for consumer durable goods, including automobiles, major appliances, furniture, and the vast assortment of goods and services associated with the coming of first and second children. Further discussion of the boom effects on the economy of the increase in young adults will be found below in our consideration of household formation.

The explosive growth of teen-age and young adult population which means expanding markets to business will not necessarily benefit other sectors of the social order. For example, even if delinquency rates remain the same, the volume of juvenile delinquency during the sixties will rise by 44 per cent by reason of the increase in the number of persons of this age. This of course means a larger clientele for reform schools, reformatories, jails, and penitentiaries, and an expansion in the work loads of the police force, the court system, probation officers, and social workers.

The great impetus to purchases of automobiles resulting from the more than 50 per cent increase in young adults will be accompanied by further frustrations as highways, despite new construction, become even more congested and parking spaces even scarcer.

The explosive rise in marriages will create pressures on virtually all public services: the physical services, such as water supply, sanitation, and drainage; the health and welfare services; the recreational services, and so forth. The explosive increase in young adults will make present shortages in housing supply more acute in many communities.

Similarly, the continued steep rise in the number of older persons requires rapid expansion of services for the aged. Gerontological services must almost double in less than a generation if even present relatively low levels are to be maintained. Pressures on obstetrical services, public and private, may be expected to rise again as the boom of newly married couples produces a new surge in the birth rate, approximately twenty years after the beginning of the postwar boom in 1946.

One of the most important effects of the changing age structure of the United States as the result of the postwar resurgence in national growth is the changing dependency ratio—that is, the number of young persons under twenty and older persons sixty-five and over per one hundred persons of working age, twenty to sixty-four. Throughout the course of the history of this nation until 1940, the dependency ratio had been declining (Table 1). In 1820, for example, for each one hundred persons of working age there were 153 dependents, 146 of whom were under twenty and about seven of whom were sixty-five and over. By 1900, as the result of the aging of the population, the number of dependents had declined to ninety-four, of whom eighty-six were young dependents and eight were old dependents. By 1940, the total number of dependents had declined to seventy-one, of whom fifty-nine were young and twelve were old.

As the result of the combination of

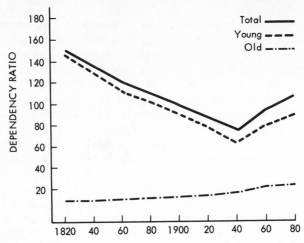

FIG. 2. Dependency rations for the United States, 1820 to 1960, and projected to 1980. *Source:* U.S. Bureau of the Census.

the rising birth rate during the forties and the continued aging of the population, dependents had increased to seventy-two by 1950, of whom fifty-eight were young and fourteen were older dependents. By 1980, if the postwar birth rate continues, the dependency ratio will have risen to ninety-five. Of the 104 dependents in 1980, younger dependents would number eighty-five, a number approximately the 1900 level of eighty-six, whereas older dependents would number nineteen, twice as many as in 1900 (Fig. 2).

Thus the resurgent birth rate during the forties and fifties has introduced changes in the age structure which, all other things being equal, would bring about the first decrease in product per head in our history. That is, prior to World War II the combination of forces affecting the age structure of the population of the United States produced "hands" faster than "mouths." As the result of the sharp upturn in birth rate in the postwar period, mouths began to be generated more rapidly than hands. The increase in dependency rates is also attributable in part to the rise in the number and

TABLE 1. Dependency Ratios for Population of the Continental United States, Selected Dates, 1820-1980.

Year	Dependents per 100 Persons of Working Age*		
	Young† and Old‡	Young Only	Old Only
Census:			
1820	153	146	7
1850	123	117	6
1900	94	86	8
1940	71	59	12
Estimate:			
1950	72	58	14
Projection:			
1960	91	74	17
1970	98	80	18
1980	104	85	19

* Working age: persons 20 to 64 years of age.
† Young: persons under 20 years of age.
‡ Old: persons 65 years of age and over.
SOURCE: computed from data in U.S. Bureau of the Census, *Current Population Reports*, Series P-25, No. 187 (November 10, 1958), p. 16, using projections based upon the assumption 1955-57 level of fertility would continue and *Historical Statistics of the United States, 1789-1945* (Washington, D.C.: U.S. Government Printing Office, 1949), Series B81-94. Also, 1820, and, in part, 1850 age distributions based upon interpolations.

proportion of older persons, which reflects past demographic behavior.

Another consequence of the changing dependency ratio will be found in its adverse effects on claims against

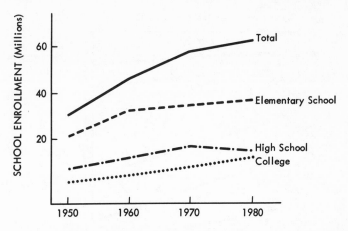

FIG. 3. School enrollment for the United States by type of school, 1950, and projected to 1980. *Source:* U.S. Bureau of the Census.

savings. An increase in younger dependents requires a larger allocation of savings for purposes of "social investment," that is, investment in the rearing and education of the young. This is achieved only at the expense, in some measure, of decreased savings allocated to "productive investment," or investment designed specifically to increase product per head. A rise in the number of older dependents increases the claims on current production of that part of the population which tends no longer to contribute to increased product. Thus apart from raising the ratio of dependents to workers, increased dependency, all other things being equal, operates in these other ways to reduce product per head and therefore to affect level of living adversely.

Without question the most visible consequence of our changing age structure during the fifties was the tremendous pressure on elementary school facilities throughout the nation. The grade schools of the United States were inundated by the tidal wave of postwar babies who reached school entrance age early in the fifties, many of whom flowed through the eight years of elementary schooling within the decade (Fig. 3). During the sixties, pressure on elementary schools will level off, reflecting the plateau in the postwar birth rate. But the tidal wave will continue its relentless surge through the high schools of the United States in the early sixties, and, later in the decade, through the colleges.

Enrollment increases . . . have not been, nor are they likely to be, accompanied by adequate expansion in school plant, facilities, and teachers. The present explosive rise in school population has undoubtedly had an adverse effect on the quality of education at the elementary and high school levels during the fifties. It will further deleteriously affect the quality of high school education, and begin the erosion of that of college education during the sixties. During the seventies the colleges and professional schools will still be reeling under the impact of rapidly increasing student enrollment. Part of the upturn in enrollment, especially in high school and college, arises from increases in rates of enrollment rather than the population explosion. Gains in enrollment rate are of course indicative of the rising level of living. The

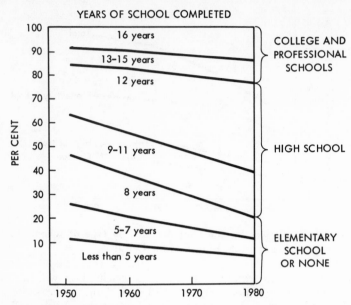

YEARS OF SCHOOL COMPLETED

COLLEGE AND PROFESSIONAL SCHOOLS

16 years
13–15 years
12 years

HIGH SCHOOL

9–11 years
8 years

ELEMENTARY SCHOOL OR NONE

5–7 years
Less than 5 years

PER CENT

1950   1960   1970   1980

FIG. 4. Educational attainment for the United States, 1950, and projected to 1980. *Source:* U.S. Bureau of the Census.

expansion of educational facilities that would be necessary to accommodate increased enrollment alone would, however, be but a fraction of the present and prospective need arising both from higher rates of enrollment and rapid population growth.

Although the exceedingly rapid rates of increase in school age population together with higher rates of enrollment have created serious problems for the schools, the increases in enrollment rates mean higher levels of education. What are the implications of the American people's rising level of formal education (Fig. 4)?

First of all, it should be noted that increased education opens up new vistas of intellectual, emotional, and aesthetic experience to the population. It means that the level of living of the people of the United States will be raised culturally as well as materially. It may also mean modifications of many present practices. For example,

the increased educational level of the American people could change the character of American politics and perhaps that of political campaigns. The kinds of appeals candidates can make to an electorate are undoubtedly of a different order when the average voter has not progressed beyond grade school than when he has at least a high school education. Similarly, the increasing educational level of the population may bring about important changes in the patterns of consumption of goods and services. There could conceivably be greater demand for the types of goods and services associated with the "egghead"—more good magazines, books, music, art, museums, and travel —and decreased demand for other goods and services, such as lurid and sensational publications, honky-tonk amusements, and fraudulent sucker products ranging from false cures for arthritis and cancer to astrological guides to behavior. Further, it may be

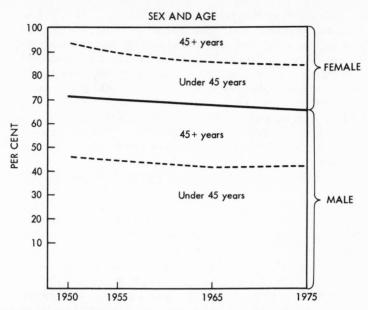

FIG. 5. Labor force of the United States by sex and broad age groups, 1950, and projected to 1975. *Source:* U.S. Bureau of the Census.

anticipated that the rising educational level of the American people will have an important impact upon the advertising profession, since both the form and the substance of advertising appeals will very likely require considerable modification.

Predictions as to the consequences of the increased educational level of the American people are necessarily speculative, but we can expect that it will alter many present aspects of life in these United States, possibly even the caliber of TV programs.

The increase in national population growth and changes in the age structure of the population, together with changes in trends in education, in retirement, and in the role of women, have markedly affected and will continue to make great changes in the composition of the nation's labor force. While the proportion of the population working or seeking work should

remain relatively constant over the next two decades, the labor force will expand tremendously and undergo important changes in composition (Fig. 5). The labor supply will have growing proportions of young and old workers, and fewer workers of intermediate age. It is likely to become more female in the next two decades. The changes in prospect have important implications for workers, employers, and the economy at large.

From the standpoint of the individual worker, it was the astute youngster who managed to be born during the depression and so entered the labor force when the new entrant group was relatively small. This favorable market situation—a seller's market from the standpoint of labor—meant relatively high entrance wage rates and opportunity for promotion. In contrast, the youngster who contrived to be born during the postwar baby boom, as part of a much larger new entrant group, is faced with a much more competitive situation. Workers seeking their first jobs will, during the sixties and seventies, encounter stiffer competition and probably relatively lower entrance wages than the smaller cohort of new workers during the fifties. They will have stiffer competition, also, all other things being equal, throughout their work careers in respect to such things as promotion and retention or layoff.

The increased number of new entrant workers could conceivably affect adversely some types of opportunities for the expanding supply of female workers. The prospective increase in new entrant workers could depress the trend toward greater labor force participation of women. Changes in this trend could of course markedly influence family income, and thereby consumption patterns. The economic contribution of women, and especially of wives, has been an important factor in home ownership, in the second TV set or car, and, in general, in the expanded market for household appliances, clothing, and a higher quality diet. Any dip in the trend toward greater labor force activity of women could have serious consequences for the American market. If the present trend continues, however, household consumption standards will continue to rise and to swell the growing United States market for goods and services.

Increases in the proportion of working wives and mothers are bound to have social as well as economic repercussions. For example, with larger proportions of children having little or no daytime parental supervision, the school, the day nursery, the church, family welfare agencies, and various recreational facilities will be confronted with an increasing and more diversified clientele.

From the employer's standpoint, the sixties will herald a new era in providing a relatively large reservoir of new employees. The change in the relative supply of new workers may ease his problems in the recruitment, training, placement, supervision, and development of workers. On the other hand, the employer will be more and more faced with the necessity of using older workers, as larger proportions of the labor supply become forty-five years of age and over.

The great increase in the size of the labor force in prospect as a consequence of national resurgent population growth has significant implications for the economy as a whole. On the one hand, it spells economic opportunity in heralding the continued growth of the economy. On the other hand, it spells challenge, in that the expansion of entrepreneurial enterprise will be needed to create enough jobs to absorb the swelling supply of labor.

As recently as the late forties, Henry Wallace's insistence that the United States economy must expand to provide 60,000,000 jobs[3] was greeted by many business and political leaders, as well as by some economists, with considerable dismay. They believed such a program to be visionary, unrealistic, and designed to embarrass business leadership. Yet Wallace's program was founded on census projections of the labor force based on anticipated growth of the total population.

As the result of the resumption of explosive national growth, the United States economy is now faced, not with the need to provide 60,000,000 jobs, a task accomplished by the civilian economy by 1950, but with the goal of about 90,000,000 jobs by 1975. To reach it, the economy must create about 20,000,000 additional jobs between 1960 and 1975. Even with our fabulous

---

[3] Henry A. Wallace, *Sixty Million Jobs* (New York: Simon and Schuster, Inc., 1945).

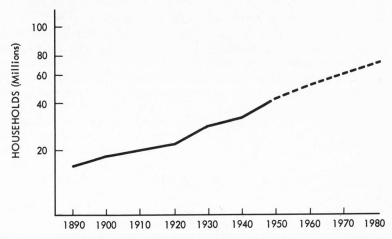

FIG. 6. Growth of households, 1800 to 1950, and projected to 1980. *Note:*
Drawn on logarithmic scale so that slope of line indicates rate of increase.
Source: U.S. Bureau of the Census.

history of economic growth, this will be a formidable task, particularly in view of the trend toward increased automation. There is no reason to regard the achievement of such an objective as impossible. But there can be little doubt that the rapid growth of the labor force deriving from the population explosion, involving as it does disproportionately great increases in younger, in older, and in female workers, will pose many problems in the years ahead—problems that will challenge the ingenuity of the nation.

The difference between rates of growth of total population and households, respectively, has important implications for all sectors of American life (Fig. 6). For example, business institutions or health and welfare agencies primarily concerned with the household as a unit must follow the pattern of household rather than of total population changes. During the fifties, while total population was rising explosively, annual increments to the number of households declined appreciably. During the sixties, in contrast,

net household formations will turn upward in an increase approximating a million a year or more.

The way in which shifts in the relative numbers of young, old, and intermediate households can affect different sectors of the economic and social order is illustrated by differences among such households in their home ownership. About half of the total household growth in the period from 1958 to 1965 will be accounted for by an increase in older households and about a fourth by a rise in younger households. The increase in young households will have relatively little effect on the demand for new home ownership. In fact, young home owners with mortgages constituted only 3 per cent of total borrowers in a recent study.[4] Older households with mortgaged homes accounted for only 8 per cent of borrowers. Eighty-nine per cent of borrowers were in households

---

[4] Miles L. Colean and Leon T. Kendall, *Who Buys the Homes: A Report on the Characteristics of Single-Family Home Buyers* (Chicago: United States Savings and Loan League, 1959).

with heads twenty-five to fifty-four years of age. The relatively great percentage rise in younger and older households may point to increased demand for apartments rather than houses during the sixties—a fact of both economic and sociological significance.

In similar fashion, all sectors of the economy in which the household is the basic consumer unit will be affected by the changes in household rather than total population growth. This consideration is of vital importance to manufacturers and distributors of durable products, such as the automobile, the refrigerator, the television, and the home laundry. The number of sets of encyclopedias and hi-fi and stereo sets will also be affected, not to mention the work loads on family service organizations, magazine salesmen, domestic employment, and obstetrical services.

So we see that the changing age structure accompanying the population explosion, together with factors affecting the transition from the large to the small family system, is greatly influencing the rate of net household formation. The rapid increase in the number of households, like the rise in total population, will mean expanded markets and higher levels of economic activity in the short run. Even in the short run, however, explosive rates of household growth also produce frictions and maladjustments in the economy by necessitating spurts of expansion after periods of decelerated growth.

Rapid household increase also means rapid change in the number and composition of families, the basic social institutions, and, therefore, in the social and cultural context in which children are reared. While the exact consequences of such changes cannot be accurately traced in the present stage of knowledge, they certainly influence the character of interpersonal relations in the family—of spouses, of parents and children, of siblings—and affect the relations of the family to the community and its various subunits. In the vortex of rapid family growth and fundamental changes in family size and composition, both the character of human nature and the mechanisms and processes by which it is formed are altered. Such modifications undoubtedly add to the frictions of social change manifest in various forms of social and personal disorganization. These short-run problems are of course augmented by the longer-run consequences of the population explosion.

III

It has been indicated that the Negro population explosion is of much greater magnitude than that of the white. The implications of present rates of growth of the Negro may be grasped by examination of projections of population by color beyond 1980. The continuation of present trends of white and nonwhite (mainly Negro) growth, respectively, would result in over 50,000,000 nonwhites by the year 2000, about 14 per cent of total population. By 2050, the trend would increase the proportion of nonwhites to about the same level as at the beginning of our national history—approximately one-fifth. That is, present growth rates indicate that of a possible total of 1,000,000,000 persons in 2050, about 200,000,000 would be nonwhite.[5] Thus in less than a century the present growth rate of the Negro could give the United States a much larger Negro population than Africa had in 1950, and almost as many

[5] Donald J. Bogue, The Population of the United States (New York: The Free Press of Glencoe, Inc., 1959), p. 761.

Negroes as there were in the entire world at mid-century.[6]

The magnitude of the explosive growth of the Negro population will undoubtedly make the problems of intergroup relations even more difficult in the coming years. That is, the complex problems of adjustment created by the great streams of Negro out-migrants from the South to the North and West, involving transition from a rural folk culture to urbanism as a way of life, will undoubtedly be aggravated by the exceedingly rapid expansion of the Negro population. This explosive growth will intensify the already acute problems facing both the communities of destination and the Negro in-migrant in respect to housing, employment, prejudice, and discriminatory practices. . . . Without question the transition would be much easier both for the Negro and the communities to which he is migrating if the tempo of growth were dampened.

The high fertility of the Negro, actually increased in recent years by his access to better health facilities and care, undoubtedly contributes to his relatively low level of living by decreasing per capita income in the Negro family. Moreover, large families combined with relatively low income mean fewer Negro children who can acquire an adequate education. Thus the Negro worker, who has a relatively low income partly because of his lack of education and skill, is handicapped in his effort to improve the educational and skill levels of his children by his high birth rate.

The foreign-born population is of course not experiencing explosive growth. The size of this population is entirely dependent on the aging and mortality of the foreign-born already here and on the volume of net immigration. . . . With present trends the foreign-born population will remain about the same size over the next several decades but become a smaller proportion of the total population (Fig. 7). It can safely be predicted that the process of assimilation of the foreign-born and their general acceptability will be furthered by the relative stability of their numbers. In contrast, problems in white-Negro intergroup relations are likely to be aggravated by the explosive growth of both the Negro and white populations. Certainly this prospect must be reckoned among the costs of the resurgence we have experienced in national population growth.

IV

In the course of our national history the frictions of rapid population growth have shifted across the nation as each section has in turn experienced great economic development. At present, and for at least several decades into the future, the opportunities afforded by rapid growth of the West Coast, the Gulf area, and the Great Lakes area, will be accompanied by the same deleterious consequences as the nation as a whole. Moreover, the areas of greatest growth will also be the areas of greatest in-migration. Many social and personal problems will be most acute in areas subject to heavy in-migration, because such change of residence means not only adjustment to life in a new area but often adjustment from a rural to an urban pattern of living as well.

Needless to say the great differentials in past and prospective population growth and the great inequalities in internal migratory flows point to im-

[6] W. S. Woytinsky and E. S. Woytinsky, *World Population and Production* (New York: Twentieth Century Fund, 1953), p. 51.

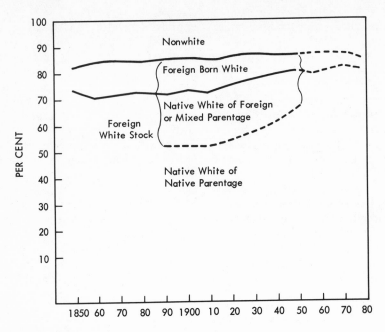

FIG. 7. Population of the United States by race and nativity, 1850 to 1950, and projected to 1980. *Source:* U.S. Bureau of the Census.

portant differences in problems in the various parts of the United States (Fig. 8). The frictions of explosive growth will of course be most acute in the more rapidly expansive areas. On the other hand, the regions of the nation which are experiencing relatively little population increase or even some decline may in this, their period of demographic maturity, have the opportunity to consolidate earlier gains and to concentrate on the qualitative rather than the quantitative aspects of living.

V

In the long run, present rates of population increase in the United States confront the same limit of space as those in prospect for the world as a whole. For the United States, with approximately the same population density as that of the world (fifty-six persons per square mile as compared with fifty-two for the world) and with

about the same rate of increase (1.7 to 1.8 per cent per year), is faced with the same outlook of a density of one person per square foot of land surface in less than 200 years. Such a period is only twice as long as that which has elapsed since the landing at Plymouth Rock.

Because of the limited human life span, it is difficult for the average person to become concerned about potential problems several centuries in the future even though in the perspective of human evolution they are almost upon us. It is impossible, however, to avoid facing the consequences of the present rate of growth of the United States to the year 2050—a date less than a century away—a date many persons now alive are destined to reach.

The continuation of our present birth rate could, by 2050, produce a population of over 1,000,000,000 (Fig. 9)!

What impact would a population of

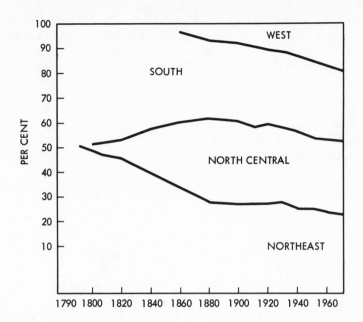

FIG. 8. Population of the United States by regions, 1790 to 1960, and projected to 1970. *Source:* U.S. Bureau of the Census.

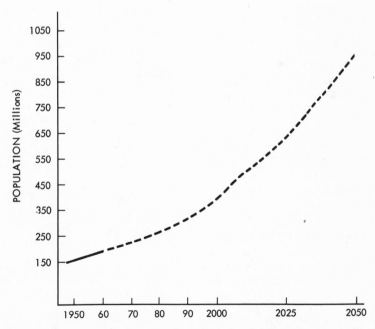

FIG. 9. Population of the United States, 1950 and 1960, and projected to 2050, assuming continuation of postwar birth rate. *Source:* U.S. Bureau of the Census.

the united states population explosion: consequences and implications **139**

1,000,000,000 have on the United States? To begin with, such a population, if ever attained, would greatly accelerate the dependence of the United States upon the rest of the world as a deficit nation in respect to many essential raw materials. Prior to 1940, the United States was a surplus nation, producing more raw materials than it consumed. During the forties this position changed.[7] At the beginning of the century the United States produced some 15 per cent more raw materials than it consumed (except for food). By the middle of the century, however, this nation was consuming about 10 per cent more raw materials than it produced. In 1952, the President's Materials Policy Commission pointed to thirty-three separate minerals on the "critical" list at that time. Nor can the United States indefinitely depend on the rest of the world for its mineral needs at present and increasing rates of consumption. Explosive population growth in this country and in the world as a whole would have profound effects upon the utilization of natural resources. Denudation of nonrenewable resources and greatly increased costs for renewable materials could seriously lower levels of living.

In respect to food supply, the United States is not likely to be in a bad way during the second half of the century, even with a population of 1,000,000,-000. But the ratio of population to acreage under cultivation would be greatly decreased. From a level of 2.1 cultivated acres per capita in 1950, a population of 1,000,000,000 would produce a mere 0.35 of a cultivated acre per capita by 2050—a ratio below that

in contemporary China.[8] In 1950 there were 509,000,000 acres under cultivation. Despite probable rises in production costs, heavy population pressure might expand this to include all the land available for crops. But the days of huge United States agricultural surpluses will have passed. A population increase of this magnitude, however, is not likely to be universally acclaimed as the most desirable solution to our problem of agricultural surplus.

After reviewing our potential consumption in relation to supply for a number of raw materials, Ordway, in disagreeing with the relatively optimistic conclusions of the President's Materials Policy Commission, develops a theory of "the limit of growth."[9] The theory is based on two premises: (1) levels of human living are constantly rising with mounting use of natural resources, and (2) despite technological progress we are spending each year more resource capital than is created. The theory maintains: "If this cycle continues long enough, basic resources will come into such short supply that rising cost will make their use for additional production unprofitable, industrial expansion will cease, and we shall have reached the limit of growth."

It is not possible to fix the precise date for such an eventuality as Ordway describes. It is clear, however, that with a population of 1,000,000,000 such a situation, if not already reached by this nation, would not be far in the future.

In the short run, then, explosive population growth contributes to economic growth and to continued pros-

[7] Samuel H. Ordway, Jr., "Possible Limits of Raw Material Consumption," in William L. Thomas, Jr., *Man's Role in Changing the Face of the Earth* (Chicago: University of Chicago Press, 1956).

[8] Chauncy D. Harris, "Agricultural Production in the United States: The Past Fifty Years and the Next," *The Geographical Review*, 47 (1957), 175-193; J. Frederick Dewhurst, *et al.*, *America's Needs and Resources, A New Survey* (New York: Twentieth Century Fund, 1955), Chap. 22.

[9] Ordway, *op. cit.*, pp. 990-992.

perity. In the longer run, however, it will become clear that these gains may have been achieved at the expense of levels of living of future generations, even in a country as fabulously wealthy and rich in resources as the United States of America.

The Triple Revolution

AD HOC COMMITTEE ON THE TRIPLE REVOLUTION

This statement is written in the recognition that mankind is at a historic conjuncture which demands a fundamental re-examination of existing values and institutions. At this time three separate and mutually reinforcing revolutions are taking place:

The Cybernation Revolution. A new era of production has begun. Its principles of organization are as different from those of the industrial era as those of the industrial era were different from the agricultural. The cybernation revolution has been brought about by the combination of the computer and the automated self-regulating machine. This results in a system of almost unlimited productive capacity which requires progressively less human labor. Cybernation is already re-

organizing the economic and social system to meet its own needs.

The Weaponry Revolution. New forms of weaponry have been developed which cannot win wars but which can obliterate civilization. We are recognizing only now that the great weapons have eliminated war as a method for resolving international conflicts. The ever-present threat of total destruction is tempered by the knowledge of the final futility of war. The need of a "warless world" is generally recognized, though achieving it will be a long and frustrating process.

The Human Rights Revolution. A universal demand for full human rights is now clearly evident. It continues to be demonstrated in the civil rights movement within the United States. But this is only the local manifestation of a worldwide movement toward the establishment of social and political regimes in which every individual will feel valued and none will feel rejected on account of his race.

We are particularly concerned in this statement with the first of these revolutionary phenomena. This is not because we underestimate the significance of the other two. On the contrary, we affirm that it is the simultaneous occurrence and interaction of all three developments which make evident the necessity for radical alterations in attitude and policy. The adop-

The Triple Revolution (March, 1964), by the Ad Hoc Committee on the Triple Revolution: Donald G. Agger, Dr. Donald B. Armstrong, James Boggs, Dr. Louis Fein, W. H. Ferry, Erich Fromm, Maxwell Geismar, Todd Gitlin, Philip Green, Roger Hagan, Michael Harrington, Tom Hayden, Robert L. Heilbroner, Ralph L. Helstein, Dr. Frances W. Herring, Brig. Gen. Hugh B. Hester, Alice Mary Hilton, Irving Howe, Everett C. Hughes, H. Stuart Hughes, Gerald W. Johnson, Irving F. Laucks, Ron M. Linton, Dwight Macdonald, Stewart Meacham, A. J. Muste, Gunnar Myrdal, Linus Pauling, Gerald Piel, Michael D. Reagan, Bayard Rustin, Ben B. Seligman, Carl F. Stover, Robert Theobald, Norman Thomas, John William Ward, and William Worthy. Reprinted by permission of the Ad Hoc Committee.

tion of just policies for coping with cybernation and for extending rights to all Americans is indispensable to the creation of an atmosphere in the United States in which the supreme issue, peace, can be reasonably debated and resolved.

The Negro claims, as a matter of simple justice, his full share in America's economic and social life. He sees adequate employment opportunities as a chief means of attaining this goal: The March on Washington demanded freedom and jobs. The Negro's claim to a job is not being met. Negroes are the hardest-hit of the many groups being exiled from the economy by cybernation. Negro unemployment rates cannot be expected to drop substantially. Promises of jobs are a cruel and dangerous hoax on hundreds of thousands of Negroes and whites alike who are especially vulnerable to cybernation because of age or inadequate education.

The demand of the civil rights movement cannot be fulfilled within the present context of society. The Negro is trying to enter a social community and a tradition of work-and-income which are in the process of vanishing even for the hitherto privileged white worker. Jobs are disappearing under the impact of highly efficient, progressively less costly machines.

The United States operates on the thesis, set out in the Employment Act of 1964, that every person will be able to obtain a job if he wishes to do so and that this job will provide him with resources adequate to live and maintain a family decently. Thus jobholding is the general mechanism through which economic resources are distributed. Those without work have access only to a minimal income, hardly sufficient to provide the necessities of life, and enabling those receiving it to function as only "minimum consumers." As a re-

sult, the goods and services which are needed by these crippled consumers, and which they would buy if they could, are not produced. This in turn deprives other workers of jobs, thus reducing their incomes and consumption.

Present excessive levels of unemployment would be multiplied several times if military and space expenditures did not continue to absorb 10 per cent of the gross national product (i.e., the total goods and services produced). Some 6,000,000 to 8,000,000 people are employed as a direct result of purchases for space and military activities. At least an equal number hold their jobs as an indirect result of military or space expenditures. In recent years, the military and space budgets have absorbed a rising proportion of national production and formed a strong support for the economy.

However, these expenditures are coming in for more and more criticism, at least partially in recognition of the fact that nuclear weapons have eliminated war as an acceptable method for resolving international conflicts. Early in 1964 President Johnson ordered a curtailment of certain military expenditures. Defense Secretary [Robert S.] McNamara is closing shipyards, airfields, and Army bases, and Congress is pressing the National [Aeronautics and] Space Administration to economize. The future of these strong props to the economy is not as clear today as it was even a year ago.

How the Cybernation Revolution Shapes Up

Cybernation is manifesting the characteristics of a revolution in production. These include the development of radically different techniques and the subsequent appearance of novel principles of the organization of production; a basic reordering of man's relationship to his environment; and a dramatic increase in total available and potential energy.

The major difference between the agricultural, industrial, and cybernation revolutions is the speed at which they developed. The agricultural revolution began several thousand years ago in the Middle East. Centuries passed in the shift from a subsistence base of hunting and food gathering to settled agriculture.

In contrast, it has been less than 200 years since the emergence of the Industrial Revolution, and direct and accurate knowledge of the new productive techniques has reached most of mankind. This swift dissemination of information is generally held to be the main factor leading to widespread industrialization.

While the major aspects of the cybernation revolution are for the moment restricted to the United States, its effects are observable almost at once throughout the industrial world and large parts of the nonindustrial world. Observation is rapidly followed by analysis and criticism. The problems posed by the cybernation revolution are part of a new era in the history of all mankind, but they are first being faced by the people of the United States. The way Americans cope with cybernation will influence the course of this phenomenon everywhere. This country is the stage on which the machines-and-man drama will first be played for the world to witness.

The fundamental problem posed by the cybernation revolution in the United States is that it invalidates the general mechanism so far employed to undergird people's rights as consumers. Up to this time economic resources have been distributed on the basis of contributions to production, with machines and men competing for employment on somewhat equal terms. In the developing cybernated system, potentially unlimited output can be achieved by systems of machines which will require little cooperation from human beings. As machines take over production from men, they absorb an increasing proportion of resources, while the men who are displaced become dependent on minimal and unrelated government measures—unemployment insurance, social security, welfare payments.

These measures are less and less able to disguise a historic paradox: That a substantial proportion of the population is subsisting on minimal incomes, often below the poverty line, at a time when sufficient productive potential is available to supply the needs of everyone in the United States.

Industrial System Fails to Provide for Abolition of Poverty

The existence of this paradox is denied or ignored by conventional economic analysis. The general economic approach argues that potential demand, which if filled would raise the number of jobs and provide incomes to those holding them, is underestimated. Most contemporary economic analysis states that all of the available labor force and industrial capacity is required to meet the needs of consumers and industry and to provide adequate public services: schools, parks, roads, homes, decent cities, and clean water and air. It is further argued that demand could be increased, by a variety of standard techniques, to any desired extent by providing money and machines to improve the conditions of the billions of impoverished people elsewhere in the world, who need food and shelter, clothes and machinery, and everything else the industrial nations take for granted.

There is no question that cybernation does increase the potential for the provision of funds to neglected public sectors. Nor is there any question that cybernation would make possible the abolition of poverty at home and abroad. But the industrial system does not possess any adequate mechanisms to permit these potentials to become realities. The industrial system was designed to produce an ever-increasing quantity of goods as efficiently as possible, and it was assumed that the distribution of the power to purchase these goods would occur almost automatically. The continuance of the income-through-jobs link as the only major mechanism for distributing effective demand—for granting the right to consume—now acts as the main brake on the almost unlimited capacity of a cybernated productive system.

Recent administrations have proposed measures aimed at achieving a better distribution of resources, and at reducing unemployment and underemployment. A few of these proposals have been enacted. More often they have failed to secure congressional support. In every case, many members of Congress have criticized the proposed measures as departing from traditional principles for the allocation of resources and the encouragement of production. Abetted by budget-balancing economists and interest groups they have argued for the maintenance of an economic machine based on ideas of scarcity to deal with the facts of abundance produced by cybernation. This time-consuming criticism has slowed the workings of Congress and has thrown out of focus for that body the interrelated effects of the triple revolution.

An adequate distribution of the potential abundance of goods and services will be achieved only when it is understood that the major economic problem is not how to increase production

but how to distribute the abundance that is the great potential of cybernation. There is an urgent need for a fundamental change in the mechanisms employed to insure consumer rights.

Facts and Figures
of the Cybernation Revolution

No responsible observer would attempt to describe the exact pace or the full sweep of a phenomenon that is developing with the speed of cybernation. Some aspects of this revolution, however, are already clear:

The rate of productivity increase has risen with the onset of cybernation.

An industrial economic system postulated on scarcity has been unable to distribute the abundant goods and services produced by a cybernated system or potential in it.

Surplus capacity and unemployment have thus coexisted at excessive levels over the last six years.

The underlying cause of excessive unemployment is the fact that the capability of machines is rising more rapidly than the capacity of many human beings to keep pace.

A permanent impoverished and jobless class is established in the midst of potential abundance.

Evidence for these statements follows:

1. The increased efficiency of machine systems is shown in the more rapid increase in productivity per man hour since 1960, a year that marks the first visible upsurge of the cybernation revolution. In 1961, 1962, and 1963, productivity per man hour rose at an average pace above 3.5 per cent—a rate well above both the historical average and the postwar rate.

Companies are finding cybernation more and more attractive. Even at the present early stage of cybernation, costs have already been lowered to a point where the price of a durable machine may be as little as one-third of the current annual wage cost of the worker it replaces. A more rapid rise in the rate of productivity increase per man hour can be expected from now on.

2. In recent years it has proved impossible to increase demand fast enough to bring about the full use of either men or plant capacities. The task of developing sufficient additional demand promises to become more difficult each year. A $30,000,000,000 annual increase in gross national product is now required to prevent unemployment rates from rising. An additional $40,000,000,000 to $60,000,000,000 increase would be required to bring unemployment rates down to an acceptable level.

3. The official rate of unemployment has remained at or above 5.5 per cent during the sixties. The unemployment rate for teen-agers has been rising steadily and now stands around 15 per cent. The unemployment rate for Negro teen-agers stands about 30 per cent. The unemployment rate for teen-agers in minority ghettoes sometimes exceeds 50 per cent. Unemployment rates for Negroes are regularly more than twice those for whites, whatever their occupation, educational level, age, or sex. The unemployment position for other racial minorities is similarly unfavorable. Unemployment rates in depressed areas often exceed 50 per cent.

Unemployment Is Far Worse than Figures Indicate

These official figures seriously underestimate the true extent of unemployment. The statistics take no notice of underemployment or featherbedding. Besides the 5.5 per cent of the labor force who are officially designated as unemployed, nearly 4 per cent of the labor force sought full-time work in 1962 but could find only part-time jobs. In addition, methods of calculating unemployment rates —a person is counted as unemployed only if he has actively sought a job recently—ignore the fact that many men and women who would like to find jobs have not looked for them because they know there are no employment opportunities.

Underestimates for this reason are pervasive among groups whose unemployment rates are high—the young, the old, and racial minorities. Many people in the depressed agricultural, mining, and industrial areas, who by official definition hold jobs but who are actually grossly underemployed, would move if there were prospects of finding work elsewhere. It is reasonable to estimate that over 8,000,000 people are not working who would like to have jobs today as compared with the 4,000,000 shown in the official statistics.

Even more serious is the fact that the number of people who have voluntarily removed themselves from the labor force is not constant but increases continuously. These people have decided to stop looking for employment and seem to have accepted the fact that they will never hold jobs again. This decision is largely irreversible, in economic and also in social and psychological terms. The older worker calls himself "retired"; he cannot accept work without affecting his social security status. The worker in his prime years is forced onto relief: In most states the requirements for becoming a relief recipient bring about such fundamental alterations in an individual's situation that a reversal of the process is always difficult and often totally unfeasible. Teen-agers, especially dropouts and Negroes, are coming to realize that there is no place for them in the labor force, but at the same time they are given no realistic alternative. These people and their dependents make up a large part of the "poverty" sector of the American population.

Statistical evidence of these trends appears in the decline in the proportion of people claiming to be in the labor force—the so-called labor force participation rate. The recent apparent stabilization of the unemployment rate around 5.5 per cent is therefore misleading: It is a reflection of the discouragement and defeat of people who cannot find employment and have withdrawn from the market rather than a measure of the economy's success in creating jobs for those who want to work.

4. An efficiently functioning industrial system is assumed to provide the great majority of new jobs through the expansion of the private enterprise sector. But well over half of the new jobs created during 1957-1962 were in the public sector—predominantly in teaching. Job creation in the private sector has now almost entirely ceased except in services; of the 4,300,000 jobs created in this period, only about 200,000 were provided by private industry through its own efforts. Many authorities anticipate that the application of cybernation to certain service industries, which is only just beginning, will be particularly effective. If this is the case, no significant job creation will take place in the private sector in coming years.

5. Cybernation raises the level of the skills of the machine. Secretary of Labor [Willard] Wirtz has recently stated that the machines being produced today have, on the average, skills equivalent to a high school diploma. If a human being is to compete with such machines, therefore, he must at least possess a high school diploma. The Department of Labor estimates, however, that on the basis of present

trends, as many as 30 per cent of all students will be high school dropouts in this decade.

6. A permanently depressed class is developing in the United States. Some 38,000,000 Americans, almost one-fifth of the nation, still live in poverty. The percentage of total income received by the poorest 20 per cent of the population was 4.9 per cent in 1944 and 4.7 per cent in 1963.

Secretary Wirtz recently summarized these trends:

The confluence of surging population and driving technology is splitting the American labor force into tens of millions of "have's" and millions of "have-nots." In our economy of 69,000,000 jobs, those with wanted skills enjoy opportunity and earning power. But the others face a new and stark problem—exclusion on a permanent basis, both as producers and consumers, from economic life. This division of people threatens to create a human slag heap. We cannot tolerate the development of a separate nation of the poor, the unskilled, the jobless, living within another nation of the well-off, the trained, and the employed.

New Consensus Needed

The stubbornness and novelty of the situation that is conveyed by these statistics is now generally accepted. Ironically, it continues to be assumed that it is possible to devise measures which will reduce unemployment to a minimum and thus preserve the over-all viability of the present productive system. Some authorities have gone so far as to suggest that the pace of technological change should be slowed down "so as to allow the industrial productive system time to adapt."

We believe, on the contrary, that the industrial productive system is no longer viable. We assert that the only way to turn technological change to the benefit of the individual and the service of the general welfare is to accept the process and to utilize it rationally and humanely. The new science of political economy will be built on the encouragement and planned expansion of cybernation. The issues raised by cybernation are particularly amenable to intelligent policy making: Cybernation itself provides the resources and tools that are needed to insure minimum hardship during the transition process.

But major changes must be made in our attitudes and institutions in the foreseeable future. Today Americans are being swept along by three simultaneous revolutions while assuming they have them under control. In the absence of real understanding of any of these phenomena, especially of technology, we may be allowing an efficient and dehumanized community to emerge by default. Gaining control of our future requires the conscious formation of the society we wish to have. Cybernation at last forces us to answer the historic questions: What is man's role when he is not dependent upon his own activities for the material basis of his life? What should be the basis for distributing individual access to national resources? Are there other proper claims on goods and services besides a job?

Because of cybernation, society no longer needs to impose repetitive and meaningless (because unnecessary) toil upon the individual. Society can now set the citizen free to make his own choice of occupation and vocation from a wide range of activities not now fostered by our value system and our accepted modes of "work." But in the absence of such a new consensus about cybernation, the nation cannot begin to take advantage of all that it promises for human betterment.

Proposal for Action

As a first step to a new consensus it is essential to recognize that the traditional link between jobs and incomes is being broken. The economy of abundance can sustain all citizens in comfort and economic security whether or not they engage in what is commonly reckoned as work. Wealth produced by machines rather than by men is still wealth. We urge, therefore, that society, through its appropriate legal and governmental institutions, undertake an unqualified commitment to provide every individual and every family with an adequate income as a matter of right.

This undertaking we consider to be essential to the emerging economic, social, and political order in this country. We regard it as the only policy by which the quarter of the nation now dispossessed and soon to be dispossessed by lack of employment can be brought within the abundant society. The unqualified right to an income would take the place of the patchwork of welfare measures—from unemployment insurance to relief—designed to insure that no citizen or resident of the United States actually starves.

We do not pretend to visualize all of the consequences of this change in our values. It is clear, however, that the distribution of abundance in a cybernated society must be based on criteria strikingly different from those of an economic system based on scarcity. In retrospect, the establishment of the right to an income will prove to have been only the first step in the reconstruction of the value system of our society brought on by the triple revolution.

The present system encourages activities which can lead to private profit and neglects those activities which can enhance the wealth and the quality of life of our society. Consequently, national policy has hitherto been aimed far more at the welfare of the productive process than at the welfare of people. The era of cybernation can reverse this emphasis. With public policy and research concentrated on people rather than processes we believe that many creative activities and interests commonly thought of as noneconomic will absorb the time and the commitment of many of those no longer needed to produce goods and services.

Society as a whole must encourage new modes of constructive, rewarding, and ennobling activity. Principal among these are activities such as teaching and learning that relate people to people rather than people to things. Education has never been primarily conducted for profit in our society; it represents the first and most obvious activity inviting the expansion of the public sector to meet the needs of this period of transition.

We are not able to predict the long-run patterns of human activity and commitment in a nation when fewer and fewer people are involved in production of goods and services, nor are we able to forecast the over-all patterns of income distribution that will replace those of the past full employment system. However, these are not speculative and fanciful matters to be contemplated at leisure for a society that may come into existence in three or four generations. The outlines of the future press sharply into the present. The problems of joblessness, inadequate incomes, and frustrated lives confront us now; the American Negro, in his rebellion, asserts the demands— and the rights—of all the disadvantaged. The Negro's is the most insistent voice today, but behind him stand the millions of impoverished who are beginning to understand that cyberna-

tion, properly understood and used, is the road out of want and toward a decent life.

The Transition[1]

We recognize that the drastic alterations in circumstances and in our way of life ushered in by cybernation and the economy of abundance will not be completed overnight. Left to the ordinary forces of the market, such change, however, will involve physical and psychological misery and perhaps political chaos. Such misery is already clearly evident among the unemployed, among relief clients into the third generation, and more and more among the young and the old for whom society appears to hold no promise of dignified or even stable lives. We must develop programs for this transition designed to give hope to the dispossessed and those cast out by the economic system, and to provide a basis for the rallying of people to bring about those changes in political and social institutions which are essential to the age of technology.

The program here suggested is not intended to be inclusive, but rather to indicate its necessary scope. We propose:

1. A massive program to build up our educational system, designed especially with the needs of the chronically undereducated in mind. We estimate that tens of thousands of employment

[1] This view of the transitional period is not shared by all the signers. Robert Theobald and James Boggs hold the two major principles of the transitional period will be (1) that machines rather than men will take up new conventional work openings and (2) that the activity of men will be directed to new forms of "work" and "leisure." Therefore, in their opinion, the specific proposals outlined in this section are more suitable for meeting the problems of the scarcity-economic system than for advancing through the period of transition into the period of abundance.

opportunities in such areas as teaching and research and development, particularly for younger people, may be thus created. Federal programs looking to the training of an additional 100,000 teachers annually are needed.

2. Massive public works. The need is to develop and put into effect programs of public works to construct dams, reservoirs, ports, water and air pollution facilities, community recreation facilities. We estimate that for each $1,000,000,000 per year spent on public works 150,000 to 200,000 jobs would be created. Two billion dollars or more a year should be spent in this way, preferably as matching funds aimed at the relief of economically distressed or dislocated areas.

3. A massive program of low-cost housing, to be built both publicly and privately, and aimed at a rate of 700,000-1,000,000 units a year.

4. Development and financing of rapid transit systems, urban and interurban, and other programs to cope with the spreading problems of the great metropolitan centers.

5. A public power system built on the abundance of coal in distressed areas, designed for low-cost power to heavy industrial and residential sections.

6. Rehabilitation of obsolete military bases for community or educational use.

7. A major revision of our tax structure aimed at redistributing income as well as apportioning the costs of the transition period equitably. To this end an expansion of the use of excess profits tax would be important. Subsidies and tax credit plans are required to ease the human suffering involved in the transition of many industries from man power to machine power.

8. The trade unions can play an important and significant role in this period in a number of ways:

(a) Use of collective bargaining to negotiate not only for people at work, but also for those thrown out of work by technological change.

(b) Bargaining for perquisites such as housing, recreational facilities, and similar programs as they have negotiated health and welfare programs.

(c) Obtaining a voice in the investment of the unions' huge pension and welfare funds, and insisting on investment policies which have as their major criteria the social use and function of the enterprise in which the investment is made.

(d) Organization of the unemployed so that these voiceless people may once more be given a voice in their own economic destinies, and strengthening of the campaigns to organize white-collar and professional workers.

9. The use of the licensing power of government to regulate the speed and direction of cybernation to minimize hardship; and the use of minimum wage power as well as taxing powers to provide the incentives for moving as rapidly as possible toward the goals indicated by this paper.

These suggestions are in no way intended to be complete or definitively formulated. They contemplate expenditures of several billions more each year than are now being spent for socially rewarding enterprises, and a larger role for the government in the economy than it has now or has been given except in times of crisis. In our opinion, this is a time of crisis, the crisis of a triple revolution. Public philosophy for the transition must rest on the conviction that our economic, social, and political institutions exist for the use of man and that man does not exist to maintain a particular economic system. This philosophy centers on an understanding that governments are instituted among men for the purpose of making possible life, liberty, and the pursuit of happiness and that government should be a creative and positive instrument toward these ends.

Change Must Be Managed

The historic discovery of the post-World War II years is that the economic destiny of the nation can be managed. Since the debate over the Employment Act of 1946 it has been increasingly understood that the federal government bears primary responsibility for the economic and social well-being of the country. The essence of management is planning. The democratic requirement is planning by public bodies for the general welfare. Planning by private bodies such as corporations for their own welfare does not automatically result in additions to the general welfare, as the impact of cybernation on jobs has already made clear.

The hardships imposed by sudden changes in technology have been acknowledged by Congress in proposals for dealing with the long- and short-run "dislocations," in legislation for depressed and "impacted" areas, retraining of workers replaced by machines, and the like. The measures so far proposed have not been "transitional" in conception. Perhaps for this reason they have had little effect on the situations they were designed to alleviate. But the primary weakness of this legislation is not ineffectiveness but incoherence. In no way can these disconnected measures be seen as a plan for remedying deep ailments, but only, so to speak, as the superficial treatment of surface wounds.

Planning agencies should constitute the network through which pass the stated needs of the people at every level of society, gradually building into a national inventory of human requirements, arrived at by democratic debate of elected representatives.

The primary tasks of the appropriate planning institutions should be:

To collect the data necessary to appraise the effects, social and economic, of cybernation at different rates of innovation.

To recommend ways, by public and private initiative, of encouraging and stimulating cybernation.

To work toward optimal allocations of human and natural resources in meeting the requirements of society.

To develop ways to smooth the transition from a society in which the norm is full employment within an economic system based on scarcity, to one in which the norm will be either nonemployment, in the traditional sense of productive work, or employment on the great variety of socially valuable but "nonproductive" tasks made possible by an economy of abundance; to bring about the conditions in which men and women no longer needed to produce goods and services may find their way to a variety of self-fulfilling and socially useful occupations.

To work out alternatives to defense and related spending that will commend themselves to citizens, entrepreneurs, and workers as a more reasonable use of common resources.

To integrate domestic and international planning. The technological revolution has related virtually every major domestic problem to a world problem. The vast inequities between the industrialized and the underdeveloped countries cannot long be sustained.

The aim throughout will be the conscious and rational direction of economic life by planning institutions under democratic control.

In this changed framework the new planning institutions will operate at every level of government—local, regional, and federal—and will be organized to elicit democratic participation in all their proceedings. These bodies will be the means for giving direction and content to the growing demand for improvement in all departments of public life. The planning institutions will show the way to turn the growing protest against ugly cities, polluted air and water, an inadequate educational system, disappearing recreational and material resources, low levels of medical care, and the haphazard economic development into an integrated effort to raise the level of general welfare.

We are encouraged by the record of the planning institutions both of the Common Market and of several European nations and believe that this country can benefit from studying their weaknesses and strengths.

A principal result of planning will be to step up investment in the public sector. Greater investment in this area is advocated because it is overdue, because the needs in this sector comprise a substantial part of the content of the general welfare, and because they can be readily afforded by an abundant society. Given the knowledge that we are now in a period of transition it would be deceptive, in our opinion, to present such activities as likely to produce full employment. The efficiencies of cybernation should be as much sought in the public as in the private sector, and a chief focus of planning would be one means of bringing this about. A central assumption of planning institutions would be the central assumption of this statement, that the nation is moving into a society in which production of goods and services is not the only or perhaps the chief means of distributing income.

The Democratization of Change

The revolution in weaponry gives some dim promise that mankind may finally eliminate institutionalized force as the method of settling international conflict and find for it political and moral equivalents leading to a better world. The Negro revolution signals the ultimate admission of this group to the American community on equal social, political, and economic terms. The cybernation revolution proffers an existence qualitatively richer in democratic as well as material values. A social order in which men make the decisions that shape their lives becomes more possible now than ever before; the unshackling of men from the bonds of unfulfilling labor frees them to become citizens, to make themselves, and to make their own history.

But these enhanced promises by no means constitute a guarantee. Illuminating and making more possible the "democratic vistas" is one thing; reaching them is quite another; for a vision of democratic life is made real not by technological change, but by men consciously moving toward that ideal and creating institutions that will realize and nourish the vision in living form.

Democracy, as we use the term, means a community of men and women who are able to understand, express, and determine their lives as dignified human beings. Democracy can only be rooted in a political and economic order in which wealth is distributed by and for people, and used for the widest social benefit. With the emergence of the era of abundance we have the economic base for a true democracy of participation, in which men no longer need to feel themselves prisoners of social forces and decisions beyond their control or comprehension.

modernization

five

The past has seen many sweeping changes that have radically transformed the lives of substantial portions of the world's population. Epidemics and plagues have vied with man's own capacity for mischief in the form of military conquests as sources of widespread impact on the course of daily lives. Technological change until the relatively recent past may appear "revolutionary" in retrospect, but generally had a relatively gradual influence if viewed in its actual, historic context. But in the modern era technological change—in the strict sense of changes in the procedures of production (and destruction)—has been linked to ideological and organizational changes in the broad process now commonly called "modernization." The strands in this skein can be unravelled, and are not always mutually consistent: political independence and the quest for administrative efficiency in the structure of the state; improvements in health and longevity and in the material conditions of life; literacy, communication, and sharing in a partially communal world cultural pool. Modernization makes previous sweeping changes seem like relatively small and isolated events.

Again we begin our selections with a view of history, for modernization did not begin as a worldwide process. Diamond's discussion of the United States in the late nineteenth century reminds us both of the historical precedents for the current upheavals in new nations and of the relative recency of what subsequently came to be called the Industrial Revolution. (Contemporary changes in developing areas probably warrant the term more aptly than did the original models.) Diamond puts meat on the bones of social theory. He reminds us that at the heart of our abstractions there are real thinking, feeling, choosing people. The later selection by Bell and Oxall illustrates the same point: as Levy would say, it is *men* who act, not societies.

To complement the emphasis in *Social Change* on the conditions and consequences of *economic* modernization, we here present three selections that deal especially with *political* change. The paper by Bell and Oxall is partly methodological—the implications of using national states as units for comparative analysis —and partly substantive—the implications of nationalism as a major factor in the course of modernization. Both Halpern and Levy deal specifically with political structures and processes. Halpern explores the meaning and measurement of "political development," whereas Levy views the concept of modernization more broadly, but then gives particular emphasis to the "political" in a dual sense: matters of the concentration and distribution of power and matters of policy. Levy's view that "we will come increasingly to resemble one another" is disputed in *Social Change,* where some persistent differences are predicted, particularly in the allocation of political power. Part of this divergence in theoretical position derives once more from attention to different segments of social reality. Part of it is genuine, and could scarcely be settled or resolved without both greater specification of assumptions and greater information on sequential patterns than the study of modernization yet affords.

The Nation Transformed

SIGMUND DIAMOND

On May 10, 1876, a gigantic throng of more than 100,000 people—tired and hot, but eager with anticipation—swarmed into Fairmount Park, Philadelphia, in quest of the excitement that only a World's Fair can offer. Fifteen bitter years had passed since the guns had boomed across the harbor at Charleston, South Carolina; and though peace had brought relief and gratitude, a nation still distracted and tormented by the problems of Reconstruction and caught fast in the grip of a relentless depression had had little cause for enthusiastic celebration. But on the morning of May 10, the season of celebration began. The great Centennial Exposition was being opened by the President of the United States; and in honoring those whose efforts had forged national unity in 1776, Americans of 1876 found at last what had so long eluded them—that pride in an accomplishment to which all had contributed might provide the basis for a new-found unity and hope. What at the beginning had been an untried form of government, a republic, had survived a century of the cruelest buffeting, of international wars and civil

Sigmund Diamond, ed., *The Nation Transformed* (New York: George Braziller, Inc., 1963), pp. 3-32. © by George Braziller, Inc. Reprinted with the permission of the publisher.

wars—and still it stood. It was reason enough for gratitude and for celebration.

But there were still other reasons, less weighty but perhaps even closer to the hearts and minds of the thousands who made their way to the exhibition hall that dwarfed the best that the expositions of Paris and Dresden had offered and that shamed even Queen Victoria's Crystal Palace. They came to gawk at the celebrities—at President Grant; at Dom Pedro, the Emperor of Brazil; at the ambassadors from the royal courts of exotic China and Austria-Hungary; and at the Tsar of all the Russias. They came to hear the President speak of "the specimens of their skill" that had been sent by "the enlightened agricultural, commercial, and manufacturing people of the world. . . ." Above all, they came to see the wonders that they and others had created. There were the exotic products of far-off places—porcelains and tapestries from France, teak and ivory from Siam, sables from Russia, delicate china from Bavaria, Japanese toys which seemed, to American eyes, only slightly more dainty than Japanese people. There were the innocent products that lent delight—miniature music boxes; a pretty black marble fountain "which sent up a constant jet of cologne water, where the tired visitor might enjoy the delightful privilege of bathing his forehead with the refreshing liquid"; the newest thing in automatic soda fountains, the Minnehaha, made of Tennessee and Italian marble and decorated with bronze dolphins and silver crowns and a lion's head from which the bubbly liquid flowed. There were the less innocent products —Gatling guns and Dahlgren torpedoes and Krupp cannon. Above all, there were the miraculous inventions that were changing the world—steel bridges, giant locomotives, and that amazing source of power, the Corliss steam engine whose 1,500 horses provided all the power needed for the Exposition.

Painting, music, and sculpture were pushed off into the wings; technology and industry held the center of the stage. "The farmer saw new machines, seeds, and processes," the official handbook of the centennial concluded; "the mechanic, ingenious inventions and tools, and products of the finest workmanship . . . the man of science, the wonders of nature and the results of the investigation of the best brains of all lands. Thus each returned to his own home with a store of information available in his own special trade or profession." There were some, a few, who wondered at the absence of exhibits of some characteristics of American life. When puzzled Columbia asked what she should display, James Russell Lowell's Brother Jonathan answered tartly:

Show 'em your Civil Service, and explain
How all men's loss is everybody's gain;
Show your new patents to increase your rents
By paying quarters for collecting cents;
Show your short cut to cure financial ills
By making paper-collars current bills;
Show your new bleaching process, cheap and brief,

To wit: a jury chosen by the thief;
Show your State Legislatures; show your Rings;
And challenge Europe to produce such things
As high officials sitting half in sight
To share the plunder and to fix things right;
If that don't fetch her, why, you only need
To show your latest style in martyrs— Tweed. . . .[1]

And there were even those who raised portentous questions about the nature of a society which could produce such an exposition. Eugene Pottier, author of *The Internationale*, living in exile in the United States, caught a glimpse of a dark and bloody future in the midst of the gaiety:

. . . Let us get to the bottom of things.
Industry, is this, then, the spectacle for which you propose
    That we judge you?
You clothe yourself in striking colors;
But we who know bloody rags,
    We will exhibit them.
Yes, we will exhibit the hollow bellies of the masses,
Their wan poverty full of dark threats
    To stability,
The poorest bowed down under the heaviest taxes,
In your topsy-turvy world revolving about the false axis
    Of Property.
Exhibit your pride. These brick Bastilles,
Powerful prisons that you call factories,
    And which we must tear down,
And the sad slaves, sealed in their cells,
Not knowing the sun and the clean country air,
Do you want to exhibit them? . . .[2]

---

[1] James Russell Lowell, "The World's Fair, 1876," *The Nation*, **21** (August 5, 1875), 82.
[2] Translated from "The Workingmen of America to the Workingmen of France," in Eugene Pottier, *Chants révolutionnaires* (Paris: 1937), pp. 205-214.

But this was still the New World, for all that the country was a century old, and most Americans were more likely to see promises than problems. For them, it was Walt Whitman who saw in the exposition the true vision of things to come.

Away with old romance!
Away with novels, plots and plays of
    foreign courts,
Away with love verses sugar'd in rhyme,
    the intrigues, amours of idlers. . . .
I raise a voice for far superber things for
    poets and for art,
To exalt the present and the real,
To teach the average man the glory of
    his daily walk and trade,
To sing in song how exercise and chemi-
    cal life are never to be baffled,
To manual work for each and all, to
    plough, hoe, dig,
To plant and tend the tree, the berry,
    vegetables, flowers,
For every man to see to it that he really
    do something, for every woman too;
To use the hammer and the saw (rip, or
    cross-cut,)
To cultivate a turn for carpentering,
    plastering, painting,
To work as tailor, tailoress, nurse, hostler,
    porter,
To invent a little, something ingenious,
    to aid the washing, cooking, cleaning,
And hold it no disgrace to take a hand at
    them themselves. . . .[3]

The American people were engaged in a great task of construction. "Mightier than Egypt's tombs . . . fairer than Roma's temples," they planned to raise a "great cathedral sacred industry, no tomb,/A keep for life for practical invention." And in the excitement of the task there was little concern for still unsolved problems of the previous half century and but dim anticipation of the new problems their own enterprise would create.

[3] [This and the following are from] "Song of the Exposition," in *The Complete Writings of Walt Whitman* (New York: G. P. Putnam's Sons, 1902), I, 238-250.

II

One day while floating along on the river, Huck Finn's raft encountered a steamboat. "She was a big one, and she was coming in a hurry, too. . . . All of a sudden she bulged out, big and scary, with a long row of wide-open furnace doors shining like red-hot teeth. . . ." For the American people, the encounter with the last third of the nineteenth century must have been like Huck's with the steamboat; strange, new forces were loose that threatened to run over the old, familiar, but flimsy shelters. A new society—an industrial society—was being created, and its creation involved the uprooting and transplanting of millions of people, the raising of new groups to power and the decline of the once-powerful, the learning of new routines and habits and disciplines, the sloughing off of old ideas. Nothing was left untouched—the state itself in its relation to citizens, the churches, the family; all were altered because the circumstances of life itself were being altered.

Behind these changes—beneficent to some, cataclysmic to others—lay a new method of production, based on factory and machine, with an increasingly refined technology that made use of ever-increasing supplies of capital and specialized labor. Regional differences remained, though with the passage of time these tended to be more important to local-colorist writers, exploiting a nostalgia for the past, than to men of affairs, for whom it was the present reality of a great national market, welded together by a network of railroads and communications, that was to be exploited. And while the face of the land was itself being made over, so, too, were the millions of men and women from rural America and from Europe, who, pouring into the new industrial centers of the nation, were subjected to the new discipline of factory labor. With startling speed, a nation of farmers and small-town merchants began to learn, if not wholly to master, the techniques of an industrial society.

During the two decades after 1870, industrial growth in the United States reached a pace the world had not yet seen. In 1870, mining and manufacturing contributed only 14 per cent to the national income; farming, 20 per cent. By the end of the century, the contribution of farming—reduced now to 16 per cent—was matched by that of finance, while the contribution of mining and manufacturing rose to 21 per cent. In that year, the world's largest producer of food and raw materials had become as well the world's largest manufacturer. Total population, benefiting from both a high birth rate and immigration, rose rapidly, from 40,000,-000 in 1870 to 76,000,000 in 1900, but the increase was not evenly distributed throughout the country; some occupations and some sections grew more rapidly than others. Just under 60 per cent of the American labor force worked on farms in 1860, but only 37 per cent in 1900; only 26 per cent worked in industry and transportation in 1860, but 46 per cent did so in 1900. If the small New England town and Middle Western river entrepot were characteristic of an earlier landscape, they were being roughly shouldered aside toward the end of the century by mill towns, steel towns, coal towns that sprang up it seemed almost everywhere.

Most spectacular of course was the growth of the great city, that most characteristic institution of an industrial society. In 1860, one-sixth of the American people lived in urban areas; in 1900, one-third. During that stretch of four decades, the population of the great cities grew more than twice as fast as that of the country as a whole.

By the end of the century New York, Chicago, and Philadelphia were all booming metropolises, each with well over 1,000,000 people. Rural Massachusetts, having pretty much disappeared from the census returns, was to be found mainly in the poems of John Greenleaf Whittier; as early as 1890, four out of every five persons in that state were town dwellers.

Nor was the landscape of the mind unaffected. When once sturdy farmers had become rural hicks, when slick traders had become captains of industry, when the hub of affairs had shifted from countinghouse to banking house, standards which had once been settled became problematic. To swim with the new tide of affairs meant to choose a new career and a new place to live, to learn new skills and new ideas. And even those who fought to preserve the old had to contend with the forces that threatened to make their world obsolete. Whether one tried to swim with the tide or hold it back or change its course made little difference. It provided the environment in which life was lived and, sometimes subtly, sometimes ruthlessly, forced men to alter the ways in which they worked and thought.

Behind these changes lay a revolution that began in transportation and communication and spread quickly to the processes of production and distribution. Railroads had long since surpassed canals in importance, but their own expansion had been slowed by the Civil War. Between 1870, however, and 1893, when the depression again slowed the momentum of development, the mileage of railroads increased from 30,000 to 170,000; by 1900, it rose to 193,000. As early as 1887, nearly 33,000 towns were served by the railroad network. It was the hope that the development of cheap transportation would permit them to reach out to distant markets that spurred the merchants of Boston, Baltimore, New York, Philadelphia, and dozens of inland towns to mobilize the capital and skills necessary to lay down the railroad network. Sometimes these hopes proved illusory, sometimes realistic, but in any case the development of the railroad was the major economic stimulus of the post-Civil War period.

First of all, railroad construction itself provided a direct stimulus to industrial production. With a labor force that mushroomed to 200,000 by the 1880's, the railroads were an enormous market for the products of stone quarries, lumber mills, and iron factories and for the excess capital of domestic and, especially, foreign investors. Most important of course was the effect on the basic iron and steel industry. In 1874, Sir Lowthian Bell, a Middlesborough ironmaster, maintained that iron would never be produced more cheaply in the United States than in Britain because of the high cost of labor and of transporting iron ore to coal.[4] Even as he spoke his forecast was being disproved. By linking the sections of the country with each other, the railroad made it possible to bring together more efficiently and cheaply the elements of industrial production. The railroad not only created the demand for rails, locomotives, rolling stock, and bridges, but it provided the conditions for satisfying the demand— a fast, cheap, certain method for bringing iron ore to coal.

By 1875, railroads consumed more than half the iron produced in the United States, and their insatiable demands were producing far-reaching technological changes within the industry. Rolling mills and blast furnaces, using coke, could turn out iron at ten times the pace of the old charcoal-fueled ovens. No longer did scarce supplies of expensive charcoal provide a limiting factor on the size of the furnace; fed on unlimited supplies of cheap coal from western Pennsylvania and stimulated by the appetite of the railroads, the size of the furnaces increased steadily. Blast furnaces which before the Civil War were producing at an average daily rate of forty tons were producing a daily average of more than 400 tons at the turn of the century. Not even the great depression of the 1870's could markedly delay the rapid growth of the steel industry. Steel production rose from 140,000 tons in 1873, to 500,000 in 1877, to 2,500,000 in 1886. By the end of the century, only twenty-five years after Sir Lowthian Bell had made his gloomy forecast of the prospects of the American steel industry, the Carnegie Steel Company alone was turning out about four-fifths as much steel as the entire British industry.

But the railroad stimulated the economy in yet another way, by creating the great national market that made mass production possible. Local producers who had dominated regional markets now faced the competition of products manufactured in distant factories and hauled to every section of the country by the railroad. The growth in size of markets encouraged businessmen to produce in larger quantities to take advantage of lower costs and to experiment in the development of low-cost mass-production methods. Andrew Carnegie's lieutenant, Charles M. Schwab, reported that Carnegie once tore down and rebuilt a new steel mill because they had learned, during its construction, how to save one dollar per ton rather than the fifty cents on the output of the first design. Spurred on to reduce costs to lower and lower levels so as to capture wider markets,

[4] Frank Thistlethwaite, *The Great Experiment* (New York: Cambridge University Press, 1955), pp. 210-211.

the steel industry brought down the price of steel rails from $160 per ton in 1875 to seventeen dollars in 1898. Other industries felt the impact of the same forces. Textile manufacturing, meat packing, canning, and flour milling, for example, had long passed the pioneering stage of mass production when it was introduced into the automobile industry so dramatically by Henry Ford in 1914.

The rapid development of American industry depended not only upon changes in technology—as in the case of mass production—but also upon changes in organization. Standardization of parts, long practiced in the Connecticut gun industry, spread to other industries—sewing machines and clocks, for example—and eventually into the standardization of the final assembly of products. Nor was the drive for rationalization confined to the workshop. Office, accounting department, and sales division were subjected to increasingly rigorous supervision in an attempt to cut costs by providing standardized methods of procedure. Organization—as well as land, labor, and capital—was seen to be a variable influencing the level of costs and productivity, and fundamental changes were made in traditional modes of assigning tasks in shop and office, supervising the activities of the work force, determining the proper relation of supervisory to production personnel, and determining the locus of authority within the business enterprise. In these circumstances, when new products and new processes were being introduced of a complexity never before encountered, the nature of work itself changed.

There was room for the handyman in the village, but not in the factory. When production depended increasingly upon the performance of specified, even measured, tasks, the Jack-of-all-trades had to yield to the specialist. And specialization was not a characteristic of a specific industry, a specific region, a specific trade. What Professor Thomas C. Cochran has called the "general entrepreneur" of the pre-Civil War period—the man who shifted his interests easily between foreign trade, wholesaling, banking, and real estate, for example—made way for the man whose career was confined to a particular industry. Specialist workmen replaced general artisans; specialist retailers replaced the general store; the investment banking houses that specialized in the flotation of stocks and bonds were different from the bankers who gave short-term credit to business. Undirected and unplanned, a farflung network of connections developed between individuals and groups whose relationships depended not on personal choice or face-to-face contact but on the particular position each occupied in the processes of production and exchange. For some, power and influence were the results; for others, apparent impotence; but so tightly woven were the relationships that few could act without affecting the lives of countless nameless others.

The problems of adjustment would have been great even if the rate of industrial progress had been steady and continuous. The fact is, however, that it was sporadic, and the combination of discontinuity in development and complexity in organization made for an increasingly unstable economy whose alternating cycles of expansion and contraction brought bewildering uncertainty. To compete successfully for markets required the application of the latest techniques of science and technology to reduce costs to competitive levels. The very costs of modernization were so great, however, that only when factories operated at or near capacity could economies of production be achieved. But to operate at that level would cause prices to fall. Every glimmer of hope for potential new markets —the establishment of a new railroad line, a new wave of immigration, the opening of new territory, the enactment of a new tariff—was desperately grasped and was followed by a frenzy of expansion, only to be followed in turn by idle plant and equipment when the markets had been saturated.

For much of the last third of the century, moreover, the headlong rush to capture new markets and to drive out competitors from old took place in an atmosphere of benign indifference to many of the methods of businessmen. Ebulliently optimistic, Americans of all ranks poured their money into ventures to build great cities where there were yet no people, to construct railroads where there were no passengers and no freight, to promote new enterprises that, at least on paper, promised to dwarf existing firms. Often it was the prospect of immediate profit from the promotion of these enterprises, not profit from the conduct of a business, that led to their creation. Often, too, insiders operating in the absence of law or in bland indifference to the law milked the treasuries and manipulated the stocks of their companies to line their own pockets. And in so doing they frequently had the acquiescence, sometimes tacit, sometimes active, of legislatures and courts at every level of government.

So powerful, indeed, had business become, so increasingly tenacious its hold on the imagination, so visible the activities of its more flamboyant practitioners, that in the period after the Civil War the businessman stepped out into the limelight as one of the prime makers of his age. The great fortunes of an earlier day—the wealth of a Girard, a Lorillard, even of the first John Jacob Astor—seemed puny compared to the new fortunes of the Fields, the Armours, the Pillsburys. What had there ever been to compare with the Vanderbilts, the Rockefellers, or with Andrew Carnegie's annual income of $25,000,000? Some, to be sure, like Rockefeller, shunned notoriety, though not even he could escape the headline of the Hepburn Committee and other investigators of monopoly. Others courted it, like George Vanderbilt, whose estate in Asheville, North Carolina, cost more than the congressional appropriation for the Department of Agriculture. In any case, whether they were held out as models to be emulated or examples to be scorned, how could they be ignored? They sat at the center of the web of influence which penetrated into every section of the country. Their decisions helped shape the environment in which all had to live and, increasingly, that environment began to rub hard against large numbers of people.

How would the American people react to that environment? What groups would emerge to new importance as a result of the strategic position they now occupied in an industrial society, and which would find only a slippery handhold? How would the first gain consciousness of their new-found importance and how would the others respond to their impotence? Would concentration of economic power be compatible with the traditional dispersion of political power? Could immigrants of all degrees of ethnic and social diversity accept the imposed discipline of industrial labor and the self-discipline of democratic society? Would life be enlarged in an industrial society—would there be a new and generous vision of what was humanly possible—or would life narrow down to a struggle to escape uncertainty? Conceivably the questions might not be answered; they could not be ignored.

Perhaps the most important lesson that was being learned as the century drew to a close was the recognition that the answers to these questions escaped individual solutions. Only as individuals formed organizations and hammered out joint programs could they attempt to impose their wills and mold the social environment to their own choosing. The first to learn this lesson, because technological change had given them the initiative, were the businessmen themselves. Heavy investments in plant and equipment were necessary to meet the competition of rivals in the search for markets, but so incredibly productive was the new technology that it tended constantly to outstrip the absorptive ability of the markets. Moreover, so great was the cost of the new technology that economies of production could be achieved only when plants operated at near capacity. But this, like the ruthless competition between industrial rivals, drove down prices and threatened the security of even the most efficient. How to escape from this cruel dilemma became an overriding concern of American businessmen toward the turn of the century, and led them into a search for "order," the major outcome of which was the discovery of the importance of organization.

First of all of course came changes within the scope of activities of the single firm. So efficient had Andrew Carnegie's operations become, for example, that he was already the dominant producer in the basic iron and steel industry when, in the 1880's, he began to reach out into all branches of the industry. Through his partnership with Henry Clay Frick he had access to coal, railroads, and coking plants. He bought into Michigan iron ore land and, finally, into the great

Mesabi iron range. He built ore ships for the Great Lakes, a port at Conneaut to handle them, and a railroad to haul the ore to Pittsburgh. Even so, however, he could not free himself from the threat of combinations in the steel-consuming industries which were powerful enough to affect his prices. In 1900, he announced plans to carry combination a long step forward by entering directly into the manufacture of steel wire, tubes, and similar products himself. In the end, he was dissuaded from doing so by the offer of J. P. Morgan to buy him out for $450,000,000, and Morgan himself, once the way was cleared, proceeded to establish order in the industry through the organization of the world's first billion-dollar company, the United States Steel Corporation.

But organizational efforts to limit the effects of competition and create stability could not, in the nature of the case, be confined to the level of the single firm. The railroads pioneered in efforts to create intercompany agreements, because it was they that first experienced the chaotic results of excessive competition. Direct mergers carried out under the sponsorship of the banking houses that financed the consolidations, as well as "traffic associations" to fix rates and share traffic, were attempted. Railroads, though, for a variety of reasons were more vulnerable than other industries, and the railroad entrepreneurs were not allowed a free hand in the efforts to achieve stability. Eventually, government regulation was invoked. Still, by 1900 the vast national railroad network had been so shaken down that only six large systems controlled 95 per cent of the mileage. Other industries followed the same path.

As early as the 1870's, "pools" were organized to divide territorial markets, fix production quotas, and set prices, but these "gentlemen's agreements"—generally organized in the black despair of the bottom of a business depression—could not withstand the tendency of their own members to violate the rules during the corrosive optimism of a business upturn which gave promise of new killings to be made. John D. Rockefeller's Standard Oil Company provided the first spectacular example of a more effective form of industrial organization—the trust. The shareholders of a number of competing firms turned over their voting stock to "trustees" in return for nonvoting, interest-bearing certificates; in this way, general pricing and marketing policies could be established for all the companies in the trust. But the trust, too, proved to be only an interim form of organization. Held to be in violation of the law, it was soon replaced, with the aid of complaisant state legislatures who provided the necessary enabling acts, by the holding company, a single company which held a controlling interest in several subordinate ones.

Nearly everywhere the attainment of these new forms of organization depended upon the cooperation of or was carried out under the sponsorship of the great investment bankers. No less than industrial managers were they fearful of excessive competition, and with the leverage provided by their financial assistance they insinuated their own people into corporate boards of directors and attempted to bend corporate policy toward conservative programs. The effort to do so involved corporation executives in activities their forebears knew not of. Time was when the successful businessman had only to concern himself with costs and prices; other variables could be taken for granted. But this was no longer true, and even costs and prices depended upon such factors as the program of political parties, the attitude of labor, the quality and degree of its organization, the temper of the legislature, belligerent or pacific, the state of public opinion—all of them variables over which the businessman could exercise only limited authority. Yet if he were to attain the environment needed to provide a climate of security in which to carry out his affairs, more and more had to be brought within his purview and made susceptible to his influence. Increasingly powerful, the businessman was also, by virtue of the way in which every area of the social environment bore in upon him, increasingly vulnerable as well. With greater power and greater vulnerability, small wonder that he became increasingly self-conscious.

If the process of industrialization elevated some, it depressed others. The same forces which locked industrial enterprises into a network of relations with others were working in the agricultural sector of the economy as well, reshaping the social environment and altering the position of the farmer. It had been only a few years since the passage of the Homestead Act, which both presupposed and presumably guaranteed the existence of the independent farmer. Yet the application of science to agriculture and transport and the increasing involvement of farmers in market relations undermined their traditional independence and forced even them, the most fiercely individualist of all sections of society, into experiments in new forms of social organization. The railroad, which carried the farmer into the new territories of the Great Plains, linked him to distant markets, where he could get cash for his crops, and to distant sources of supply, where he could satisfy his needs more cheaply than with household production. Whatever his degree of self-sufficiency before, he was now simply another specialist exchanging his products for those of others. Technology itself contributed to the change. With sickle and flail a man could reap only about seven and one-half acres, but with a mechanical reaper he could handle a hundred or more. Heavy steel plows, barbed wire for fencing, mechanical reapers and binders, and steam traction engines contributed to an amazing expansion of productivity. Though agriculture lost 3,500,000 workers between 1870 and 1900, efficiency rose by 86 per cent during the same period.

Yet there was a debit side to the ledger. Technological aids were indispensable for survival, but not all could afford them. By the turn of the century, it has been estimated, the cost of establishing even a modest farm was in the neighborhood of $1,000. The need for capital was becoming increasingly great, but not always was it possible to obtain. Some of the problems that bedeviled farmers—like winter blizzards and summer droughts and plagues of grasshoppers—they could not control. Nor, at least at the start, was there much that could be done to offset the social consequences of the very pattern of land settlement—the unbearable monotony and loneliness that resulted from the wide dispersion of homesteads and the absence of centers of social interaction. But some of the problems of the farmer were in the order of society, not in the order of nature; these, presumably, might be understood and solved.

The root of the problem lay in the relation of costs to prices. The farmer sold his cotton, his wheat, and his corn on a world market, and the prices he obtained—which he could do little to influence—seemed to bear little relation to his costs of production. He sold in an unprotected world market; he bought in a national market where tariffs and combinations seemed to

single him out for victimization. The railroad, which controlled transportation to distant markets, imposed steep freight rates, partly because of the high cost of shipping bulky, seasonal freight one-way without compensating return freight, partly because of its tendency to charge what the traffic would bear in the absence of competing means of transportation. For every bushel of corn the farmer shipped from Nebraska to Chicago, it took another bushel to pay the freight charges. Freight rates west of the Missouri were double those from Chicago to the East. The farmer's conviction that railroad rates were excessive seemed confirmed by the spectacle of railroad rate wars and special low rates granted to favored customers who could guarantee large shipments over long hauls. The grain elevator company, too, seemed in the business of exploiting the farmer; it charged excessive rates and downgraded the quality of his grain. The prices of machinery, manufactured by companies organized in trusts or protected by tariffs, seemed exorbitant, and so did the cost of credit.

Most farmers, lacking adequate financial resources, carried on by buying machinery on credit and by mortgaging land, crops, buildings, and equipment. This was supportable as long as prices maintained a fairly stable level, but a series of crop failures in the late 1880's and the industrial depression of 1893 ushered in a prolonged period of agricultural instability and unrest. In western Kansas alone twenty towns were depopulated, and all over the Great Plains marginal lands were abandoned and farms were consolidated. Lands which had been mortgaged fell into the hands of banks and finance companies, and former proprietors—when they did not leave the land entirely—were reduced to the ranks of tenant farmers. In 1880, when the first national census of tenancy was taken, 25 per cent of all American farms were tenant-operated; by 1900, somewhat over one-third were operated by tenants.

It was clear that for farmers, as well as businessmen, new forms of organization were needed to keep the jaws of the cost-price vise from closing. For some, escape could be found by organizing agricultural production on a vast scale—as on the great "bonanza farms" of Minnesota—so that full advantage could be taken of the economies of machine production; but few farmers had the capital necessary to buy the required land and equipment. Others might shift their production from staple crops to truck gardening or dairy farming, but this, too, required capital and technical knowledge. For the majority, escape seemed possible, as in the case of industry, only by interfarm organization, though the most appropriate form of organization and the decision as to whether economic or political action would be most effective took years to determine. The struggle of the farmers to organize and to work out their relationship to an industrial society provided some of the sharpest and most characteristic political controversies of the post-Civil War period.

The first of the great national farm movements to be organized was the Patrons of Husbandry, or the Grange, founded in 1867 by Oliver H. Kelley, a former clerk in the Department of Agriculture. Designed originally to help farmers break down the impoverished isolation of their lives and to provide social and intellectual nourishment, it was soon converted—out of the farmers' own interest in the problems that pressed most heavily upon them—into an organization that concerned itself with ameliorating the economic conditions of rural life. Cooperative enterprises came to occupy the center of their attention. Cooperative grain elevators, cooperative stores, cooperative schemes for purchasing supplies and marketing products, even cooperatives to manufacture farm machinery were organized, but these found tough sledding against the entrenched opposition of better organized, richer competitors. One factor in the farmer's cost of production proved not to be amenable to economic pressure—the railroad; and the farmers were forced, almost despite themselves, to organize politically. Working in some states through the existing political parties, in others through antimonopoly parties of their own, farmers succeeded in enacting "Granger laws" regulating railroad rates. These state acts were first held to be constitutional by the United States Supreme Court in 1876, then unconstitutional when the Court reversed itself in 1886, but the political momentum they generated led eventually to federal regulation of railroads. By the 1870's the Grange had declined in effectiveness and in popular support, but its place was taken by more militant groups—the Farmers' Alliances of the West and South—which showed that they had not forgotten the importance of organization for economic and political action.

Demanding the nationalization of railroads and telegraph lines, recovery of unused railroad land grants, graduated income tax, an end to alien ownership of land, and currency inflation through the coinage of silver, the farmers' movement—organized politically as the Populist party—made rapid progress in the South and West in the depressed economic circumstances of the early 1890's. The Populist party won striking successes in the elections of 1890 and 1892, but in 1896 the combination of an upturn in business, the capture of the party by the Democrats, and an aggressive campaign by the Republicans led to their defeat. At the end of the century, the farmers—though they had influenced the character of much state and national legislation—had not yet succeeded in attaining the program or the degree of organizational strength that permitted them to achieve the position they wanted. But they had learned that without organization their case was hopeless, they had begun to redefine themselves in relation to other groups in their society, and increasingly they began to see their plight more in terms of present realities than outworn myths.

Industrialists and farmers were not alone in having to puzzle out their relationship to a new universe of national markets and rapid technological innovations. Industrial labor, too, had to work out its mode of accommodation and, of all groups, it was perhaps the one most directly under the gun of industrial pressures.

If organization was the prerequisite of survival, industrial workers began the struggle under special handicaps. There was, first of all, the question of definition: What did it mean to be a worker and what did it portend? Clearly the semiskilled tender of a machine in a factory was a very different person from the skilled artisan who worked by and for himself, but what conception did he have of his own role and what relation did this bear to the strategy he adopted to govern his relations with others? Different conceptions suggested different strategies, each with different implications for the kind of organization that was felt to be desirable and for whether organization was felt to be desirable at all. If, for example, the sewing-machine operator, the steel puddler, the carpenter felt himself forever tied to his position, he might have responded by developing a

sense of common purpose and common destiny with others of his same rank. But where any industrial or clerical job was conceived as only a steppingstone to something higher, where, in fact, the worker was urged by both precept and example to identify himself not with his peers but with the successful in whose steps he or his children might one day stand, a powerful psychological solvent existed to destroy that self-conception which might result in unity of action with others.

There were, moreover, certain characteristics of late nineteenth-century industrial society itself which reinforced this psychology. The isolation of markets had once protected workers in one area from the competition of others in more remote areas, but the development of the transportation network brought even workers in the most distant places into competition. And when competition between trades and areas seemed to be correlated with ethnic differences, the problem of achieving organizational unity seemed almost insurmountable. Finally, that endemic feature of industrial civilization, the business cycle, served to compound the difficulties of achieving a viable organization. On the business upswing workers, like farmers, felt squeezed between relatively fixed wages and mounting living costs, and they might be moved to organize and to protest. But on the business downturn, the reverse occurred; loath to protest because of the fear of unemployment, they were reluctant to antagonize their employers and jeopardize their jobs by making new demands.

There were, then, both psychological and structural impediments to organization even had there been no opposition from employers and a clear-cut program on the part of labor itself. But of course there was employer opposition, as the widespread use of the strikebreaker, the lockout, the black-list, and industrial espionage testifies. And there was no clear-cut program on the part of labor with respect either to organizational form or long-range goals.

The earliest of the labor organizations to appear after the Civil War, the National Labor Union and the Knights of Labor, were concerned more with devising methods to escape from industrialism than with coming to grips with it. Cooperation was to be the way. The trade unions had failed, Uriah Stephens, president of the Knights maintained, because they had concerned themselves too narrowly with the problems of workingmen. It was cooperation, his successor, Terence V. Powderly, argued, that would "eventually make every man his own master—every man his own employee. . . . There is no good reason why labor cannot, through cooperation, own and operate mines, factories, and railroads."[5]

The Knights grew rapidly, especially after 1885, when they succeeded in forcing Jay Gould to negotiate a contract with the employees of his railroad; but the fact is that the leadership of the Knights, believing in the harmony of all social groups, was reluctant to follow a militant program in support of trade union interests. Even their very organizational form militated against the use of economic pressures on employers. Their goal was the organization of all producers into a single, irresistible coalition that would abolish the wage system and usher in a new society, and their structure—reflecting that goal—grouped all workers, regardless of craft, into a single territorial unit. It was a structure better adapted to agitation and political action than to bargaining with employers,

[5] Terence V. Powderly, *The Path I Trod* (New York: Columbia University Press, 1940), pp. 266-270.

and when Powderly himself expressed his disapproval of militant trade union actions during the Chicago strikes of 1886, disillusioned members turned away by the thousands.

Even before the formation of the American Federation of Labor in 1886 it was apparent that fundamental differences in philosophy—and therefore in strategy and organization—existed within the Knights of Labor. Aligned against the official leadership was a group of national unions, organized on craft lines, which was less interested in the reform of a social order than in the achievement of better conditions for workmen even while they remained workmen. It was the bargaining function of labor that was to be pre-eminent, not its political function; hence its organization on craft rather than territorial lines, its concern with immediate economic issues rather than general programs of reform, the importance of strikes and boycotts in the arsenal of labor's weapons. Industrial disputes did not end with the achievement of this new organizational form; indeed they became even more bitter, as strikes on railroads and in steel mills, packing houses, mines, and factories testified. But the importance of labor organization was not to be measured in terms of strikes won or lost. It lay in the fact that behind the emerging form of organization was a definition of status and a strategy of action. The status—the worker as indispensable member of an industrial order. The strategy—collective action to improve the conditions of life.

To speak of the importance of organization as the mode of adjusting to the conditions of industrial life, to speak of the new self-consciousness of both groups thrust up into significance by the economic changes of the late nineteenth century and of those cast down, is not only to speak from the perspective of a later age but somehow to deprive the period of the passion it possessed. For organizations were not created without bitter struggles between men and in the minds of men and, once achieved, they were involved in dramatic efforts to influence the shape of the environment. The attempt of persons to understand the forces remaking their world and, by organization, to control them, constitutes, indeed, the major motif of the social history of the late nineteenth century.

By the last decade of the century there seemed little enough to give hope that an acceptable solution to the problems of industrialization could be found. A later generation was to speak blithely of the "Gay Nineties," but to most of those who were then alive it was more a period of *fin de siècle* despair than of buoyant optimism. The American people had long since developed elaborate explanations to account for their special place in human history, to explain why they were not condemned to suffer the same history and the same destiny as the nations of Europe. But there seemed much in the circumstances of the 1890's to belie this optimistic version of the past and forecast of the future.

Poverty was one of these circumstances. Even in 1890, possibly the peak year of prosperity before the First World War, one contemporary estimated that of the 12,500,000 families in the United States, 11,000,000 had an average income of less than $380 a year. Andrew Carnegie defied any man to show that there was pauperism in the United States, but a few years after he spoke one out of every ten persons who died on the Island of Manhattan was being buried in Potter's Field. The gap between rich and poor—growing more visible every day—may have been the most glaring cleav-age in American society, but it was not the only one. City people mocked country folk, who were at once envious and angry. Native Americans wondered at what was to be done with hundreds of thousands of Irish, German, Scandinavian, Italian, and Polish immigrants, and the latter found it no less difficult to make common cause with each other. Nor was the conflict only potential. Violent outbursts at the Haymarket riots of 1886 and the great strikes at Homestead and Pullman gave evidence of the savagery of industrial warfare and led many to conjure up visions of a new and bloodier Paris Commune on American soil.

No institution of the industrial age gave greater grounds for anxiety than its most characteristic product—the city; nowhere were its main attractions greater, nowhere were its sins more apparent, nowhere its conflicts more violent. "The turbid air," wrote Henry James, describing New York, "the tramp, the whole quality and allure, the consummate monotonous commonness, of the pushing male crowd, moving in its dense mass—with the confusion carried to chaos for any intelligence, any perception; a welter of objects and sounds in which relief, detachment, dignity, meaning perished utterly and lost all rights. . . . All the signs of the heaped industrial battlefield, all the sounds and silences, grim, pushing, intruding silences, too, of the universal will to move—to move, move, move as an end in itself, an appetite at any price."

It was in the city that the contrast between Fifth Avenue luxury and Bowery squalor was most apparent; it was in the city that National Guard armories—great Gothic castles with crenelated walls—were built to protect the propertied from the imminent onslaught of the poor; it was in the city that teeming multitudes, alien and native, looked at each other with fear; and it was in the city that were to be found the beneficiaries and the derelicts of industrial society. Increasingly, too, the city came to make its weight felt in the political arena, but the way in which its power was organized served only to intensify the fears of an older generation. To the respectable, the urban political machine was a mechanism of graft and corruption. To the immigrant, it was Santa Claus wintertime and summertime—an avenue to power and influence, a helping hand in time of need, the purveyor of jobs and the provider of excitement. For such as had been reared in the tradition of the small town as a college of the virtuous, the industrial, polyglot city was a center of infection.

As optimism was the temper of the start of the period, fear was the keynote of its close. The reality of overt strife could not be ignored; neither could the overwhelming evidence of brooding hostility between social classes and ethnic and racial groups. How was it all to be explained? By the will of God? But surely even the most pious Christian must feel a pang of guilt at the thought of millions condemned to misery. By the survival of the fittest? Perhaps, but did not a truer understanding of the theory of evolution suggest that man need not passively submit to the pressures of his environment, that intelligence might be used to control the course of his development? By the rigorous laws of competition? But private striving, the theorists had said, would lead to public welfare, and where, in the midst of rural poverty and urban squalor, could that be found? By the theories of Marxism? By the corrupting influence of materialism? Older explanations were clearly inadequate, but no new theory could win universal assent. The palpable facts of industrialization were in themselves

disturbing; what made them frightening was that, in the absence of an adequate theory, it was difficult to read the future.

It was not, however, a record of failure. Even as their world was disintegrating, the American people at the turn of the century had begun the task of adjusting to the new order of things. Technology and urbanization were not to be wiped away, they were to be lived with; and already many had learned the lesson that if men do not organize they cannot solve their social problems or achieve their social goals.

III

In 1904 the United States was host to another great international exposition. Coincident with the Universal Exposition of St. Louis, held to mark the centennial of the Louisiana Purchase, hundreds of the most renowned scientists and scholars of every country in the world met at an International Congress of Arts and Science to discuss the problem of the unity of knowledge. Yet not only scientific problems were discussed. No aspect of human activity was left untouched, and the roster of social problems touched upon by the scholars at St. Louis in 1904 makes the Philadelphia Exposition of 1876 seem almost arcadian. Race relations, the cooperative movement, the struggle of social classes, slums and settlement houses, government regulation of industry, imperialism and the quest for colonies—the problems that had not been foreseen by a more innocent generation were now high on the agenda.

The great German sociologist Max Weber, musing upon the future, saw a gradual convergence of American with European history. "For while it is correct to say that the burden of historical tradition does not overwhelm the United States," he said,

and that the problems originating from the power of tradition do not exist here, yet the effects of the power of capitalism are the stronger and will, sooner or later, further the development of land monopolies. When the land has become sufficiently dear so as to secure a certain rent, when the accumulation of large fortunes has reached a still higher point than today, when, at the same time, the possibility of gaining proportionate profits by constant new investments in trade and industry has been diminished so far that the "captains of industry," as has occurred everywhere in the world, begin to strive for hereditary preservation of their possessions instead of new investments that bring both gain and danger, then, indeed, the desire of the capitalistic families to form a "nobility" will arise. . . .[6]

The equally eminent German economist Werner Sombart was even more apprehensive:

What capitalism has tossed together, in crowds, in great cities and centers of industry, is . . . an inarticulate mass of individuals who have completely broken with the past, who have cut themselves loose from all communal ties, from home, village, and kindred, beginning life anew with a complete destruction of their old ideals. The laborer's only support is the comrade of his fate. . . . Hence arises a host of confederates who are distinguished by one thing above all others, not by individuality, not by common tradition, but by their mass, their massiveness. . . . And if we would picture to ourselves the social movement of our day, it invariably appears to us as an inexhaustible stream of men hardly one of whom stands out clearly, flowing over the whole land as

[6] [This and the following] quotations are from the speeches by Weber, Sombart, and Ross in *Congress of Arts and Science, Universal Exposition, St. Louis, 1904*, ed. Howard J. Rogers (Boston: Houghton Mifflin Company, 1906-1907), VII, 744, 796; V, 876, 882, 877.

far as the eye can see, to the farthest horizon where the last of them roll away into darkness.

The two German scholars saw little future for representative democracy in the United States; it was to be swept away by the masses, hungering for power, or by the élite, determined to keep what it had.

They were answered by a less eminent, but perhaps more prescient, American scholar, the sociologist Edward Alsworth Ross. "How is the attitude of a man toward the rest of his class affected by the fact that socioeconomic classes are in a hierarchy, and individuals are constantly escaping from one class into a higher?" he asked.

Does not the secret hope of rising prompt many a man to identify himself in imagination with the class he hopes to belong to rather than the class he actually belongs to? Are not the conflicts that, in view of their clear oppositions of interest, one would expect to break out . . . between working men and employees, frequently averted because the natural leaders and molders of opinion among the working men hope to become capitalists . . . ? In this epoch of democracy and deliquescence, society by no means falls apart into neat segments, as it did two centuries ago. Caste has had its day, and the compartment society, with thick bulkheads of privileges, prejudice, nonintercourse, and nonintermarriage separating the classes, is well-nigh extinct. Today the imprint each manner of life tends to leave on those who lead it is continually effaced by such assimilating influences as church, school, press, party, voluntary association, and public opinion.

But not even for Ross was this the best of all possible worlds. In a world of increasing organization—

what will be the fate of personal individuality? Will there be more room for spontaneity and choice, or is the individual doomed to shrivel as social aggregates enlarge . . . ? As that cockleshell, the individual soul, leaving the tranquil pool of tribal life, passes first into the sheltered lake of some city community, then into the perilous sea of national life, does it enjoy an ever-widening scope for free movement and self-direction, or does it, too frail to navigate the vaster expanses, become more and more the sport of irresistible waves and currents?

We ponder his question—a legacy of the nineteenth century—even yet.

The Nation-State as a Unit
in the Comparative Study of Social Change

WENDELL BELL   IVAR OXAAL

It cannot be said today, as a number of writers charged a decade ago, that American sociologists are congenitally blind to the power dimension in their studies of social structure, nor that they are uninterested in social change. That the study of power has become fashionable—perhaps too fashionable—is witnessed by the steady production of monographs exploring the system of power of dozens of communities. While these individual case studies have resulted in a tremendous increase in methodological ingenuity and conceptual sophistication, their contribution to macrosociological concerns has been limited by the parochial nature of the subject matter. Individual trees have been felled, but the national forest remains, on the whole, uncharted. This is certainly understandable, because from both a theoretical and practical research standpoint we tend to be overawed by the myriad operations and interconnections of the modern nation-state. The small community, or even the city, is far less intimidating than the apparently inac-

cessible decision-making structures of the national power élites.

We propose, however, to suggest that the sociologist need not limit his intellectual function primarily to the investigation of subsystems within the nation-state, but that he can in fact bring his technical competence to bear on the issues of power and social change at the national level. To do so he need not become an historian, but he will be compelled to investigate some of the same issues which historians have traditionally regarded as important. "History," as it is commonly practiced, deals precisely with the changes which overtake national social systems, but the lack of systematic training in the theory and methods of social science—and their inapplicability in most instances—often seems to leave the historian with a suspicion of all theory, or else stranded with the brave assumption that Freud or Parsons can be adopted for a bit of *ad hoc* theorizing. A comparative study of social change at the national level must do better than this; but its subject matter—the variables it seeks to explain—is, we would argue, based on the same implicit criteria of significance adopted by many historians. In this connection, we view history not as some sort of nomothetic residue to be

Prepared especially for this volume. For further elaboration of these themes see Wendell Bell and Ivar Oxaal, *Decisions of Nationhood: Political and Social Development in the British Caribbean* (Denver: Social Science Foundation, University of Denver, 1964).

considered by sociologists apart from the study of social structure; rather, it is a description of the structure in the process of changing itself.

Some interrelations between power and social change on the national level are of course inscrutable and not open to full social science inquiry. Unlike the historian, however, the sociologist cannot wait impatiently in the ante-room of history until the archives are opened, the memoirs published, and the need for secrecy evaporated. The best tools of sociology can only be applied *in medias res* in order to catch living men in the act of committing history. The techniques for such investigations exist and have already been applied by a few social scientists;[1] what has been missing, perhaps for the reasons just suggested, is a serviceable conceptual orientation toward the nation-state as a unit of sociological inquiry. This paper will address itself to that question, and represents our attempt to clarify and generalize our own recent research into the problematics of social change in a new nation-state which didn't quite come into existence, but might have: the West Indies Federation.[2]

---

[1] It is a curious fact that macrosocial science has been the dominant orientation of students of the developing nations while it remains a minority viewpoint in the United States itself. It appears that either macrosocial scientists are willing to go abroad, or else, as happened to the present writers, once they get to the new nation they are forced to try to make sense out of the basic social and political facts of the environment—facts which they tend to take for granted in their own culture.

[2] The provisional West Indies Federation was established in 1958 and dissolved in 1962. Jamaica and Trinidad and Tobago became politically independent in August, 1962, while the other members of the Federation—the British islands in the Leeward and Windward chain—continued to be ruled as British colonies. British Guiana, on the South American mainland, was never a member of

Theoretical Guidelines: "The Decisions of Nationhood"

The transition from colony to nation-state involves the formal transfer of political power from an old élite representing the established interests, especially from officials representing the imperial power, to a new élite composed predominantly of nationalist politicians representing new national citizenries. Despite the rapid and possibly confused changes which occur during this period of "modernization," it is actually an excellent time in which to analyze and clarify just what, from a sociological standpoint, a nation-state is. The reason for this is simple: nation-states do not just happen, they are made to happen by men who must, if they are to be successful, at least implicitly pay heed to the organizational principles—the functional requisites and strains—inherent in this form of social organization. They are forced by the logic of the situation in which they find themselves to cope, often simultaneously, with many or all of the issues which we will term "the decisions of nationhood."

The political, economic, and social facts of the new states since World War II, combined with the ideologies of the modern world, have resulted in the leaders' adoption of what can be described as a rational decision-making model. This is not to evaluate objectively the degree of rationality with respect to some extrinsic criterion, but simply to say that the new national leaders' *definitions of the situation* are such that they view themselves as conscious actors within a set of conditions, means, ends, and motives—as actors who are to some extent manipulators of the present and creators of the future. Thus we extract the decisions of

---

the Federation and it, too, remains a colony as of 1965.

nationhood in part from our knowledge of the maps of social reality, only more or less accurate to varying and unknown degrees, carried in the minds of the new élites. Such perceptions of reality of course are consequential both for the terms of emphasis in which political, economic, and social problems will be specified and for the nature of the solutions which will be implemented. Real consequences follow from the leaders' perceptions of the tasks before them. Thus our formulation of the decisions of nationhood results in part from our effort to see the new nations through the eyes of the persons who are establishing them (or in some cases trying to prevent their establishment), and we have asked: What do men *think* they must do and *think* they must become in order to establish and maintain what they *think* is the type of organization called a nation-state? The answer of course may not be a single subjective reality, but may be multiple subjective realities if different actors have different perceptions of the situation.

Additionally, our specification of decisions of nationhood follows from an analysis of the functional requisites of nation-states. Not everything is *perception* of reality; there is also *reality itself*, real stones on which to stub one's collective toe—as well as those one perceives. Nation-states have some features they share with all social organizations, such as the problem of the maintenance of boundaries and the regulation of the relations with other organizations; they have others which are distinctive, such as those that result from their claim to be that social unit which legitimately demands the highest priority and overriding loyalty from its individual members.

The sociological notion of functional requisites compels us to ask: What must men really do and really become

in order to establish and maintain the type of organization called a nation-state? The answer defines some of the specific problems that require solutions if men are to build a nation successfully. What men *think* they must do and what they really must do from an independent observer's point of view of course are not necessarily the same thing, and here and there in the course of our studies in the West Indies we were able to show that real constraints, causes, and effects existed in contradistinction to the subjective meanings of social reality held by some of the West Indian leaders.[3]

We do not think, however, that the way in which functional analysis has often been used to explain particular outcomes in the new states is generally valid. It has often created perceptions of obstacles and necessities where none existed. Too much weight has been placed on incomplete, faulty, or inaccurate functionalism, and too little on revealing the definitions of the situation and the values, to be discussed below, of the responsible men in leadership positions. For example, from a functional analysis, we conclude that *some form of government is necessary to establish a nation-state*, but we reject a functional analysis that goes so far as to explain *why a particular form of government must be established or must fail*, the fashionable conclusion being of course from this latter view that political democracy *must* fail under the economic, social, or cultural conditions of the new states. Such conclusions may rest a good deal more on an investigator's own *beliefs* about the nature and effectiveness of different

---

[3] For a further discussion of this point the reader should consult Wendell Bell, *Jamaican Leaders* (Berkeley: University of California Press, 1964); also, Wendell Bell, ed., *The Democratic Revolution in the West Indies*, forthcoming.

alternative forms of government and his own *perceptions* of the conditions under which the government will be expected to function than they do on an objective analysis of actual functional requisites.

Furthermore, we arrived at the decisions of nationhood from our analysis of the underlying values of the people of the emerging nations of the British Caribbean. "Values," writes Neil J. Smelser, "are the major premises of the social order; they set the bearings of society toward general kinds of ends and legitimize these ends by a particular view of man, nature, and society."[4] As we have stated elsewhere:

Values at this high level of generality and societal importance are not the same thing as functional requisites of a national society. The difference lies in the distinction between how men must behave in order to create and maintain a nation-state and the various purposes which they may give for doing so. The relationship between the two is an empirical problem. Often it appears that new societal values emerge when major changes in the overall institutional order are being undertaken. On the other hand, there is likewise a tendency to legitimize innovations in the name of the old verities. . . .

. . . Nonetheless, it may be observed that when men do things which importantly change, or attempt to change, the boundaries, membership, autonomy, coalitions, organizational structure, internal relationships, history, and personal character of an organization (and all these things are involved in building a new nation), they generally advance what they believe to be important reasons for doing so. Societal values, therefore, can be regarded as including the more generalized qualities of an image of the future toward which historical action is

directed. As such, they are what the big decisions of nationhood are often about.[5]

Finally, the decisions-of-nationhood approach grew out of our consideration of a variety of works, including prominently the decision-making approach as formulated by Richard C. Snyder and others,[6] developmental analysis as delineated by H. D. Lasswell,[7] and the concept of the image of the future as elaborated by Frederik L. Polak.[8]

For the purpose of exposition, and in keeping with our attempt to recreate the logic of the situation of the decision maker, we phrase the decisions of nationhood as a series of questions that require some answer, if a nation-state is to be created. Often national debate representing basic cleavages and differences within the society surrounds a decision, thus pushing it into the forefront of public consciousness. At other times, a particular outcome or an answer is so taken for granted that it does not even appear as if anything so dramatic or clear-cut as a "decision" has been made. No alternative possibilities may be considered, there may be no controversy, and any issues that

[4] Neil J. Smelser, *Theory of Collective Behavior* (New York: The Free Press of Glencoe, Inc., 1963), p. 35.

[5] Wendell Bell and Ivar Oxaal, *Decisions of Nationhood: Political and Social Development in the British Caribbean* (Denver: Social Science Foundation, University of Denver, 1964), p. 6.

[6] Richard C. Snyder, "A Decision-Making Approach to the Study of Political Phenomena," in Roland Young, ed., *Approaches to the Study of Politics* (Evanston, Ill.: Northwestern University Press, 1958), p. 15. Also see, Richard C. Snyder, H. W. Bruck, and Burton Sapin, *Decision-Making as an Approach to the Study of International Politics* (Foreign Policy Analysis Series No. 3, Organizational Behavior Section, Princeton University, June, 1954).

[7] For example, see Heinz Eulau, "H. D. Lasswell's Developmental Analysis," *Western Political Quarterly*, 11 (June, 1958), 229-242.

[8] Frederik L. Polak, *The Image of the Future*, Vols. I and II (Dobbs Ferry, N.Y.: Oceana Publications, Inc., 1961).

may be contained in the nature of the outcome may remain buried deep within the public unconscious. Among the different new states of course there are, because of varying historical circumstances, variations in the amount of public concern and disagreement over the outcomes of particular decisions.

Our list of the decisions of nationhood, which we regard as preliminary, is as follows:

1. *Should we become a politically independent nation?*[9] This decision may have priority over all the others in time, since the other decisions of nationhood may never arise if this one doesn't, and in importance, since the purposes and objectives behind the desire to create a politically independent state have implications for particular preferences with respect to the alternative outcomes of the other decisions. Needless to say, opinion within as well as without the territory of a potential nation-state has been far from unanimous regarding the desirability of independence. There have been active individuals who were dedicated to the idea of independence and who participated in the nationalist movements, but there have been equally active individuals in many countries dedicated to preventing independence and expressing antinationalist sentiments. And of course there have been others—often large numbers of the general population in some countries—who have been relatively indifferent to political change. We asked: Who fought for nationhood and who opposed it? What rea-

sons did they give for doing so? How did their images of the future conflict? How did the nature of the existing polity, economy, society, and culture generate or suppress particular attitudes and actions? Thus involved in deciding to be independent are ideas —potentially conflicting, sometimes subtly, sometimes wildly, different— about what an entire society should aspire to be, ideas that are carried by individuals and groups that have been shaped by the past, sustained by the present, and influenced by the images of the future toward which their action is directed.

In the West Indies, for example, as our colleague Charles C. Moskos, Jr. found on the basis of structured interviews with 112 top leaders, there was considerable disagreement over the desirability of political independence, and while that disagreement to a great extent was correlated with the basic cleavages in the social structure, it was more closely associated with the broader values of individuals regardless of social position. From a content analysis of the respondents' attitudes and activities regarding political independence, three basic types were identified: *colonialists, acquiescing nationalists,* and *true nationalists.*[10]

Colonialists were those leaders who opposed political independence for the West Indies in the present or future and favored an indefinite continuation of colonial rule. Usually, however, they did not express such sentiment publicly because of their belief that theirs was a lost cause, that independence was inevitable, and that the climate of opinion was hostile to such views. There were exceptions to this posture of colonialist political disaffiliation,

---

[9] Here, as in the other paraphrases of the decisions, the reader can readily rephrase the question so as to apply to older national politics, or even, in many instances, to other types of organizations. For example, in established nations the present question may become "Should we *remain* a politically independent nation?"

[10] A full report of Moskos' study will be included in *The Democratic Revolution in the West Indies.*

particularly in British Guiana, where colonialists openly espoused an anti-independence position.

Acquiescing nationalists were differentiated into three subtypes. Some were found to be *reluctant nationalists* because, while they expressed a desire for political independence as a long-range goal, they disavowed it for the near future. They temporized by saying, for example, that the West Indies were not ready for independence, that economic development should come first, and that the people lacked political maturity. They were not prepared, however, to form an open opposition to the nationalist movement but expressed the notion that events were moving too quickly. Another acquiescing group were the *dutiful nationalists*, leaders motivated to aid the nationalist movement out of a sense of *noblesse oblige*. Some of these men were mavericks from the traditional upper classes who did not view political independence as desirable but who nonetheless were willing to bend with the "inevitable" by using their skills and influence to alleviate the strains of the transition from colony to independent nation-state. A third acquiescing type was identified, the *opportunistic nationalists*, who, although privately opposed to independence, publicly engaged in pro-independence activity in the belief that they would gain personally by doing so.

True nationalists were defined as those leaders who favored immediate independence and who backed their expressed convictions by open support of the nationalist cause, including such activities as membership in nationalist parties, public speaking, and pamphleteering in favor of independence.

The distribution of these types among the top West Indian leaders was as follows:

Nationalist Types		Percentage
True nationalists		39
Acquiescing nationalists		25
reluctant	11	
dutiful	5	
opportunistic	9	
Colonialists		36
Total		100
Number of Cases		(112)

Slightly more than one-third each of the West Indian leaders were either true nationalists or colonialists. The remainder, one-fourth of the total, were acquiescing nationalists. These findings can be viewed in either of two ways. From one perspective, much less than a majority of the West Indian élites were genuinely committed to political independence. But the apparently low number of true nationalists may be a result of the narrow definition of this type which involved private as well as open support for immediate political independence. Thus by keeping in mind the acquiescing nationalists, it can be said that close to two-thirds of the leaders exhibited some amount of pro-independence sentiment. The colonialists were generally very well-off economically, being found chiefly among the more prosperous planters and merchants. Because economic status is associated with skin color in the West Indies, most whites and near-whites were also found to be colonialists. In contrast to the true nationalists, colonialists were statistically likely to be older, to adhere most closely to Anglo-European styles of life, and to have been educated to the secondary school level rather than having received more or less education. True nationalists, on the other hand, were younger, tended toward a more provincial, middle-class West Indian variant of European life styles, and were likely to have either a university degree or an education not extending beyond elementary school. Moreover, the true nationalists were typically dark brown or black (and East Indian in British Guiana) and leaders of mass-based organizations such as trade unions or political parties. The true nationalists, therefore, included relatively few members of the traditional white oligarchy, but at the same time their numbers were not overly reflective of a basically lower-class origin.

Acquiescing nationalists tended to have intermediate background characteristics, although they were notably persons who occupied important positions in governmental service or in the mass media. Many of the opportunistic nationalists among the acquiescing type were old-style colonial politicians who apparently were not leading so much as they were following the crowd down the path toward independence.

More highly correlated with the nationalist types than the above social background characteristics were the economic ideologies of the leaders. Moskos classified the leaders into five categories according to their views on the proper role of the government in the economy of their territories: *reactionaries*—those who thought the state's role should be about what it was before the rise of the nationalist movements and should not extend beyond providing basic services, such as a postal system, roads, police and fire protection; *conservatives*—those who wished to maintain the present situation, with the state in addition to providing basic services also being respon-

sible for welfare schemes for the ill, aged, and unemployed, for public works, and for a general educational system, but with the reservations that taxation should be less discriminatory against the entrepreneurial class and that government should be less protective of the labor union interests; *populists*—those who lacked long-range economic policies, and who were pragmatically concerned with immediate bread-and-butter issues, although accepting a belief in a market economy geared to the demands of labor unions or mass-based political organizations; *liberals*—those who wanted greater intervention of the government in the economy, but who did not foresee radical changes beyond the achievement of modern welfare capitalism; and the *radicals*—those who advocated fundamental changes in the present system so that the state would become the major factor in determining local economic life, with the extreme radicals seeking the abolishment of all private property.

The distribution of these economic ideologies among the nationalist types is reported below.

The table below shows an unmistakable connection between nationalist behavior and economic ideologies. Among West Indian leaders, "Left" economic ideologies went with true nationalism and "Right" economic ideologies went with support for the colonial system: all of the radicals were true nationalists, and none of the reactionaries or conservatives were.

Economic Ideologies	Percentages of West Indian Leaders Who Were:				
	Colonialists	Acquiescing Nationalists	True Nationalists	Total	Number of Cases
Reactionaries	86	14	0	100	(22)
Conservatives	58	42	0	100	(33)
Populists	18	36	46	100	(11)
Liberals	0	28	72	100	(25)
Radicals	0	0	100	100	(21)

the nation-state as a unit in the comparative study of social change **175**

Moreover, the acquiescing nationalists tended to be concentrated in the intermediate economic ideologies.

We have cited Moskos' findings here simply to supply one example of what we mean when we say that the techniques of sociological inquiry can be brought to bear on the issues of power and social change on the national level. Lack of space prevents us from similar illustrations of other decisions, where we will be confined to general discussion.

2. *How much national sovereignty should the new nation have?* This question is explicitly stated among the big decisions of nationhood in recognition of the fact that potentially there are various degrees of independence, although most of the new nations since World War II, just as the older nations had at an earlier time, decided on full autonomy as far as their national *political* status is concerned. Few were very inventive on this question, and ironically they followed the path of the older European nations whose shackles they were trying to throw off in the search for their own distinctive identity. And they did this at a time when the older European nations were experimenting with the workability of supranational organizations, such as the Common Market and Euratom, which could result eventually in the erosion of the national sovereignty of European countries. There have been a few countries, however, that have stopped short of full political independence. The notable case in point is Puerto Rico, which is a free state in association with the United States and which has achieved with remarkable success most of the goals that the modern nationalist movements set for themselves. Unless independence is viewed as an end in itself rather than as a means to an end, an independent observer may wonder why more thought was not given by the new nationalist leaders throughout the world to alternatives to complete political autonomy.

Militarily and economically of course the new nations are less independent than they are in formal political status. Not having adequate military power to protect their own lands from actual or potential threats from more powerful enemies, some—the late Malaysian state comes to mind as a prominent example—call upon the military strength of the former imperial power or upon that of some powerful friend for assistance. In some cases, this call for aid has been the result of an inability to control internal disorder among their own peoples, such as in the case of Kenya and British Guiana to mention just two examples. Furthermore, economic autonomy has been striven for by some of the new nations through expropriation, nationalization, or otherwise increasing control over foreign-owned land and enterprise within their borders, but many have devised policies designed more to lure the former imperial rascals in than to throw them out—Trinidad and Tobago in the West Indies being a case in point.

In any event some outcome is necessary to the questions of how much national sovereignty the new nation should have; and it will often significantly affect, or place limitations upon, the most probable outcomes of other decisions.

3. *What should the geographical boundaries of the new nation be?* Given notions about what constitutes a nation-state and the fact that human life is concentrated on the surface of a sphere, the problem of drawing lines on the sphere to create the boundaries between one nation-state and another arises. When a collectivity of people seek to establish a nation-state, they must decide, if they are going to succeed in their task, on the geographical

boundaries that are to delimit the new state. This decision, like the others, is made only more or less by the new national leaders themselves. The heritage of colonialism enters in as well, to some extent in the form of advice, more or less insistent as a condition for permitting early independence, voiced by the European colonial officials during the transition to independence, and to some extent by the historical facts of European domination that have over the years set certain patterns of language, communication, transportation, association, and orientation in the former colonies. The facts of existing territorial divisions which demarcated European empires and which resulted from wars between European powers, for example, were of great importance in explaining where many of the geographical boundaries of the new nations were to be established. They help explain why Gambia, a former British colony nearly surrounded by Senegal, a former French colony, in West Africa, is even in existence as a separate state and why in many ways it is nearer to London than to Senegal, while Senegal is nearer to Paris than Gambia; and they help explain why some islands that can be seen with the naked eye from others in the Caribbean are nearer their European metropole thousands of miles away than they are to each other.

Forces both for consolidation and fragmentation have been at work among the imperial purposes as well as among the emergent national circumstances. Federations—like the West Indies in 1962 or Malaysia in 1965—were formed and collapsed; sometimes cultural groups were cut asunder and divided between different nations, and other times many diverse groups were placed together within the same colonial administrative districts, the boundaries of which were carried over into nationhood. Many of the problems of selecting boundaries—or dealing with existing boundaries once they had been selected—are related to the next big decision of nationhood to be discussed.

4. *Should the state and the nation be coterminous?* This question pertains to the degree of cultural homogeneity that the new state should strive to attain. Here we must use the term "state" strictly to refer to the legal and political definition in order to distinguish it in the discussion from the cultural, linguistic, religious, or communal connotations contained in the term "nation." Should the state have the exact same scale as the nation, and should the nation have the exact same scale as the state? That is, should the political boundaries defining the new state be coterminous with the boundaries of some culturally distinct and homogeneous group?

Such a decision is obviously related to the decision regarding geographical boundaries, since the correlation between culture and geography makes juggling the boundaries one way of making the state and nation coterminous, as was done, for example, in the split between India and Pakistan. Another way of course is the mass migration of people from one location to another.

The boundaries that have been set up have sometimes made the state smaller in scale than the nation at least for some of the groups within the state, but frequently have done the reverse, and have created a state larger in scale than the nation. For example, one writer summarizes the situation as follows:

In South-Southeast Asia, the former colonial area with the longest history of political independence, not a single country has escaped the problem of dissident groups. Pakistan has her frontier peoples; Ceylon, the Tamil-Sinhalese conflict; Burma, her hill peoples; Thailand, her Chinese and southern Malayans; Laos, the non-Mekong Lao; Cambodia, the Vietnamese; Vietnam, the Cambodians and other ethnic and religious groups; Malaysia, a delicate balance among Malayans, Chinese, and Indians; while India, the Philippines, and Indonesia must cope with a multitude of different ethnic, language, and religious groups. In many Middle Eastern countries, tensions have arisen over alienated groups, such as the Kurds, the Armenians, and various Muslim sects. In Africa, many of the new states are torn by tribal rivalries.[11]

Most of the leaders of the new states have answered "yes" to the question of state and nation cotermineity, although they don't always agree on how to bring it about. Some have succeeded or still hope to succeed by fragmentation, taking some primordial group smaller in scale than the state and creating a state coterminous with it by secession from a larger state. Others, confronting a culturally plural state, hope to create a nation by breaking down communal ties within the state and building up the priority of loyalty to the state over subgroup loyalties by bringing a statewide culture into dominance, a subject that will be discussed below under cultural traditions. And a few seem to have considered the possibility of rejecting the melting-pot concept in favor of a cultural mosaic, as Canada did at an earlier time, in which ethnic minorities are encouraged to maintain their cultural identities while the unity of the state is achieved through legal rules of the game and political cooperation.

5. *What form of government should the new nation have?* For the new nations of the twentieth century, perhaps the most important aspect of this ques-

tion has been whether or not to have a political democracy, by which we mean a representative system based upon wide participation in the political community and the maintenance of public liberties. In such a system, dissent is not only possible, but more probably institutionalized. But countries such as Indonesia and Ghana, to name just two examples among the new states, despite considerable democratic rhetoric have opted for authoritarian systems which fail to fulfill the definition of a democratic political system as understood in the West. Often the explanation is given that the mobilization of effort that is needed to lift the relatively poor new states out of the economic doldrums into the mainstream of self-sustained economic progress cannot be achieved under a democratic political system. Debate and division of opinion, according to this view, must give way to unity in order to maximize the success of achieving collective national goals. Yet other nations, such as India, facing much the same conditions of poverty and underdevelopment, strive to maintain political democracy.

The new and near nations of the British Caribbean are particularly instructive in this regard, since they have managed so far to establish and maintain political democracies based on universal adult suffrage while at the same time, at least in the cases of Jamaica and Trinidad, succeeding in their attempts to grow economically at relatively rapid rates.

As we stated earlier, we do not view the functional requisites of a nation-state as requiring any particular type of political system; they demand only that *some* form of government be established and maintained. Rather the particular type of system that is created will depend on the complex interaction of many factors, including importantly

---

[11] F. R. von der Mehden, *Politics of the Developing Nations* (Englewood Cliffs, N.J.: Prentice-Hall, Inc., 1964), p. 2.

the patterns of priorities given within a new nation to civil and political rights on the one hand *vs.* economic, social, and cultural rights on the other. To those people who place higher priority on the former, political democracy tends to become an end in itself, a feature of the good society toward which they should strive; to those who place higher priority on the latter, the political system may be viewed as a means to an end to such a degree that any political system is acceptable, even an authoritarian one, as long as it is effective in producing the desired level of economic progress and economic, social, and cultural equality.

6. *What role should the government play in the affairs of the society and of the economy?* Whether or not the government plays a large role in other institutional sectors of course is a question that can vary quite independently of the question regarding the *form* of government. An authoritarian regime can play either a large or small role in the lives of the people and so can a democratic regime. These two things are commonly confused by the tendency to equate an authoritarian regime with a government that has elaborated and extended its control and services throughout the society and economy and to identify a democratic regime with a government that offers a minimum of functions and services. In fact, such thinking is promoted by those persons who oppose the extension of government services and control, since they frequently argue that such extension represents a trend toward authoritarianism. But this correlation is false empirically, since we have cases to the contrary—for example, authoritarian and economically stagnant Haiti compared to democratic and economically advanced Sweden—and fallacious theoretically.

In most of the new states, the lead-ers are committed to the modernization of their countries, and, whether authoritarian or democratic in their present political policies, they are often deeply dedicated to the welfare of their people—*all* of their people—and tend to view their new control over the governmental machinery as well as an increase in the power of that machinery itself as being among the most important ways—some go so far as to say *the* most important way—of achieving it. It was, after all, the control of the *political* institutions that was placed into the hands of the new national leaders, and it has been through the utilization of the resulting new political power that such leaders' influence on other sectors of society, whether by persuasion, threat, or force, has been most evident.

7. *What should the new nation's external affairs be?* Another example of a decision every new nation must face

. . . concerns the new nations' entry into international relations. Prior to political independence, these countries had little or no control over their foreign affairs. As colonies, their contacts with the outside world, apart from those with the imperial power itself, were indirect and circuitous. But with the successful drive toward nationhood the question of the most desirable and beneficial international relations could be raised from the point of view of the emergent nation's own welfare. Although there were limitations imposed by economic ties, as well as by bounds of sentiment and culture, to the European power that had dominated them during the years of colonial rule, the new national élites faced the outside world with considerable freedom of choice to formulate their new nations' foreign policies.[12]

[12] Charles C. Moskos, Jr., and Wendell Bell, "Emergent Caribbean Nations Face the Outside World," *Social Problems*, **12** (Summer, 1964), 24-41.

External affairs are perhaps dominated by a nation's relationships with other nation-states, by international relations. But they also include relationships with supranational organizations at the global and regional level, and in some cases they include relationships with subnational units, such as those with ethnic communities or local governmental bodies.

We have examples of new states that are more aligned with the Communist bloc—now either Chinese or Russian versions—than with the Western democracies, others that seem to be fence-straddling, trying to play each side of the cold war off against the other, and still others more inclined toward the West than the East. As the new nations have grown in number and stepped onto the stage of world affairs, however, a distinctive result of their foreign policies has been the emergence of the so-called neutralist bloc of countries, generally committed neither to Communist or Western viewpoints but to their own particular interests and world views.

In the West Indian territories we studied there was considerably more sentiment for alignment with the West than with the Communist countries, although favorable attitudes toward a neutralist role seemed to be on the increase from at least 1958 to 1962. Only in British Guiana, where nearly a third of the top leaders preferred alignment with Communist countries, was there much support for establishing a position within the Eastern bloc. The desire for becoming a member of the neutralist bloc, however, was connected with the desire for independence and differential images of the future in a very definite way. Those leaders who were true nationalists tended toward neutrality and didn't wish to be tied either to the Western or to the Eastern bloc, and those leaders who were most committed to the higher ideals of Western civilization, such as liberty, equality, and fraternity, were less likely to want to align with the Western nations than were leaders who were authoritarians, inegalitarians, and exclusivists.

8. *What type of social structure should the new nation have?* 9. *What should the new nation's cultural traditions be?* 10. *What should the national character of the new nation's people be?* We have lumped these three decisions of nationhood together because they have certain similar features that make it convenient to discuss them together. The first seven decisions are primarily political decisions, while the last three are mostly nonpolitical, although this is not to say that the political system is not involved in the decisional process with respect to these issues. Far from it. But they can be properly thought of as containing problems that are primarily *sociological* in the case of the question on social structure, *anthropological* with respect to the question on cultural traditions, and *social-psychological* with regard to the question on national character. Of course the facts of the past leave any society in the present with a particular social structure, a set of cultural traditions, and a typical psychological type of person; and the new national leaders, no matter how divergent their aspirations for the future are from the actualities of the present, cannot create a new social order, a new culture, or a new basic personality structure among themselves and their people very quickly. Yet most of the new national leaders have set about the tasks of just so transforming their new states. It may take decades, more probably generations, but the effects of their policies can already be observed in many countries. In fact, in large part the new nationalist movements prom-

ised as the essence of their meaning just such transformations. They promised more egalitarian and socially inclusive social structures; more distinctive, unified, impressive, and purposive cultural traditions—more modern while also being linked with their *own* pasts; and new national men and women within whose characters would be embodied new hope for perfection within this earthly world. There were exceptions of course: nationalist movements that represented splintering; exclusive movements; and even in the case of the nationalist movements that professed the highest humanitarian ideals, the threat of the deflection toward limited and parochial goals remains.

Summary and Conclusions

We have suggested that the decisions of nationhood are both unavoidable problems in the minds of national decision makers as well as—or because they are—abstractions derived from a functional analysis of the nation-state as a type of social organization. The nation-state must, if it is to come into, or continue in, existence, in some sense "solve" the problems raised by its own nature. As we have seen, these problems center on the values which motivate the creation and maintenance of the nation-state, the issues of geographical and demographic boundaries, the question of autonomy and coalition in an environment composed of other nation-states, and the internal character of the society. The structure and role of the government in relation to other institutions must somehow be defined; group traditions establishing the legitimacy of certain solutions must be related to considerations of cultural traditions, social structure, and national character. We have not been able to go into many of these problems in detail; rather our purpose, based on what might perhaps be called "voluntaristic-functionalist" reasoning has been taxonomic and exploratory and therefore we have probably raised more questions than we have answered.

Our claim and plea, however, is that we have identified the most significant variables in the life of all nations and that social scientists might therefore be persuaded to direct their energies to the study of how and why changes in the "solution" to particular decisions come about and, more importantly, how these variables interact in different nation-states. From the latter enterprise—in which one of the authors is at present engaged—we should be able to move from a purely classificatory orientation to empirical generalization based on comparative data and, ultimately, to a comprehensive overview and theory of social change on a global level. This is the real task of comparative analysis on the scale suggested here, and competing models and theories can in the process be applied to the variables identified above.

The Rate and Costs of Political Development

That we can now catalogue five or ten different ways of understanding political development is evidence of our backwardness.[1] There is demonstrable, if varying, value in all these approaches, even as there are virtues to be found in societies still backward in political development. The trouble is that our modes of analysis so far have failed to tell us just how fundamental a revolution is entailed by "political development" in the modern world. My argument is that the type of change characterizing the revolution of modernization is much more uprooting, and the rate of change involved in this type of political development much faster, than we commonly realize in analysis or action. Hence I conclude that the next decades are likely to witness the politics of competent development.[2]

The Nature of the Revolution of Modernization

The search for capacity to direct the rate and course of change in modern

Manfred Halpern, "The Rate and Costs of Political Development," *The Annals of the American Academy of Political and Social Science*, **358** (March, 1965), 20-28. Reprinted by permission of the author and *The Annals*.

[1] For such helpful analytical catalogues see Lucian W. Pye's essay in [the abovementioned] volume of *The Annals*, and Robert A. Packenham, "Approaches to the Study of Political Development," *World Politics*, **18** (October, 1964), 108-120.

[2] This essay reflects initial explorations by the author in the theory of the revolution of modernization, being conducted under the auspices of Princeton University's Center of International Studies.

times demands more than alterations or growth in selected institutions and processes. "Change" or "development" can, in any period of history, take place incrementally. Modernization cannot. To become modern does not simply mean to attain rapidly and geometrically more of what some already possess—more power over men, ideas, and things more efficiently exercised and in greater security, to the greater profit of the greater number. Such is the Capitalist-Communist-Socialist and Post-Ideological vision of modernity. It must therefore be reckoned with, if not as the wholeness of our dream, at least as the commonly accepted aim of political development. But such a description does not yet constitute analysis of the basic requirements of modernization and its costs. Such a view is misleading also if it is taken, as so often it is, as a prescription. To suppose that the development of a modern polity and society means only more satisfaction of more demands for more, better, and, only in certain specific fields, different performance is to miss the revolution already underway and the revolution yet required. Modernization is nothing as simple as magnification or improvement; its movement is not a straighter, wider, stronger line along the path already being traveled by most developing nations. Instead, the revolution of modernization involves transformation—the transformation of all systems by which man organizes his society, that is, his political, social, economic, intellectual, religious, and psychological systems.

Transformation does not mean that

there is, or needs to be, in all instances a break with the past. On the contrary, many of the elements and linkages which constituted the premodern system tend to continue into the present and likely also long into the future. Transformation constitutes a more subtle and more difficult change than the destruction of the past, and is no less radical. If modernization requires of society the will to maintain continuously that capacity which the species *lepidoptera rhopalocera* loses after having been successively transformed from caterpillar to chrysalis to butterfly, it is because, by now, the revolution of modernization is already transforming traditional systems around the world, whether men wish it or not. Increasingly, sons can no longer profit from extended families as principal collective bargaining units with the rest of the world. Thanks to their opinions, lack of connections, or sheer number, such men can also no longer hope to find a place in the traditional matrix of their society as a whole. They can be contained neither by its norms nor by its politics based on a calculus of personal relations. When new élites based on a modern, salaried middle class in army, bureaucracy, and corporations come into power, the new men find that their own individual success brings no security. To maintain status, power, and prosperity for themselves they must for the first time create institutions which mobilize an entire nation, linking all individuals in consciousness and material fact. Men who wish to avoid becoming the victims of the revolution of modernization—of the uncontrolled forces of social change—will need consciously to organize the revolution of modernization themselves.

The revolution of modernization is, however, the first revolution of mankind to set a new price upon stability in any system of society—namely, it requires an enduring capacity to generate and absorb persistent transformation. This capacity represents at the same time the minimum and maximum requirements for wedding stability and change once crucial elements and linkages of a traditional system cease to function. To maintain such a capacity for transformation constitutes both the uniquely modern opportunity —which many élites desire—and the uniquely modern requirement—which many élites may fail to meet—for succeeding in the fundamental revolution of our times. Traditional societies, by contrast, were not faced continuously by system-transforming demands. When, usually only after centuries, they were confronted by a particular challenge of this kind, they were capable of responding only by disintegrating or by creating a new closed system.

Modernization demands of all systems of society the capacity which the scientific community already possesses: the ability to persist continuously in the enterprise of responding to the challenge of new questions, new facts, and inadequate solutions by developing, maintaining, modifying, and disintegrating systems of theory. That such scientific revolutions, even under the best of circumstances, tend to be discontinuous, conflict-ridden, and marked by considerable intervals of concentration on refining and enlarging existing systems, helps to make scientific revolutions particularly characteristic examples of the revolution of modernization.[3]

What we need to know in order to understand any political system in relation to the revolution of modernization is the interaction among three elements: the *imbalances* existing within

[3] See Thomas S. Kuhn, *The Structure of Scientific Revolutions* (Chicago: University of Chicago Press, 1962).

and among the systems of a society—for example, the disparity between population and resources, between educated men and the jobs available for them, between modern problems and theories relevant for understanding them—and the *will* and *capacity* of a society to transform these imbalances so that it may generate and absorb continuing transformation. The most important question is whether, and at what cost, any particular policy or event facilitates the process of transformation in the system as a whole, or in the relationship of any one system to other systems in society.[4]

Imbalances Created by the Rate of Change

If these are the tasks of political development, most nations are likely to fail at them, again and again, at least during the remainder of this century. The rest of this essay will therefore concern itself with the reasons for such failures, and with alternative responses to failure.

Three among the reasons for failure are so obvious that one need only point to them: too little knowledge, too many people, too many high and early expectations. Yet it may be helpful to assess their destabilizing impact on the revolution of modernization in a less familiar light—as rapidly creating growing imbalances in rates of change among crucial social forces.

[4] I have developed some of these, still tentative, perspectives at greater length in "Notes on the Revolution of Modernization in National and International Society," to be published in the NOMOS *Yearbook on Revolution*, as part of a series sponsored by the American Society for Political and Legal Philosophy. Portions of the preceding material were also drawn from my essay "Toward Further Modernization of the Study of New Nations," World Politics, **17** (October, 1964), 157-181.

None of the most dramatic social transformations of our century—the Soviet Union, China, Turkey, Egypt, Israel, Tunisia, Germany, and the United States among them—have yet been utilized to provide us with a theory of social change based on an inquiry into the imbalances that had to be faced, and the improvisation, plans, costs, and rejected alternatives that helped to shape the present outcome. No longer do all Communists fail to acknowledge the worldwide lack of an adequate theory for understanding or controlling the process of institutionalizing change. Never before has there been as rapidly growing a gap between what we do, as it affects an increasingly interrelated society, and what we know. Never before in history has the quality of so many lives depended on a good theory.

Although for some 99.999 per cent of the earth's history, no man lived here, this is not the first time that a grave crisis has been provoked by man's extraordinary will to survive his extraordinary capacity to be fruitful and multiply. What is new is a rapidly increasing gap among rapidly increasing forces—more posttraditional men seeking more and new kinds of goals in a growing mobilization of discontent, since these aspirations are unlikely to be achieved by most of the newly expectant people.

In Iran, one of the best endowed of Middle Eastern countries, most university graduates can find no jobs today. Yet already three-quarters of all applicants for university study must be turned away for lack of space, and this pressure for knowledge and position in the posttraditional world will surely increase once that two-thirds of Iranian children will without any elementary school training also begin to press for mobility. If India's third Five-Year Plan succeeds, it anticipates having more unemployed then than when it first began its economic reconstruction. These are typical illustrations of the gap between actual "development" and the required transformation. P. N. Rosenstein-Rodan has estimated that if the underdeveloped nations of the world receive all the aid which they can economically absorb and utilize skillfully in combination with their own likely savings, their average annual per capita GNP would increase from $140 after twenty-five years to $196. By that time, per capita income in the United States may be at least twenty times higher than the average of the great majority of the world. It will cost that majority much to attain so little, for economic development is and must be destabilizing before it can stabilize a new capacity for growth, for unless old habits, values, and institutions are transformed into new, investments cannot be creative or even secure. But neither in relative nor absolute terms will individual shares of about $200 annually come close to meeting present aspirations, or provide sufficient means for overcoming the imbalances created by the uncontrolled forces of the revolution of modernization.

The rate of change that is crucial is not growth of economic production or literacy or institutional specialization or efficiency—whether separately or as a cluster of indices. It is the rate at which the various systems by which man organizes his society attain the capacity to overcome imbalances sufficiently to guide the permanent revolution of modernization. Power, profit, and solidarity are therefore not signs that a nation has finally arrived, but rather that it at last possesses means to keep moving in deliberate response to the persisting forces of transformation.

The cost of modernization therefore increases as time passes: that is another rate of change that frustrates the capacity to control this revolution. As times passes, more mouths immediately consume a larger proportion of economic gains; more men are uprooted from a traditional environment to raise new kinds of demands; more interests and attitudes that began as temporary adjustments to particular moments of transition harden, become organized, and defend themselves against the threat of transforming change; the willingness to sacrifice and postpone rewards slackens; capital equipment adequate for competition in world markets becomes more expensive to buy and more difficult to maintain with locally available skills; the ground lost relative to the more modernized nations becomes ever more painfully obvious; frustrations left festering too long may break out in violence that increases the cost of repression or concession; vulnerability to intervention from outside grows; both stability and change come to cost more in terms of freedom.

It may be, though I doubt it, that even under these pressures, the majority will remain politically passive. That would not be politically the most relevant fact. The political coup that marked the beginning of the deliberate revolution of modernization was effected by less than fifty men each in most instances during the twentieth century. Rarely were the supporting elements—whether composed of army segments, parties led by members of the salaried or would-be salaried middle class or professions, students, workers, or peasants—either large in proportion to the rest of the population or compelled to fight for long to achieve victory. The uncontrolled forces of the revolution of modernization need not touch all men of a society before a minority among them feels impelled deliberately to increase the rate of change.

The very magnitude of the task is an incitement to action. A nation cannot be built on unproductive toil, parochial loyalties, and on misery that has come to be recognized as remediable injustice. Thus the per capita annual income of Moroccan peasants has remained steadily at about fifty dollars; they are in great majority illiterate; the normal cycle of droughts came to destroy half their harvest in 1960; the government has so far done little to modernize agriculture. "The agrarian revolution," said a Moroccan opposition leader recently, "required two centuries in Western Europe; it cost 8,000,000 deaths in the Soviet Union. We do not want to wait so long, nor act so brutally."[5] The same impetus toward rapid change thus need not be the result of purposeful political initiative, but of its absence. In Iran, the Shah has turned most land over to peasants but, suspicious of the loyalties of the salaried middle class, neglects the organization of cooperatives, credit, training, and political movements which would, inevitably, require the leadership of a new educated salariat. As a result, peasants are unlikely to be able to increase their productivity, may well lose their land to the usurer, and in their new disappointments greatly swell the ranks of the urban and rural discontent.

If the modernizing minority is frustrated in its hopes, its shortfall is not to be ascribed to its having wanted too much. Rather, they will have failed to do what others have shown the will and capacity—or else have been helped to attain the capacity—already to accomplish. Once all the world has been conscious of the success of moderniza-

tion in a few nations, it is useless politically and unwarranted rationally to denounce as Utopians those who are just starting out.

Ideology as an Instrument of Modernization

To overcome the incapacity of their society to guide change, and narrow the gap between themselves and the more modern nations, political leaders require an ideology.[6] There are, however, at least three common conceptions of ideology which make this a recipe for mischief. Ideology can become the substitute for traditional religion, and, as myth, magic formula, ritual, and balm, become the officially manufactured opiate for the masses. Ideology can become a political dogma, freezing a particular moment of partial insight. (Even pragmatism can thus become a political dogma when it refuses to generalize but holds fast only to particular experience.) Ideology can also be construed as the usually misleading rationalization of the right of an élite to rule. There are, in addition, two frequent conceptions of ideology that are merely unhelpful to modernization but, like the first three, more relevant to the maintenance of a system than to its transformation. Ideology can be thought of as the implicit pattern of beliefs and valuation at any given moment. Or ideology can be defined as an explicit statement of ideal

[5] Mehdi ben Barka, quoted by I. William Zartman in *Problems of New Power: Morocco* (New York: Atherton Press, 1964), p. 118.

[6] The ideas contained in the remainder of this essay were further crystallized in the course of meetings at a Conference on Political Development sponsored by the University of Pennsylvania in November, 1964. The discussion group to which I am particularly indebted included A. U. Ahmed, A. Burks, T. Davy, H. Glickman, F. Haviland, D. Smith, A. Smithies, H. Teune, R. Andrews, D. Keiner, B. L. Maheshwari, B. McAfee, and D. Williams. To all of them I am grateful, but they must not be held responsible for this particular formulation.

patterns, though only at the cost of reflecting the inadequacies of most current ideologies to the tasks of modernization.

A sixth and quite different conception of ideology is that of instrument of modernization. Based upon a theory of social change, such ideology is an explicit framework of means and ends capable of stimulating policy-oriented analysis, inspiring action, and constituting the normative and practical touchstone of accomplishments. Its instrumental purpose is to help create, as quickly as possible, a new political culture to substitute for the disintegrating traditional way of life. It is intended to stimulate new orientations about the individual and society and new patterns of behavior relevant to modernization.

Alternative Costs of Failing and Succeeding

Against this conception of the kind of ideology required for political modernization, one may raise objections on empirical and prudential grounds. Observation suggests that many political leaders around the world are concerned only with short-term gains derived from brokerage or invidious aggregation among existing interests. Prudence may also urge that politicians faced with scarcities concentrate on cutting the ends to suit the means at hand. To be content in this fashion, however, is to fail in modernization; given the uncontrolled rates of change already discussed, it is even to fail in conserving power or stability that may now exist.

Nonetheless, the skeptics are probably right. One of the principal scarcities in the world remains the shortage of leaders, ideologies, and theories devoted to systemic transformation. One

therefore needs to ask: What are the alternative ways of avoiding modernization? Two alternatives are out altogether. It is no longer possible to return to the age before the new consciousness, demands, and forces for change came into being. Given such pressures, it is also no longer possible merely to stay put and maintain things as they are, except at increasing cost. But it is possible, in a variety of ways, to "change" or "develop" politically without attaining a sustained capacity to generate and absorb continuing transformation.

Nations can opt to maintain as long as possible traditional behavior, orientations, and institutions as stabilizing compartments within an increasingly modern society; for example, as in the paternalism of Japanese factory life. However, not all traditional societies possess such usable elements, and even in Japan and India, such compartmentalization has exacted its costs and is not likely to endure in its present agglutinated form.

A second alternative involves not the maintenance, but the resurgence in new form of selected traditional elements. In one form, as in the growth of Methodist evangelism in early industrial England, such a revitalization in new form may draw people away from immediate political concerns. Even in traditional societies, however, such a turn toward quietism often prepared the ground for a deeper emotional and moral commitment to a subsequent rebellion for justice. In modern times this transformation, whether in England, or in Africa among the Separatist Christian sects, usually arrived more surely and quickly.

In a quite different form, and as a third alternative, resurging traditional elements may seek instead through institutionalized terror to recover selected dogmas and bonds of the past in a bitter if foredoomed struggle against modernization.

A fourth possible alternative may be drawn as an enlargement of Marion J. Levy's concept of politics as recreation: namely, official encouragement of private hedonism. In addition to circuses, demonstrations, and wars limited largely to excursions and alarms, this mode can be practiced by small groups which require little organizational or capital investment.

The obverse of hedonism—asceticism—is perhaps the most obvious alternative when confronted by hard work amid grim scarcities. But just as obviously, no alternative is less popular in the world today, not even among the descendants of Puritans, or among more recent Puritans, the Communists of Eastern Europe. Only China today is a conscious example of enforced asceticism. Given the growing burden, as well as the growing sensitivity to, scarcity in the world today, China may be the first example of a generic kind of enforced asceticism, but not for long its sole or best model. For does even China know how to compel the sacrifices in norms and habits that may be required to fulfill its government's particular set of expectations? Is it possible to develop types of asceticism that could, even in our age, once more alter a people's sense of the high value of time?

Another alternative is willingness to live with unsolved problems, uncertainty, frustrations, modest expectations, and acquiescence for the sake of order in the provision of more satisfactions for politically crucial segments of society than for others. This may be the counsel of perfect imperfection advocated by the extremist center. It may prove much less acceptable in the less comfortable quarters of the world.

There is an ancient alternative: to harness growing discontent for aggression abroad. Under present international conditions, most countries can be deterred from making any but the most carefully administered and limited wars against each other. Another form of aggression may become much more common in the future: assassination and sabotage abroad. The more modernized a country, the more vulnerable it is to the selective destruction of its managers, machines, and communications. If the gap between the rich and the poor nations continues to widen, and the incapacity of the latter to solve their problems by themselves becomes more painfully apparent, such warfare within the international community cannot be excluded, whether highly organized or as a more spontaneous symptom of delinquent politics.

There is one last alternative left to discuss. It involves a transformation not only of national but of international capacity to deal with modernization. I doubt that most nations will be able to modernize themselves unaided except at an enormous cost in freedom and suffering. Certainly many of them will continue to "develop"—if all that concerns us are incremental changes unrelated to the capacity of a society at last to shape its own transformation. The cost of modernization is far greater than the cost of such "development." A national leadership committed to modernization is unlikely to persuade its people to forgo this quest if the decisive reason for failure is the backwardness of the international system to solve what may only be soluble on this larger level. There is no reason to believe that the poorer nations of the world will lack the shrewdness and strength any more than have the poor of each nation in modern times to press their claims with rapidly increasing effectiveness upon the rich.

To meet this demand of the revolution of modernization would demand certain transformations also of the United States. It would mean for us, as for most nations, a departure from what Edward C. Banfield exposed as the retarding effects of amoral familism in Southern Italy but championed for the American nation in a more recent essay denying that any community beyond our borders had any moral or political grounds for claims on our resources.[7] It would demand that we give more aid to more nations—not merely, as now, 80 per cent of our aid to twenty nations—but more of it to increase for more nations their *political* generative and absorptive capacity, and not only their economic absorptive capacity.[8] It would mean forgoing our

accustomed short-term pragmatism and acting on theoretical prognosis of the forces and trends inherent in the revolution of modernization, perhaps at some risk to what we regard as our present achievements in diplomatic ties and positions of seeming strength. We would have to become increasingly willing to give more aid and involve ourselves more thoroughly in the historical transformations of other nations under increasingly unattractive circumstances—namely, when leaders come into office after the rate of change has further magnified the imbalances of their society, and who, therefore, feel compelled to mobilize more power while giving vent to frustrations more boldly than we are now accustomed to accept.

In the unforeseeable future, there may be reasons for hope about men's perceptions, diagnosis, and readiness for acting on the revolutionary costs of creating stability in modern times, but in the era that seems foreshadowed, the stronger indications are for the growth of politicized despair.

---

[7] The first reference is to Edward C. Banfield, *The Moral Basis of a Backward Society* (Chicago: University of Chicago Press, 1958), the second to "American Foreign Aid Doctrines," in *Public Policy*, ed. C. J. Friedrich and Seymour Harris (Cambridge: Harvard University Press, 1963), pp. 64-105.

[8] The twenty nations who in fiscal year 1964 were expected to receive 80 per cent of our total economic assistance are: India, Pakistan, Turkey, Brazil, Vietnam, Korea, Colombia, Nigeria, Argentina, Chile, Mexico, Congo, Jordan, Bolivia, Sudan, Peru, Laos, Afghanistan, Iran, and Tunisia. (Testimony by David Bell, hearings before the Commit-

tee on Foreign Relations, U.S. Senate, June 26, 1963, p. 577.)

Social Patterns (Structures) and Problems of Modernization

MARION J. LEVY, JR.

Introduction

Modernization as a Peculiar Problem in Social History

A *general social solvent.* In discussing the problems of "modernization" for

the developing nations—whatever term or euphemism we use—we deal with a

An abridged version of this paper appears in *The Annals of the American Academy of Political and Social Science,* **358** (March, 1965), 29-40, under the title "Patterns (Structures) of Modernization and Political Development." In considerably expanded form it appears in M. J. Levy, Jr., *Modernization and the Structure of Societies* (Princeton: Princeton University Press, 1965), 2 vols.

peculiar problem in social history. We are confronted—whether for good or for bad—with a universal social solvent. The patterns of the relatively modernized societies, once developed, have shown a universal tendency to penetrate any social context whose participants have come in contact with them. From many points of view it makes little difference whether these patterns penetrate at least partially by the will and preference of relatively nonmodernized peoples or whether they have the patterns thrust upon them. The patterns always penetrate; once the penetration has begun, the previous indigenous patterns always change; and they always change in the direction of some of the patterns of the relatively modernized society. The changes, once begun, are by no means necessarily successful from the point of view of either outsiders or insiders, but lack of success and dissatisfaction with them hardly impede the disruption of the previous patterns—rather the opposite. There have been "world conquests" before,[1] but even in the areas conquered, the one-way change in social structure that we see in the world today did not exist. The Mongols in their conquest were more changed than changing. The further out Alexander the Great got the more Hellenistic and the less Greek his influence became

until finally at the far reaches of the Indus it was the drapery of Greek sculpture which left its trace rather than the social structure in general.

A *nonbinary distinction.* Throughout this paper I shall invoke a distinction between relatively modernized and relatively nonmodernized societies. I conceive of these categories as locations along a continuum. I wish to avoid, for purposes here, any discussion of just where the dividing point lies. Certain examples of societies or nations are sufficiently far on one side or the other of such a point as to make discussions reasonably clear, if one sticks to examples of that sort. Thus I would consider the United States to represent a relatively modernized society. I would consider the society of Tokugawa, Japan, or traditional China or modern China or modern India, for that matter, to be examples of relatively nonmodernized societies. For purposes of definition—note, not for purposes of description and not as the most significant causal element—solely for purposes of definition—I would consider any society the more modernized the greater the ratio of inanimate to animate sources of power and the greater the extent to which human efforts are multiplied by the use of tools. I would consider any society relatively modernized if comparatively small changes increasing the ratio of animate to inanimate sources of power would have very far-reaching implications for the general social structure. In this sense there are no societies totally lacking in all elements of modernization, and that is the reason I have used quotation marks around the word modernization when it first appeared above. All remarks in this paper, unless specifically noted to the contrary, refer to cases well on one side or the other of any dividing line in such a continuum. At least it is my hypothesis that they do. I have deliber-

---

[1] Actually there have never been "world conquests" before. What are described as world conquests never encompass more than what the author then considered the most important parts of the world. Sometimes he considered the world to have been conquered when whole areas, such as China, were left relatively untouched or completely untouched. The patterns of the relatively modernized societies have been one of the great antidotes to this sort of parochialism. The average graduate student in the social sciences and the disciplines of history avoids this sort of parochialism with a taken for granted ease that completely eluded scholars of even the calibre of Professor Werner Jaeger.

ately chosen a definitional element which is a continuum even though I intend to confine my attention to quite extreme distinctions along that continuum. I feel that many elements of misunderstanding with regard to the problems of development are a function of the fact that current misuses of binary concepts in the social sciences have begged many of the most important questions of modernization by the fallacy of misplaced dichotomies.

Common elements and variations. It is an assumption here that on the most general levels of consideration all societies must be identical and that all variations at less abstract levels constitute overlays on these common elements. Furthermore, all relatively modernized societies have developed out of relatively nonmodernized ones. Some of them developed with only minor importations from abroad. All relatively nonmodernized societies have more in common as regards social structure than any one of them has with any case of a relatively modernized society and vice versa. For example, it is an hypothesis here that, despite the fact that modern English society developed out of thirteenth-century English society, thirteenth-century English society had more in common with the society of the Trobriand Islanders than it does with that of modern England.

Some General Considerations

Hypothesis about the facts. All of the statements made throughout this paper, except those made by way of illustrations, will be on extremely general levels and will, I hope, be made in terms of extremely small numbers of variables. The statements made will ordinarily refer to such general levels as: all societies, all relatively nonmodernized societies, all relatively modernized societies, all relatively nonmodernized societies into which patterns of

relatively modernized societies have been introduced, etc. For few if any of these statements has definitive evidence been assembled. In all such cases —and in all cases introduced by way of illustration—the statements made should be considered to be hypothesis about the facts. I do not knowingly present any such hypotheses without believing them to be tenable, but my beliefs are not to be confused with proof.

Common elements and variations. As indicated above, it is part of the general point of view underlying this essay that all societies have some elements in common—that otherwise we would not be able to conduct sessions of this sort at all. Furthermore I would assert, for reasons which need not detain the argument here, that all of the variations which concern us in any particular society are always overlays on the common elements to which I have referred. This consideration alone makes the fallacy of misplaced dichotomies a matter of danger.

Requisites and prerequisites. I shall consider anything to be a requisite of a given phenomenon if in the absence of that element the phenomenon cannot continue to exist. I will consider an element to be a prerequisite of a given phenomenon if in the absence of the elements concerned the phenomenon cannot come into existence. It is flatly teleological in the fallacious sense of the term to attribute the existence of any element to the fact or hypothesis that it is a requisite or a prerequisite of some phenomenon. This always involves as a minimum the unproved and frequently unprovable hypothesis that the phenomenon itself must exist or come into existence. In the last analysis, this in turn always involves questions of ontology.

Ideal and actual patterns. Throughout this paper I shall make references to ideal and actual patterns. There are no ethical connotations to the word ideal as used here. I define a pattern as an ideal pattern if some specifiable set of individuals regard these patterns as being preferable, right, proper, etc. I define the patterns as actual if some theoretically omniscient scientific observer sees that they are in fact the pattern in terms of which some specifiable set of individuals behave. This distinction is an important one because a whole set of generalizations can be drawn up in terms of them. For present purposes I would like to assert five of them:

1. All peoples distinguish between ideal and actual patterns. There are no peoples who do not in some respects distinguish between the way things are and the way they would prefer them to be.

2. The ideal and actual patterns never coincide completely. That is to say that there are always some discrepancies between ideal and actual patterns.

3. The members of a society are always to some extent aware of the fact that their ideal and actual patterns do not coincide perfectly.

4. Some of the sources of stress and strain characteristic of any society are a function of the fact that the ideal and actual patterns do not coincide perfectly. Not only are the members of every society aware that they or others do not always behave as they feel they should or would prefer to but to some extent they are upset by it.

5. Some of the possibilities of integration inhere in the fact that the ideal and actual patterns do not coincide perfectly. This generalization is not paradoxical relative to the preceding one. One of the reasons ideal and actual patterns do not coincide perfectly is that the ideal patterns are not always mutually consistent. Some ideal patterns are approximated only to the

extent that certain other ones are not approximated. For example, the traditional Chinese were able to approximate their ideal pattern of equal division of property among all sons only because they were not able to approximate their ideal patterns with regard to the number of sons they wished to have survive per family.

Sources of Naïveté About Problems of Modernization

Requisites—prerequisites. Most of the errors of policy programs which are not simply a function of strict empirical error about the customs of the people concerned fall into one of three categories.

1. They ignore the fact that the requisites of relatively modernized societies are not necessarily the same as the prerequisites for achieving such a state. You cannot simply look at the patterns of a relatively modernized society and say that is what society so and so must do now in order to become modernized.

2. The prerequisites for latecomers to the process are not necessarily the same as the prerequisites for those societies whose members achieved these patterns largely indigenously and above all gradually in a situation in which they have not been previously developed. That is to say you cannot simply look at the prerequisites for the development of a relatively modernized society in Great Britain and assume that those constitute what the members of a relatively nonmodernized society today must do. For example, in the early part of Great Britain's development universal education was not a prerequisite. In the British case a loosening of the patterns of governmental control probably was a prerequisite. The increase of governmental centralization is a prerequisite for latecomers.

3. The prerequisites of one set of late-

comers are not necessarily the same as prerequisites of another set of latecomers. The differences from one case to another will be a function primarily of the different historical bases from which change takes place. Thus one cannot simply look at the prerequisites in the case of Japan and assume that that is what other latecomers must do.

Failure to take these matters into account would not be difficult to correct were it not for the fact, alas!, that some of the requisites for relatively modernized society are the same as the prerequisites for becoming relatively modernized. Some of the prerequisites for latecomers are the same as those for the indigenous developers, and some of the prerequisites for one set of latecomers are the same as those of another. Furthermore, the closer the periods of history on which attention is focused, the greater is the likelihood that the requisites and prerequisites for a given phenomenon will coincide. The failure to distinguish between latecomers and indigenous developers and between one latecomer and another as far as the stages of modernization are concerned—the implication that the process is in all important respects the same for everyone is one of the most serious errors we face. In part, whether intended or no, some of the prevalence of this latter difficulty is a function of the fact that Professor Rostow, in his now famous work, made the point that there were differences in the time of starting but gave the quite general impression that the process was essentially the same for all.[2] He is of course absolutely correct in one sense. On the most general possible level it is always the same—but our attention is never focused for any save problem of intellectual and scientific interest on that level alone.

The fallacy of misplaced dichotomies. Binary distinctions are powerful and important tools, both for scientists and those of a more pragmatic turn of mind. It is only necessary to mention the fact that there are those who regard us as only just now coming into the age of the computer. Alas, there remain, especially as far as social science concepts are concerned, misuses as well as proper uses of the law of excluded middle. Thus, for example, it is misleading rather than helpful—quite apart [from] the geographical idiocy involved—to refer to the governments of "non-Western societies" (i.e., the governments of relatively nonmodernized societies) as characterized by cliques. The implication (or explication) here is that the "government of Western societies" (i.e., the governments of relatively modernized societies) are not characterized by cliques. People who write this way have something in mind and guarantee by this way of putting it that it will not be understood. The distinction between relatively modernized and relatively nonmodernized societies is not the presence or absence of cliques. Rather it is the way in which clique patterns fit into the general social structure, the attitude of the members of the society toward them, the bases for the formation of cliques, etc. The differences may be of many sorts. For example, the actual patterns may be the same in most respects but the ideal patterns radically different. This will in turn have implications for some other actual patterns.

One of the most misleading of the distinctions currently used as a binary one is the distinction between rational and traditional ways of looking at things. It makes an enormous amount

2 W. W. Rostow, *The Stages of Economic Growth* (Cambridge: Cambridge University Press, 1960).

of difference whether people emphasize the continuation of certain patterns because this is supported by tradition as opposed to being justified presumably by scientifically meaningful knowledge. But the implication is frequently given that the traditional is irrational or varies randomly relative to rationality. Nothing could be further from the truth. In many social contexts things which are done for traditional justifications coincide to a high degree with what it is rational to do with the means available. Indeed one of the special problems may be a function of the fact that what is (or was) traditional coincides with what is rational given the means at the disposal of the people concerned. One of the things that is important about doing things with traditional justifications is the fact that, if the means change, one is likely to continue to do things which, though previously rational, are now irrational— and continue for the same reasons given before. The emphasis on rationality rather than on tradition is more important for a prediction of what will happen if the available means change than in a prediction that what is presently being done is rational *versus* irrational.

Spiritual versus *materialistic orientations.* The use of different adjectival endings is interesting in this. It has become one of the clichés of modern criticism in connection with this whole process to distinguish between those who are presumably spiritually oriented and those who are materialistically oriented. This is so special a case of the fallacy of misplaced dichotomies as to require separate listing. There are no peoples completely lacking in what are generally referred to as spiritual interests and it is even more striking that—sanctimony to one side—there are no peoples completely lacking in materialistic orientations. This misuse of a binary distinc-

tion is given separate listing here specifically because a careful consideration of problems under this heading uncovers one of the basic sources of appeal of the patterns of the relatively modernized societies. Here again one may state a set of generalizations that apply to any and all peoples regardless of variations in their social patterns:

1. No peoples are indifferent to material factors.
2. No peoples fail to differentiate in some fashion between being relatively better off and relatively worse off materially.
3. Peoples everywhere always exhibit some preferences for being better off as opposed to being worse off materially.
4. Peoples do vary widely, both within a given social context and from one social context to another, with regard to the prices they are prepared to pay in order to be relatively better off— materially and even more importantly —in the horizons they envisage about the possibilities of being relatively better off. Indeed, failure to envisage possibilities of improvement probably explain more of the many alleged spiritual qualities than spiritual criteria which make people explicitly unwilling to pay prices for material improvement.

Whatever else one may say about the patterns of the relatively modernized societies, the material productivity of those who operate in terms of them materially is inordinately greater than that of those who operate in terms of the patterns of relatively nonmodernized societies. Thus insofar as there is always some minimal interest in material improvement amongst all peoples, there is always something in it for someone, once contact with patterns of relatively modernized societies have been made. To this extent an enormous number of the practices generally regarded as vicious and lumped together under the heading "imperialism" have been largely irrelevant. Even without the nastiness that we generally agree to associate with the phenomena of imperialism, these patterns would have penetrated; they would have subverted the status quo; they would have resulted in considerable amounts of dissatisfaction and unease. In the process of movement toward relatively modernized patterns, someone, usually very large numbers of people, always gets hurt. Furthermore, as previously pointed out, neither the movement nor the hurt necessarily results in success as that is envisioned.

Combining the best of the East and the West. Once again it is necessary to ignore the geographical idiocy involved in this formulation. This is an exceedingly popular form of solution to these problems. This is the great form of modern romanticism on the subject. This view has its official philosopher, and recently a modern sociologist has been reported (perhaps erroneously) as having told a meeting of African specialists that "the pattern of modernization in Africa would not follow the European pattern *and would not involve the abolition of traditions*" (italics added). No one of course is foolish enough to maintain that all previously existing traditions in any given relatively nonmodernized society vanish overnight with these contacts or that *all* ever vanish. Some persist much longer than others. What is difficult about this form of romanticism is that it is usually difficult to get careful specifications of what is regarded as the best of the East and what is regarded as the best of the West. Insofar as specification is available, what is generally regarded as the best of the East usually turns out to be most radically incompatible with what is regarded as the best of the West.

The East and the West. There are several difficulties about this distinction; the first is that it preserves the flavor of the "mysterious Orient" which turns out never to have been anything but a euphemism for a difficult language barrier. Second, if one pays close attention to the distinction, it lumps together such current cases as Portugal and Western Germany. Third, it lumps together such cases as Merovingian France—indisputably Western—and modern England. Fourth, it implies that there are few if any differences among the relatively nonmodernized societies as far as implications for modernization are concerned. There may be some sense in which India, Japan, and China all represent cases of preoccupation with the "undifferentiated aesthetic continuum," if any meaning can be specified for that, but those societies vary from one another about as widely as is possible—either within the category of relatively nonmodernized societies if one is considering them before the achievement of relatively modernized patterns in Japan or as much as one would expect once Japan became a relatively modernized society, while India and China remained relatively nonmodernized.

Prior internal pressures. So peremptory have been the problems of the members of relatively nonmodernized societies once they have come in contact with the patterns of relatively modernized societies that many of us lose sight of the fact that these peoples were not without their problems before these contacts were meaningful to them. These were not necessarily welladjusted, highly integrated societies devoid of internal pressures until the apple of discord was thrown among their members. Some of these societies were in various stages of change. But more importantly, some that gave the most dramatic outward appearances of stability were stable because the pre-existing patterns were such that elements of stress and strain were powerfully contained—not because they were absent.

Foci of Differences Between Relatively Modernized and Relatively Nonmodernized Societies

Specialization of Organizations

There is a type of specialization—not unknown in relatively nonmodernized contexts—but carried very much further in relatively modernized contexts. This specialization is quite independent of the kind of products produced or operations performed in terms of the organization. This kind of specialization increases in relatively modernized contexts. The kind of specialization referred to here is a specialized orientation to a single aspect of behavior. Predominantly economically oriented organizations, such as business firms or factories, predominantly politically oriented organizations, such as governments and political parties, predominantly educationally oriented organizations, such as schools, predominantly religiously oriented organizations, predominantly recreationally oriented organizations—all these are enormously elaborated in relatively modernized contexts. Relatively nonspecialized organizations, such as family units, are not eliminated in such contexts, nor do they become unimportant. Nevertheless, one of the critical differences between relatively modernized and relatively nonmodernized societies lies in the fact that when such specialized organizations exist in the relatively nonmodernized contexts, only a relatively small proportion of the general population operate often or for much of their careers in terms of such organizations. The vast majority of the members of any relatively modernized society operate continuously in terms of such organizations, in addition to the operations they continue to carry out in other contexts. One aspect of the increase of such organizational contexts is of course what is sometimes referred to as the "compartmentalization" of life in highly modernized contexts. This change alone has far-reaching implications for people accustomed to carrying out the vast majority of their activities in relatively nonspecialized contexts. This not only represents a new sort of context for many, it changes the implications of behavior in terms of the relatively nonspecialized contexts in which they continue to act. The increase of such contexts at one and the same time undermines previous family stability and increases the relevance of the family in certain respects. For example, for the person accustomed to roving ceaselessly in and out of such specialized contexts, the family may come to be the one context in which he is considered as a whole man—the only "castle of the me" for modern man.

Interdependency

A close correlate of the increased specialization of organizations is the high level of interdependency characteristic of relatively modernized society. In no society are there organizations whose members are capable of complete self-sufficiency, but the levels of self-sufficiency attained in terms of organizations such as the family, the village, etc., is frequently high. The level of self-sufficiency of the members of all organizations up to and including nations continues to decline with increases in modernization.

Relationship Emphases

Relatively modernized by contrast with relatively nonmodernized contexts are featured by great emphases both ideally and actually on what have come in the trade to be known as the patterns of rationality, universalism, and functional specificity as opposed to emphases on tradition, particularism, and functional diffuseness. Explicit emphases in many contexts on using knowledge that is presumably scientifically justified (rationality), of selecting people and judging them on the basis of what they can do that is relevant as opposed to who they are (universalism), and on precisely defined and delimited relationships (functional specificity) are requisites for a relatively modernized society. The most common form of the fallacy of misplaced dichotomy is to imply or assert that in such relatively modernized contexts there are no or negligible emphases on tradition, particularism, and functional diffuseness. The family context, for example, as will be noted below, is always relevant for these societies, and that context in all societies is predominantly traditional, predominantly particularistic, and predominantly functionally diffuse. Actually speaking, in relatively nonmodernized contexts there are often some emphases on rationality, universalism, and functional specificity, and sometimes there are ideal patterns of this sort as well—as witness the examination patterns of the Chinese bureaucracy. Nevertheless both ideally and actually the vast majority of the members of all of the relatively nonmodernized societies operated in nearly all their organizational contexts on predominantly traditional, predominantly particularistic, and predominantly functionally diffuse bases. I have already pointed out above that what is done because it is predominantly traditional is not necessarily irrational, and indeed frequently coincides with rationality given the means at the disposal of the people concerned. The same cannot be said of the other two aspects, although here, given the contexts in which they are emphasized, they may not make the kind of differences that one might suppose. For example, predominantly particularistic criteria for employment do not necessarily under these circumstances lower the level of efficiency of the personnel engaged in a given job.

Patterns of Centralization

All relatively nonmodernized societies stable over relatively long periods of time are examples of quite specific combinations of centralization and decentralization. Moreover, however much the patterns of centralization may have been emphasized, these systems as a whole were never overwhelmingly centralized, if stable. It is only with the patterns of relatively modernized societies that the logistics of overwhelming centralization become either feasible or economic—regardless of ethical considerations. In all of the relatively modernized contexts the levels of centralization continually rise over long periods of time. Because of our preoccupation with specialized organizational contexts, we tend to think of all centralization as heading up in governmental organizations. Increasingly this is the case with relatively modernized societies, but it is by no means exclusively the case. Most observers would probably agree that the centralization of the government of the Soviet Union has been carried to considerably greater lengths than that of the government of the United States, but there are also many senses in which the much greater development of communication facilities alone constitute greater over-all centralization of United States society than is characteristic of the Soviet Union.

What is most important about this question of centralization is that for latecomers to the process the requirements of coordination and control are always strategic, and they are always strategic at a point in time in which the probability is overwhelming that the previously existing patterns of co-ordination and control will be radically undercut. So far in history only the patterns of Tokugawa, Japan, have shown "virtuosity" in avoiding these effects.

Generalized Media of Exchange and Markets

All relatively modernized contexts require much greater emphases on monetary devices and markets. Media of exchange—monies—vary enormously in the level of generalization character-istic of them. That is to say, the num-ber of things that can be exchanged or evaluated in terms of money vary enormously. Characteristically in feu-dal contexts land is not subject to free and easy purchase and sale. Therefore the level of generalization of such media of exchange as exist in those contexts does not include land.

The whole subject of money is a matter about which academics are ex-ceedingly skittish, and even nonaca-demics seem to feel that a preoccupa-tion with money is one of the crassest forms of materialism. None of us hesi-tates to affirm the opinion that travel is broadening, but so is the use of money. Few things so affect a people's horizons of the possible as the increased use of money. Above all it spreads comparisons. Whether one likes it or not, if one knows that a Rembrandt painting has sold for $2,500,000 and the latest edition of *Fanny Hill* sells for $2.50—regardless of ideology—a relation of the one as 10^6 more costly than the other has been established. Correspondingly, to tell a peasant who has never even considered the possibil-ity of getting an education for his son that an education costs a given amount —even if that amount is one that he does not think he has any prospect of achieving—tells him that, if he can make certain accumulations, he can achieve an education for his son. (It is not entirely correct that money can-not buy an education.) By contrast with any relatively nonmodernized con-text the generalization of the media of exchange and the use of money in gen-eral always increases. It will continue to do so until or unless a completely managed and centralized organization for allocation of goods and services under government auspices is achieved. Such centralization, however, in turn implies other problems—especially a problem of adequate knowledge— which will be taken up later.

Markets are by no means unknown in relatively nonmodernized contexts but they always proliferate enormously in relatively modernized contexts. There are by definition always some degrees of freedom associated with a market. These degrees of freedom, if broad enough and if the number of participants in the market is great enough, spreads out and hence mini-mizes the problem of error and always poses problems of control. In the ab-sence of adequate knowledge for effi-cient rationality about direct allocation of goods and services, a market device minimizes the problem of errors in judgment by diffusing them among a relatively large and less powerful set. Of course this cannot be done without to some degree leaving to the individ-ual members of the market the power to be wrong and the possibility of using their allocations in ways that may not be deemed desirable. It is one of the ironies of modern ideological disputes that "capitalism" and the associated presence of very high degrees of free-dom in the markets concerned is sup-posed quite broadly to increase the implications of allocations of goods and services for the allocations of power and responsibility. Actually such patterns are perhaps the most efficient device found by man to minimize such implications. Societies which may be described as feudal, Fascist, and Socialist are always ones in terms of which allocations of power and responsibility and allocations of goods and services are more directly and immediately interdependent than capitalistic societies.

Fit in General Structure

The implication of a given pattern may vary enormously depending on how that pattern fits into the general social structure. Although there were important differences, the many common emphases of Japanese and Chinese family patterns were enormously modified by virtue of the fact that the Chinese was expected to give his loyalty first and last to his family, whereas the Japanese of the corresponding period—if the opportunity offered—was ideally speaking prepared to sacrifice his family interests for those of his overlord. Correspondingly, in this process even the retention of previously existing patterns does not mean that they have the same implications as before nor does it mean that a given pattern may be taken over directly and used efficiently. All relatively modernized societies must be ones whose members stress social mobility, but the ideal patterns of social mobility in China, initially at least, had negative implication of the modernization process, whereas the closed-class patterns of Japan as a background had positive implications. Although positions in the Tokugawa civil service system were ostensibly inherited, whereas those in the Chinese bureaucracy were achieved by prowess in examinations, the Japanese in fact had a sort of civil service by adoption which may have been even more efficient and less vulnerable to corruption than the patterns of the Chinese.

Bureaucracy

This whole question is so frequently commented upon that it need not detain the argument here. Suffice it to say that the bureaucracies in relatively modernized contexts must be on a different basis than those in relatively nonmodernized contexts. In relatively modernized contexts members of bureaucracies are not only faced by the necessity of high levels of ingenuity and skill in devising both patterns of government and physical plant. They are also faced by the twin problems of rapid obsolescence and far-reaching implications of relatively minor failures in maintenance. The rapidity of technological change and the high levels of interdependency characteristic of these societies are relevant here.

One of the critical questions for members of all relatively modernized societies is how to recruit and maintain such organizations. Members of all societies with such organizations share the problem of how one is to insulate the members from other contexts. For latecomers to the process this poses a special problem. Not only are the previous contexts with overwhelming emphasis on nonbureaucratic criteria still very much present, but the bureaucrats themselves constitute one of the great sources of dissidence. Bureaucrats in general are easily frustrated, and in the process of modernization the new bureaucrats are first made both ideally and actually élite, and then are likely to be radically frustrated.

Family Considerations

From a theoretical point of view the family is an interesting organization. It is the one organization that we feel sure has existed in all known societies. Furthermore, the overwhelming majority of members of all known societies, including the most modernized, have roles in some family or other throughout their life histories. The family context is interesting in yet another respect. All nonfamily organizations can be divided into two categories. The first is those relative to which, ideally speaking, family considerations are supposed to make a difference. Most of the relatively nonmodernized societies are ones whose members regard nepotism as a virtue rather than as a vice. Under these circumstances it is better than an even money bet, very much better, that both ideally and actually what happens to one in terms of one's family will affect the way in which one behaves in the nonfamily context in which he acts. The other type of nonfamily organization is that in terms of which family considerations are not supposed to affect how one behaves. The proliferation of such organizations in relatively modernized contexts is enormous. Most of the specialized organizations referred to are of this sort, and all of the bureaucracies, ideally speaking, are. In the context of these organizations, ideally speaking, what happens to one in terms of one's family does not affect one's behavior. But actually speaking, it is exceedingly likely to affect the way one behaves in important respects. It takes, for example, a virtuoso of professorial objectivity to keep serious domestic difficulties from interfering with the way in which a member of the faculty treats his students. Finally, in the context of all known societies much of the basic learning (i.e., much of the learning that every individual member is expected to acquire at some time in his life cycle) is acquired in family contexts. Even in the most highly modernized societies, where the "functions of the family" are alleged to be eaten

away, the overwhelming majority of the individuals learn to walk, to talk, to eat, to sleep, to control bodily functions, to adjust to patterns of authority and allocations of goods and services, to receive and give affection, etc., in a family context. Thus for all known societies the family organization is always present; the vast majority of individuals belong to some such organization throughout their life histories; and what they do in terms of all other organizations either ideally and/or actually is affected by what happens to them in their family contexts. And they acquire their basic learning or a considerable portion of it in such contexts. Family organizations are not likely to be negligible matters for understanding any social setting.

Moreover, in all relatively nonmodernized contexts the vast majority of all behavior of all individuals is actually likely to be family oriented even if it is not ideally so. That is to say, the average member of such societies rarely operates outside a family context. Even when he operates in a village context it is usually simultaneously in a family context as well. Furthermore, the average member of all relatively nonmodernized societies acquires the vast majority of all of the learning that he acquires throughout his life cycle—not just his basic learning—in a family context. The various bases of precedence in the family context ordinarily reinforce one and another. The family head is ordinarily the representative of the oldest generation, is in fact the oldest individual, and a male if customarily precedence is on the basis of generation, age, and sex. Furthermore, insofar as individuals are controlled, the vast majority of individuals in relatively nonmodernized contexts are controlled on a family basis. The major form of decentralization of control is to the family head in such contexts. This is one of the reasons why the general problems of social control for all the latecomers to this process are so closely related to questions of family disintegration. The fact that, with the introduction of the new patterns, the individual may for the first time have learned something of importance to his performance of adult roles from someone other than an older member of his own family may undermine the ordinary reinforcement of respect for the control of the older members. From the point of view of such individuals, lack of defiance may be more a function of lack of conceived alternatives than of a lack of dissatisfaction with the forms of control as they exist. This as much as anything else is relevant to the explosive disintegration of so many social patterns under the impact of modernization.

Town-Village Interdependencies

The vast majority of all of the members of all of the relatively nonmodernized societies are rural rather than urban. They are villagers rather than townspeople. They are also overwhelmingly preoccupied with sedentary forms of agriculture. If the societies are of considerable scale in terms of numbers of members and territorial limits, they are without exception—never mind how they came to be—accustomed to some level of what they regard as essentially a one-way flow of goods and services from rural to urban contexts. The main forms of such flows are of course rent, taxes, interest, and profits. All of these may be substituted by feudal dues or other devices. In general the rurals take this as a way of life. They do not ordinarily defy or resist unless there is some increase beyond customary limits. In general they do not regard themselves as recipients of a continuous flow of goods and serv-

ices from urban contexts. Above all, they are not accustomed to the urban contexts as a source of goods or devices or ideas that systematically increase productivity per acre in the rural areas. This latter expectation is one of the most revolutionary features of relatively modernized societies and has reached its most extraordinary development in the case of modern United States society. Our great comparative advantage in problems of modernization is surely our agrarian know-how. It is relatively speaking much easier to reproduce our factories than our productivity per acre.

The Difference It Makes

Change

Once contact is made with members of a relatively modernized society, change in that direction begins—even if the change from the point of view of all concerned is a dismal failure.

Families and Strains

Family contexts always are a focus of strain. And the new possibilities of learning and alternative form of employment furnish explosive outlets for those strains.

Problems of Control

The problems of control are maximized just as most of the bases for control are undercut—especially the bases of family control. In some sense all of the latecomers, as they modernize, are in for political instability. Furthermore, initial successes in control are not necessarily harbingers of success in these respects. There is hardly a case in which there is not sufficient control initially to get some more or less spectacular increases in productivity, in the form of a factory here or an improved communications facility there. The real trick is to coordinate such increases in productivity and such changes once a large number of them have come into existence. So far, many more latecomers have tried than have succeeded. This is what makes the case of Japan so very spectacular.

Individualism by Default

There is likely to be individualism by default in all cases of modernization rather than stable forms of individualism by ideal. That is to say, people are [more] likely to be radically cut loose as far as their horizons of what they can do or attempt is concerned than to pick up the kind of patterns of individualism that we tend to think of. The individualist by default, not so much because he feels that the average individual "should stand on his own two feet," but rather because the context in terms of which he has ordinarily made his decisions—most usually the family context—is either no longer available to him or not relevant. Individualism by default always increases the possibilities of ruthless behavior. If this is sufficiently widespread, like a market system, it can minimize the implications of certain forms of error, but it is likely to be concentrated among virtuosi of individualism by default. Such concentration considerably complicates problems of control.

Advantages and Disadvantages of Latecomers

Advantages. Latecomers to the process have certain obvious advantages. For one thing they are not traveling in terra incognita. Unlike the indigenous developers of these patterns they have conceptions, right or wrong, about where they are going. Second, there exists the possibility of borrowing initial expertise in planning, capital accumulation, skills, patterns of organization, etc. Third, there is the possibility of skipping some of the early stages associated with the process elsewhere.

Fourth, the leaders among latecomers —because the problem is not terra incognita—may be able to solidify their leadership by holding out prospects elsewhere achieved. Fifth, latecomers are always to some extent in a position to take over the fruits of the process elsewhere without the cost of invention or previous obsolescence. Not only are the latecomers likely to ask for assistance, but regardless of motivation those who have previously achieved in these respects are likely to offer or insist on assistance.

Disadvantages. The disadvantages of latecomers are in general of three sorts. There are problems of scale, problems of conversion, and problems of disappointment. Latecomers, in order to get into the process at all, must do some things from the very outset on a fairly large scale. Characteristically these are things which the indigenous developers were able to carry out over long periods of time in relatively small steps. Most spectacular among these are the development of modern communication and educational facilities. Universal literacy, for example, is something that "needs" achieving for these people as soon as possible. The larger the problems of scale, the greater the implications of any failures in coordination and control.

The second disadvantage of latecomers has to do with the problem of conversion of resources, materials, skills, etc., from one employment to another. For those who modernized gradually over long periods of time the materials and skills at hand were converted into the new ones. In Great Britain the carpenters, the blacksmiths, and the wrights of one period working with the materials at hand created the materials and skills for the next stage. For the latecomers the problem is different. No amount of ingenuity and skill permits one to use the carpenters, blacksmiths, and wrights at hand plus the materials available to make a modern milling machine. Some of the conversions to be made are of this order. Short of everything needed in this fashion being an outright gift from abroad (and that poses problems of a different sort), as a minimum there is the problem of re-orientation of pre-existing forms of productivity so as to accumulate foreign exchange or its equivalent. The Chinese anthropologist, Fei Hsiao-t'ung, once wrote a marvelous account of how a whole village of south China got tied into the world economy and ended up in the 1929 depression with a large number of unmarried young women overage and out of hand because of the effect of the depression on the export market for raw silk (this was that long-ago never-never land in which one of the major uses of raw silk was for such luxury items as silk underclothes and stockings).

The third disadvantage of latecomers is that of disappointment. To some extent these people get involved in the process with a view to what it will do for them. To some extent they and their leaders lead themselves to certain expectations which really did not exist for the indigenous developers, but in the process someone always gets hurt. Things do not always turn out according to either expectations or hopes. In some cases there is the illusion of falling further and further behind, even though in relative terms one is gaining. Sooner or later an 8 or 10 per cent in capital formation anywhere in the world would overtake the United States rate of 3 per cent or slightly more. But in absolute terms that 3 per cent is overwhelmingly greater than the 8 or 10 per cent. Latecomers are exceedingly likely to experience the frustration of running harder and harder only to seem to fall further and further behind.

Fundamentalist Reactions

In this process someone always gets hurt. Someone is always disappointed. In the midst of the disintegration of the old someone always sees villainy as the introduction of the new. The cry that things were better in the good old days always occurs to someone, always appeals to someone, and someone always acts on it. The attempt to turn the clock back is no less radical in its implications than the attempt to push the clock forward beyond one's means. The main difference lies in the fact that the former are unintentionally radical and the latter are often unthinkingly radical.

Mobs

One of the earliest importations now is always radical improvement in the means of communication—and with that the probability of mass appeals—and with that the possibility of the use of mobs. The temptation to use mobs is something that should be indulged in by those out of power seeking to gain it but never attempted by those in power. For those in power the use of mobs means instability. One can endow the members of a mob with power but one cannot hold them effectively responsible. The former is more likely to be seen as the short-cut means to the ends of some of the leaders involved.

The Problem of Adequate Knowledge

The more highly centralized a given system becomes, the more strategic is adequate knowledge to the levels of explicit planning necessary. For latecomers to the process, with their special disadvantages and their special problems of coordination and control, adequate knowledge is a critical problem. Usually neither they nor we know much about their own societies. Certainly far less is known explicitly than is necessary to take fully into account the bases from which change takes place. Furthermore, given the state of the social sciences, with certain notable exceptions in particular areas of the field of economics, the prospects are not favorable that we will soon come into possession of the knowledge we need. The state of theory in most of these fields is a scandal, and we need more analysis of a high order of these problems than seems in immediate prospect. In the world in which we live today radicalism has little to do with the ideology of left and right. Increasingly radicals take the form of conservative radicals who would unwittingly cut the levels of centralization below the minimum requisite for the kinds of contexts in which they live, and the liberal radicals who would increase the level of centralization beyond the limits of adequate knowledge for operating effectively in terms of centralized patterns. In the absence of improvements in the social sciences well beyond sophisticated techniques of gathering and assessing data, members of both highly modernized and relatively nonmodernized societies alike are in far greater danger from ignorance than from population explosions.

Changes in Fit

The fit of one set of social patterns into another can be altered—and usually is—unintentionally. Levels of interdependency build up in a cumulative and accelerated fashion. I have tried to illustrate this point by the example of the teaching of new techniques undermining general family control. There are other ways in which such undermining takes place. It may well be that in villages balances of predominantly particularistic interests have resulted in predominantly universalistic results. By trying to teach people explicitly to pay attention to what a person can do that is relevant rather than who he is, the

previously existing balances of interests may be undermined without techniques of predominantly universalistic assessment having been well learned.

Possible Avenues of Control

Alterations of Town-Village Imbalances

As indicated above, these societies are overwhelmingly likely to be predominantly agrarian. For most people in the past the terms modernization and industrialization have been considered almost synonymous. Only recently have the revolutionary implications of highly modernized agrarian productivity been recognized for what they are. At almost every turn in all of the relatively nonmodernized cases, when one speaks of capital formation, of controlling people—whatever one speaks of—one speaks of handling farmers. It is no longer possible to satisfy farmers in these areas by the strategy of allocating titles of land to them. For the remainder of this century the major strategy of modernization for latecomers will have to be increasingly an attempt to improve productivity per acre systematically and continuously first, and to increase productivity in industry in the ordinary sense in urban settings no more rapidly than is necessary to support such increases in productivity per acre in the rural areas. One of the major obstacles to this at present is that to the latecomers themselves it is the factories, the automobiles, the computers that symbolize modernization, and not the somewhat more subtle continuous increases in productivity per acre.

Creative Use of Armed Forces

Both academics and Americans have been provincial in their views of armed forces. We tend to consider them as essentially negative in their impact and available primarily for external use alone. For most people in the world and increasingly in the future, the relevance of armed forces for the maintenance of internal order will, short of a holocaust, be more important than their uses in external forays. The members of these societies are going to maintain armed forces—the more modern the better as far as they are concerned. Our real disability in this respect is primarily a function of the fact that we have not generally considered the armed forces for what they are. Under relatively nonmodernized conditions, the armed forces are more likely to be a focus of preoccupation with rationality, universalism, functional specificity, etc., than anything else. Furthermore, in the modernization situation armed forces offer certain advantages. First, the things that the leaders of the countries concerned will want the members of their armed forces to be good at are usually directly convertible to nonmilitary contexts. Driving a military truck is not in principle different from driving a civilian truck, and indeed driving a military tank is not in principle different from many other techniques in handling heavy machinery. Second, problems of control of the members of armed forces are usually minimal. Mass mutinies are relatively rare in history and do not occur save in the context of general social disintegration. The real problem with handling armed forces is the problem of containing palace revolutions engineered by armed force officers or other cliques. Third, armed forces are likely to be set up on the basis of universal conscription from among the members of the society, and that affords those in control the possibility of the selection of the ablest people both physically and mentally for the impact of the training to be given in an armed force context. Fourth, for reasons having to do with

the focusing of attention, elimination of interference, etc., the inculcation of new patterns in an armed force context is almost always carried out in "camps." These involve, potentially at least, high levels of isolation from the population at large, and creative thought in the matter could probably increase those rates. This means that the armed forces probably offer a more promising context for the maximization of new elements of modernization with a minimization of problems of uncontrolled feedback than any other single social device. The feedback from armed force contexts will not be eliminated, but it is more amenable to control than most. One is aided in this by the inevitable emphasis on discipline characteristic of armed force contexts. Furthermore, armed forces as such are not the only adaptations that can be made. Modified versions, such as the Civilian Conservation Corps of the United States in the 1930's, are possibilities. Our distaste for military and paramilitary organizations given the uses to which they have been put in the recent past in Europe and elsewhere in the world must not close our minds to alternative possibilities with regard to such organizations.

Nationalism

Nationalism is the major envelope curve for particularisms open to the members of relatively nonmodernized societies. Increasingly the levels of interdependency characteristic of life on our planet makes a mockery of the doctrines of national sovereignty as conceived in the eighteenth century, but in many of these areas the only basis of choice of people for most purposes will be from among fellow nationals. Thus particularism on a nationalistic basis is less likely to interfere with efficiency than elements of particularism on other bases. At the same time nationalism as a basis for emotional devotion is well known. It has its uses as a basis for control. Associated with this of course are the problems of chauvinism. Injudicious uses of nationalism lead to the development of superpatriots and chauvinism in general with consequent irrationalities. These results on occasions may well outweigh the implications of control gained by nationalistic appeals.

Politics as Recreation

. . . One of the most important changes in American institutional life has been a switch from politics as recreation to recreation as politics. There was a time in this country when alternative forms of specialized recreation were relatively little developed. Furthermore, this was the period in which something approaching mass participation in the specialized political contexts of life was a new and heady experience. During the last century politics was a major form of entertainment for large audiences. That was the day of the two- to three-hour political speech. That was the day of people who came with their entire families in their wagons with their lunches and picnics to hear the politicians of their day. Except for occasional flurries today, such as debates between presidential candidates, party conventions when televised for the first time, etc., politics is no longer a major form of recreation. Recreation becomes a special form of politics when each party has its own Hollywood folk, and when an increasing number of people with leisure at their command find political participation as amateurs at the grass-root level more fascinating than bridge. With the introduction of mass communication media there is likely to be among all of the latecomers a considerable period of politics as recreation. Ideology may be terribly important, but one

can hardly witness or look at films of the demonstrations of the 1960's in Japan, of the freedom chanters in Africa or elsewhere, without being struck by the recreational aspects of these occasions. If this is at all correct, it holds the prospect of substituting other forms of recreation for politics as recreation. The counterploy for youth intrigued and active in one political camp may well be nonideologically oriented driving schools or the furtherance of dating patterns rather than alternative ideological themes in an alternative political context. Mass participation in anything except labor corvées has been rare throughout social history, let alone mass participation in the specialized political contexts of life. It is exceedingly likely to be heady stuff. It is not frivolous to think of the recreational implications of political participation.

The Trickle Effect

The trickle effect is an increasing possibility as income distribution becomes more unimodal and as the standard of living continues to improve. Some of the implications of the trickle effect were first suggested by Professor Lloyd Fallers.[3] Relatively modernized contexts are likely to emphasize social mobility to a higher degree than their members achieve it. If new and relatively costly consumer goods are continuously generated, if they are first used by people in higher income brackets, if there is enough of a continuity in income distribution for them to trickle down to lower and lower income brackets as they catch on, their cost can be reduced by larger markets so that they will trickle down even faster. They will first have acquired an aura of upperclass usage and prestige. If there is a

---

[3] See L. Fallers, "A Note on the Trickle Effect," *Public Opinion Quarterly,* **18** (1954) 314-321.

continuous flow of such goods trickling down through income levels, Fallers maintained that one would get from this an illusion of social mobility even in the absence of actual social mobility. He reasoned that this would operate much in the same way that a man sitting stationary in a train on one side of the platform has the illusion of moving in the opposite direction when a train on the opposite side of the platform pulls out. It may be possible to use the trickle effect as a method of control, as an offset to some of the problems of frustration previously mentioned. If this is true, it is vital that one have an increasingly distributed per capita income, not just an increasingly earned per capita income. It is also implicit in the trickle effect that very early attempts at equalization of income or attempts, however nugatory, to block the association of higher income with higher prestige would be great mistakes. Such attempts cannot be successful, but they can be made.

Conclusion

In the previous part of this paper I have concentrated increasingly on what seem to me to be some of the policy implications of the theorizing that has preceded. The policy ideas are themselves hypotheses and perhaps of some interest as such even though impractical. But there is more to this than theorizing. Neither we nor they have a real alternative to trying to carry out modernization. We are not going to be able to modernize primarily in terms of the traditional patterns of the societies concerned or to preserve those patterns to any considerable extent. As time goes on, they and we will come increasingly to resemble one another—not necessarily because they come to be more like what we are now, but because the patterns of modernization are such that

the more highly modernized societies become, the more they resemble one another. We and the Japanese, for example, may be more like one another in the year 1990 than either of us will be like what we are today. Furthermore, in addition to the problems of adequate knowledge for latecomers and for the members of relatively modernized societies already stressed, we face —all of us—increasingly another special problem, and this is truly new under the sun. We face the problem of socialization for an unknown future. The rate of social change in both relatively modernized and modernizing contexts is itself revolutionary. Prior to our day the vast majority of all individuals in world history lived out their lives in the expectation that their lots would be roughly modeled on the lots of their parents and their children's lots would be modeled on theirs. Both as an ideal and as an actuality we expect the lives of our children as adults to be removed from ours. But how does one educate children for an unknown future? What kind of adequate knowledge does one need for that? It is not a matter of chance that what we call juvenile delinquency is characteristic of all of the relatively modernized and all of the modernizing societies. And one of the queries of those youths, deeper than ignorance of the law, is always "How was I to know?"

However pessimistic one may be about the state of the social sciences, at least things do not seem to be getting worse. In some fields theory has advanced notably. And in most of the others at least the marshaling and the analysis of data have advanced. We do have increasing knowledge of how to induce radical changes in productivity and perhaps even ideas of how to increase patterns of control with which we could live. There is in principle no barrier to our learning how to create new controls—especially if we do not insist on thinking primarily in terms of ideology—either theirs or ours—since neither makes much sense in terms of the world as it exists today. There is also open to us another possibility. The strategy of scientific analysis has proved to be enormously powerful in the application of its findings, even those findings for which fewest applications were envisaged at the time of interest in the discovery. Fundamental to that strategy of analysis has been an attempt to get as far as possible on as general a level as possible with as small a number of variables as possible as long as that number exceeded one. Our preoccupation with individual cases is our worst disability in this effort. Preoccupation with responsible policy objectives rather than fruitful scientific hypotheses will do more to delay creation of those responsible policy findings than most other things we can do—we as social scientists, I mean, for most of us here have the responsibility of coming up with ideas that will be fruitful rather than right.

social evolution

six

If modernization represents the large-scale social change for which we have the largest amount of information—which grows apace—an even broader (and much longer-term) process of *social evolution* is urged by some scholars as an encompassing theory of change. For this view there is a good deal less than universal assent, as some of the following selections demonstrate. The first two papers are by biologists, each seeking to see beyond his own discipline. The biological analogy is an old one, but became discredited by being pushed too far in such works as those by Herbert Spencer which rely on "organismic" models of society, and attempt to show far too much sequential uniformity in social change. The current renewal of interest in social evolution, of which our selections are only a sample, rests on a more sophisticated theory of evolution. Moreover, as Blum says, we are less ready to "confuse analogy with identity."

Blum does not argue for social evolution as comprising all significant change, but rather for a particular aspect of cumulative change over the long run. Stebbins is more hesitant about cumulative evolution, being more confident of the utility of evolutionary concepts in accounting for diversity. Cautionary notes are sounded by the sociologists Nisbet and Moore. Nisbet doubts that the analogy is tenable at all, and Moore thinks that it is, but doubts that it has substantial utility as a theory having predictive power.

Since happy endings in the form of universal consensus on what we know and do not know could only be illusory, a current controversy is an appropriate ending to our overview of social change.

On the Origin and Evolution of Human Culture *

HAROLD F. BLUM

Perhaps we make our world picture with a beginning and end because we have conceived too narrowly of our beginnings and ends.

J. Z. YOUNG

Just a few years ago I heard debated by some leading authorities the prob-

lem of distinguishing the earliest man from his fellow primates. One criterion suggested was brain size; another, the ability to make tools. Agreement was not reached. And at that time evidence

Harold F. Blum, "On the Origin and Evolution of Human Culture," *American Scientist*, **51** (March, 1963), 32-47. Reprinted by permission of the author and *American Scientist*.

* I wish to thank the Bollingen Foundation for assistance which made possible the development of the ideas in this paper.

was accumulating that primates with smaller brains made tools earlier than had been supposed—seeming to push the origin of man back considerably in time, and making distinguishing criteria even more uncertain. But after all, should we expect, using any criteria whatsoever, to be able to pinpoint the exact moment of origin of man, any more than could Archbishop Usscher, who placed it at 4004 B.C.? More than a few genetic steps must separate man from his nearest known primate relatives, and even though each step itself was an abrupt one, all did not occur, or manifest themselves, simultaneously. So any choice of a moment of emergence must be arbitrary, and may be misleading if we let it color our ideas of subsequent events. Is it not better to think of this, and other evolutionary origins, as vague periods of transition at the end of which categories have appeared that could not have been distinguished before, and the exact path to which is not traceable?[1]

From fossil remains the more man-like *Australopithecus* may be easily distinguished from, say, the more apelike *Oreopithecus* as a separate though related species having common ancestry.[2] But even if the one were derived more or less directly from the other there must have been many intermediate forms that have not been discovered, since the fossils that have been collected can be only a meager sample of the populations that have existed. By

[1] Recently . . . I pointed out some of the difficulties of assigning a moment of origin for living systems. See Harold F. Blum, "On the Origin and Evolution of Living Machines," *American Scientist*, **49** (1961), 474-501.
[2] W. E. Le Gros Clark, *The Fossil Evidence for Human Evolution* (Chicago: University of Chicago Press, 1955); E. L. Simons, "New Fossil Primates: A Review of the Past Decade," *American Scientist*, **48** (1960), 179-192.

diligent search, fossils of some of these intermediates may be found; but not all, for it is not to be expected that each genetic step will be reflected in gross anatomical features that may be recognized in the fossil record. The transition from one species to another would probably appear quite gradual if we had the whole record before us instead of only those fragments accidentally preserved.

But in the case of man there is concerned something more than his biological status—something that distinguishes him profoundly from all other animals, including his fellow primates. For man's highly developed culture is a part of man, and this did not emerge suddenly. Looking back, the development of this culture seems continuous over many thousands of years —starting very slowly but gaining impetus as it goes along, until today it accelerates at an almost frightening rate.

Acceleration in Cultural Evolution

To view man's cultural evolution in proper perspective one must peer back over a tremendous stretch of time. The accompanying chart may be an aid in this, but its categories and dates are to be accepted only as the roughest approximations. If cultural evolution has followed a continuous curve, distinctions between cultures must be based on inflections that give the impression of more or less sharp breaks, perhaps emphasized by the fragmentary nature of the record, making separation into cultural periods somewhat arbitrary at best. Cultures in different areas may overlap in time, and dating encounter stratigraphic uncertainties. Although the Carbon 14 method has provided means of obtaining more accurate dates for points in the last 60,000 years, the correlation of dates

TABLE 1   Approximate Chronological Chart*

Period	Duration (years before the present)	Dominant Species of Hominid
Historic	0 to 5,000	
Neolithic and Mesolithic	5,000 to 13,000	Modern man
Late Palaeolithic	13,000 to 40,000	
Middle Palaeolithic	40,000 to 200,000	Neanderthaloid
Early Palaeolithic	200,000 to 500,000+	Pithecanthropecine Australopithecine

* The dates in this chart are based, roughly, on R. Turner, *The Great Cultural Traditions* (New York: McGraw-Hill Book Company, 1941); H. L. Movius, "Radiocarbon Dates and Upper Paleolithic Archaeology in Central and Western Europe," *Current Anthropology*, 1 (1960), 355–391, and 2 (1960), 427–454; J. Maringer, *The Gods of Prehistoric Man* (New York: Alfred A. Knopf, Inc., 1960); S. L. Washburn, ed., *The Social Life of Early Man* (Chicago: Aldine Publishing Co., 1961).

and cultures is still far from complete.[3] Difficulties in earlier dating are discussed by Straus and Hunt[4] with regard to the Australopithecine, *Zinjanthropus*, described by Leaky.[5]

Recorded history extends back about 5,000 years. Beyond this the Neolithic and Mesolithic occupy another 8,000 years or so; during these periods man learned many things—to polish his stone tools, to make ceramics, to work metals to some extent, and to till the soil. Next, looking back, is the Late Paleolithic. It is during this period that man's first artistic creations—paintings, engravings, and sculptures—enter the record. From the beginning of the Late Paleolithic to the present, the dominant species of hominid has been modern man, *Homo sapiens*. Neanderthaloid Man, whom we associate with a particular stone tool culture, the Mousterian, may have been dominant during the Middle Paleolithic, but disappears

[3] H. L. Movius, "Radiocarbon Dates and Upper Paleozoic Archaeology in Central and Western Europe," *Current Anthropology*, 1 (1960), 355-391, and 2 (1960), 427-454.

[4] W. L. Straus, Jr., and C. B. Hunt, "Age of Zinjanthropus," *Science*, 136 (1962), 293-295.

[5] L. S. B. Leaky, "A New Fossil Skull from Olduvai," *Nature*, 184 (1959), 491-493; "Recent Discoveries at Olduvai," *Nature*, 188 (1960), 1050-1052; and "New Finds at Olduvai Gorge," *Nature*, 189 (1961), 640-650.

as a biological entity around the end of that period. How far Neanderthaloid Man extends into the Late Paleolithic or how far *Homo sapiens* extends back into the Middle Paleolithic are questions that may be unanswerable, since sharp discontinuities are not to be expected. Beyond, in the Early Paleolithic, Pithecanthropecines may have dominated, and before them Australopithecines;[6] but as we go back relationships become increasingly blurred, and dating less certain.

At some time in these early years, say, several hundred thousand years ago, some hominid began to make stone tools, fashioning them crudely at first, then with more refinement as time went on. But just when this happened, and the sequence of the early steps, is vague. Only a few types of tools are recognized in the Early Paleolithic, and their number does not greatly increase for a long time, perhaps a few hundred thousand years. Then, toward the end of this period and in the beginning of the Middle Paleolithic, the number rises markedly and the record becomes relatively com-

[6] C. Arambourg, "Le Gisement de Ternifine et l'Anthropus," *Bulletin de la Société Préhistorique Française*, 52 (1955), 94-95; R. A. Dart, *Adventures with the Missing Link* (New York: Harper & Row, Publishers, 1959); Leaky, works previously cited.

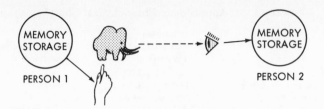

TRANSFER OF CULTURAL INFORMATION

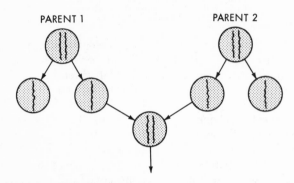

TRANSFER OF BIOLOGICAL INFORMATION

FIG. 1. Schematic diagram contrasting transfer of cultural information with transfer of biological inheritance.

plex.[7] In the Late Paleolithic the diversification of tool forms increases greatly, even though many fewer years elapse. During this period tools of bone and antler are added, and then in the Mesolithic and Neolithic come numerous innovations, including use of ceramics and metals. Upon this accelerating accumulation of technical achievement man eventually built during historic times the machine culture, which developed faster and faster, and still mounts.

Sometime in the Late Paleolithic, perhaps 30,000 years ago, appears the first evidence of man's artistic creativity. This begins with a representational

style,[8] to which is added, particularly in the Mesolithic and Neolithic, an increasing schematization and abstraction.[9] There then seem to develop—over a matter of millennia—the pictogram, then hieroglyphics, and only about 3,500 years ago a phonetic alphabet from which all those we use today have origin. Looking back in this perspective brings realization that the depicted image and the written word were rather lately and slowly introduced, yet they have subsequently

---

[7] K. Oakley, Man the Toolmaker, 4th ed. (Norwich, England: Jarrold & Sons, Ltd., 1958); F. Bordes, "Mousterian Cultures of France," Science, 134 (1961), 803-810.

[8] H. Breuil, Four Hundred Years of Cave Art (Montignac, France: Centre d'Etude et de Documentation Préhistorique, 1952); P. Graziosi, Paleolithic Art (New York: McGraw-Hill Book Company, 1960).

[9] H Kuhn, The Rock Pictures of Europe, A. H. Brodrick, trans. (Fair Lawn, N.J.: Essential Books, Inc., 1956).

played all-important roles in the accelerating evolution of human communication.

Clearly this kind of evolution cannot be closely tied to genetic mutation and natural selection. Toolmaking seems to have continued to develop without respect for genetic type recognizable by anatomical differences, in the hands of Australopithecines, Pithecanthropecines, Neanderthaloids, and *Homo sapiens*. During the reign of the latter, culture has bloomed as never before; but does this mean that he is comparably advanced beyond his ancestors in the potential equipment for gaining culture, and that the others could not have gone further had they survived? It seems no more likely that the increased elaboration of toolmaking and the beginning of artistic creation which characterize the Upper Paleolithic after *Homo sapiens* took over, signal the advent of a more effective genetic species than does the flowering of technology in the short space of the nineteenth and twentieth centuries. Both, as I read the record, represent short periods in the course of a long, accelerating evolution which should be described by some form of exponential curve.

Mechanisms of Cultural and Genetic Inheritance: Comparison and Contrast

But if cultural evolution accelerates as it goes on, why is this true? An explicit answer would require more understanding of the underlying process than we have at present. We still lack a general concept comparable to that of biological evolution by mutation and natural selection, and the essentials of a basic physical mechanism such as modern biology gives us for replication and mutation. One may say that cultural evolution proceeds by means of learning and the transmission of learned ideas; but just what does this mean? Somehow images get recorded in the memory of one person and passed on to another person who forms a more or less similar image. But what is the remembered image? The answers to these questions are beyond our reach at present; but we may nevertheless make some attempt to analyze the process of cultural evolution, comparing and contrasting it with biological evolution, where mechanisms are better understood.

Basic to evolution by natural selection is the passing on of patterns of information from one generation to the next. These patterns we think of as embodied in "templates" within the cells, composed of molecules of desoxyribose nucleic acid, or DNA, long polymers made up of a relatively few kinds of monomer units that can be arranged in a great variety of ways. By means of the machinery of the cell these templates are accurately replicated with each cell division so that daughter cells receive like patterns. In the higher forms the information for constructing the adult organism is carried in the fertilized egg, the templates in which are furnished from the sex cells of both parents, each contributing half. This inheritance is schematized in the lower part of Figure 1, where the wiggly lines within the circles are supposed to represent templates or patterns of information within the sex cells—my biological colleagues will understand that these are not chromosomes, and will forgive the oversimplification. What I have wished to illustrate is not the details of biological inheritance, but that it is based on quite rigid transmission of information—on the replication and transfer of patterns of intra- and intermolecular structure. Fortunately for evolution, the patterns are subject, although rarely, to errors that may be replicated and passed on; these are the mutations which make possible evolution by natural selection.

In contrast to biological inheritance, the transfer of cultural information is not by means of an exact molecular pattern and much more variation is permitted. The transfer of information about a visual image is schematized in the upper part of Figure 1; transfer of information by sound, as in spoken language, or another sensory motor mechanism might have been chosen instead as an example. The circles labeled memory storage are supposed to represent the recording and maintaining of memory images somewhere in the brains of two persons concerned in the transfer.[10] Memory storage has been likened to the recording of information on the drum or tape of an electronic computer by orienting the molecules of the metal, through magnetic forces, into specific arrangements of pattern; it has been proposed, in analogy to biological templates, that storage in the brain is in large polymer molecules. Alternatively, it has been suggested that the brain functions in a way comparable to a complex of electronic relay units, where storage of memory images consists in the facilitation of certain patterns of circuit pathways. Whatever the mechanism of storage, we must think of the image as being transferred by means of nerve impulses into a pattern of motor action, without loss of the original stored image. This is suggested in Figure 1 by the hand which reproduces, in the form of a drawing, a replica of an object whose image has been stored in the memory of the first person; the drawing could be a mammoth graved in stone, or a mathematical symbol written in chalk. At this

point the image is transferred through the air to the eye of a second person. From the retina of the second person the image is transferred, again by nerve impulses, to his brain, where it is stored. In these operations there is no transfer of a molecular entity carrying a pattern of information, and there would seem to be opportunity for modification of the memory image at more than one point in the pathway from one brain to the other. Starting with the image stored in the brain of the first person, there is the possibility of divergence of the pattern in the transfer to the hand and the execution of the drawing. In the next step, even if the geometrical arrangement of the lines of the drawing is accurately transferred to the retina of the eye, transmission of the information by nerve impulses from retina to brain may entail some uncertainty; and further departure from the original pattern may enter with the interpretation and storage of the message in the brain.

Templates of the sex cells of higher organisms, replicated closely at each cell division, are passed on in the fertilized egg, thus insuring the continuance of genetic information for constructing the new organism. If mutation occurs in one of the sex cells, the mutant template may be replicated and passed on, so providing the basis for a possible step in evolution by natural selection, but if one of the many other cells of the body undergoes mutation this has no effect on the sex cells or on evolution. Similarly, there is no known means by which an acquired memory image can affect directly the genetic information in templates of the sex cells to induce genetic changes specifically related to the memory image. Obviously there is no direct relationship between the upper and lower parts of Figure 1; specific learned facets of

---

[10] The term memory image is used throughout this paper to include all the kinds of information that may be stored in the brain, whether relating to action, behavior, beliefs, aesthetic concepts, or whatever.

culture are not inherited through the genetic system.

Biologically each newborn human being is constructed according to information from template patterns, half of which he has received from each of his two parents and cannot alter of his own volition; half the patterns, combined with half from another parent, will provide the templates for a new human being. Thus, except for reshuffling, cutting the deck, and infrequently a mutation, the templates are passed on unchanged from one generation to the next. But the personal collection of memory images belonging to any human being—which provides the information on which his cultural behavior is based—he must assemble for himself during his own lifetime; the zero point being, presumably, somewhere in fetal life. This personal collection of memory images will not be passed on to his offspring directly by means of a template, but will cease to exist with his death. Persistence of any of his memory images beyond his lifetime must be by transfer in one way or another to the brains of other persons who survive him. This wiping clean of the slate and building anew for each individual generation would seem to lend great fluidity to cultural transmission and evolution, marking a great difference from the relatively rigid transfer of information in genetic inheritance.

To aid in the following discussion I shall introduce the term *mnemotype* to describe the personal collection of memory images in a single brain. This will correspond to the accepted use of the term *genotype* to describe the genetic makeup of a single individual of a species, which we may think of as a template pattern that contains the information for building the organism— the overt expression of this information in the morphology and physiology of the organism is referred to as the *phenotype*.

Thinking genetically we may regard a given species as a population of genotypes that are basically very similar, yet differ in minor aspects. As the species reproduces itself in its offspring there is constant reshuffling of the templates that will be delivered to each member from his parents. In addition there are mutations, which may be thought of as changes and rearrangements of template elements, guided by chance within the restrictions set by molecular structure; such changes are rare and perforce minor as regards the template as a whole, because too drastic ones will yield templates not compatible with a viable organism (lethal mutations). The result of all this is a distribution of genotypes grouping around a mean; and it is in terms of such an idealized distribution, and the corresponding distribution of phenotypes that we may hope to describe the species and distinguish it from others. Anything that brings about the isolation of a group of members of the species, for example, migration, may bring about a shift in distribution of genotypes tending toward greater genetic resemblance within the group than in the species as a whole. Constant change in the population of genotypes, with the innovations provided by mutation, makes possible evolution by natural selection; that is, bearers of patterns of heredity that confer on them better adaptation to the prevailing environment are favored in the struggle for existence, may outmultiply their less favored kin, and ultimately replace them. Thus we see the population of templates in constant flux, but maintained in a sort of dynamic, near-steady state. Departures from the average of genotypes are relatively small because of the relative inflexibility of the molecular structure of the templates; but the minor changes that do occur make gradual evolution possible.

Unless one is willing to invoke some directing factor unknown to science and hence not susceptible to analysis, it seems necessary to assume that the information determining the cultural pattern of a society resides in the brains of its members, where it is stored as personal sets of memory images, or mnemotypes. Storage of information may of course be supplemented by such devices as the written word or pictorial representation, but these operate through memory images in individual brains. Mnemotypes will differ among members of the society; but since the memory images belonging to one person are, for the most part, acquired from other members of his society, there must be rather close resemblance. Greater similarity is to be expected among closely associated members, as in families and clans, than within the society as a whole; but nevertheless one may imagine a given society to be describable in terms of a population of mnemotypes distributed around a mean with few extreme deviations. Such a population I shall refer to as a *collective mnemotype*. The overt behavior of the individual members of the society will be determined by their individual mnemotypes, the behavior of the society as a whole by the collective mnemotype. We may distinguish conceptually between societies, and between groups within societies, in terms of their collective mnemotypes; and we may think of human society as a whole in terms of a collective mnemotype which is a composite of those of all existing societies. This treatment parallels the description of a biological species in terms of a population of genotypes and their corresponding phenotypes, but the two things are of course very different.

Cultural evolution of a society would seem to be based on changes in the collective mnemotype, innovations coming through changes in the individual mnemotypes which compose it. New memory images could arise from new experiences related to the outside world, or from modification and merging during storage or in transfer between members of the society. Addition of new memory images together with new combinations of the old would result in a constantly changing collective mnemotype, which we may picture in a dynamic, near-steady state comparable to that of the genotype distribution of a biological species—but much more fluid.

For evolution to occur, new memory images would have to be copied into the brains of a considerable part of the population, but this need not wait for a new biological generation; the whole mnemotype need not be copied of course, but only that part from which arises a new facet of culture. The facility with which such a divergent unit of memory pattern can be copied into a given population must be an important factor in the evolutionary success of a cultural innovation. This introduces a kind of selection. If a cultural innovation is immediately useful, and this is obvious to a considerable part of the society, it may be readily adopted, which means that the corresponding memory image is rapidly copied until it becomes characteristic of the mnemotype population. Innovations that are recognized as useful by only a small part of the members of the society may be copied very slowly at first yet ultimately accepted, or they may be lost. Innovations that have no utility but are associated with advantageous ones, or which appeal for less tangible reasons, may be incorporated, while others are rejected. On the whole one would expect a tendency to keep the mnemotype relatively close to the mean, and to reject innovations that depart too much therefrom; this could result in the conservation of many facets of culture having little or no practical value to the society, and the retention of some long after they have become obsolete because of subsequent innovation.

It would seem thus that the character of the existing collective mnemotype restricts both the likelihood of wide departure of mnemotype from the mean and the kind of memory images that will be selected and copied, thus affecting both the rate and direction of cultural evolution. But innovation must come in the first place from an altered memory pattern in an individual brain. Thus it seems necessary to think of cultural change as a function of both the collective mnemotype and an individual mnemotype that diverges therefrom in some particular way—the soil must be ready for a particular innovation, but there needs also to be an innovator. This seems nonetheless true because great innovations often come in successive steps, each usually involving one person, although there are many instances where the name of one man is associated with a sudden cultural change. The development of quantum theory at the beginning of the century is a good example from the field of science, where a single mind produced an idea that permitted the correlation of observations previously made by other scientists. This explanation was quickly followed by further applications of the theory by still others, and evolution of scientific thought in a new direction was soon under way. The formulation of modern genetic theory comes from nearly the same date, when three men arrived independently and almost simultaneously at basic principles that had been outlined about forty years earlier by yet another man, but not then ac-cepted into contemporary scientific thought. According to his particular point of view—of his particular mnemotype, if you wish—one may tend toward the apotheosis of the individual or to emphasize the role of the cultural milieu. A correct view would seem to include an essential place for both.

Correlation Between Cultural and Genetic Pattern

It should not be forgotten that the members of a human society are genetically related, and that reasoning about biological species and their evolution also applies at this level. Because of similarity of genetic pattern, greater biological similarity is to be expected between closely related members of the society—within races or between families within racial groups. The most obvious resemblances are anatomical ones, such as complexion, details of facial structure, and body proportions; and these are common criteria by which we judge racial and family relationships. But corresponding resemblances are also to be expected between the mnemotypes of more closely associated members of a society, for reasons pointed out above. A certain correlation would thus be expected between physical characteristics and items of social behavior; yet this need indicate no functional relationship between the two. Nevertheless, the association of physical and social characteristics may lead us, without strict reason, to attribute them to a common cause; and such association, having been tacit in our thinking for a long time, may be the basis for a good deal of confusion of biological and cultural aspects of human behavior.

To be sure, the genetic templates may carry information that determines physiological and even subtle psychological differences, as well as the more obvious anatomical ones, and this may contribute to the similarity of behavior of racial and family groups. It might be extremely difficult by any method of scientific measurement to separate rigidly the genetically inherited component of social behavior from the culturally acquired component, but the need to distinguish conceptually between the two seems obvious when the basic differences in mechanism of transmission of information are taken into account. When we try to weigh these components it seems necessary to credit the greater role to cultural acquisition; yet we seem to emphasize the genetic aspects in so much of our social thinking, and this may lead to an exaggeratedly deterministic view of man's behavior and his society.

Rate of Evolution

It would seem that any cultural innovation makes further innovation possible. The invention of one kind of tool opens the way for further developments, whether it be struck from a stone or fashioned with elaborate techniques and calculations from metal and plastic. But the chances of either thing happening must depend upon the existing cultural milieu and the possibilities it offers—the complicated tool could not have been constructed at the time when the simpler one emerged. Under these circumstances human culture may be expected to expand at increasing rate as time goes on and new facets accumulate. Thinking of this accelerating evolutionary process as based on number of kinds of memory image possessed by society, we may describe it loosely in quantitative fashion, even though exact measurements are unobtainable.

Let us think in terms of total number of kinds of memory image, regardless of how many times the same image

may be repeated in the population that constitutes the collective mnemotype. The probability of introducing a new kind of memory image may then be treated as a function of the total number already present. For simplicity we may assume that the rate of cultural evolution is directly proportional to the rate of introduction of new kinds of memory images, writing

$$\text{rate of cultural evolution} = \frac{dt}{dl} = rI \quad (1)$$

where I is number of kinds of memory image, t is time, and r is a constant which we adopt for simplicity while recognizing that it should be some more complex function. What this expression says is that the rate of addition to the total collection of memory images is proportional to their number at any given time.

The corresponding expression for the accumulation of memory images as time goes on is given by

$$I = I_0 e^{rt} \quad (2)$$

where I_0 is an initial number of images, e being the base of natural logarithms.

I have already spoken of the difficulty of selecting starting points, and of course we have no way of enumerating all the memory image units that have entered the collective mnemotype of society as a whole in the course of the millennia man has inhabited the earth. But it is fun to make a few guesses, as I have done in drawing Figure 2, where I have chosen to start my curves 150,000 years ago, when humanity must have possessed a relatively small number of memory images compared to today. In the curve labelled 10^3, I have assumed that man has in the meantime increased this early number, whatever it may have been, by a thousandfold. Allowing for only this small amount of advancement the number increases only ten times in the

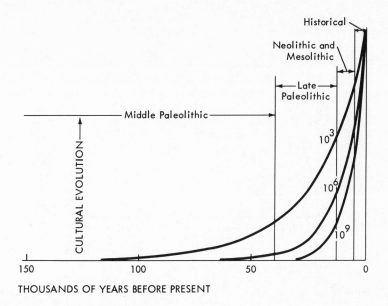

FIG. 2. Types of curves to be expected if cultural evolution increased in simple proportion to the extent of existing culture.

first 100,000 years, but rises one hundred times this in the next 50,000. Increase of a millionfold is assumed in the curve labelled 10^6, which rises so slowly at the beginning that it cannot be represented on the graph, and so seems to begin quite late in the time man has been on earth. In the curve labelled 10^9, where an increase of one billion has been assumed, there appears to be no rise at all until about 30,000 years ago. These estimates can have no real meaning, to be sure, but the curves suggest the kind of accelerating course exemplified in, say, toolmaking. At the earliest time represented on the graph man made a relatively small number of tools, and the number probably did not increase more than a few fold until the Late Paleolithic—compare this rate of increase with the number of tools that have come to man's disposal within the last century. The curves illustrate how easily one can be misled into assuming abrupt beginnings when dealing with exponential curves.

Following similar quantitative reasoning, the course of man's biological evolution might be expected to differ markedly from that of his cultural evolution. From what we are learning about biological templates, we may assume that the genetic equipment of a species is limited to a given amount of DNA, and hence a limited number of possible coded arrangements of nucleotides contained therein. This number may be very great, but for a given species it should be nevertheless finite; so as evolution eliminates nonadaptive mutations by the process of natural selection, the number of possibilities for mutations would be gradually spent. If we wish to write an expression comparable to that essayed for cultural evolution (2), it should look something like this,

$$M_t = M_0(1 - e^{-st}) \qquad (3)$$

where M_t is the number of mutations that have occurred at time t, after some initial moment when the number

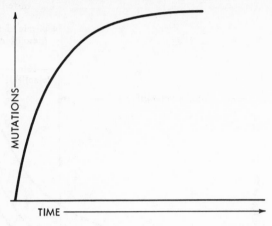

FIG. 3. Type of curve to be expected if there were a limit to the number of possible mutations.

of mutations possible was M_0, and s is a constant. The curve in Figure 3, based on this equation, tends toward a level at which all possibilities of mutation will have been exhausted. Such a curve never shows acceleration as do those in Figure 2—at most it is nearly linear in its early course. I doubt very much that such a curve describes biological evolution as a whole; but it is the kind to be expected unless there is some mechanism by which the number of facets of genetic information increases as evolution goes along, say by increasing the amount of DNA available in the genetic system from time to time. It seems most unlikely that the first living organism—which it would be difficult to locate in time[11]—contained all the possibilities for genetic information needed to evolve into all the vast array of living species; but the way in which more possibilities were acquired is not clear. It seems, though, that the kind of curve shown in Figure 3 might be expected to apply to mutation within a limited array of living forms, as, say, the hominids, where man finds himself.

[11] See Blum, *op. cit.*

Returning to cultural evolution, let us suppose that for some reason a limit were imposed upon the kinds of memory images that could be introduced into the collective mnemotype of a society. Then the curve of cultural evolution for this society might approach more nearly the form in Figure 3, at least for a time, than those in Figure 2. Conceivably this might happen when a small group separates off from the main stem and moves into a new environment where resources are limited and the struggle for survival claims too much time and effort for frequent innovation. Or, again, this might result from taboos that suppress innovation by demanding too strict conformity. It seems also that evolution of a society may regress at times, in the sense of loss of given facets of culture and their corresponding memory images. Isolated groups in which evolution has progressed slowly might be regarded as "primitive" by the more rapidly evolving body of society, although the former had continued to evolve far beyond its state at the time of departure from the main stem. Considering all these possibilities it seems likely that cultural evolution follows a curve that combines both the forms represented in Figures 2 and 3, showing slow and fast periods, but an over-all acceleration. Such a curve, being subject to more or less abrupt changes, would not be described by a simple, continuous function.

Obviously none of these curves can describe the true course of evolution, where numerous factors enter, including the isolation, growth, and reintegration of societies, climatic and other environmental changes, and the increase in total world population with the many changes this entails. That cultural evolution has increased progressively in rate over many thousands of years can hardly be denied, however, when viewed in that perspective, or even in the relatively short reaches of historic time; neither can it be denied that cultural evolution has seen many minor fluctuations of rate with time and place. The prospect that exhaustion of the possibility for further innovation may lead to ultimate leveling off of all cultural evolution in the manner of the curve in Figure 3 is a possibility that may be considered.[12] If this comes, it would seem more likely to result from factors outside the human brain, such as the exhaustion of resources or from aberrations of the collective mnemotype, than from saturation of individual memory image capacity.[13] As with a computer at the beginning of a given operation, the human brain is cleared of memory images at the beginning of each generation. It may be more difficult to clear the larger

collective mnemotype, but there seems no obvious reason why this cannot be achieved a step at a time.

Discussion

Although cultural and biological evolution resemble each other in numerous ways, and are to an extent interdependent, they may best be regarded as distinct phenomena that depend on very different ways of copying and transferring information. For example, the use of fire distinguishes us from all other animal species, yet I think no geneticist would venture that there is a gene—a template—for fire-making. This is something we have discovered, exploited, and passed along culturally, with profound effect on our evolution. Chimpanzees have been taught to light matches; but none has come upon this without the example of man, or manufactured a match. Chimps have also made paintings and have sold them with the help of their close primate relatives; but there seems nothing to indicate that these apes have ever in their evolution come upon the idea of depiction on their own account.

There are important biological differences between ourselves and our nearest primate relatives; but by far the greatest difference seems to be in the cultures we have developed. Our culture has been won in many steps, the occurrence of which has been in a sense fortuitous, although since each step makes others possible there is something of direction. The cumulative effect of successful steps accounts for the accelerated character of our cultural evolution and its rapid divergence from that of other primates. One may wonder if the artistically inclined chimpanzees or the exhibitionistically athletic gibbons might, with a little luck, have evolved societies more compa-

---

[12] R. Seidenberg, *Prehistoric Man* (Chapel Hill: University of North Carolina Press, 1950), and *Anatomy of the Future* (Chapel Hill: University of North Carolina Press, 1961).

[13] H. Blum, "Time's Arrow and the Evolution of Sociology," *University, A Princeton Magazine*, 9 (1961), 9-13.

rable to ours—and had we not blocked their progress by getting started first. I do not mean to suggest that there are not very important genetic differences between us that may have influenced the direction taken by our respective cultures, or that no basic behavior patterns are inherited. But the portion of human culture that is genetically inherited is surely much less than that which has been culturally acquired. There may well be genetically inherited characters unique to man that have facilitated the development of his great culture, and the lack of which has held back his nearest relatives. Any factor that tended to enhance the making of memory images, for example, should have had powerful effect on cultural evolution. This could be some subtle biochemical factor that escapes our knowledge.[14] Or again, the matter of brain size could be important, if this were a good index of the number of functional elements. But what the underlying genetic differences might be, and at just what points they have crept into man's evolution, are questions unanswerable at present. All in all, I suspect that even with something of a head start man has had a remarkable run of luck to have left his fellow primates so far behind. Man's cultural evolution seems to have taken the bit in its teeth a long time ago, and to have run far beyond his biological evolution.

We often employ the term "human nature" as though this were something fixed in man's makeup, something introduced at a particular moment in his evolution and not since altered. As I view it, many aspects that are attributed to human nature today are probably very different from their counter-

parts of 20,000 years ago, or twenty centuries ago; and the differences are to be credited overwhelmingly to cultural evolution. For this reason it seems risky to extrapolate back, as is sometimes done, from existing, so-called "primitive," societies to those of "stone age" times—the farther the extrapolation is carried back the more risky. Such existing societies have evolved and sophisticated cultures, which even the heavy chains of tradition are not likely to have kept unaltered for so long. Still more to be distrusted, it would seem, are extrapolations to human behavior from the behavior of other animals of very different species, or even those quite nearly related.

When we compare biological and cultural evolution they seem to have so little in common, although the latter is clearly restricted by the former. Yet one may draw many analogies between the two, as has been indicated in the preceding pages. And here lies a danger because it is easy to confuse analogy with identity. I am afraid that this happens all too often; and I find it difficult in reading some authors to be sure that they are not confusing biological and cultural evolution. The confusion is most likely to occur in "popular" writings, although not altogether absent from more erudite ones. Emphasis on the animal aspect of man, so common in current literature, and a generally fatalistic attitude regarding human behavior may be symptoms of false concepts and applications of Darwinian evolution.

An idea seems to be in the air at present, that, knowing so much more about genetic inheritance than we did a few years ago, we may soon be in a position to modify man's genetic heredity and hence his evolution. The aim of such modification seems vague. Is it toward a superior race that would automatically be endowed with a su-

---

[14] E. W. Caspari, "Some Genetic Implications of Human Evolution," in S. L. Washburn, ed., *The Social Life of Early Man* (Chicago: Aldine Publishing Co., 1961).

perior culture? Surely not, for culture —as truly a part of man as his genes—is something he is continually modifying

—templates or not—for better or for worse.

Pitfalls and Guideposts in Comparing Organic and Social Evolution

G. LEDYARD STEBBINS

More than any other period in the history of mankind, ours is a time of change. Among the welter of ideas and theories about modern society and where it is going, this one truism, above all, stands unchallenged. Anybody who has lived for half a century or even less is so personally aware of this change that it is bound to have a strong influence on his entire outlook toward life. A biologist in this modern world, whose thoughts are centered almost entirely about either his personal affairs, those of the body politic around him, or about the nature of the living world outside of man, cannot help making constant comparisons and analogies between social change and those changes in populations of animals, plants, and micro-organisms which, following Darwin, he has learned to call evolution. Are these comparisons and analogies nothing but an interesting parlor game, useless and misleading to anyone who is seriously studying the nature and future prospects of modern society, or can at least some of them be used to give us a deeper insight into the trends of social change? This is the question which I shall try to answer in this paper.

In previous discussions of this sub-

G. Ledyard Stebbins, "Pitfalls and Guideposts in Comparing Organic and Social Evolution," *Pacific Sociological Review*, 8 (Spring, 1965), 3-10. Reprinted by permission of the *Pacific Sociological Review*.

ject with anthropologists and sociologists, the strongest impression I have gained is of the misconceptions which are widely, perhaps generally, held about the nature and course of organic evolution. The words "evolution" and "evolutionism" are often used in a derogatory sense, and refer to the belief that human culture has changed in a linear and progressive fashion, with many close parallels between the course of evolution of entire cultures in different parts of the earth. The idea that cultures have evolved progressively toward what we call civilization, and that one function of anthropologists and sociologists is to classify each culture into one of several progressive stages of this evolution, was being developed simultaneously with Darwin's studies on the evolution of the organic world. These two ideas of organic and cultural evolution became inevitably interwoven shortly after the publication of the *Origin of Species*. With the dawn of the twentieth century, both organic evolution and cultural change began to be approached in a more pragmatic and objective fashion. Consequently, in both fields, the excesses of generalization committed by the previous generation of scientists became increasingly apparent. Biologists of the twentieth century distrusted more and more the "phylogenetic trees" which their forebears had erected in order to place in a supposed evolutionary succession the various modern phyla, orders, and families of plants and animals. Anthropologists and sociologists discarded completely the concept of "cultural stages," and many of them spoke only of diversity and change, rejecting completely any implication that cultures advanced or regressed as wholes during the time of man's existence on the earth. Moreover, they did not associate organic evolution with the experimental studies of evolutionary processes, which began in 1900 with deVries' discovery of mutations, and the rediscovery of Mendel's laws of heredity, and which now dominate scientific research on the evolution of contemporary organisms. They were more familiar with the descriptive and speculative phylogenetic comparisons which were in vogue among biologists of the previous generation, but which were being looked upon with increasing skepticism by the new generation of biologists.

Many contemporary students of human culture, such as Steward[1] and Hallowell[2] use the concept of evolution in much the same way as do modern biologists. The viewpoint to whicл they adhere, and which I shall now summarize, is often called the modern, synthetic theory of evolution. It is set forth by G. G. Simpson,[3] T. Dobzhansky,[4] Sir Julian Huxley,[5] and in a series of symposia held in 1959, the centenary of the publication of Darwin's *Origin of Species*. The most elaborate of these,[6] at the University of Chicago, presented discussions of cultural as well as organic evolution.

The Modern Theory of Organic Evolution

The modern synthetic theory of organic evolution accepts the occurrence of evolutionary change as a fact, for which the evidence is as strong as it can be for any series of historical events which can never be exactly repeated. Furthermore, the supporters of this theory are reluctant to speculate about the course of evolution, or phylogeny, on the basis of the supposed primitiveness or advancement of modern forms of life. Nearly all modern organisms are specialized in at least some respects, and in groups of which the fossil record is reasonably good, the extinct probable ancestor of any two or more modern groups looks so different from its contemporary descendants that its nature could not have possibly been reconstructed solely from comparisons between these descendants, without reference to fossils of extinct types. Since, however, most of the analogies made in the past between organic and cultural evolution have been phylogenetic in nature, a summary of the present opinions of biologists and particularly paleontologists about the course of evolution is needed as an introduction to the present topic.

As seen from the fossil record of those organisms in which it is most complete, particularly the vertebrates and molluscs, the course of evolution is

---

[1] J. H. Steward, "Evolutionary Principles and Social Types," in *Evolution After Darwin*, Vol. II: *The Evolution of Man: Mind, Culture, Society*, ed. S. Tax (Chicago: University of Chicago Press, 1960), pp. 169-186.

[2] A. I. Hallowell, "Self, Society and Culture in Phylogenetic Perspective," in *ibid.*, pp. 309-371.

[3] G. G. Simpson, *The Meaning of Evolution* (New Haven: Yale University Press, 1949).

[4] T. Dobzhansky, *Evolution, Genetics and Man* (New York: John Wiley & Sons, Inc., 1955), and *Mankind Evolving* (New Haven: Yale University Press, 1962).

[5] J. S. Huxley, *Evolution, the Modern Synthesis* (New York: Harper & Row, Publishers, 1942).

[6] S. Tax, ed., *Evolution After Darwin*, Vol. I: *The Evolution of Life* (Chicago: University of Chicago Press, 1959), Vol. II.

better described as a succession of adaptive radiations into different habitats and different ways of exploiting similar habitats, than as a steady progress toward a particular goal. Let us look, for instance, at some of the major features of the evolution of vertebrates. During the Devonian Period, about 300,000,000 years ago, the earliest fishes and their relatives radiated into a variety of habitats; oceans and lakes, rivers, and small streams. Some became larger and anticipated the evolution of modern sharks, others developed large scales and evolved in the direction of sturgeons, while several other groups evolved along specialized pathways which led to "blind alleys" and extinction. Two groups of these radiants became adapted to living in shallow, fresh water lakes of tropical and subtropical climates, in which the water often became poor in oxygen and even tended to dry up during seasons of drought. These forms, as fishes, were obviously highly specialized and aberrant. In them, genetic changes, guided by natural selection, favored the acquisition of air pouches or bladders, enabling the fish to gulp in oxygen from the air when that in the water was exhausted. In one group (the Crossopterygians), further adaptation to changes in water level was acquired by the evolution of strong fins by means of which the fish could waddle toward deeper water as its lake was drying up. As the climate became increasingly drier, larger air pouches and stronger fins were favored until the fish could make short journeys over land from one completely dried up lake to another which still contained some water. This was the probable way in which the conquest of the land began.

Given the ability to live at least some of the time on land, four-footed animals (amphibians) radiated into a number of ecological niches and ways of exploiting their habitat, but were at first restricted in their ability to do this because they had to lay their eggs and spend their larval life in the water. One of the first of these radiants evolved an egg which contained inside it, protected by a tough outer coat, the liquid medium required for early development of its embryos. This acquisition triggered off a much larger radiation, that of the reptiles, which dominated the earth for 100,000,000 years or more. At an early stage in this second radiation, one of its branch lines consisted of small, tree-living animals with specialized jaws and teeth, and perhaps with warm blood. These gave rise to the mammals, which at a much later date, about 60,000,000 years ago, diversified and radiated to become eventually the various kinds of animals which dominate the earth today.

This brief sample of some features of vertebrate evolution can be supplemented by reading Colbert's *Evolution of the Vertebrates*.[7] From it, one can clearly see the predominance of successive patterns of adaptive radiation. Advances in complexity and more efficient ways of exploiting the environment were made whenever one particular radiant acquired some special adaptive device, such as lungs, leg and feet, the amniote egg, and warm blood. In a few rare instances an evolutionary line acquired two or three of these specializations which complemented each other. By this means, the descendants of this line advanced to a high level of organization, and radiated anew into various ecological niches by virtue of their more efficient ways of exploiting their environment.

From this brief account, one can see that an impression of progressive advancement toward a particular goal can

[7] E. H. Colbert, *Evolution of the Vertebrates* (New York: John Wiley & Sons, Inc., 1955).

be gained only if we start with a type which we consider advanced, such as man, and reconstruct for it a family tree of the particular ancestors of that group, disregarding the immensely greater number of collaterals which never evolved to a state regarded by us as advanced, even though their descendants survive to the present time. The impression of progress is dissipated even further when we consider differential rates of evolution, both between different groups of organisms and between different characteristics of the same evolving group. For instance, a group of Devonian fishes related to the ancestors of the first land animals acquired a different adaptation to the vagaries of the climate and changes in water level. Possessed of very small, weak fins, they simply increased their tolerance for foul, stagnant water. Some of their descendants acquired the ability to encase themselves in mud and become dormant during periods of drought when their lakes dried up. These fishes became adapted to increasing drought by extending their dormant period. After a short evolutionary spurt which adapted them perfectly to this narrow, specialized ecological niche, their rate of evolution slowed down and almost stopped. The modern lungfishes of Africa are hardly different from their ancestors which existed 150,000,000 years ago.

When we compare vertebrates with other forms of animals, our impression of steady evolutionary progress toward more complex, highly developed forms becomes even further dissipated. We are accustomed to thinking of insects as considerably lower forms of life than mammals, particularly man. Yet the amount of change in bodily form and structure which took place in the evolution of insects from their remote, one-celled ancestors was certainly as great [as] and probably greater than

that of mammals. Furthermore, when we study the elaborate instincts and social behavior of bees, ants, and wasps, we realize that their nervous systems are equally highly evolved. The course of evolution from primitive forms of life to man on the one hand and higher insects on the other differed greatly in kind and direction, but little in degree. Even if we define evolution as change in populations of organisms toward greater complexity (a definition which is unacceptable, as I shall point out), then ants and bees are as highly evolved as we are.

When we turn toward the class of insects, however, we recognize that a considerable number of evolutionary lines have not changed toward greater complexity. Fleas, aphids (plant lice), and thrips differ almost as much from the primitive common ancestor of insects as do butterflies and bees. Yet the later evolutionary history of these groups of insects has been one of progressive simplification. Similar lines of evolution toward greater simplicity can be found in many groups of animals and plants, particularly those which have become parasitic.

Unequal rates of evolution are equally apparent, both in comparing different groups of insects with each other and in comparisons between insects and mammals. Bees have evolved a tremendous number of diverse types during the last 10,000,000 to 20,000,000 years; modern cockroaches are hardly different from their ancestors of 150,000,000 to 200,000,000 years ago. Insects as a whole have evolved relatively little during the past 40,000,000 years; the marvellously preserved fossil fauna of insects from the Baltic amber is essentially modern in composition. Yet when these modern insects were inhabiting the forests of northern Europe, the mammals of the same fauna were still very primitive. Forms resembling modern cattle, deer, cats, foxes, and horses did not appear until 20,000,000 to 30,000,000 years later.

We see the same unevenness of evolutionary change when we compare different characteristics in animals belonging to separate lines of evolution. The head structure of elephants has been greatly modified by evolution, but their legs and feet are far less specialized than those of horses or deer. In nearly every group of animals we can find some organs which are greatly modified and others which have changed much less. The course of evolution as a whole has been devious, uneven, and opportunistic. The fact that the forms of life which now dominate the earth have, on the whole, a more complex organization than those which have preceded them in previous geologic epochs is due not to any evolutionary urge toward greater complexity, but to the fact that certain types of more complex structure and behavior enable their bearers to achieve more complete dominance over their environment, both the physical world about them and the other forms of life with which they are associated. The two evolutionists who in recent times have seriously debated the question as to whether or not progress can be recognized in evolutionary change are G. G. Simpson[8] and Sir Julian Huxley.[9] Simpson reached the conclusion that progress can be recognized only by defining it in anthropomorphic terms. Huxley defines progress as evolution toward increasing dominance over the environment, both inanimate and living. On the basis of this definition, he regards mankind as the most progressive form of life, since our control over our environment is greater than that possessed by any other organism.

Organic Evolution and Social Change

When we compare this survey of evolutionary change in the animal kingdom with that of social change in human cultures, such as has been recently discussed by Wilbert Moore,[10] the similarity between the two is obvious. The course of change in human cultures has been devious, uneven, and on the whole opportunistic. In the words of Moore: "The course of change may be gradual or rapid, peaceful or violent, continuous or spasmodic, orderly or erratic."[11] As in organic evolution, the progress in cultural change is not self-evident. It may be defined in ethnocentric terms, i.e., progress toward that particular form of society in which the writer lives, or, following Huxley, in terms of greater dominance of man over his environment, including people belonging to different cultural groups. This definition is most likely to be adopted by members of dominant societies.

Sahlins[12] has developed a most interesting pair of concepts which may be applied to organic as well as cultural evolution. He speaks of diversity through adaptive radiation as Specific Evolution; and the rise of "higher forms," which he defines, like Huxley, in terms of dominance over their environment, as General Evolution. His diagram to show the relationship between these two phenomena is entirely in agreement with the ideas which I am presenting today.

[8] *Op. cit.*
[9] *Op. cit.*

[10] Wilbert Moore, *Social Change* (Englewood Cliffs, N.J.: Prentice-Hall, Inc., 1963).
[11] *Ibid.*, p. 33.
[12] M. D. Sahlins and E. R. Service, *Evolution and Culture* (Ann Arbor: University of Michigan Press, 1960).

The Process of Organic Evolution and Social Change

Faced with this undoubted similarity between the course of organic evolution and of social change, we naturally ask ourselves whether an equal resemblance exists between the processes which have brought about organic evolution and those responsible for social change. This question is particularly timely at present, since our knowledge of the dynamics of organic evolution has greatly increased during the last thirty years. Books and articles published during the past five years have revealed a remarkable agreement among most serious students of evolutionary processes, even though they have been studying very different groups of organisms from diverse points of view. They agree that the major processes of evolution are known to us; we need no longer search for hidden causes. These major processes are genetic mutations, chromosomal changes, and genetic recombination, which provide the source of variability; and natural selection and reproductive isolation between species, which canalize and direct this variability into adaptive systems.

In considering these processes, we must emphasize the fact that all of them are equally essential to evolutionary change. Furthermore, they interact with each other in such numerous and complex ways that none of them can be considered separately from the others. Their interrelationships can be expressed by the following analogy. We can compare a line of organisms evolving through time to an automobile moving along a highway. The mutations and chromosomal changes can be compared to the gasoline in the tank. They are the ultimate source of change, but do not contribute directly to it, since most of the mutations

toward greater adaptive fitness have such small effects by themselves that they are significant only in combination with other genes. The mechanisms of Mendelian heredity, which is responsible for genetic recombination, can be compared to the engine, since it provides the direct source of variability which natural selection, through interaction between organisms and environment, guides into channels of adaptive fitness. In this analogy, therefore, natural selection can be compared to the driver of the vehicle. Reproductive isolation, a general term applied to a great variety of mechanisms which prevent or restrict successful hybridization between members of different species, may be likened to the highway, with its boundaries and directive signs, enabling a large number of "vehicles," or evolutionary lines, to follow similar or opposing directions in the same general habitat, without mixing or colliding.

Before comparing these processes of organic evolution with those which have guided social change, I must first point out and clarify some widespread misconceptions about the processes of organic evolution, particularly natural selection. Darwin's dramatic phrase "the struggle for existence" has given to many nonbiologists the impression that the chief mode of action of natural selection is by direct conflict between the different individuals of a population, which causes the death of the less fit individuals. Even Darwin recognized, however, that this is only one of the numerous ways in which natural selection can act, and modern studies have emphasized increasingly the importance of other ways. Once we recognize that heredity is determined by essentially constant, particulate units, the genes and chromosomes, we realize that the basis of evolutionary change is differential alteration in the frequency of particulate genes rather than of individual genotypes. This places differential reproductive capacity in the key position, rather than differential survival. One of my students, Joshua Lee,[13] performed an experiment with cultivated barley which showed clearly that one variety can supplant another through differential fecundity, even though every seed which germinates grows up to an adult plant that bears some seed. If, on a particular plot of ground, equal numbers of plants of two varieties exist initially, but the plants of one variety produce a larger amount of seed on the average than the other, then if all destruction of seeds and plants is at random, the more fecund variety will displace the less fecund one in a few generations. The same rule would apply to animal populations, particularly those like many marine fishes which produce enormous numbers of eggs and young, the great bulk of which are destroyed at random. The key to success of such species, and probably of the majority of species of organisms, lies not in direct competition with other organisms, but in developing more efficient ways of converting the resources of their environment into growth and reproduction of their kind. A commonplace fact of ecology is that in any biotic community the largest number of individuals and the greatest diversity of species, both of which could be taken as good indices of evolutionary success, are possessed by the herbivores, which go quietly about their way, eating, reproducing, and avoiding enemies. The competitive carnivores, at the pinnacle of the food chain, are the fewest in number of individuals, and their evolutionary lines

have evolved fewer species. In his recent book, *Animal Species and Evolution*,[14] Ernst Mayr presents much evidence to show that an important direction of evolution in many different lines of animals has been toward avoidance of competition with other animals in the same community. These facts show that even if analogies between organic evolution and social change can validly be made, those of Herbert Spencer and others, which were the foundation of the so-called "Social Darwinism" of the nineteenth century, were based upon a misconception of the mechanism of organic evolution.

Whether or not valid analogies can be made between organic evolution and social change depends largely upon the degree of similarity which exists between the processes governing the two types of change. We must, therefore, ask ourselves whether processes comparable to genetic mutation, recombination, natural selection, and reproductive isolation are responsible for social change. The processes are undoubtedly different, but do they have enough characteristics in common so that they can be compared? I believe that they do.

In social change or cultural evolution, as in organic evolution, there are some factors which contribute to variability and make change possible, as well as others which sort out the possible changes and give direction to them. Variability depends largely upon the invention of new tools, machines, and styles of clothing and architecture, as well as the development of new laws and customs. These processes are comparable to mutation. Transmission of this variability depends upon learning and tradition, while its spread to new

[13] Joshua A. Lee, "A Study of Plant Competition in Relation to Development," *Evolution*, 14 (March, 1960), 18-28.

[14] Ernst Mayr, *Animal Species and Evolution* (Cambridge: Harvard University Press, 1963).

cultures depends upon cultural diffusion. These processes are, therefore, comparable to hereditary transmission and gene flow in organic evolution. Selection also operates to effect cultural change, but the analogy with natural selection is indirect. Cultural selection may involve differential survival, but this usually affects whole cultures rather than the individuals composing them. The more spectacular examples of this are wars and revolutions, but changed conditions of life have probably been the more effective way of favoring the spread of one culture as compared to others in the same region. The reduction of the Indian population in parts of temperate North and South America was due much more to their susceptibility to disease and their inability to adapt themselves to the changes produced by European culture than to defeat in battle. Equally important has been conscious selection of new inventions, laws, or customs, by members of a society which is changing itself, usually by imitation, following cultural diffusion.

The second method of canalization which operates in organic evolution, reproductive isolation, has no counterpart or at best a feebly developed and temporary substitute among the processes of social change. Any member of the human species can potentially mate with any other of the opposite sex. Social barriers exist in most cultures which reduce intercultural unions, but these are never irreversible, as are the barriers of reproductive isolation between species of animals and plants. Barriers to cultural diffusion have sometimes been erected, in the form of physical barriers, like the Great Wall of China, or of censorship and propaganda against foreign ways. These have always been temporary, and present means of communication are likely to reduce their effectiveness more and more as time goes on.

On the basis of these similarities and differences between organic evolution and cultural change, what analogies should we avoid, and what, if any, can we make that will help us to understand the processes of social change?

The first problem is the validity of the analogy implied by designating social change as cultural or social evolution. This has now been done by a number of biologists, particularly Huxley, Dobzhansky, Waddington, and the writer, and by such anthropologists and sociologists as White, Steward, and Hallowell. Other social scientists have been reluctant to apply the term, largely because of the connotation which it acquired as a result of the speculations of nineteenth-century anthropologists and philosophers. I believe that it is justified principally by the striking similarity between the course of organic evolution and of social change. Furthermore, the most important events in organic evolution have been the successive appearance of those adaptive systems which have enabled their bearers to exploit their environment in a more complex and efficient way, and thus have increased the independence of and dominance over the inanimate environment which is one of the most significant characteristics of life as a whole. One cannot deny the fact that during the past 25,000 years mankind has increased his independence of and dominance over his physical environment to a greater degree than has any other evolutionary line of organisms, even over periods of many millions of years. This increase has been accompanied by an almost negligible change in those biological characteristics, such as intelligence, powers of speech, and manual dexterity, which are the basic prerequisites for it to occur. As a method of increasing dominance over the environment, organic evolution has in mankind been replaced by social change or, as I prefer to call it, cultural evolution.

In the past, many anthropologists who used the term cultural evolution for change in man's way of life believed that this enabled them to arrange all of the diverse contemporary societies into stages of cultural advancement, and on the basis of such seriation to predict the future of cultural systems. Such predictions have not been realized. In addition, a true comparison between the course of organic and of cultural evolution must emphasize the fact that major advances in organic evolution have been so rare and sporadic that no amount of study of those organisms which existed before these major events occurred would have made possible their prediction. For instance, if an intelligent being had been transplanted to the world of life existing in the Triassic period, when the reptiles were in their most active stage of adaptive radiation, he could not possibly have constructed the body plan and behavioral pattern of a bird or placental mammal, much less have predicted that these classes would, several million years later, almost completely displace the dominant reptiles. A social scientist who looks to an organic evolutionist to help him predict what will happen to society in the future is a blind man seeking help from another who is equally blind.

Three Analogies

Rather than ending upon this pessimistic note, I should like to conclude by bringing up three analogies which may give better insight into the problems of both organic evolutionists and sociologists. Two of them have to do with processes of evolution, the third with its course.

The first analogy, suggested by Service[15] is called by him the Law of Evolutionary Potential and deals with the course of evolution. He refers at first to the statement made by a number of biologists, particularly Julian Huxley, that animals with a high degree of specialization cannot give rise to new types. By analogy, he reasons that the more specialized and adapted is a particular culture, the less likely it is to give rise to a new culture with a different, more progressive way of life. According to him, this generalization applies to particular cultural traits, such as writing, as well as to entire cultures.

I do not have the necessary knowledge and experience to say whether or not this generalization is sound from the anthropological and sociological point of view. I should like to point out, however, that its biological basis is doubtful if not actually false. Simpson[16] has pointed out that new adaptive types have in many instances arisen from groups which, at the time of their appearance, were among the most advanced and specialized of the then-existing types. The lungfish types with strong fins (Crossopterygians) which gave rise to the first amphibians, as well as the tree-climbing reptiles (Ictidosaurs) which were the ancestors of mammals, are both good examples. The belief, which has been expressed by many evolutionists, that only generalized forms can give rise to entirely new adaptive types, is apparently based upon comparisons between the probable ancestors of new groups and the later and more specialized descendants of some of their collateral relatives.

The second analogy is developed by W. B. Cannon in the last chapter of

---

[15] Op. cit., Chap. 5.
[16] Op. cit.

his book, *The Wisdom of the Body*.[17] An eminent human physiologist, he pointed out in the principal portion of his book the need of the human body to maintain a steady state, or "homeostasis," of its basic functions, which may involve the "brain and nerves, the heart, lungs, kidney, and spleen, all working cooperatively." In order to maintain this basic stability, the body requires both efficient systems of communication between all of its parts—provided by the blood stream, nervous system, and hormones of the endocrine system—and the ability of each separate organ to change the rate of particular accessory reactions which are needed to restore any unbalance of the basic stability which arises when the organism faces various kinds of unusual environments. In the Epilogue of his book, Dr. Cannon makes an analogy between the homeostatic adjustments of the human body and similar adjustments which are needed to maintain the steady state of the body politic. From his analogy he concludes that "the organism suggests that *stability is of prime importance*. It is more important than economy." Later he suggests that "the hope is not unreasonable that the distress arising from catastrophes can be greatly mitigated, and that suffering due to lack of necessary things which is attendant on great economic fluctuations can be obviated, by carefully planning and by intelligently regulating the processes of production and distribution." A final word of wisdom is that "the main service of social homeostasis would be to support bodily homeostasis. It would therefore help to release the highest activities of the nervous system for adventure and achievement. With essential needs secured, the priceless unessentials could be freely sought."[18]

I understand that this analogy of Dr. Cannon's has been much discussed by sociologists, although I have not been able to find specific references to such discussions. I believe that it should be studied carefully by both biologists and sociologists. Perhaps an expansion of it could do much to develop a reasonable philosophy of modern life and help to ease our apprehensions about the future of the body politic.

The final analogy is one about which I have been thinking for some time. It is based upon an evolutionary principle which was originally worked out by the English geneticist C. D. Darlington[19] and which biologists have found to be an increasingly valuable guide to understanding the diversity of systems which exist in various groups of plants and animals for achieving genetic stability or variability. This is the principle of compromise between immediate fitness and evolutionary flexibility. In higher animals and plants, with their complex bodily structures and elaborate systems of adaptation, mutation is far too slow and haphazard to serve by itself as a means of providing the necessary variability by which natural selection can enable these organisms to adjust to changing environments. Consequently, all cross-fertilizing populations of higher organisms have acquired a large store of concealed genetic variability, in the form of recessive genes and gene combinations, which becomes revealed when they are inbred. All of these genes lower the adaptation of the population to its immediate environment, but some of them can contribute toward adjusting the population to rapid changes which

---

[17] W. B. Cannon, *The Wisdom of the Body* (New York: W. W. Norton & Company, Inc., 1932).

[18] *Ibid.*, pp. 304-305.

[19] C. D. Darlington, *The Evolution of Genetic Systems* (New York: Cambridge University Press, 1939).

it may face in the future. In a few instances, populations of flies and hamsters have become adjusted to seasonal variations in climate by means of alternate gene combinations, one of which becomes relatively frequent in summer, and the other in winter or spring.

This genetic variability is never completely hidden, and from time to time causes the appearance of inferior individuals, thus lowering the average fitness of the population. It must be regarded as a sort of *genetic insurance*, without which evolutionary lines are doomed to eventual extinction. Many groups of organisms have, however, dispensed with most or all of this insurance by substituting asexual for sexual reproduction, by various devices which favor inbreeding or self fertilization, or by altering the chromosomal mechanism in such a way that genetic linkage is strongly reinforced, and recombination correspondingly diminished. These organisms have also evolved in the direction of shorter life, less complex adjustments to their environment, and particularly to the ability to colonize rapidly unoccupied habitats. Among plants, this reduction of genetic variability, sacrificing evolutionary flexibility for the sake of immediate fitness, is found most commonly in weeds. These plants are highly successful in certain restricted habitats, and many of them have persisted for long periods of time, but they are apparently unable to evolve entirely new adaptations to their environment. Their variation patterns are restricted to fluctuations about a theme which was already outlined in their cross-fertilizing ancestors. If a radical alteration of the environment should occur, they are much more likely to become extinct than to advance toward a new level of evolutionary adaptation.

I should like to suggest that societies, like populations of higher organisms, must make a compromise in their cultural system between the needs of immediate fitness and those of long-term flexibility. As long as the environment of a community is constant, its stability and smooth functioning are best maintained if its members adhere to a rigid code of ethics which have worked in the past. Such a code is easily passed on from one generation to the next. Everyone knows his place, is not worrying either about his position in society or what is in store for himself or his children in the future, and goes contentedly about his assigned task. Such systems, whether they originate as devices for protecting the wealth and power of a ruling class, or as utopias founded by idealists, can succeed only if their environment, cultural and biological as well as physical, remains essentially constant, so that the leaders can predict coming events. The eventual disintegration of such societies in the face of changing conditions has occurred so many times as to be a commonplace event in history.

Any society which is to remain healthy through such upheavals as the industrial revolution and the atomic revolution must take out a certain amount of *cultural insurance*. This should consist of ideas, inventions, and legal or constitutional provisions which may appear to be useless or even harmful in the immediate present, but which may form the basis of rapid adjustment to changed conditions. Furthermore, complex societies in a constantly changing world must value and give credit to those of their members who are capable of unorthodox thinking, and who by their vision and foresight can produce and make available the components of this cultural insurance. On the other hand, if all members of society are permitted to have an unlimited range of unorthodox thinking and behavior, the homeostatic stability of the body politic will decline, and its functioning will be seriously impaired. A compromise must be found between blind faith and unbridled free thinking, between mechanical adherence to outworn tools and methods *versus* reliance upon untried new tools and machines, between unimaginative provision for present needs and idealistic reliance on hoped-for social changes. Most important, as the structure of society and its relationships with other societies becomes more complex, the old compromises, which worked in the past, will no longer do. New compromises must be found before the stability is irreparably lost.

A biologist, who has only a superficial acquaintance with the workings of society, can only suggest that this problem exists. I hope that it has given my readers who are sociologists a new outlook on some of the specific problems in their field.

The Irreducibility of Social Change: A Comment on Professor Stebbins' Paper

ROBERT A. NISBET

The heart of Professor Stebbins' paper lies—for sociologists, at least—in the following passage:

Whether or not valid analogies can be made between organic evolution and social change depends largely upon the degree of similarity which exists between the processes governing the two types of change. We must, therefore, ask ourselves whether processes comparable to genetic mutation, recombination, natural selection, and reproductive isolation are responsible for social change. The processes are undoubtedly different, but do they have enough characteristics in common so that they can be compared? I believe they do.

The gist of my comment can be summarized in the dissenting statement that they *cannot* be compared; not in any way that has operational, as opposed to metaphorical, meaning for those whose primary concern is change

Robert A. Nisbet, "The Irreducibility of Social Change: A Comment on Professor Stebbins' Paper," *Pacific Sociological Review*, 8 (March, 1965), 12-15. Reprinted by permission of the *Pacific Sociological Review*.

in institutions, groups, traditions, and life styles. The differences between types of data, perspectives of time, processes of persistence and modification, and relation between object and environment are altogether too great in the biological and sociological worlds, it seems to me, for any use of common phrases to have other than minimal significance.

I do not question the fact that insights and images may now and then be drawn by the sociologist from biological theory which, when subjected to the alembic of imagination, may be the source of productive thought. But this is a *conceptual act,* one that is not different from the frequently recorded phenomenon in all imaginative work, scientific or other, of deriving the final creative "push" or breakthrough from observations in areas totally removed from the problem at hand. It is very different when we take on a large-scale theory from another, older science and allow ourselves to be persuaded by occasional similarities of data that this theory is genuinely useful to us. Here we run the risk of what is best called evaporative reductionism: under the spell of the borrowed theory, the really crucial data are lost in vaporous haze.

We need not blame biologists for their benevolent imperialism. Evolution for them is a golden thread, one that has a symbolic significance (as does Darwin himself) quite unlike anything else, I believe, to be found in modern science. But this is their business. The danger in any case does not come from the occasional Stebbins, Dobzhansky, or Simpson—brilliant evolutionists all, who from sheer exuberance are unable to resist carrying their burden to underdeveloped areas of knowledge. The danger comes from social scientists who, unable to shake off the heritage of centuries-old concepts of developmentalism, continuity, and teleology in the study of man, are all too prone to seize upon the modern theory of biological evolution as, so to speak, confirmation of what they have accepted independently.

If some of us in the social sciences resist the biologist's entreaty to hear the comfortable words of biological evolutionism as we face the hardships and perplexities of social change, we are entitled surely to the biologist's understanding. For today biologists are under the pressure of physicists to scuttle the autonomy of their own theory of natural selection, and to view it simply as one more expression of the second law of thermodynamics. The biologist Ernst Mayr's reply to such efforts might be heeded by sociologists: "To drag the second law of thermodynamics into the discussion of evolutionary irreversibility confuses two distant levels of integration, the atomic level and the level of the phenotype."[1] So, equally, does the effort to drag the

[1] Ernst Mayr, *Animal Species and Evolution* (Cambridge: Harvard University Press, 1963), p. 6.

theories of biological variation, mutation, and natural selection into the discussion of social change. Notwithstanding, more than a few social scientists are doing this in their desire to reach an "autonomous" theory of change, one resting on so-called variations within the institution or group.

The essence of the modern theory of biological evolution lies, as Professor Stebbins makes clear, *not* in vistas of stages, unilinear or multilinear, proceeding from primitive and simple to modern and complex types. The real essence of evolution lies in what the theory has to say about the *mechanism* of change: specifically, about the processes of genetic variation and natural selection. Common ignorance of the real nature of both processes on the part of social scientists is the basis of their frequent supposition that they are in fact dealing with "variations" and "selection" in their studies of kinship, class, tribe, or nation.

But the biological theory of evolution has something very precise indeed in mind when it uses these terms, and Professor Stebbins goes to the point of the matter when he writes: "Once we recognize that heredity is determined by essentially constant, particulate units, the genes and chromosomes, we realize that the basis of evolutionary change is *differential alteration in the frequency of particulate genes* rather than of individual genotypes. This places differential *reproductive capacity* in the key position, rather than differential survival" (italics added). Now if we conceive natural selection in this accurate way, realizing that it is *only* in these terms that a self-resident, "autonomous" theory of change makes sense, we will perhaps the sooner abandon wistful illusions of analogy between what biologists are talking about and what we are dealing with, as sociologists, when we turn to processes like conflict and competition, to "role tensions" within groups, or to inventions in human culture.

There are, it seems to me, three central ways in which the differences between biological evolutionary change and social change are manifest: (1) the type of *data* the two disciplines work with, (2) the altogether different role of *time* in each, and (3) the relation between *process and event*.

Type of Data

The biologist's theory of natural selection, as one may infer from Professor Stebbins' text, is first and last a population—rather than type—oriented theory. The validity of the theory and even its meaning disappear promptly for the modern biologist once it is directly applied to fixed "types," such as species and varieties. The theory is limited in applicability to the biologist's rather special and wholly statistical concept of population. Ernst Mayr has written on this point clearly, and Professor Stebbins would not dissent, I am sure:

All organisms and organic phenomena are composed of unique features and can be described collectively *only* in statistical terms. Individuals, or any kind of organic entities, form populations of which we can determine the arithmetic mean and the statistics of variation. Averages are merely statistical abstractions; only the individuals of which the populations are composed have reality. The ultimate conclusions of the population thinker and of the typologist are precisely the opposite. . . . The replacement of typological thinking by population thinking is perhaps the greatest conceptual revolution that has taken place in biology. Many of the basic concepts of synthetic theory, *such as that of natural selection and that of the population*, are meaningless for the typologist.[2]

The social scientist, however, cannot escape being in large degree a typologist. (I recognize that there is, even within the social sciences, bad as well as good typology, just as there is bad as well as good teleology). The biologist is able to make genetic sense of his theory of natural selection only because he dispenses with species and varieties in the sense of existential types, in the sense of things "real," of structures determining or conditioning the behavior of organisms within. The sociologist, however, can hardly escape the reality of types—institutions like kinship, church, state, and caste. Each of these, as we know, is a pattern of norms, authorities, functions, and allegiances which, once coming into distinctive existence, may remain for centuries, even millennia, as with caste in India or Christianity in the West, profoundly affecting human behavior and making the sociologist's "population" a very different thing from the biologist's. To be sure, there are philosophers who now and then question the substance of institutions (realities or only names?), but to them we may recommend Dr. Johnson's famous reply to Bishop Berkeley's epistemology.

In sum, if the theory of natural selection is comprehensible only in terms of population thinking, in the biologist's sense—and this would appear incontestable—it is hard to suppose that sociologists are doing other than verbalizing when they talk of "selection" and "survival." Man the organism is, to be sure, subject to genetic laws of selection in the biologist's sense. As the biologists Paul R. Ehrlich and Richard W. Holm have reminded us in a recent, arresting article, it is a gross error to suppose that natural selection is "some sort of weight or burden which can be lifted from the back of a poor struggling population."[3] This view, as the authors go

------

[2] Ernst Mayr, *op. cit.*, pp. 5-6 (italics added).

[3] Paul R. Ehrlich and Richard W. Holm,

on to say, "is most evident in works on human evolution where we find that man has finally been freed from the dire load of natural selection." He has not, nor will he be. But here we are dealing with natural selection ("differential reproductive contributions of different genotypes greater than or less than one would expect from sampling error") with respect to human organisms conceived in the biologist's sense of population, *not* with man in culture, man in society—that is, with institutions and social groups.

Time

Now let us pass to the problem of time, to the two different worlds of time in which the biologists and the sociologists live. Plainly, the biologist is not dealing with time, in his evolutionary theories, in any sense that has much meaning for those of us who are compelled, by the nature of our data, to recognize not merely the linear before-and-after relationship of things but also time in the sense of *when* things happen. Ideally, we can date when things happen, but even when, as is much more often the case, we cannot date them, we are still constrained by the "when-ness" of things in human history. It is insensitivity to time as well as place that makes the study of institutions as "natural systems" seem more like exercises than insights into reality. Man is not only a time-binding creature; he is also a time-specifying creature. The biological evolutionist, as someone in the nineteenth century once observed, is dealing with a nearly unlimited bank of time to which he can take any amount of scientific paper for discount. When either laboratory or field observations suggest that a given transition in biological evolution must be set back—or forward—a few

"Patterns and Populations," *Science*, 137 (August, 1962), 652ff.

million years, it does not matter much. For the biologist is not in any event working with time in the sense of the number of years involved (his rough specifications here are concessions to the layman rather than aids to himself). Where the sociologist-historian must be bound by not only limits of time but also the specifications of time, the biologist is, in a very real and very important sense, free of the discipline of time. The sociologist, like the poet Andrew Marvell, always hears "time's winged chariot hurrying near." He must adapt his processes of change, whether in the study of the Renaissance, the modern nation, or the American family, to chronological termini that cannot, under any circumstances, be obliterated. He is, so to say, stuck with "1066 and all that."

Sociologists, we may recall painfully, have on occasion pretended that time does not matter, that, as in the case of biological vistas, social vistas may be presented in which time is absent, in which processes of adaptation and modification are strung out like so many beads on a string in a never-never land of the uniform and the universal. It was indeed this form of time-free, "abstract" or "natural" history, with its blithe disregard of the "when-ness" of things and its often preposterous sequences, that led to the modern reaction in the social sciences against not merely evolutionism but the study of change in general. The social world, the world of social change, unlike the biologist's world, is time-saturated, time-bound, and time-oriented. To paraphrase F. W. Maitland, the study of social change either will be historical (in the sense of "when-ness") or it will be nothing. As social scientists, we sometimes play with concepts of the "natural life cycle" of, say, revolutions. But these come out best, it would appear, when done by a Crane Brinton who has not forgotten the dates and places of his revolutions rather than by those for whom dates and places are nonscientific irrelevancies.

Process and Event

Here we come to what is, I think, the major area of difference between the biological and sociological worlds. The basic framework of the theory of biological evolution, as Ernst Mayr has written, and Professor Stebbins would agree, is that it is a two-stage phenomenon: the production of variations and the sorting of variation by natural selection. I am primarily interested in the nature of variations as this nature might be transferred to the study of social change. It was in Darwin's insistence upon the centrality of variations— infinitesimal and cumulative variations —that broke with, not only the creational theories of man but also, and this is for present purposes the only important point, *saltatory* theories: those resting on the centrality of sudden, major leaps in the biological process of change, leaps that would perpetuate themselves. Darwin's theory won the field in the late nineteenth century, and it has, I gather, held the field with ever-increasing certainty since— the "mutational revolt" of men like Bateson earlier in the century having been put down almost as firmly as Lamarckianism. What we are left with is a theory based on the fact of a near-infinity of variations within the biological population, some of which prove more efficient in reproductive fertility than others and therefore are selected by the environment in a way that inefficient variations are not. Furthermore, with due recognition of the innumerable blind alleys and manifestations of stagnant evolution, the efficient variations may be seen as lineally linked and producing, for example, over an enormous period of evolutionary time,

legs where there had been only fins. In this process, environmental changes were of course involved. Had it not been for the drying up of vast areas, the process of cumulative selection leading eventually to legs could hardly have taken place. But the essence of the modern synthetic theory of evolution (and of Darwin's own theory) lies in the vital fact that the drying up of the environment did not *cause* the variations which resulted in legs, for these exist in a world of their own—the world of the genotype—but only, as we say, *selected* useful or relevant variations from those that were nonadaptable to the altered condition of environment. The nature of modern scientific genetics, and its profound difference from Lamarckianism (not to mention Lysenkoism) consists at bottom in this crucial view of the relation between environment and change.

It is this same crucial view that renders the theory of variation and natural selection largely inapplicable to the study of social change. In studying the gross manifestations of social change—rise of new nations, fall of empires, dislocations of caste and class, disappearance of patriarchalism, and so on—it is tempting of course to seek to make these changes the consequence of "internal" variations caused, let us say, by role dysfunctions or tensions. And here lies the first pitfall. As sociologists, we are forced, as I have said, to think typologically, and the result is that we frequently write as though the "variations" among individuals *within* a social type accumulate lineally over periods of time (decades and generations rather than the millions of years biologists can call on), leading eventually, it is argued, to structural alterations of the *type*—caste, family system, tribe, or nation. Sociologists may suppose that in this methodological use of internal variations they are doing what contemporary biologists do, but if so they err. For the evolutionary biologist is *not* dealing with types and structures but only populations, and, as Mayr emphasized in the passage quoted above, the whole theory of evolution breaks down if conceived typologically.

The really important difference, however, between biological evolution and social change lies in the significance of what contemporary geneticists call random events; that is, the relation between ordinary processes of variation and selection, on the one hand, and sudden, unforeseeable happenings of genetic character on the other. The study of random events and of "explosive evolution" is, Ernst Mayr tells us, one of the major areas of contemporary biological inquiry. For good reason I remain strictly out of this matter as it pertains to biology, and it may well be universally and lastingly true, as Professor Stebbins has elsewhere written, that "selective pressures are almost always strong enough so that random events not associated with selection are either nonexistent or of little consequence."

But in the social world random events are neither nonexistent nor of little consequence. They are, on the contrary, absolutely inseparable from the study of institutional change, and any effort to reduce structural changes to microscopic variations of role or behavior within a structure is doomed to futility. A generation ago, F. J. Teggart made this point the very basis of his brilliant writings, and no effective answer to the point has yet been made. Despite this, a whole host of writings on such subjects as caste, race relations, kinship, tribe, and religion are testimony to the lure that continues to be exerted by the model of a "systematic" theory of change in which gross changes in the social structure are accounted for in terms of cumulative minor variations within the structure.

Here I take the liberty of quoting from an article I wrote thirteen years ago on the subject of social structure and change:

The chief danger of contemporary functionalist approaches seems to me to lie in search for causes *within the social system*, as though the social system were, like a biological entity, governed by autonomous, inner drives toward cumulative change. There is the added fact that these alleged causes take on, increasingly, a psychological character. Both tendencies—the search for inner, autonomous causes of change, and the concentration upon psychological processes as causative forces—seem to me unfortunate. . . .

Instead of dealing with the problem of structural change in historical and institutional terms, which is to say in terms of the total relation of the structure to its environment (temporal and spatial), we find sociologists and ethnologists, first, seeking the causes of change in allegedly autonomous mechanisms within the structure and, second, throwing the weight of causal analysis upon such actually *derivative* phenomena as psychological strains and stresses within the social structure.[4]

There may be those today who believe the search for internal, autonomous, and systematic causes of change in society to be modern. It is not. It is the oldest, most tenacious, and universal approach to the problem in the whole history of Western thought. From Aristotle's preoccupation with the self-resident and the continuous in family, community, and state down to Auguste Comte's fascination with a scientific "eventless" history to be constructed (in the light of biology) on the basis of "slow, continuous, accumulation of successive changes" this search has been the very substance of

---

[4] Robert A. Nisbet, "Social Structure and Social Change," *Research Studies of the State College of Washington*, **20** (June, 1952).

Western man's study of change. A "non-Euclidean" sociology of change is still before us.

The gulf between biological evolution, as a theoretical model, and the actual requirements of any proper study of social change is, then, unbridgeable save in purely metaphorical terms. And the reason lies, as I have tried to indicate in these remarks, in, first, the radically different character of the nature of the *data*; second, in the ineffaceable demands imposed on the social scientist by *time*; and, third, and most important, in the utterly contrasting relationship in the two areas between *process* and *event*. Sociologists who would seek surcease from events in autonomous and internal processes of variation would be like a Margaret Fuller who had decided *not* to accept the universe.

Some Misgivings About Evolutionary Theory: A Comment on Professor Stebbins' Paper

WILBERT E. MOORE

I find myself in what must be, for a discussant, an awkward position, for I agree with most of what Professor Stebbins has said, and I could not have seen the main point on which I disagree without his excellent exposition. I thank him for the sound scientific sense he has displayed for us here. . . .

Especially valuable to my mind is the clarification of what modern biological conceptions of evolution are *not* and the clear identification of the limited number of variables which *define* evolution and which, in their combination, *produce* it. Evolutionary theory does not attempt to order existent species into a single sequence of stages, say from simple to complex. It has other, and better, explanations for cross-sectional diversity—diversity that was always embarrassing to cultural evolutionists who sought to fit lateral differentiation into a scheme of sequences. Second, evolutionary theory

Wilbert E. Moore, "Some Misgivings About Evolutionary Theory: A Comment on Professor Stebbins' Paper," *Pacific Sociological Review*, 8 (March, 1965), 10-11. Reprinted by permission of the *Pacific Sociological Review*.

is not concerned with structural differences among individuals, save as these are of demonstrable significance either in terms of genetic drift or in terms of differential adaptation. On a third point, the experts are not agreed, namely, whether there are clear and anthropomorphically neutral tests of progress, that is, of relative degrees of development or advancement. Professor Stebbins chooses his language with care when he says that supporters of the synthetic theory of organic evolution "are *reluctant* [my emphasis] to speculate on the course of evolution, or phylogeny, on the basis of the supposed primitiveness or advancement of modern forms of life."

Here I believe we have an issue that can be identified, joined, and hopefully clarified. Can the same theory explain, first, both great and persistent structural differentiation and varieties of adaptive mechanisms; second, order these variations in terms of some objective criteria of relative advancement, which would imply, third, a retrospective *and* prospective interpretation of evolutionary course for at least part of the array of variations in terms of *differences* in adaptive capacity?

The sources of Professor Stebbins' pessimism on points two and three are worth reiterating. He properly discounts the simplicity-complexity scale as offering prospects for a scale either of viability and survival or of prospective further structural change. He also notes the difficulties of predicting what he refers to as "major advances in organic evolution," which he refers to as having been rare and sporadic.

Yet Professor Stebbins does not reject totally the idea of an evolutionary scale. He says that "the most important events in organic evolution have been the successive appearance of those adaptive systems which have enabled their bearers to exploit their environment in a more complex and efficient way." He also notes the test of numerical expansion in the competition for life space and other resources. Thus he has in fact subscribed to the *developmental* conception of evolution that several sociologists including myself have found useful for explaining a *part* of social change.

I emphasize "part" of social change, because I think that the very ambiguity which I think I have detected in Professor Stebbins' position highlights the difficulties of the evolutionary frame of reference in *both* biology and sociology. Professor Stebbins would simply equate social change with cultural evolution, and the only serious objection to that is precisely the attempt to account for both lateral differentiation and the long-term course of organic species or social systems by the same explanatory principles. The point here is rather a subtle one, for it is not the distinction between static and dynamic, since differentiation arises from variability and selective adaptation just as does cumulative change. No, the difference is between persistent structural differentiation, the structural varieties surviving as long as the environment is relatively stable, and developmental adaptation which is cumulative in its mastery and its change of the environment through interaction with it.

Just to bring this into some main streams of current sociological discourse, functionalism in sociology is clearly, though usually implicitly, evolutionary in the first sense in that the emergence of differentiated patterns having certain requisites for survival must have involved selective adaptation to natural environments as well as interactive adaptation of the nonhuman and human environment. But functionalism has not been evolutionary in the sense of cumulative developmental adaptation, for theoretical reasons that several of us have been stating for some time.

Now appeareth before the sociological tribunal the June, 1964, issue of the *American Sociological Review*, with five leading articles on social change, three—by Talcott Parsons, Robert Bellah, and Schmuel Eisenstadt —explicitly on the theme of evolution, and a fourth, by myself, containing a couple of paragraphs on evolution. Though none of my three colleagues took the trouble to define what he meant by evolution, in all three cases it was clear that the authors were concerned precisely with cumulative, developmental change, and not with differentiation as such. I gave a bow to evolutionary theory as acceptable for some purposes but not for mine, which was the prediction of discontinuities in social change. My expressed avoidance (not rejection) of evolutionary theory was in terms of its being too grand for the finer detail I sought. The opportunity of commenting on Professor Stebbins' paper has provoked me into further thought on the matter. I should now say that I should have two misgivings about use of evolutionary theory for predicting discontinuities. The first is, I believe, akin to Professor Stebbins' caution about predicting major structural or adaptive changes from prior historical records. Here, however, I did note my opinion that the sociologists have a better explanatory base for *innovations* as the source of variability than the biologists do for genetic mutation. And I should add that I think both Professor Stebbins and I would have profited from reading Parsons' paper on "evolutionary universals," for he deals with discontinuous innovations—I should have preferred to say "emergents"—that are likely to be hit upon across species or social systems.

My second misgiving about evolutionary theory for the purposes I had I should now rephrase as its excessive permissiveness. It allows for variability at a moment of time and for change through time but it lacks predictive bite except for very large-scale and long-run changes.

I should like to add a few more points as quickly as possible. . . .

Professor Stebbins refers to "the reduction of the Indian population of temperate North and South America," and I suspect that this is simply wrong, at least over the long run to the present. Rather, Indian survival appears to have involved new and viable forms of adaptation, including notably peaceful ones and some having a distinctly symbiotic relation to the dominant civilization.

On a more important matter I want to underscore and applaud the discussion of adaptation to a *changeful* environment. This is what seems to me to be the most useful part of evolutionary principles, whether in biology or sociology. That leads me to reiterate my view that "environmental mastery" is *the* criterion of developmental evolution and its principal, phylogenetic basis for prediction. But I should add a caution about a discontinuity of another sort—that between phenomenal systems. Much of human action is purposive, and a case can be made for the *evolutionary* growth of deliberate change. Thus one can sympathize with and even commend the critical cautions of those who came to distrust the teleological assumptions of the older evolutionary theories. But contemporary cultures are organized in such a way that the teleology is explicit and overt, and it commands large resources. Human effort is directed to changing the future state of affairs by rational acts and also to predicting the uncontrolled future and making anticipatory adaptations—a process Arnold Feldman and I persist in calling teleonomy. This emergent, that of deliberate and anticipatory action, only part of which is technological in the narrower sense, is certainly irreversible, but failure to adapt constructively to new powers may make it lethal.

Yes, Virginia, there is social evolution, and we are beholden to [Professor Stebbins] for his sober explication of its biological foundations and counterparts.